CHINESE WALLS
IN TIME AND SPACE

CHINESE WALLS IN TIME AND SPACE

A MULTIDISCIPLINARY PERSPECTIVE

EDITORS

Roger Des Forges, Minglu Gao,
Liu Chiao-mei, Haun Saussy,
with Thomas Burkman

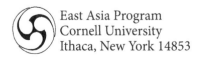
East Asia Program
Cornell University
Ithaca, New York 14853

The Cornell East Asia Series is published by the Cornell University East Asia Program (distinct from Cornell University Press). We publish books on a variety of scholarly topics relating to East Asia as a service to the academic community and the general public. Standing Orders, which provide for automatic notification and invoicing of each title in the series upon publication are accepted.

If after review by internal and external readers a manuscript is accepted for publication, it is published on the basis of camera-ready copy provided by the author who is responsible for any copyediting and manuscript formatting. Alternative arrangements should be made with approval of the Series. Address submission inquiries to CEAS Editorial Board, East Asia Program, Cornell University, Ithaca, New York 14853-7601.

Cover photo: Used by permission of Mr. Zhao Gang. Picture taken in Jincheng, Shanxi, on his trip to the prominent sites of ancient buildings that are particularly rich in this province. See back cover for full image.

Number 144 in the Cornell East Asia Series
Copyright ©2009 by Roger Des Forges, Gao Minglu, Liu Chiao-mei, Haun Saussy, Thomas Burkman (the editors). All rights reserved.
ISSN: 1050-2955
ISBN: 978-1-933947-14-3 hc
ISBN: 978-1-933947-44-0 pb
Library of Congress Control Number: 2009925854

24 23 22 21 20 19 18 17 16 15 14 13 12 11 10 09   9 8 7 6 5 4 3 2 1

The paper in this book meets the requirements for permanence of ISO 9706:1994.

Contents

List of Illustrations

Chapter 5

Chapter 6

Chapter 7

Chapter 10

Chapter 12

List of Principal Chinese Polities

Xia, semilegendary, ca 2000–
    ca 1750 BCE

Shang, ca 1750–ca 1050

Zhou, ca 1050–256
    Western, ca 1050–770
    Eastern, 770–256
        Spring and Autumn, 722–
        481
        Warring States, 403–221

Qin, 256–206

Han, 206 BCE–220 CE
    Western or Former, 206
        BCE–8 CE
    Xin, 8–23
    Eastern or Later, 25–220

Six Dynasties, 220–589
    Three Kingdoms, 220–265,
        Wei, Shu-Han, Wu
    Jin, 265–420
        Western, 265–317
        Eastern, 317–420
    North and South Dynasties,
        317–589, eg. Northern
        Wei, Liang
Sui, 589–617

Tang, 618–907

Five Dynasties, Ten Kingdoms,
    907–960

Liao, 947–1125

Northern Song, 960–1126

Jin, 1126–1234

Southern Song, 1126–1279

Xi Xia, 990–1227

Yuan, 1279–1368

Ming, 1368–1644

Qing, 1636–1911

Republic, 1911–1949 on mainland,
    to present on Taiwan
    Militarists, 1916–1927
    Mongolian People's Republic,
        1924–1992, Mongolian
        Republic, 1922–present
    Nanjing government, 1927–
        1937
    Japanese invasion, 1937–1945
    Civil War, 1945–1949

People's Republic, 1949–present,
    except Taiwan,
    Mongolian Republic

Preface

ART HISTORIANS MINGLU GAO AND BINGYI HUANG FIRST conceived the idea of this book. They curated an exhibition titled "The Wall: Reshaping Contemporary Chinese Art" that opened in Beijing in the summer of 2005 and moved to Buffalo, New York, in the fall. It was the largest display of contemporary Chinese art ever to leave the People's Republic and appear in the United States. Gao, who was then at the University at Buffalo, and Huang, who was soon to succeed him there, asked some of the rest of us to help organize an academic conference that would accompany the exhibition in Buffalo. Our first expression of gratitude, therefore, goes to Minglu and Bingyi for describing and contextualizing the exhibition in an important bilingual book, *The Wall: Reshaping Contemporary Chinese Art/Qiang: Zhongguo dangdai yishu de lishi yu bianjie*. That book actually went far beyond serving as a catalogue for the exhibition to provide a comprehensive analysis of many different forms of contemporary Chinese art. In that same spirit, we soon envisioned a second volume that would track the theme of the wall beyond art history to what turned out to be a dozen disciplines.

The academic conference titled "The Roles and Representations of Walls in the Reshaping of Chinese Modernity" that accompanied the exhibition in Buffalo would not have been possible without the enthusiastic support of many individuals, institutions, and sponsors. Sandra Olsen, Director of the University at Buffalo Art Galleries, and Holly Hughes, Director of the Wall Project at the Albright-Knox Art Gallery, were driving forces behind the exhibition and included the conference in their fund-raising. Lynn Mather, Director of the Baldy Center for Law and Social Policy, and Laura Mangan, Assistant Director, provided crucial intellectual inspiration and channeled further support for the project. The University at Buffalo Asian Studies Program directed by Thomas Burkman; the College of Arts and Sciences under Dean Uday Sukhatme; the Department of Art under Chair David Shirm, Department of Art History under Chair Charles Carman, and Department of History under Chair Tamara Thornton; the Humanities Institute directed by Ewa Ziarek; and the Julian Park Chair in Comparative Literature all provided scholarly and monetary assistance in organizing the conference. The Mentholatum Company and the W. L. S. Spencer Foundation contributed additional funding.

Many scholars helped make the conference a success by presenting papers and serving as panel chairs and discussants. Those who gave papers that are not printed in the present volume but have appeared or may appear in other publications include Julia Andrews, Timothy Billings, Qiang Fang, Magnus Fiskesjö, Hu Cheng, Xiao Hu, Bingyi Huang, Kuiyi Shen, Shui Tianzhong, Eugene Yuejin Wang, Margaret Woo, Xu Hong, Yue Zhang, and Ming Fang Zheng. Douglas Dreishpoon, Chief Curator at the Albright-Knox, and University at Buffalo professors Rebecca French, Shubha Ghosh, Tsan Huang, and Claude Welch served ably as chairs and discussants and made comments that enriched the exchanges. Arthur Waldron gave the opening keynote address, Haun Saussy served as commentator-at-large, and Minglu Gao delivered the closing summary address. Because Gao's reflections appeared in his book they are not repeated here, but we will refer to them extensively in the Introduction. We thank all of these good colleagues from near and far whose active participation in the conference helped to shape the content and the structure of this book.

In the process of preparing the book manuscript, we were assisted by Lynne Mather, Director of the Baldy Center; Kristin Stapleton, incoming Director of the Asian Studies Program; Mary Anne Lang and Elizabeth Felmet, successive office managers of the Asian Studies Program; and H. Lorraine Oak, Associate Dean of the College of Arts and Sciences. The College of Arts and Sciences and the Asian Studies Program at Buffalo, the Council on East Asian Studies and the MacMillan Center for International Studies at Yale, and the History Department of National Taiwan University all provided generous subventions to help defray the cost of publishing this book. We are also grateful to Sherman Cochran, Hu Shi Professor of Chinese History at Cornell, who encouraged the publication of the work; two anonymous readers who made very constructive suggestions for fine-tuning the manuscript; Liu Chiao-mei for compiling the Glossary; Benjamin Van Dyke, Millie Chen, and Keyang Tang contributed valuable concepts toward the cover design, incorporating a photograph taken in Shanxi by Zhao Gang, a photographer long associated with *The National Geographic*; Mai Shaikhanuar-Cota, Managing Editor of the Cornell East Asia Series, who supervised publication; and copyeditor Mike Sola, who helped us to achieve consistency in the final text.

An earlier version of Chapter 11 was published as "Reconstructing World History in the People's Republic of China since the 1980s," *Journal of World History*, 18.3 (Sept. 2007):325–50. An earlier form of Chapter 13 appeared as "Writing on the Wall: Brice Marden's Chinese Work and Modernism," in *Taida lishi xuebao*, 40 (Dec. 2007):201–37. We are grateful to those two journals for granting us permission to include significantly updated versions of these essays in this volume.

We have followed the Chinese practice of putting family names before personal names in the case of Chinese living primarily in China; we have reversed the order for Chinese living most of the time in North America.

TWB for the editors, August 2009

Introduction

The Persistence and Significance of Walls

THE GREAT WALL OF CHINA is one of the largest, most venerable, and most widely known of human constructions. Whether judged colossal, prodigious, hermetic, archaic, or irrational, in the popular imagination it often stands for China. Recent scholarship with its analytic tools has cut the Great Wall down to size, casting doubt on the very existence of a single, continuous, historic, large, and solid wall, and attributing the creation of the Great Wall legend to outsiders who confused the "long walls" of antiquity with the Ming Dynasty's complex of border defenses. Even the story, confidently repeated for generations, that the Wall is visible to the human eye from the moon turns out to be a myth.[1] Many of the other alleged features of China's long walls, including their age and size, are subject to ongoing research and debate.[2] And yet, even if we are to put little faith in the singular definite article we sometimes use to refer to "the" Great Wall and the capital letters with which we often give it the status of a proper name, there is, undeniably, a Great Wall, not only in hundreds of miles of restored Ming-era fortifications but also in the collective imagination of humanity. In addition, much remains to be said about other walls and the roles they have played throughout China's long history. The building of walls, levees, and other barriers was a primary responsibility of every civic authority in China for thousands of years. Walls in China have long enclosed cities, towns, and villages as well as administrative

---

1   Waldron, *The Great Wall*; Lovell, *The Great Wall*.
2   Roberts and Barmé, *The Great Wall*.

sectors, public compounds, and courtyard homes.[3] These walls—
including physical and juridical dimensions—are less well known to
the outside world, but to most of the Chinese people—who at times
have constituted up to a quarter of humanity—they may have been
more significant than the "long" or "great" walls that stretched across
north China.

Like walls anywhere, Chinese walls have generally functioned to
keep some things in and other things out. They have typically been
accompanied by passes, gates, or other openings where comings and
goings may be supervised and controlled. There is no clear barrier—no
self-evident "wall"—between the physical/social and virtual/imaginary
kinds of barriers. Walls can assume such varied forms as printed
drawings, cellular membranes, and electronic shields. These, too,
China has had in abundance. As in the case of more bluntly material
walls, questions have arisen as to just how effective such soft barriers
have been in attaining the ends for which they have been designed.
Within the large territory of China and between China and the rest of
the world, people have also constructed linguistic and literary, ethnic
and racial, regional and disciplinary walls. Such boundaries have
sometimes been ignored, circumvented, or transcended, but they have
rarely been dismantled, dissolved, or eliminated. The Chinese, like the
rest of humanity, have also regularly created and breached social and
cultural walls in such aesthetic domains as film and painting—media
that typically adhere to a wall-like surface.

In this book we seek to expand and deepen our understanding of
the persistence and significance of various kinds of walls in the long-
term evolution of Chinese civilization. To anticipate, we challenge the
reigning paradigms that associate walls with ancient, medieval, feudal,
traditional, or imperial times and that depict them as constraining,
isolating, divisive, and xenophobic.[4] Instead we attempt to free walls
from any singular or fixed role in time and space and to see them as

---

3   Xu, *The Chinese City*, ch. 4; Naquin, *Peking*, 2000. See also the journal *Chengshi/Wall
     and Market*.

4   For two recent treatments of walls as largely negative, understandable under the cir-
     cumstances, see then-Senator Barack Obama's address in Berlin in July 2008 on the
     United States' role of the in the world and film director Zhang Yimou's depiction of
     "the Great Wall" at the opening of the Olympics in Beijing in August 2008.

various, multifunctional, and dynamic, rising and falling in yet to be described patterns. When we go beyond material walls to virtual ones and beyond history to many other domains, we cannot expect to find a single integrating theme that will make simple sense of all the rich data that we encounter. Yet we believe that many and perhaps most of the findings in this study support the notion of a fairly coherent multidisciplinary perspective—not simply unrelated views—on walls and one with significance going far beyond "the past" or "China" and speaking to issues of importance to all of contemporary humanity.

We first came together over three years ago in conjunction with an exhibition that resulted in the book *The Wall: Reshaping Contemporary Chinese Art/Qiang: Zhongguo dangdai yishu de lishi yu bianjie*. The exhibition opened first in the summer of 2005 at the Millennium Art Museum in Beijing. It was remounted in only slightly altered form again in the fall of that year at the University at Buffalo and Albright-Knox art galleries in Buffalo. The exhibitions consisted of a wide array of cutting-edge works, including paintings, video, film, installation art, and behavioral art. The resulting catalog/book described the immediate content and context of the items in the exhibition and offered a comprehensive history of contemporary Chinese art during the "new era" of "reform and opening" in the People's Republic since 1979.[5] In that volume written in both Chinese and English on the theme of "the wall" in Chinese contemporary art, curator Minglu Gao and assistant-curator Bingyi Huang raised many fresh questions, offered many persuasive answers, and left some important issues open for further exploration. The accompanying conference, held simultaneously at the University at Buffalo and the Albright-Knox art galleries under the title "The Roles and Representations of Walls in the Reshaping of Chinese Modernity," addressed some of those questions and raised others of its own.[6]

The present book includes thirteen of the conference papers that have been considerably revised through intercommunication among the editors, authors, and outside readers over the last three years. It contains our considered reflections on issues raised by Gao and Huang

---

5   Gao, *The Wall*.
6   For a brief overview, see Des Forges, "Roles and Representations."

and by all of the participants in the conference, and it seeks to provide a synthetic, multidisciplinary analysis based on original research that will be useful to faculty and specialists and accessible to students and the public. The volume ranges over all of Chinese history from earliest recorded times to the present but devotes special attention to the years since 1979, the "new era" of "reform and opening," in the People's Republic. It examines the territory of what is called China today but narrows to certain key regions, such as the "central plain," where Chinese civilization originated as an amalgam of cultures, and expands to include the entire world, where people of Chinese descent and/or culture are increasingly in evidence. We believe that a profound and comprehensive understanding of Chinese walls in their global context is an essential step toward anticipating the future roles of such persistent and significant barriers or demarcations in China and in the world at large.[7]

Perhaps the biggest and most important question Minglu Gao raised was how to conceptualize time and space with respect to Chinese art. Although in general eschewing all simple dichotomies and binaries, such as tradition/modernity and China/West, Gao nonetheless observed that China's historical experience differed significantly from that of Europe. As a result, he writes, the "Western" "temporal logic of pre-modern, modern, and postmodern does not exist" in "China," at least not to the extent it does in the "West." In other words, "these temporalizations, which are rooted in Euro-American history, might not apply neatly to Chinese history," even if many Chinese have appropriated them for their own purposes. "In China," Gao continues, "'modernity' more often refers to the spirit of the times, not to a concrete span of historical time." Thus, in Gao's view, modern and avant-garde have come to mean the same thing in China. "Chinese avant-garde," he continues, "always tries to combine traditional and modern, past and present. . . . As a result, historical memory enters into

---

7   For the argument that China was historically more open to other cultures and more subject to recurrent change than is often recognized, see Hansen, *The Open Empire*; Des Forges, *Cultural Centrality*. For two recent works associating walls with xenophobia and closure to greater and lesser degrees, see Lovell, *The Great Wall*, p. 334; Naquin, *Peking*, p. 6.

a dialogue with the present, creating a new artistic space."[8] In other words, in China, "contemporaneity (*dangdaixing*) and modernity (*xiandaixing*) are one and the same." In Gao's words, "modernity is a constantly evolving state of contemporaneity, a succession of instances as encapsulated by Hu Shi in his formulation 'a particular time, specific space, and my truth.'"[9]

Yet, perhaps because of Gao's background in the People's Republic and the power of both Marxian and Weberian conceptions of time and space in many influential Chinese minds on both sides of the Taiwan strait (as well as in Europe and America), he and his collaborator Huang continue to use the terms "ancient," "feudal," "traditional," "premodern," "early modern," "capitalist," "bourgeois," "modern," "modernization," and "postmodern" not just as important contemporary Chinese ways of thinking about time and space but as universal paradigms needing no definition and little qualification.[10] These two art historians are keenly aware that the concepts of modernity, modernization, modernism, and postmodernism are frequently wielded to posit the West as "advanced" and normative and the East as "backward" and exceptional. But they believe that the solution to this problem is to take Chinese modernity and modernism seriously as (in Gao's words again) "critical reflections on the current pattern and the global system." "From that point of view," he writes, "we could regard modernity as an interactive relationship between the culture and society of a particular region and the other cultures and societies that influence it." More specifically, Gao continues to regard China as a "developing," "modernizing," "non-Western," "Third World," country. This view, which he shares with many others, Chinese and non-Chinese, is keenly aware of inequities in the global division of labor and distribution of wealth and fully cognizant of the

---

8   Gao, *The Wall*, pp. 43, 44, 47, 48. For contemporary Chinese artists' and art critics' use of such terms as "traditional," "premodern," "modern," and "postmodern," see Wu, *Transience*, pp. 24, 41, 43, 130, 133, 135, 140, 141, 163, 167.

9   Gao, *The Wall*, p. 239. Hu Shi was the Anhui-born, Cornell- and Columbia-educated, Dewey-inspired liberal pragmatist of the May 4 movement who became the Republic of China's ambassador to the United States and played an important leadership role in the academic establishment in Taiwan after 1949.

10 Ibid., pp. 41, 42, 91, 124, 125, 127, 192, 197, 199, 202, 212, 213, 239, 277, 292.

inhumanity of certain aspects of Chinese society and economy.[11] In Gao's words, "Only through constructing … [a] new discursive standard can non-Western avant-gardes and modernities declare their own equal worth." He adds: "My goal is to try to find a narrative style and critical standard with which to discuss the modernity and avant-garde nature of Chinese art."[12]

The Wall raises in our minds a question that we address in this book: Is it possible to develop narrative styles and critical standards in the study of Chinese walls that are even less teleological, Eurocentric, and Orientalist than those used in Gao and Huang's recent analysis of contemporary Chinese art? We think that there may be—and that Gao and Huang have already pointed us in the right direction.

They have done so, first, by writing in Chinese as well as in English, and by paying close attention to terminology. Thus, while the English title of their catalog may inevitably suggest to the average English-language reader a sharp focus on the *Great* Wall (itself a special rendering of the Chinese term *changcheng*, lit. "long walls") and attention to the reshaping of *today's* Chinese art (probably as a result of *Western* influence), the Chinese title actually uses the more generic term for "wall" (*qiang*, a word that applies as well to the inner walls of a house or compound). The Chinese title promises an account of an entire genre of physical and metaphysical barriers and markers and calls our attention to both the *history* (i.e., the past) and the *frontiers* (i.e., here suggesting the future) of contemporary Chinese art.

Gao and Huang make good on that promise in a variety of ways. They consider walls as both borders and spaces, they create their own terms for periodizing Chinese art since 1979, they choose "avant-garde" over "experimental" to describe the art (although not consistently the film), and they distinguish among various kinds of "humanism" and between those humanisms and various kinds of "individualism." In a very Chinese way, they note the play on the homophones avant-garde (*qianwei*) and money-oriented (*qianwei*[2]), they eschew misleading dichotomies such as that between avant-garde and official, they point out the differences between performance and behavioral art (their

---

11   Ibid., pp. 47, 53, 232, 239, 262.
12   Ibid. p. 53.

social content), and they distinguish between dignity under hardship and masochism to attract attention. They meditate on the ambiguities of development and progress, value the coexistence of abstraction and spirituality, and consider womanism as well as feminism in interpreting gendered art.[13]

In passing, *The Wall* also recounts numerous instances of Chinese contemporary artists' drawing on the full range of Chinese historical experience to create their own art that comments on conditions in the late-twentieth-century world. The book points out that Lü Shengzhong specializes in cutting little red men out of paper, a practice that goes back to the religious life of early times and persists in folk culture even today.[14] It remarks that He Yunchang's *Diary on Shanghai Water* alludes to the Confucian *Analects'* comparison of life to a river, while He's *Appointment Grasping the Column* references a story of a faithful lover in the Daoist text *Zhuangzi*.[15] *The Wall* mentions that a love story in the film *In Expectation* set in the Yangzi town of Wushan (lit. shaman mountain), about to be submerged by the reservoir created by the Three Gorges Dam, harks back to an affair of the Han ruler Wudi celebrated by the Han poet (and eloper) Sima Xiangru.[16]

We read that the Zhejiang Academy of conceptual art is inspired by the Zen master Hui Neng of the early Tang period.[17] We are reminded that the contemporary artists Gu Wenda and Ding Fang favor the painting of the Northern Song while Li Zhanyang is drawn to painting street scenes on the model of *Spring Festival on the River*, the famous scroll depicting daily life in the Northern Song capital of Kaifeng as it was remembered (and idealized) in the Southern Song and later ages.[18]

---

13   Ibid., pp. 41, 42, 43, 50–51, 52, 81, 162, 175, 232, 262. For an earlier argument in favor of "experimental" over "avant-garde," see Wu, *Transience*, p. 15. For a slightly different interpretation of contemporary women's art, see Xu, "Feminist Art."
14   Gao, *The Wall*, pp. 241–42, Plate 38.
15   Ibid, pp. 225, 227.
16   Ibid., pp. 273–74.
17   Ibid., p. 128.
18   Ibid., pp. 97, 220, 241; see also the influence of the Northern Song poet Su Dongpo on the film set in Hangzhou in *Estranged Paradise*, p. 285, and the influence of the Kaifeng scroll on the film *Xiao Wu* (lit. Little Martial), p. 280.

The prominent contemporary artist Xu Bing cites the late-Ming early-Qing scholar Gu Yanwu on the inefficacy of long walls in resisting invasions by frontier people, a common judgment that will merit further discussion in our Chapter 1.[19] Qin Yufen incorporates Beijing Opera as well as Western Classical music into her artwork to approach the Chinese ideal of "joining the sky and the earth."[20] Wu Jian's impressionist paintings have traces of the early Qing "individualist" Bada Shanren.[21] The film *Sanyuanli* implicitly contrasts the heroes who fought off the British in the Opium War of 1840 with the drug addicts who inhabit that "village suburb" of Canton in the present era. The film *Tiexi* (*West of the Rails*) contrasts the prosperity of the Soviet-supported industrialization of the 1950s with the unemployment characteristic of the deindustrializing Shenzhen suburb today, a point hardly welcome to the apostles of "modernization" in today's China.[22]

Although Chinese art of the eras of Deng Xiaoping and Jiang Zemin was very much a reaction against the socialist realism and revolutionary romanticism of Mao's reign, the continuing force of the first three decades of the People's Republic is readily apparent in the self-proclaimed new period of reform and opening. Xu Bing acknowledges that Mao at least tried to make art serve the people. The Star Group initiated the avant-garde in 1979 with big character posters in the style of the Cultural Revolution, a medium soon thereafter banned by a revised constitution. The New History group celebrated the centennial of Mao's birth in 1993 with a march to Mao's hometown of Shaoshan, painting walls along the way. The Three Step Studio in Shanxi led groups of artists to rural areas in the fashion of the Cultural Revolution movement "down to the countryside."[23] The persistence or, perhaps better, the recurrence of fundamental Chinese notions of the cosmos is evident in the artist Xu Hongming's adoption of the multipoint perspective that, he says, "transcends time and space." (This perspective was challenged and sometimes replaced by arguably "Western" notions of space as early as the eighteenth century.) Resonance with earlier

---

19   Ibid., p. 199.
20   Ibid., p. 258.
21   Ibid., p. 247.
22   Ibid., p. 286.
23   Ibid., pp. 49, 134, 149, 169–70.

ideas is evident too in Minglu Gao's suggestion that Chinese women artists have wanted not so much to "alter their place in a dichotomous framework" as to achieve "a true balance between yin and yang."[24]

Whatever the validity or acceptability of these Chinese claims of identification with the past (some of which might risk appearing to accept a too simple kind of East–West binary), they certainly destroy the idea of a sharp break between any supposed Chinese artistic "tradition" and any putative Chinese "modernity." Instead they strongly support the idea of a continuing dialogue between the present and the past—or, more precisely, various dialogues among various presents and various pasts—that Gao has suggested is (or are) part and parcel of Chinese modernity. Indeed, we would go further to propose that such dialogues have always characterized the history of Chinese aesthetics (as perhaps they have the histories of other aesthetics) and of other domains of Chinese (and of other) civilizations. The present volume, at least, explores these possibilities in several domains through a variety of disciplines.

As we embark on this wider inquiry, *The Wall* offers us further valuable guidance and raises other provocative questions. Chief Curator of the Albright-Knox Art Museum Douglas Dreishpoon writes, quite accurately, "No wall in China possesses a more magisterial, and yet ambiguous, status than the Great Wall."[25] For example, some may wish to regard the historical long walls that lie behind the mythical Great Wall simply as symbols of division, repression, and conservatism, similar to the Berlin Wall, the dismantling of which in 1989, according to Dreishpoon, "signaled a momentous liberation not only for Germany but the world at large."[26] But Mao Zedong, whose attitude toward China's long walls was highly ambivalent, seems to have been equally uncertain about how to appraise the Berlin Wall. According to one account, in 1956 he actually recommended to Walter Ulbricht, leader of the German Democratic Republic, that he build a wall to defend his state by "keeping out people like 'fascists.' "[27] But in 1961 when Khrushchev actually built the Berlin Wall, Mao reportedly told the East

---

24   Ibid., pp. 52, 246–47.

25   Ibid., p. 30.

26   Ibid.

27   Meissner, *Die DDR*, pp. 85, 87, cited in Chang and Halliday, *Mao*, pp. 384, 561, 706.

Germans that it was a sign of Soviet capitulation to the United States.[28] Apparently at this point Mao saw the Berlin Wall as a static, defensive structure, inimical to the cause of world revolution.

Chinese interest in the Berlin wall outlived Chairman Mao. In 1989 the artist Song Haidong as part of the *China/Avant Garde* exhibition in Beijing constructed *The Earth in the Eye of Extraterrestrials,* which featured a globe with a toy wall mounted on the border between East and West Germany. The East German ambassador and an official of the Chinese government asked Gao Minglu, the curator of the exhibition, to remove the artwork on the grounds that it interfered in the internal politics of Germany. As it happened, the entire exhibition was soon shut down for a variety of reasons, but Song's work was prophetic: the Berlin Wall came down five months later.[29] Whatever the relative reliability of some of the sources of these stories, they together suggest the close interaction between China and the rest of the world, and, in that context, the intimate relationship between art and politics posited in *The Wall.* Such accounts raise quite dramatically the question of how to understand the origins and development of the myth(s) of the Great Wall, the topic of our first chapter.[30]

Dreishpoon also commented perceptively that "walls are immanent carriers of urban memory, which makes their accelerated demolition in the Chinese cities and municipalities . . . unsettling." He continued: "If urbanization continues at the present pace, China's burgeoning cities may ultimately exist as entities without memory."[31] Pointing to the same phenomenon, Gao records that the total volume of

---

28 Brie interview, cited in Chang and Halliday, *Mao,* pp. 466, 643, 718.

29 Gao, *The Wall,* pp. 69–70.

30 Dreishpoon writes: "Walls such as the Great Wall in China or the Wailing Wall in Jerusalem, sacred sites of mythic proportions, defy the perils of time even as they continue to impact cultural perception." See Gao, *The Wall,* p. 30. For recent ruminations on the Israel-Palestine imbroglio, which is currently producing another kind of wall, see "Two Wailing Walls."

31 Gao, *The Wall,* p. 30. For similar arguments about the destruction of the walls of Beijing and "the rapid disappearance of the traditional city," see Zhang, "From Demolition"; Wu, *Transience,* pp. 24, 114–19. The number of city walls extant in China depends on one's definition of "extant" as well as one's definition of "China." A recent study includes seventeen relatively well-preserved city walls on the mainland as well as four in Taiwan. Zhao and Gu, *Zhongguo chengqiang.*

construction work in China during the past two decades is said to be equal to that of the preceding millennium. Two-thirds of the world's cement and scaffolding are reported to be in China.[32] This helps to explain the focus of many contemporary artists on scenes of the destruction of the old walls of cities, compounds, shops, and houses, and on the construction of new metropolises without walls and featuring buildings that are often indistinguishable from those of other global cities. The film *Sanyuanli* emphasizes the new forms of transportation—trains, cars, and airplanes—that have often resulted in the alteration, destruction, and/or transcendence of walls and gates while also causing quantum increases in traffic accidents and industrial pollution.[33] Examples of artwork depicting this environment include Li Zhanyang's *Street Scene No. 3—An Accident, 2001*; Wang Jinsong's *A Hundred Chai—to be demolished*; and Zhang Dali's ubiquitous self-profile (associated with an AK47 machine gun) on walls slated for, or in process of, destruction.[34] In view of this work, Gao raises key questions that seem (properly, in our view) to be rhetorical: "Does the rapid urbanization of space necessarily imply modern and humanistic progress? Does indifference to historical context and natural environment aid in our pursuit of the most fundamental human values?"[35]

Chapters 2 and 3 of this book attempt to show how such questions have been answered in Henan Province. This province takes its name from the fact that it straddles and lies largely south of the Yellow River (*Huanghe*), another icon (along with long walls) often associated with Chinese identity. Significantly, Henan is also known as the central province (*zhongzhou*) because it is located in the center of the central plain (*zhongyuan*). The central plain, in turn, was where early Chinese civilization (including the cultivation of millet and rice, the construction of cities and states, the manufacturing of bronze and writing) first developed. The central plain, therefore, is often used as a synecdoche of the central state(s) (*zhongguo*), one of the oldest, most

---

32 Ibid., p. 218.
33 Ibid., pp. 290–91.
34 Ibid., pp. 220, 222, 224, 319 (Plate 22-1). For an appraisal of Zhang Dali's art, see Wang, "The Spectral Head."
35 Gao, *The Wall*, p. 232.

common, and most durable indigenous names for what Westerners call "China."

While these two chapters focus on the cities and towns of a specific region, they therefore have implications for much of the rest of territorial China. We begin their stories in the not-so-distant (both in time and in style) past, the Ming period, and we take them down to the present. Thanks in part to archaeological evidence, a sometime beneficiary as well as frequent victim of construction projects, we shall find that the closer we approach the present the more we can use evidence from the distant past to help discount, confirm, modify, or develop our historical memories.

Walls around lower levels of urban society in other parts of China—such as the famous wards of Chang'an city (the Tang capital near present-day Xi'an in Shaanxi province) and the Sino-foreign jurisdictions of Shanghai (the late Qing and Republican metropolis in Jiangsu province)—may be studied with less or no assistance from archaeology. In those cases, which we take up in Part II, we must rely on literary and legal sources in our effort to understand how walls and gates, physical and metaphorical, influenced the lives of individuals and groups in societies undergoing significant change over time and space. In Chapters 4 and 5 we assess the interaction between state institutions of social control and the daily lives of the urbanites they were designed to order. In the process we raise questions about the vaunted power of the Chinese state and the oppressive nature of Western imperialism.

One of the reasons adduced for skepticism about the historicity of the Great Wall, or even about the military importance of long walls, is that they were only infrequently depicted by Chinese writers and artists.[36] Even Minglu Gao, who clearly recognized the importance of the idea and fact of long walls (and even of the Great Wall after the Japanese invasion of northeast China in the 1930s), commented: "During the era of Mao Zedong [1949–1976], works illustrating the Great Wall were rare and in the few ink paintings that do exist, the Wall

---

36 Perhaps this was in part because they were often in ruins, a state of being generally avoided by Chinese artists. Wu, "Ruins"; Wu, *Transience*, pp. 25, 80.

is not the focal point."[37] While this was presumably true of painting and other fine arts, it turns out not to be the case when it comes to political cartoons.

In Part III we turn to the ways in which walls are used to contain threats and are periodically breached. In Chapter 6, we analyze for the first time in print a significant cache of political cartoons from the early People's Republic that invoked walls as icons with many different meanings. Walls served as sites of failure to resist the Japanese in the northeast ("Manchuria"), as symbols of success in resisting the Americans in the same general region (Korea), and as harbingers of cooperation with the Soviet Union (a neighbor that not only recognized but assisted the new Chinese state). One question here is whether the People's Republic was reacting rationally to real threats and opportunities or was instead exaggerating the likelihood of U.S. invasion and the prospect for U.S.S.R. support to enhance its political authority and pursue its own social agenda.

In her recent study of the Great Wall, Julia Lovell, no unconditional admirer of the structure, states provocatively that "the very lack of walls" may have contributed to the collapse of Mongol rule in 1368."[38] Unlike some contemporary Chinese scholars, Lovell associates walls with restraints on trade and migration, and she argues that the destruction of—or at least the lack of attention to—frontier walls in the Yuan dynasty led to an increase in the movement of people, other animals, and commodities between the steppe and the sown regions of China. One result, she thinks, was the spread of plague from Inner Asia to central China (and eventually to Europe). That epidemic, in turn, resulted in depopulation, famine, and rebellion, which ultimately brought down the Yuan. Whatever the validity of that argument (which may seem far-fetched but deserves to be tested), it raises the issue of the quality of the effort of the People's Republic, in the midst of a period of

---

37   Gao, *The Wall*, p. 194. We should note, though, that a large mural depicting the Great Wall accompanied by the slogan "We Have Friends throughout the World" greeted visitors to Mao's China who stayed in the Beijing Hotel near Tiananmen Square, just as a different representation of that icon, but one also emphasizing both sides of the edifice, has welcomed passengers arriving at the international airport in Beijing in recent years.

38   Lovell, *The Great Wall*, p. 178.

"openness" (but one also inspired by the call to "love our China and restore our long walls") to deal with the origins and spread of the Severe Acute Respiratory Syndrome (SARS), which first appeared in November 2002 and spread to the world through mid-2003.

According to Douglas Dreishpoon, who arrived in China in March 2003, the Communist party did little to stop the threatening epidemic. Although he acknowledges that it may be human nature to minimize impending disaster and "perhaps traditional codes of honor made foreign intervention undesirable," he records that Chinese officials, "instead of seeking outside assistance . . . retrenched behind a wall of secrecy."[39] In a word, they stonewalled. The implication here, as with accounts by many other foreign observers, was that the Chinese state was highly inefficient if not woefully irresponsible in not publicizing and dealing forthrightly with the crisis. This interpretation was shared by many Chinese. Hu Jintao, then still under the shadow of his predecessor Jiang Zemin, gained added stature as the new president, general secretary, and chair of the Military Affairs Commission when he finally won support from the military to go public with the problem. The crisis also helped to legitimate the administrative reform that accelerated in its aftermath.[40]

On the other hand, Dreishpoon acknowledges, "a virus like SARS, capable of traversing vast distances through human and animal hosts, vaporizes any kind of barrier [structural, social, cultural]."[41] This raises the question of just how such a lethal disease originates and how, once it exists, humans can best combat it. The issue was more than academic for the Hong Kong–based woman artist Man Fungyi, whose pregnant sister fell ill with SARS in 2003. Man responded by continuing to burn incense (instead of using needles, the normal method, which she happened to dislike) to "embroider" silk scrolls. She now considered the process to be not just an artistic technique but a spiritual ritual designed to help her sister recover.[42] When her sister's baby was born

---

39   Gao, *The Wall*, p. 29.

40   Talk by Professor Liang Zhanjun of Capital Normal University at "Asia at Noon," in Buffalo, spring 2004; Lam, *Chinese Politics*, pp. 27, 42, 139–40, 221.

41   Gao, *The Wall*, p. 29.

42   Ibid., pp. 259–60. The artist apparently used the burning incense to mark the scrolls as well as to enhance communication with the spirits.

normally (if prematurely) and her sister recovered from SARS, Man was probably confirmed in her belief in the need to "fuse extroverted Western culture [i.e., Western medical science?] . . . with Eastern culture [religious ritual?] that explores the deeper and more primal nature of life."[43] Given her family experience and the difficulty of overcoming the new disease, Man may be excused for accepting and perpetuating one of the grandest of cultural overgeneralizations: a spiritual East contrasted with a material West. In any case, this story sparks our interest in getting more details on the way such diseases emerge, why this one spread so far so fast, and how it was apparently contained within a year with relatively low human mortality. As we discuss in our Chapter 7, the appearance of a similar disease, Avian Influenza, in the same region of the world only a couple of years later, both compounded and helped to clarify these questions.

The origins and spread of electronic communication, too, raise important questions about the functionality of walls and the existence of gates, both attended and unattended, the topic of our Chapter 8. Once again Dreishpoon has observed an interesting coincidence: the appearance of Microsoft Windows 3.0 some six months after the fall of the Berlin Wall on November 9, 1989. (The fall of the wall was an event, we may add, that followed by only five months the June 4 suppression of urban demonstrations in China).[44] If the Internet, perhaps the most lucrative by-product of U.S. military research to date, can serve as a symbol of openness in the supposed post–Cold War era, it is also not immune to supervision either in China or in the rest of the world. As Dreishpoon notes, "Even at the frontier of globalization there exists another wall in the form of a firewall—the first line of defense for any cyber-based network."[45] Although the Internet originated in the West and the United States sought to monitor its spread to China, the Chinese response was highly enthusiastic and rapid, perhaps reflecting the government's confidence in inventing and using what we might call intellectual technology (shades of paper, printing, and the abacus). In any case, technological transfer in this case was extremely rapid and it

43   Ibid, p. 259.
44   Gao, *The Wall*, p. 30.
45   Ibid., p. 34.

looks as if China will move into the forefront of both using and managing the Internet in the near future. The question, then, is not how quickly the PRC will " catch up" and perhaps "surpass" the United States in using the world wide web for its own purposes. It is rather how effectively the Chinese (along with others such as Yahoo and Google, not to speak of the Pentagon) will be able to monitor and control the net to prevent its use contrary to their perceived interests. Here again the question arises: are we facing a whole new world of "free" and "open" sources of information or only the most recent variation on past systems of communication and on methods of controlling them?

We have already noted that *The Wall* pays exemplary attention to the issues of terminology and translation. We take up these matters in our Part IV, "China in the World," and particularly in its first chapter, on translating Chinese poetry into English. Here we explore the questions posed by Wai-lim Yip: whether Chinese poetry, inspired by Daoism, effectively breaches the walls between the natural world and the human perception of it; and whether good translations can break down the walls between "Eastern" and "Western" concepts of the cosmos. Our Chapter 9 explores the strengths and weaknesses of Yip's approaches.

According to Hou Hanru, talking about contemporary Chinese art, "it is no longer possible to isolate it from the current restructuring of contemporary art and culture on a global scale today, let alone attempt to draw any borderline around it, whether such a borderline is a geographic, cultural, or material one."[46] Minglu Gao has followed up by asking: "In aesthetic terms, how have the traditional aesthetic 'walls' between East and West, ancient and modern, given way to less certain standards of delineation?"[47] In Chapter 10 we explore that issue further by looking at the performance (or, more precisely, behavioral) art of several Chinese who originated in different places, extending from the central province of Henan outward to the near periphery of Hong Kong and Taiwan, and on to the far periphery of California. In this "greater China," an aesthetic world that includes all of those places and

---

46 Hou, "Beyond the 'Chinese,'" p. 34, cited in Gao, *The Wall*, p. 33.

47 Gao, *The Wall*, p. 42.

more, we examine the particularities of life histories as keys to the problem of cultural authenticity.

If the borders among cultures and ethnic groups are blurring and fading (though not disappearing), the boundaries of nation-states and of disciplines seem to persist.[48] As Dreishpoon puts it, "A world without walls seems improbable when separation through differentiation is crucial to the existence of life. And as the nature of life's game continues to change, new walls will inevitably arise." He adds: "This need not be a bad thing where creativity is concerned; engaged art thrives on resistance. Indeed, the last bastion of resistance may well be the wall that persists in one's mind, as fleeting as a dream or as onerous as a mountain."[49] In Chapter 11 we explore persistent boundaries in the art (and/or science) of Chinese historiography. These boundaries are the familiar ones between the old (feudal or traditional) and the new (capitalist or modern) and between the subdisciplines of national history and world history. We seek to explain the resilience of these walls despite the rapid translation into Chinese of increasingly powerful "Western" critiques of historical teleology and cultural Eurocentricity. If there is a problem here, is it because Chinese historians remain stuck in their Marxian/Weberian paradigms and in their subdisciplines of Chinese and world history or because the new models of world history emanating from the "West," despite their creators' best efforts, continue to be marred by assumptions about historical change and cultural centrality?[50]

Even as walls break down between East and West in film and painting, they persist as models and metaphors in those same domains as we shall see in Part V. Minglu Gao has argued that the Chinese avant-garde has attempted over these last three decades to prove its "modernity" (in Gao's terms) by "erasing the boundary between art and life." If so, it will have to thank, among others, the French New Wave cinema, which has clearly influenced what Huang Bingyi calls

---

48   For the recurrence of various kinds of nationalism in Chinese contemporary art, for example, see Shui, "Nationalism."

49   Gao, The Wall, p. 34.

50   For a recent study exemplifying as well as exploring the achievements and the limitations of Western critiques of Western histories of the world, see Goody, The Theft. We are grateful to Claire Schen for bringing this study to our attention.

"Chinese experimental films."[51] According to the critic Michel Marie, this New Wave features: "*auteurs*" who both write and direct; improvisation in dialogue and acting; crews that are small, young, and nonprofessional; and settings that are natural in sight and sound.[52] In Chapter 12 we analyze an example of this kind of film that uses a variety of walls to portray the everyday lives and challenges of men, women, and children who have been marginalized in China's drive for "development" and "modernization." One question here is whether the growth in social inequality is essential to the creation of greater wealth or whether it is instead merely a feature of a particular world system that currently goes under the often unexamined title of "globalization." If the latter is the case, is it possible even to conceive of—let alone to realize—an alternative system?

In Gao's view, the major "Western" art critic who helped to define "modernism" in the United States, Clement Greenberg, tended to tout art for art's sake, whereas the prominent "Chinese" cultural critic of the May 4 era, Cai Yuanpei, called for aesthetic education that involved concern for the life and suffering of ordinary people.[53] But Greenberg also argued that "the two-dimensional reality of paint was far more real and advanced than three-dimensional representation," a point that went back to Plato and one that the Chinese have long understood and continue to believe.[54] The question arises, then, What would happen if an American artist trained in the modernism defined by Greenberg but confronting Western challenges to that view became aware of Chinese approaches to art? In our thirteenth and final chapter, we explore this question in the case of Brice Marden, who reacted against the Western postmodern idea of "the death of painting" and turned to various Chinese arts, including calligraphy and paintings on walls, to revitalize "modernism" and extend its life into the twenty-first century. Thus, "Chinese" aesthetic approaches that have their roots deep in the past and remain viable to this day may have helped to restore the painting culture of the "modern West" that some thought destined for extinction only a decade or two ago. The interaction of Chinese

51   Gao, *The Wall,* pp. 47, 265.
52   Ibid., p. 275.
53   Ibid., p. 46.
54   Ibid., p. 245.

aesthetics—and other cultural domains—with those of the West would appear likely to continue in the present century with positive effects on both ends of Eurasia and on both hemispheres of the globe. Marden's exploration and questioning of the two-dimensional space of the wall suggests a role for walls other than walling in and walling out: that of the screen, a plane for the projection of collective imagination.

RVD for the editors

Works Cited

Brie Horst. Interview at the embassy of the German Democratic Republic in Beijing, cited in Chang and Halliday, *Mao*, pp. 466, 643, 718.

Chang, Jung, and Jon Halliday. *Mao: The Unknown Story*. New York: Alfred A. Knopf, 2005.

Chengshi/Wall and Market/Chinese Urban History News, Kristin Stapleton, ed., University of Kentucky, Vols. 1–5 (1996–2000).

Des Forges, Roger. *Cultural Centrality and Political Change: Northeast Henan in the Fall of the Ming*. Stanford: Stanford University Press, 2003.

———. "The Roles and Representations of Walls in the Reshaping of Chinese Modernity," *Asian Studies Newsletter*, 51.1 (Annual Meeting Issue, spring 2006), pp. 12–13.

Gao, Minglu, ed. *The Wall: Reshaping Contemporary Chinese Art/Qiang: Zhongguo dangdai yishu de lishi yu bianjie*. Beijing and Buffalo: The Millennium Museum and University at Buffalo Art Galleries, Albright-Knox Art Gallery, 2005.

Goody, Jack. *The Theft of History*. Cambridge: Cambridge University Press, 2006.

Hansen, Valerie. *The Open Empire: A History of China to 1600*. New York: W. W. Norton, 2000.

Hou, Hanru. "Beyond the 'Chinese,'" *Chinese Art at the End of the Millennium: Chinese-art.com 1998–1999*, John Clark, ed. Hong Kong: New Art Media Limited, 2000.

Lam, Willy Wo-Lap. *Chinese Politics in the Hu Jintao Era: New Leaders, New Challenges*. Armonk, New York: M. E. Sharpe, 2006.

Lovell, Julia. *The Great Wall: China against the World, 1000 BC–AD 2000*. New York: Grove, 2006.

Meissner, Werner, ed. *Die DDR und China 1949 bis 1990*. Berlin: Akademie Verlag, 1995.

Naquin, Susan. *Peking: Temples and City Life, 1400–1900.* Berkeley: University of California Press, 2000.

Roberts, Claire, and Geremie R. Barmé, eds. *The Great Wall of China.* Sydney: Powerhouse, 2006.

Shui, Tianzhong. "'Nationalism' in Chinese Aesthetics Today," paper delivered at the Conference on The Roles and Representations of Walls in the Reshaping of Chinese Modernity, University at Buffalo and Albright-Knox Art Galleries, October 22, 2005. (Cited with the author's permission.)

"Two Wailing Walls: Forty Years of Occupation: Two Views," Meron Benvenisti, "The Case for Shared Sovereignty," and Saree Makdisi, "For a Secular Democratic State," *Nation,* June 18, 2007, pp. 11, 13–14, 16.

Waldron, Arthur. *The Great Wall of China: From History to Myth.* Cambridge: Cambridge University Press, 1990.

Wang, Eugene Yuejin. "The Spectral Head on the Wall: Zhang Dali's 'Graffiti' in Beijing," paper delivered at the Conference on The Roles and Representations of Walls in the Reshaping of Chinese Modernity, University at Buffalo and Albright-Knox Art Galleries, October 21, 2005. (Cited with the author's permission.)

Wu, Hung. "Ruins, Fragmentation, and the Chinese Modern/Postmodern," in Gao Minglu, ed. *Inside Out: New Chinese Art.* San Francisco and New York: San Francisco Museum of Modern Art and Asia Society Galleries, 1998, pp. 59–66.

––––. *Transience: Chinese Experimental Art at the End of the Twentieth Century.* Chicago: University of Chicago Press, 2004

Xu, Hong. "Feminist Art in China Today," paper delivered at the Conference on The Roles and Representations of Walls in the Reshaping of Chinese Modernity, University at Buffalo and Albright-Knox Art Galleries, October 22, 2005. (Cited with the author's permission.)

Xu, Yinong. *The Chinese City in Space and Time: The Development of Urban Form in Suzhou.* Honolulu: University of Hawai'i Press, 2000.

Zhang, Yue. "From Demolition to Restoration: The Story of the Old City Walls of Beijing, 1949–2005," paper delivered at the Conference on The Roles and Representations of Walls in the Reshaping of Chinese Modernity, University at Buffalo and Albright-Knox Art Galleries, October 21, 2005. (Cited with the author's permission.)

Zhao Suosheng, and Gu Yangeng. *Zhongguo chengqiang* [China's City Walls]. Nanjing: Jiangsu jiangyu chubanshe, 2000.

PART ONE
The Building and Unbuilding of Walls

CHINESE WALLS, LIKE THE WALLS of Uruk and Jericho in the Middle East or walls anywhere, were and are first and foremost material edifices erected, torn down, and restored by humans. One of the Chinese words for walls, *cheng*, with its earth radical and association with becoming and completing, was used for the massive and long fortifications across northern China (and to a much lesser extent in southern China). The term was also used for the structures that enclosed major sites of demographic, commercial, political, and cultural concentration, that is, cities such as Beijing, Nanjing, Shanghai, and Canton, or in this book, more modestly, Kaifeng, Guide (pronounced Guey-duh)/ Shangqiu, and Zhengzhou. Walls (*cheng*) also surrounded smaller conurbations such as prefectural and county capitals, which could be as large as cities and as small as towns (using these terms heuristically without any clear distinction between them).

In Part I, we examine the histories of the long walls that stretched across much of northern China from early times to the present, the city walls that enclosed three communities of varying size but roughly equal importance over time in northeastern Henan province, and the walls that were constructed around two dozen county capitals, including some that might qualify as cities but most of which were more modest in size and importance and therefore called by us towns. (There were also more strictly speaking walled towns [*zhen*], of more commercial than administrative significance that increased in importance over time, and there were even walled villages, especially in times of disorder, but these sorts of walled communities fall outside the purview of this book.)

1

The construction, destruction, and reconstruction of walls in China occurred in patterns that we are only beginning to explore. Existing paradigms that associate walls with a feudal, traditional, and/or imperial past and their destruction with a capitalist or socialist, modern, and/or republican present, do not help much in tracking and understanding the actual incidence of wall building and unbuilding in the Chinese case. Instead we need a fresh conceptualization of the issue allowing for more productive empirical research and more precise comparisons over time and space. China's long walls, city walls, and town walls were quite different in many ways, such as size and shape, but they also shared many characteristics, such as how and why they were constructed and, as it turns out, the pattern of their appearance and disappearance over time and space.

Although we can hardly claim to have conducted a comprehensive study of these issues, we have surveyed most of the existing literature on the long walls separating (or joining—the issue is contested) the steppe and sown or pastoral China from (or to) agricultural China. Our treatment of city and town walls is perforce much less comprehensive, but the region we have chosen to focus on is Henan, the so-called central province (*zhongzhou*), in the heart of the central plain (*zhongyuan*), a common synecdoche for the central states (*zhongguo*) that is one of the hoariest and most ubiquitous indigenous terms for what Westerners have come to call "China." Our studies of city and town walls therefore, while circumscribed in time and in space, should have implications for other parts of the Chinese world if not for the world as a whole.

CHAPTER ONE

"The Great Wall of China"

An Author's Reflections after Twenty Years

*Arthur Waldron**

THE PROBLEM OF THE SO-CALLED Great Wall of China first came to my attention when I was a graduate student preparing my dissertation on a great debate in the mid–Ming dynasty. The debate was over whether to drive the Mongols out of the plain and desert in the great loop of the Yellow River. My hypothesis was that the Ming could have resolved its conflict with the Mongols more peacefully if it had been willing to trade with them and to accord them legitimate status. My advisor, the late Joseph Fletcher, disagreed. He adduced many anthropological arguments about the inherent conflict between settled cultivators and horse nomads around the world and pointed to "the existence of the Great Wall for thousands of years" as evidence of it in the Chinese case.[1] So I decided to find out everything I could about the structure that my professor took as a key example in the argument.

* The author would like to express his profound gratitude for the extensive assistance of the editors, most importantly Roger Des Forges, in the hard work of rewriting and editing what had been an informal talk into this essay.

1 The brilliant, charismatic, multilingual Fletcher died at age forty-nine in 1984, but not before recognizing some of the mythical elements of the received story of the Great Wall. For a posthumous collection of his writings, see Fletcher, *Studies*.

Upon looking into the history of the "Great Wall," however, I discovered, to my astonishment, that relatively little scholarly research treated the topic. Certainly no definitive work existed in any language. As for Fletcher's views, their roots could be found in the work of the pioneer specialist in Inner Asian history, Owen Lattimore.[2] Lattimore had pointed to differences in topography, climate, economy, languages, and ethnicities to argue that what he called "the general line of the Great Wall" was "one of the most absolute frontiers in the world."[3] More recently, Joseph Needham, the polymath historian of Chinese science and civilization, had acknowledged the paucity of serious work on the Great Wall in his own relatively brief treatment of the topic.[4] But even he did not question the received story, concluding that under the founder of the Qin dynasty in the third century BCE, walls built by individual states were "joined together to form a continuous defence, the Great Wall (Wan Li Chhang Chheng), the building of which has remained a focal point in Chinese folklore ever since."[5] Although both Lattimore and Needham had been aware of some of the complexity of the history of the fortifications established in the vast region where the steppe meets the sown in north China (and although Needham referred explicitly to "folklore"), they both adopted the term "the Great Wall" and stressed the continuity of its development over the course of more than two millennia. They thus failed to dent—and may actually have reinforced—the image that most people in China and the rest of the world have long embraced and that apparently still influenced the thinking of major scholars in the field of Chinese history, of the wall as a single continuously existing structure, defining an unchanging border, and begun in ancient times.[6]

After reading more in the primary and secondary sources, I became convinced that the concept of a Great Wall of China that had

2   Lattimore, *Inner Asian Frontiers*, pp. 21–25, 429–68, maps on p. 22 and 530.
3   Ibid., p. 21; Lattimore, *Studies*, pp. 101–5.
4   Needham, *Science and Civilisation*, IV.3, pp. 47, n.f.; 53.
5   Needham, *Science and Civilisation*, I, pp. 92, 100. Needham used his own Romanization for *wanli changcheng*, lit. "the 10,000 li-long wall," a term that first appeared (as a metaphor) during the Liu Song dynasty (420–79 CE). Waldron, *Great Wall*, p. 202.
6   These scholars included my one-time colleagues Frederick Mote, Marius Jansen, James T. C. Liu, and Denis Twitchett, now all deceased, as well as Ying-shih Yu.

come down to us by the mid–twentieth century contained a great deal of myth.[7] Some writers on the wall were aware of the problems, and even pointed them out, but the myths proved well nigh unstoppable, at least at the popular level, in both China and the rest of the world. This was so much the case that the prominent Chinese journalist Liang Qichao took mistaken beliefs about the wall in the early twentieth as a prime example of historical misinterpretation in his influential book about historical method.[8] Given "the degree to which our understanding of Chinese history has been and is distorted by confusion about the Great Wall," I decided to draft a paper to summarize the myths in one place.[9]

In the resulting article, published in 1983, I argued that the Qin established long walls (*changcheng*) but they did not lay down the routes for defensive lines built by the succeeding states. Like most long walls before and after the Qin, they were made largely of tamped earth that decayed quickly. Hence, in addition to being located in remote areas, they left little if any physical traces that could have directly affected succeeding generations of Chinese wall builders. The Qin fortification of the frontier was mentioned only a few times in passing in Sima Qian's *Historical Records* and there was to the time of my writing little archaeological evidence for them. The succeeding Han dynasty proved unable to maintain the Qin presence (including its walls) in the north. Although the Han used some parts of the Qin wall to divide the frontier territory with the neighboring Xiongnu people and repaired some parts of the inherited wall, in general it emphasized watchtowers more than walls. Evidence that the Han had a 10,000 li (about 3,000 mile) Great Wall, I wrote, was "extremely limited."[10] There were only scat-

---

7   Secondary scholarly works included, notably, Luo et al., *Great Wall*; Luo and Zhao, *Great Wall*; Wang, *Zhongguo changcheng*; Shou, *Lidai changcheng*; and *Zhongguo changcheng.* My preliminary presentation at Princeton University based on these and other sources was met with some surprise but also interest; it was confirmed by the Korean scholar Gari Ledyard at Columbia University, who found little evidence of any Chinese long walls in Korean sources.

8   Liang, *Zhongguo.* Liang's treatment indicated the importance of the concept of the Great Wall in many Chinese minds and, equally significant, it did not succeed in its effort to diminish it.

9   Waldron, "Problem," p. 645.

10 Ibid., p. 652.

tered references to various kinds of border fortifications in a few later
dynasties—(Northern Wei, Eastern Wei (534–550), Northern Qi (550–
577), and the Later Zhou (950–959). The Sui, which did emphasize long
walls, did not last long. I expressed my puzzlement at the lack, at the
time, of archaeological documentation of any of these constructions,
all far more recent than whatever the Qin or Han might have built.
Moreover the Sui was followed by the Tang and the Song, which did
not build long walls, let alone any Great Wall. The Song never even
controlled the territory around modern Beijing, north of which the
walls lie. Although the Jin did build walls, "The Mongols encountered
no Great Wall when they conquered China."[11] Moreover the Mongol-
dominated Yuan dynasty built no frontier walls. At the time I was doing my research, work in the field was extremely difficult so my field-
work was necessarily limited, though I did visit key places.

Furthermore, there were the linguistic difficulties involved in the
term "*changcheng*" mentioned above. It could be either singular—a
stretch of long wall—or plural—a series of long walls. It contained no
implication of "greatness"—both *chang* and *cheng* are common, everyday words. Furthermore, when local gazetteers mention the presence
of *changcheng* at a given place, the meaning is clearly that a stretch of
long wall is to be found there, not that, somehow, "the Great Wall of
China" is there.

Had we today only the remains of pre-Ming fortifications, I argued,
Chinese wall building might be an area studied by a few specialized
archaeologists, some folklorists aware of the ancient ballads about the
hardships of wall-building, and students of poetry that lamented military service on the frontier, but no concept of an ancient and defining
"Great Wall of China" would cast its shadow backward over the history
of that country. For it was only in the mid-Ming that the much larger
and often stone-faced walls, with towers and crenellations, were constructed, and it was they, rather than earlier fortifications, that defined
the commonly accepted image of China's "Great Wall." These walls
were not begun until after the new dynasty, which emulated the offensive tactics of the Mongols under its early rulers, had tried conquest
without success, and ruled out the sort of trade to which nomads had

11   Ibid., p. 656.

been accustomed as demeaning to the rulers in Beijing. The Ming finally turned to building extensive frontier fortifications, to be sure, but they called them "frontier walls" (*bianqiang*), not long walls (*changcheng*), which term was odious owing to its close association with the reviled tyranny of the Qin. The Ming frontier walls followed no master plan. They were first suggested for the northwestern frontier at the end of the fifteenth century, in response to a local threat. Later they were built in other places. They did not follow Qin routes. However, as the dynasty progressed, frontier fortification became more and more elaborate, until in the sixteenth century walls were regularly constructed with brick and stone facing and stone fill (rather than of tamped earth, as previously), by professional masons rather than by corvée labor, and were paid for by silver obtained from taxes levied by the central government. The veritable records (*shilu*) of the dynasty, which detailed projects and disbursements, as well as local records, revealed that it was only in the late Ming that the extensive fortifications at such key points as Shanhaiguan and Badaling, visited by tourists today, were finally constructed. An impressive series of snaking masonry fortifications was thus created, bit by bit with no single blueprint. They not surprisingly acquired the mythic title *wanli changcheng* "the ten thousand li wall"—for the Ming ruins are indeed impressive—that was soon to become, in English, "the Great Wall of China." At the time, however, these fortifications attracted the same scorn that their Qin and other predecessors had. They symbolized dynastic weakness toward foreign foes and oppression of the ordinary people forced to build them. Despite their ubiquity, they were, significantly, never the subject of contemporary painting.

To be sure, accounts of a Great Wall existed in folk tradition well before the Ming. The best example is the story of Meng Jiangnü, the widow who wept for her husband (who died building the Qin wall), thereby causing part of the wall to collapse and reveal his bones, which she then carried to his native place for a proper burial.[12] Chinese regularly interpret this tale as being about the oppression of the ordinary Chinese by their rulers. They note that the people were clever in their

---

12   For a pioneering study, see Wang, "Transformation"; for a more recent account of the origins, development, and significance of the legend, see Idema and Lee, *Meng Jiangnü*.

choice of subject: a long ballad about death building a palace or an imperial tomb would have crossed the line; a tale of grief at a distant frontier project did not. And myths can take on lives of their own that influence history. As my own teacher Lien-sheng Yang had put it, in words that I placed alone on a page at the very beginning of my book, "In studying the Chinese world order it is important to distinguish myth from reality wherever possible. Both can be influential." With this injunction in mind, my purpose was to chip the myth of the historicity of the single Great Wall away from the underlying realities of Chinese border defense, and more broadly, national definition and character. So I asserted that "militarily significant walls, then, not to mention anything remotely like the Great Wall of popular imagination, did not exist for most of Chinese history."[13] Even in the early Ming, I wrote, "Nowhere is a Great Wall mentioned."[14] In sum, I argued, "While it [the myth of the Great Wall] is a promising subject for students of folklore and myth, it can only mislead the historian."[15]

Chinese history and literature provided one taproot of the myth of the Great Wall. But a second, perhaps more important source consisted of Western images of China that began as early as Marco Polo, grew enormously with the Jesuits in the late Ming and early Qing (late sixteenth and seventeenth centuries), and then broke all tethers with reality in the age of Western dominance that began in the nineteenth century and carried over into the early decades of the twentieth. This proved so absorbing a cultural topic that it seemed worth a second article, published in 1988, which addressed the way in which Chinese myths about the Great Wall were developed in the West and returned to China in the twentieth century.[16] This piece began: "The way that we

---

13   Waldron, "Problem," p. 657.

14   Ibid., p. 660.

15   Ibid., p. 663. A less categorical distinction between history and myth was made by leading Chinese historians of the wall who, nonetheless, shared the idea that the Great Wall that exists in ruins today can be traced only to the Ming. Luo and Zhao, *Great Wall*.

16   Waldron, "Great Wall Myth." Meanwhile, apparently independently, Chinese historians continued to trace the origins of long walls to the Spring and Autumn period but they also emphasized the importance of the Ming period of development. See Feng and He, *Liaoning gu changcheng*; Hua Xia Zi, *Ming changcheng*.

understand and interpret these walls, not the fact of their existence in Chinese history, is at issue here."[17] According to the prevalent myth, the Chinese built a single brick and stone wall in the third century BCE that they maintained over the course of two millennia and that therefore became their northern national boundary. In fact, insofar as any concept of a Great Wall existed, the "traditional" Chinese view was that it had been constructed at the expense of the people and with little positive effect by the Qin dynasty, which proved short-lived. Dynasties that followed in that tradition, such as the Northern Qi and Sui, were similarly ephemeral. As a result, the wall was little treated in literature and art and became an "unambiguously negative symbol" of despotism in the eyes of the literati.[18] It was a whole series of Western observers who first turned the Great Wall into a more positive symbol of the antiquity and continuity of Chinese civilization, and it was twentieth-century nationalists such as Sun Yat-sen and Mao Zedong who then refashioned it into an icon of Chinese national identity. To interpret these developments, I suggested that "China was traditionally defined as a culture; now it is being transformed into a nation."[19] But as a symbol of a culture that had been cosmopolitan as often as it was closed, the Great Wall was singularly inappropriate. It represented well, perhaps, Chinese conservatism, ethnocentrism, political immobility, and even nationalism. But it was pernicious and misleading insofar as it overshadowed other more creditable characteristics of the civilization, while seeming to render the national definition of China as unproblematic.[20]

Having distinguished between what was history and what was myth in the Great Wall concept, I next focused on discussing the actual military function of walls during their widely acknowledged heyday of the Ming. The resulting book manuscript made three points.[21] The first

---

17   Waldron, "Great Wall Myth," p. 68. In an effort to weaken the grip of the myth, I also wrote: "In fact, nothing in the pre-modern Chinese vocabulary corresponds exactly to that Western phrase," although its modern equivalent, *wanli changcheng*, did appear in poetic contexts. Ibid., p. 74.

18   Ibid., p. 71.

19   Ibid., p. 89.

20   Ibid., p. 68.

21   Waldron, *Great Wall*.

was that the idea of a single Great Wall, marking the northern boundary of China, having a continuous history of more than two millennia,
is misleading and inaccurate. The second was that the fortifications
that defined this idea of a "Great Wall of China," namely, the extensive
stone and brick border walls built from the fifteenth to the early seventeenth century by the Ming, were the product not of some fundamental incompatibility between nomads and settled peoples but rather of
court politics, in which literary and cultural concepts of Chinese civilization were used extensively. The third point was that the concept of
the Great Wall of China did not exist in Chinese historical writing until the twentieth century, when it was picked up from the West and
turned into a symbol of Chinese cultural continuity and national greatness. The book, first published by Cambridge in 1990, became part of
the Canto series (of selected paperbacks) in 1992, and was translated
into Italian in 1993. In 2008 a translation was published in China.[22] In
the eyes of many, the book has become a minor classic in the field of
Great Wall studies and China's relations with the rest of the world.

The book made no great claims to originality, but its findings sur-
prised me and many distinguished Western colleagues. Whatever intellectual success it enjoyed was owed, in the first place, to my gathering together of every scrap of evidence that could be found on the
topic, in Chinese and in other Asian and European languages. That
was possible with the help of a number of Chinese scholars who passed
on then *neibu* or "classified" archaeological studies from China. One of
those scholars was the late Professor Kwang-chih Chang of Harvard;
others worked in universities and institutes in China. My gratitude to
them was and is profound. Contrary to contemporary critical theory,
which accepts that all narratives are "constructed," I found that once all
that material was assembled it supported only one conclusion: the
myth-laden interpretation was incompatible with the available evidence.

The first task thus became the demolition of myths that, although
recognized as such by some specialists, persisted in other supposedly
scholarly and authoritative works. For example, both an American dictionary and a Russian newspaper not very long before had perpetuated

---

22   Woerdelun, *Changcheng*.

the myth that the wall defines the "historical boundary between China and Mongolia." (In fact many long walls, mostly difficult to detect today, cut across what is today Inner Mongolia, an autonomous region that is an integral part of today's China.) Somehow a myth developed that the Wall was the only human structure visible from the moon, or even Mars—a saying that had become widespread in the early decades of the twentieth century, long before even aviation had developed very much.[23] (If there are human edifices visible from the moon they do not include the Great Wall, which is hardly more striking from the air than the New York Thruway.) The origins of this myth, I think, take us deep into the human imagination that explored the possibilities of life by conceiving of what it might be like on other planets and what such creatures might have constructed, e.g., the famous "canals" of Mars, mapped by Percival Lowell, but not in fact real.[24]

Some recent editions of early Chinese histories sometimes sidescore the characters for long walls (*changcheng*) as if they were a proper noun. Supposedly authoritative Chinese maps include trajectories of walls that have not been documented by archaeology.[25] Estimates of the length of the walls vary from 1,500 to 31,250 miles, but they cannot be known because no comprehensive survey has been done, perhaps because there can be no agreement on how to define the subject over two millennia of history.[26] With respect to the Ming walls, their construction began to be considered by the dynasty only after attempted conquests of the Mongols failed decisively with the capture of the emperor in the battle of Tumu in 1449.[27] Most historical maps of China in print at the time I was working supplied the line of the Ming walls as part of the infrastructure extant even as the dynasty began. The conclusion seemed inescapable that the Ming could have had peace—or at

---

23   Waldron, *Great Wall*, pp. 1–2.
24   Lowell had a strong interest in Asia, about which he wrote several books, but this side of him, possibly a key to his imagination, is not given much attention in the best available biography: Hoyt, *Lowell*. Somewhere in the immense literature on the canals a comparison may exist, suggesting that they are visible to us just as the Great Wall of China may be visible to the inhabitants of Mars.
25   Waldron, *Great Wall*, p. 229
26   Ibid., p. 5.
27   Ibid., pp. 57ff.

least a greatly reduced threat—if they had negotiated and traded with the nomads, a view that largely accords with anthropological literature on the problem in general. The Ming refusal to do so (at least until the period of influence of Zhang Juzheng in the late sixteenth century, when such policies were adopted, and worked) appeared to be an example of a more general Chinese reluctance to deal with nomads as equal partners. In the words of my book, "Such damaging unwillingness to compromise . . . is part of a larger pattern in Chinese foreign policy."[28]

The argument was that once we abolish a single, stable, Great Wall as the boundary of China from our minds, we will be better able to see that the Ming, like all other dynasties, faced the fundamental question of where its "territory should end." This matter was subject to debate not only during the entire Ming dynasty but also during the life of every polity before and since that has secured the mandate to rule even part of China. In sum, I wrote: "Disassembling 'The Great Wall' . . . over time and space, will show us more completely than before the range of implications that the issue of boundary demarcation has had, and continues to have, in the Chinese world."[29] Similarly, documenting the development of the myth of The Great Wall since the Ming would reveal the extensive interaction between China and the rest of the world during the last three centuries and the key role of foreigners in helping to shape the definition and specify the characteristics of Chineseness. Or, as the book concluded: "Whatever the future brings, the Great Wall, useless militarily even when it was first built, seems guaranteed to keep its position as a multivalent symbol of Chineseness, and to mirror for the rest of us our fantasies about that society."[30]

Regardless of the military utility of the long walls (a question to which we shall return shortly), the importance of the Great Wall as a topic of study and as a symbol of Chinese identity continued into the 1990s. In another paper, which I published as a book chapter in 1993, I pointed out that an official Chinese Great Wall Studies Association that had been founded in 1987 was organizing an international confer-

---

28   Ibid., p. 8.
29   Ibid., p. 10.
30   Ibid., p. 226.

ence on the study of the Great Wall.[31] At the same time the Great Wall continued to be a highly contested public symbol. Just as the idea of the Great Wall helped to fill a vacuum after the overthrow of the Qing dynasty in 1911, so it had come back as a valuable and valued part of the cultural heritage in the wake of the Cultural Revolution. Most recently in the 1980s, there had been a "cultural fever," producing a wave of works questioning the very foundations of Chinese civilization in the spirit of the May 4 Movement of 1919. One of the products of this period was the television series film *River Elegy* (*Heshang*), which depicted the Great Wall (along with the Yellow River) as a symbol of conservatism and closure.[32] After several showings, the series was banned as an example of "total Westernization" and "bourgeois liberalism." That occurred even before the outbreak of urban demonstrations in spring 1989, which were violently suppressed on June 4 of that year. Under those circumstances, the Great Wall resurfaced as a potentially problematic symbol. Did it sum up the oppressive stream in Chinese civilization (as those who still chant ballads about Meng Jiangnü might think) or was it increasingly a symbol of the Chinese polity's largely defensive and peaceful intentions toward its neighbors (as the official media stressed)? While noting definite parallels between the Former Han period and contemporary PRC scholarly criticism of the Great Wall as a symbol of tyranny and the relative authenticity of the wall as a definite material object, I emphasized the inability of dissident intellectuals like Su Xiaokang, one of the producers of *River Elegy*, to understand either Chinese "tradition" or the "Communist" present and

---

31 Waldron, "Representing China," pp. 36–37. The society includes some experienced specialists who nevertheless lack academic qualifications, such as Luo Zhewen, as well as many retired officials and genuine amateurs, and it has its own website: www. chinagreatwall.org. Doar, "Delimited Boundaries," p. 119. One highly professional archaeologist who has been helpful to me, Professor Xu Pingfang at the Chinese Academy of Social Sciences, is not a member. Unlike the official Great Wall Society, which sponsors many gatherings and publications, and key universities in China today, which are well funded, the Academy of Social Sciences continues to be underfunded, impeding serious archaeological work.

32 As noted in the introduction to this book, this negative image of the long walls resurfaced in Zhang Yimou's depiction of Chinese cultural history in the opening of the 2008 summer Olympics in Beijing.

the inability of the People's Republic either to negate or to replace "traditional culture."[33]

While the Great Wall reemerged as a symbol of "traditional Chinese culture" in China and elsewhere, debates also arose over the more concrete issue of whether Ming wall building was a rational and effective policy.[34] My book attracted some attention from political scientists who were students of Chinese strategy. Many of them believed Chinese policy in general to be "rational"—a word that I would prefer not to define—broadly following the lines laid out by the "realist" school of writers, such as Hans Morgenthau and Kenneth Waltz.[35] They did not welcome my stress in the book on court politics, traditional stereotypes of nomads, and military means as explanations of Ming frontier policy. But a number of political scientists who rejected realism, such as Bruce Bueno de Mesquita, were very favorable, pointing out that my account of how the decision was made, in response to political as well as strategic exigencies rather than in accordance with objectively ascertainable imperatives, was truer to how the world really works.[36]

In any case, the projected international conference on the Great Wall was held in China in 1994 on the tenth anniversary of Deng Xiaoping's public call to "love our China and restore our long walls." The symposium resulted in papers that shed light on contemporary Chinese views of the Great Wall as a largely defensive structure entirely compatible with trade and cultural exchanges and, in general, conducive to peaceful relations among various Chinese states and their neighbors, or in contemporary Chinese parlance among China's "nationalities."[37] After attending the conference I wrote a report on it pointing out the degree to which the officially anointed cult of the

---

33   Waldron, "Representing China," pp. 38, 40, 42–43, 46–60.

34   Chu and Ju, *Great Wall.*

35   The late Hans J. Morgenthau wrote extensively about international relations, arguing that fundamental factors of military power balance and other "realistic" concerns were far more important in the making of policy than were culture, belief, political system, and so forth. His important early book was *Politics Among Nations.* Kenneth N. Waltz is perhaps the most influential contemporary advocate of this approach, most fully spelled out in his *Theory of International Politics.* For an influential study arguing for Ming (and, in general, Chinese) militarism as "realism," see Johnston, *Cultural Realism.*

36   Author's personal communications.

37   Zhongguo changcheng xuehui, *Changcheng guoji.* This anniversary was also the occasion of the publication of an encyclopedia on the wall: Zhongguo changcheng

Great Wall—as patriotic symbol—was part of a larger, post-1989 "patriotic education campaign" in which often incompatible elements were pulled together for purposes of building a sense of regime legitimacy, even though scholars would understand that these pieces did not in fact fit together.[38]

During the late 1990s Chinese scholars published a spate of books that concurred with my point that the Great Wall (or long walls) did not serve as a national boundary.[39] They nonetheless insisted that China's long walls were significant and distinctive in the continuity of their development (over 2,000 years) and the total accumulated distance they covered (an estimated 50,000 kilometers).[40] According to one study, there were five waves in the construction of frontier walls: Spring and Autumn; Qin–Han; the Northern Dynasties through Sui; Jin; and Ming.[41] The walls were built by dynasties headed by frontier peoples (such as the Tuoba and Jurchen) as well as by the "Han Chinese," so that they were clearly not always meant to separate the people of the central plain from those on the frontier, but to protect the political center—and whoever occupied it—from frontier raids.[42] The walls of the Han, Jin, and Ming were the longest and most fully developed, and there is evidence that the Ming followed the Han example in constructing its system.[43] In the short term, rulers such as Qin Shihuang, Han Wudi, and Sui Yangdi could use walls aggressively to expand the realm at the expense of neighboring peoples, but more often China (or, more precisely, the central states) mobilized infantry and built walls to resist military incursions from more mobile frontier peoples. (I had also pointed this out in my discussion of the strategic and historical significance of the Ordos and the great northwestern loop of the Yellow River.)[44] Clearly some Chinese polities assumed a constant or even growing territory defended by long walls. In retrospect, however, I

---

xuehui, *Changcheng baikequanshu*. Its 1,220 pages are not entirely scholarly; the emphasis is on tourism. Doar, "Delimited Boundaries," p. 119.

38   Waldron, "Scholarship and Patriotic."

39   Zhang, *Gudai changcheng*, p. 7.

40   Liu and Li, with Luo, *Changcheng cidian*, p. 1.

41   Zhang, *Gudai changcheng*, p. 3.

42   Ibid., p. 8. The concepts of the "Han Chinese" and of the "minority nationalities" that are current in China are much debated in the West.

43   Xie, *Wanli changcheng*, pp. 3, 44–45; Zhang, *Gudai changcheng*, p. 6, 10–13.

44   Xie, *Wanli changcheng*, p. 3; Waldron, *Great Wall*, pp. 39–42, 91–102, and elsewhere.

would acknowledge that, for the most part, frontier walls were defensive structures. In the long term, they actually contracted, first from the Qin to the Han, and later from the Jin to the Ming. As a result, the Ming defense perimeter ran considerably further south than the Han one had run.

Although on balance defensive, walls were not necessarily passive or negative. Some Chinese scholars argue that the numerous passes (some one thousand in the Ming period) piercing the wall helped to guarantee peace, which was conducive to trade, colonization, development, and cultural exchange.[45] But this ignores, I believe, the centrality in Ming politics of how to deal with repeated nomadic incursions, and the relative unwillingness of high officials to permit trade or normal diplomacy with the nomads. Whereas I have emphasized the relative paucity of references to the Great or long walls in literature and art, Chinese scholars have located and published a large number of poems that refer to the walls either directly (in a few cases) or indirectly (in many others).[46] While many of the poems were critical of conditions obtaining on the frontier, they were evidence of the importance of the walls as loci of frontier defense. Perhaps most importantly however, I would argue, they expressed the ineffable sorrow of leaving one's homeland by passing beyond the legendary "Jade Gate" in the Gansu corridor, or dying far from home, where eventually one's bones would disappear in the sand. The military efficacy of the long walls is difficult to weigh, but there is evidence that years of wall building were often followed by decades of peace (as in the reigns of Han Xuandi and Ming Longqing), though it must be observed that Ming fortifications of Beijing were still being constructed as the Manchus moved in to take control. Sun Yat-sen may have exaggerated the walls' achievement of keeping the central plain free of control by frontier peoples, but it seems likely—to publishing Chinese historians, at least—that such groups would have held power in China for longer periods than they did if no frontier walls had been constructed.[47] We may entertain this thesis, but

---

45   Ibid., p. 5; Zhang, *Gudai changcheng*, pp. 8–15; Liu and Li with Luo, *Changcheng cidian*, p. 3.

46   Zhang, *Gudai changcheng*, pp. 16–19; Liu and Li with Luo, *Changcheng cidian*, pp. 346–550.

47   Xie, *Wanli changcheng*, pp. 3–4.

we do not need to accept the faulty notions of linear social development from pastoral to settled agriculture or the ideas of "Han" ethnic and cultural essentialism and superiority that often continue to accompany it. These conceptions, after all, neglect the importance of Chinese institutions derived from steppe and nomadic sources.[48]

In 1997, anniversaries continued to provide guidance to Chinese scholarship as well as politics. On the tenth anniversary of UNESCO's recognition of the Great Wall of China as a part of the world's cultural heritage, a book of photographs of the edifice appeared.[49] In the same year, coincidentally, the first academically sound English-language children's book on Chinese walls was published.[50]

At the turn of the twenty-first century with the American/NATO attacks on the Chinese embassy in Belgrade and a pharmaceutical plant in Sudan, and, not long after, Al Qaeda's attacks on the World Trade Center in New York and the Pentagon in Washington, interest in various kinds of walls exploded around the world. On the very day of the bombing of the embassy, May 8, 1999, a young Chinese by the name of Zhang Jun launched a website for Chinese wall enthusiasts (www.thegreatwall.com.cn).[51] This website contains a mixture of archaeological news, stories about destruction and preservation, and patriotic exhortations (such as to "remember Japanese aggression"). In 2001 authorities responsible for protecting historical sites produced a volume of studies on preserving walls. The essay on long walls significantly contained only two maps, one of the Qin-Han complex and one of the Ming system, suggesting, again, the importance of these two periods in Chinese accounts of the evolution of the long walls.[52] In this year, too, an American scholar of Chinese literature, Haun Saussy, observed the need "to engage with the Great Wall as event, retrace its formation, observe its cognitive weight on the minds and actions of

---

48   Ibid., p. 5.

49   Beijing Oriental Pearl, *World Cultural.*

50   Mann, *Great Wall.*

51   When asked why he acted on that day, Zhang replied: "You could say that the Great Wall was built to protect China." Hessler, "Letter from China," p. 64.

52   Yang, "Changcheng de lishi," pp. 47–49. This essay emphasized the need to "pay back" the walls for the protection they had afforded agricultural China by using the funds obtained from tourism to protect and reconstruct them.

people who deal with the geography of Northern China, take it nomi-
nalistically or normatively; what we should not do is restrict the Great
Wall's field of operation to the evidence of the senses."[53] These inter-
ventions demonstrated the continuing importance of long walls as
symbols of "national" defense and as virtual edifices in the popular
mentality.

The following year, the *New York Times* printed several articles surveying contemporary efforts on three continents to use long walls to
control frontiers. The first, in January, discussed plans for a barrier of
concertina wire to run 1,800 miles along the Indian border with Pakistan at a cost of $68,000 a mile.[54] The second, in April, described the
walls Israel is building to control the Palestinians in the West Bank,
insisting that they are a "physical barrier" and "not meant to be a political one."[55] The author of this article also mentioned the United
States' use of high technology, such as night-vision goggles, global positioning devices, and infrared trip wires, to control movement across
its Mexican and Canadian borders. The third article, in May, cast its
net more widely, surveying the functions and fates of long walls in time
and space. It traced Western walls back to the Trojans and Romans and
remarked that Hadrian's Wall in 122 CE kept out the "barbarians" for a
century. But it cited the world historian William McNeill to the effect
that the Chinese Great Wall was ineffective because it was "too
long" (!) and peace was only ever attained through political and economic accommodation.[56] This position was quite close to my own but
was somewhat at odds with contemporary Chinese scholarship, which,
as we have seen, tends to depict wall building as productive of peace,
trade, and gradual acculturation. In my view, this Chinese notion owes
more to socialist theories of nationalism and the peace that comes
when socialist rule has rendered ethnic conflict outdated and unneces-

---

53   Saussy, *Great Walls of Discourse*, p. 188.
54   Sengupta, "Wrath and Wire."
55   Dao, "Refining an Idea."
56   Weisman, "Walls Throughout History." See also the more recent U.S.-built walls in
     Baghdad, Weiner, "Walling."

sary, than to ideas found in traditional Chinese writings, although it is arguably rather consistent with Confucianism.[57]

The *Times* article also mentioned the development of siege artillery, the key innovation that would make existing walls obsolete in the West—as was shown when cannon, built with European assistance by the Ottoman Turks, breached the Aurelian walls of Constantinople, more than a thousand years old, in 1453. The result was a new approach to fortification, which made walls low and thick, to absorb the shock of shot rather than to shatter, and gave them complex geometrical configurations (the "trace Italienne" designed to prevent enfilading fire) of whom the greatest pioneer was Vauban in the service of Louis XIV. (Such walls, the author noted, have their current analogue in the Demilitarized Zone dividing the Korea peninsula into two rival states.) Concurring with points I have made in my work, the author of this article noted that the Maginot Line did not keep France safe in 1940: the Germans swept through the "impassable" hilly terrain of the dense Ardennes Forest, where no fortifications had been constructed, and only a reserve division had been deployed for defense. The Berlin Wall became a symbol of tyranny. In complete consistency with the thrust of my book on the Great Wall, the writer of the article just mentioned concluded: "Putting up a wall is not so much a strategy as a symbol for the absence of one."[58]

If the Great or long walls in their material form were, as I tend to think, relatively ineffective in attaining the goals for which they were constructed in Chinese history, they have been much more successful in capturing the world's attention and imagination in the last three years. Xu Pingfang and other Chinese archaeologists working on long walls have shown that, as I suspected, the central states of the Spring and Autumn and Warring States periods constructed long walls as much to defend against each other as to ward off nomads on the north-

---

57 See for example Conner, *National Question,* and Schwarzmantel, *Socialism.*
58 Weissman, "Walls Throughout History." For an account emphasizing Ottoman military enterprise, see Goody, *Theft,* pp. 102–6. For the relatively small impact of new firearms, including cannons, on Chinese walls that had been relatively low and thick from early times, see Chapter 2 in this volume.

ern frontier.[59] But Xu and his colleagues have also found, as I thought they might not, the remains of walls conforming to their description in Sima Qian's *Historical Records*, including the Qin extended line of defense, the Qin walls repaired and developed by the Han, the Han walls built before Wudi's reign, and Wudi's walls constructed to open up the Western Regions (Xiyu) and divide the Xiongnu from the Qiang.[60] (Xu has observed, however, that the Qin walls do not follow the Warring States wall lines, as was regularly asserted.) Xu also argues, somewhat contrary to the thrust of my own work, "For 276 years, the Ming project of building and repairing the walls continued without interruption." He is most likely referring to the deployment of troops at key passes and strong points, done early in the dynasty, and probably accompanied by some construction.

The archaeological finds of Xu and his colleagues would seem to confirm the resonance between the Han, which, for example, established "four prefectures" in the northwest, and the Ming, which, a millennium and a half later, established "four commanderies" in the northeast.[61] This parallel would seem to illustrate the tortured and brilliant twentieth-century writer Lu Xun's point that the Great Wall's "significance was that it was both fixed and changing, as was Chinese culture itself."[62]

In 2006 the College of Asia and the Pacific at Australian National University launched the Chinese Heritage Project with its own website, www.chinaheritagequarterly.org. This site offered a rather comprehensive bibliography of scholarly publications about Chinese walls as well as some superb interpretive articles on topics ranging from issues of historic preservation to the changing ways officials seek to ap-

---

59   Xu, "Archaeology"; Doar, "Delimited Boundaries," p. 121; Zhang, "Zhongyuan gu changcheng." This is not, of course, a new idea, nor are the two kinds of walls mutually exclusive, although those designed to ward off nomadic raiders were usually constructed on the northern borders of the states concerned. For the early origins of the conflict between the peoples of the central plain and the steppe, see DiCosmo, *Ancient China*.

60   More work remains to be done to confirm (or disconfirm) by archaeological finds the supposed 10,000 li of Han period walls extending toward the east described in literary sources. Doar, "Delimited Boundaries," p. 124; Luo, "Great Walls," p. 44.

61   Xu, "Archaeology," pp. 53–55.

62   Cited in Waldron, "Representing China," p. 54.

propriate the quintessential popular heroine, Meng Jiangnü. In the same year a major exhibition was mounted in Sydney and Melbourne titled *The Great Wall of China: Dragon, Dynasties, and Warriors*. This project was sponsored, unpromisingly, by the Beijing Badaling Cablecar Company Limited, but it turned out to have real merit. The excellent catalogue puts the long walls of northern China into the context of all of "imperial" Chinese history.[63]

According to the scholar and translator Bruce Doar, Chinese researchers complement their empirical work with efforts to develop a satisfactory periodization of the history of the Great or long walls. Li Wenlong, for example, has proposed four periods: origins of walls and civilization; initial long walls of the Spring and Autumn and Warring States; flourishing feudalism from the Northern Dynasties through Tang; and the culmination of long walls in the Jin and Ming. Another Chinese scholar has objected to the inclusion of the Tang in this scheme on the grounds that it built no long walls. Doar, on the other hand, argues that long walls retained their significance even in periods like the Tang when they were not built anew. (A similar point about the Song period is made by a Western scholar, Nicholas Tackett.) Indeed, Doar points out that the exclusion of the Yuan and the Qing from Li Wenlong's periodization ignores the Mongols' demonstrated ability to besiege walls and the Manchus' borrowing of Ming military techniques, including the use of beacons and bells and the maintenance of the willow palisade in the northeast. Another Chinese scholar describes the Qing as an innovative ethnic construct, suggesting a possible line of inquiry away from the tired description of the Qing and all other major Chinese polities as "empires." In conformity with the general trend to recognize regional as well as temporal differences in methods of long wall construction, Doar notes that the Manchus also drew on the stone wall traditions of the northeast, which were exemplified in the long walls of the early Gaogouli/Goguryo polity straddling the Yalu River. While the Korean specialist Gari Ledyard confirmed my early thesis doubting the historicity of the Great Wall of

---

63   Roberts and Barmé, eds., *Great Wall*. For doubts about the common practice of describing two—or even sometimes four—millennia of Chinese polities as "imperial," see Chapter 2 in this volume.

China, other scholars of Korea have recently turned their attention to what we may call a Sino-Korean tradition of long wall construction.[64] The year 2006 also saw the publication of the first comprehensive English-language history of the Great or long walls since the appearance of my book in 1990.[65] This well-written volume by Julia Lovell draws openly and heavily on my own work and is addressed to a more general readership. Ignoring, for lack of space, many of the points on which this study agrees with my own, I would point out first some of its more original contributions to the field of Great Wall studies. It accepts the term *changcheng,* which appeared in Qin-Han times, as equivalent to the Great Wall (or Walls), thus simplifying (but I would say oversimplifying) the terminological and conceptual complexities involved in the analysis of successive frontier barriers from Zhou times to the present. It uses a collection of poetry about long walls published since the appearance of my book to argue for the greater saliency of the wall and related institutions and events in the literary record than I had suggested.[66] It draws on archaeological data reported on at the official international walls conference in 1995 to affirm the historicity and frequent overlapping of walls in the Warring States, Qin, and Han eras. It shows that the Northern Wei built its walls on the base of the earlier Zhao walls and prefigured (in its double walls) the basic design of the later Ming system.[67] It notes that the Qin destroyed some of the long walls and city walls of other states as well as built its own. It uses the walls encyclopedia of 1994 to show that the Jin built some of its walls on the Qin base.[68] It draws on a recent Chinese monograph to offer a

64   For the periodization issue, see Doar, "Delimited Boundaries," p. 123; for a spate of scholarship on the walls of Gaogouli/Goguryo, see ibid., pp. 123, 278, n. 26; for the Song, see Tackett, "Great Wall"; for a recent example of describing Qing China as an empire without any effort to examine the term, see Waley-Cohen's otherwise excellent *Culture of War.*

65   Lovell, *Great Wall.*

66   Ibid., passim; Liu, *Zhongguo lidai.* The greater visibility of those walls in works of art is also suggested by two important representations of the late-Ming wall network dating to the late Ming; see Roberts and Barmé, *Great Wall,* pp. 193–99.

67   Lovell, *Great Wall,* pp. 57–58, 71, 83, 105, 107, based on *Changcheng guoji,* pp. 36, 105, 134, 243.

68   Lovell, *Great Wall,* p. 101, based on *Changcheng baike,* p. 79.

more detailed account of Sui Yangdi's wall building, which was modeled on that of the Qin.[69]

The author notes that poetry associated with state ritual and with the northern border since Zhou times had a resurgence in the Tang, when frontier verse became an independent literary genre.[70] She uses the 1995 symposium to describe the Jin walls that extended nearly 2,000 kilometers across the northeast.[71] She agrees with me that, in general, long walls were ineffective—perhaps even counterproductive—but she also suggests—incongruously to my mind—that the Mongol Yuan's decision not to build walls may have contributed to the spread of the plague from Inner Asia to China. (In my view the Mongol empire was a single entity, extending far to the north of present-day China. Karakorum, in today's Mongolia, and Khanbalik, the future Beijing, were the two capitals of the Yuan, though regular fighting went on between rival claimants, such as Khaidu and others, until Khubilai finally prevailed in 1264. It would have made little sense for the Mongols to build a wall to defend against other Mongols.[72]) But other nomadic groups did build walls. Indeed several of the *changcheng* lines were built by such peoples. As for the plague, it is sometimes said to have been one cause of the depopulation, poverty, and rebellion that ultimately brought down the Yuan dynasty. But plague studies, even for Europe where they are most developed, are a scholarly minefield. This problem with sources, however, does not prove that the plague had no impact on Chinese population and politics.[73]

Lovell also insists, following DiCosmo and *pace* Chinese scholars, that Chinese frontier wall building was more aggressive and imperialistic than passive and defensive in character. Yet, in explaining the

---

69   Lovell, *Great Wall*, pp. 133–35.

70   Ibid., pp. 149–50. This is consistent with the pattern of wall building and unbuilding hypothesized in Chapter 2 in this book.

71   Ibid., p. 166, based on *Changcheng guoji*, pp. 154–58.

72   See Waldron, *Great Wall*, p. 68–69. See also Dardess, "Mongol Empire," pp. 117–65. Of course, the Mongols might have built a wall to separate their core on the steppe from the periphery of agricultural China, but it is unclear how that would have impeded the spread of plague from central Asia to much of Eurasia.

73   Lovell, *Great Wall*, pp. 176–79. The issue of plague in East Asia, indeed even in the West, remains underdocumented and often overgeneralized—not unlike the history of Chinese walls.

Ming fixation on building frontier walls, she notes that the "Ming emperors never forgot the humiliation of Mongol occupation."[74] This concern for security had two quite different results. On the one hand, until
the fifteenth century the Ming largely modeled itself on the Yuan,
adopting many of its institutions, even its style of dress and many
words from its language. It even considered an all-out effort to sup-
plant the descendants of Chingghis Khan as master of all the former
Yuan territories as far north as Karakorum and beyond.[75] Such a Ming
plan is perhaps the best explanation for the moving of the capital from
Nanjing in the south to Beijing, the old Mongol capital.[76] When this
policy proved too costly in manpower and treasure, the remaining
Mongols reconstituted themselves in the fifteenth century and posed a
real continuing threat to the Ming. This helps to explain that dynasty's
search for effective methods of containing the threat while stopping
short of conquering the steppe.

Although Lovell generally criticizes the supposedly general Han
Chinese characterization of frontier peoples as "barbarians" (yi or hu,
presumably), she allows that the tributary system often involved economic loss for China and correctly describes it as a system in which,
essentially, China got face for money.[77] Of course, as I have pointed
out, tribute worked best with frontier peoples who, usually because
they had already been conquered, were unable to resist the power of
the central states (China).[78] Those who could establish demographic,
economic, cultural, and military parity with the reigning Chinese dynasty could refuse to pay tribute to it; but, in that case, they could also
have difficulty establishing commercial relations with it (as the British
would discover in the eighteenth century).

Tracing the development of the Great Wall myth, Lovell pinpoints
the first appearance of the term "Great Wall" in Du Halde's history
published in 1738. Following me, she discusses how Sun Yat-sen translated the "Western misreading of the wall" into Chinese.[79] She reveals

---

Ibid., p. 186.

75 Dreyer, *Early Ming China*.

76 Waldron, *Great Wall*, pp. 74–76.

77 Lovell, *Great Wall*, p. 190.

78 See Waldron, *Great Wall*, p. 31, esp. note 92.

79 Lovell, *Great Wall*, pp. 214–15,

that the leading party intellectual Guo Moruo provided the impetus behind the decision to refurbish Badaling as a tourist site in 1952.[80] Lovell concludes her study with a brief overview of the growth of Chinese electronic communication, noting that in the first email sent in 1987 a professor called on compatriots to "Go beyond the Great Wall, March toward the World."[81] A decade later, however, the Chinese government initiated the "Great Firewall" (*da huo qiang*) which used packet sniffers and other advanced equipment, mostly of Western origin, to detect and block officially problematic words. The Chinese soon persuaded Google to join in the censoring.[82] The appearance of the Great Firewall, an active effort to defend state security by manning a virtual defense perimeter, suggests that parallels between the Han, Ming, and PRC may involve more than simply repairing the brick and stone walls in the north.[83] In any case, emphasizing the strength of the long wall tradition in China, Lovell concludes, one hopes incorrectly, that "China will, it seems, always have its Great Walls."[84]

Unfortunately, this work depends heavily on secondary and largely English-language sources. In some respects, despite its best efforts, it may refurbish some elements of the Great Wall myth and set back the effort to understand the actual roles of long walls in Chinese and world history. By adopting the title "the Great Wall," as I did and almost all other writers (and editors) continue to do, the author (and probably the press) missed the opportunity to use a less well known but more accurate alternative, such as "the long wall" or, better "long walls," a more precise translation of *changcheng* and the many different walls it represents. These are the terms that some Chinese scholars have begun to use and that we are generally using in this volume. More perniciously, by choosing the subtitle "China Against the World," the writer (and/or, again, the editors), have reinforced the age-old foreign image

80   Ibid., pp. 273, 304, 317.
81   Ibid., p. 339.
82   Ibid., p. 341. For more on this, see Chapter 8 in this volume.
83   For the Han as a model for ethnic melding in the PRC, see Bulog, "Great Wall Embodied," pp. 218, 219. Pace Bulog, this parallel may not be "anachronistic," especially if the pattern of mural history outlined in Chapter 2 in this volume is taken seriously. For the Russians as "the Xiongnu of the 1950s," see Huang, *Qinhuang*, p. 2.
84   Waldron, *Great Wall*, p. 350.

of China as a walled kingdom isolated from the rest of the world and hostile to all foreigners.[85] This, to my mind, overinterprets walls that were, after all, mostly extemporized military structures, not cultural statements; it also fails to recognize the powerful cosmopolitan elements in Chinese civilization. This is a civilization, after all, that has repeatedly shown itself open to foreign influences—from the adoption of nomadic cavalry tactics in the Warring States, to Buddhism starting in the late Han, to the cultures of the highly pluralistic societies of the Tang and Yuan, culminating with an opening to the cultures of the rest of the world starting in the seventeenth century and reaching a crescendo in the twentieth—and now picking up speed again.[86] From a cultural and intellectual standpoint, the most recent high tide of cosmopolitanism came in the richly creative and dynamic first four decades of the twentieth century, so often caricatured, quite wrongly, as a time of poverty, oppression, and cultural darkness.[87] The cosmopolitanism of China today, moreover, is evident everywhere, including, in 2005, in the translation into Chinese of William Edgar Geil's *The Great Wall of China*, originally published in New York in 1909—the source of much misinformation but also an attempt to describe the walls based on actual exploration.[88] More important, the catalogue of the Chinese-cosponsored exhibition in Australia depicts numerous examples of

85   For another example of a title that conveys an image that may not be supported by the contents of the book, see Rodzinski, *Walled Kingdom*.

86   For a recent exposition of this view at least through the early Ming period, see Hansen, *The Open Empire*.

87   Of course, this was also an era of war, autocracy, and revolution. I have discussed aspects of this period in Waldron, *From War to Nationalism*. See also Dikötter, "China before Closure," and Waldron, *Chinese*.

88   Geil, *Great Wall*, translated as Gailuo, *Zhongguo changcheng*. This work was apparently a major source of the myth that the long walls could be seen by the naked eye from the moon. It also, more reasonably, touted the walls as evidence of China's largely restrained approach to the rest of the world. Geil was an extraordinary character, whom innkeepers recalled to a traveler in the 1920s as striding into their caravansarais, drawing a pistol, putting it to their head, and demanding in heavily accented Chinese, "Jidan! Jidan!" i.e., "[please make me some] eggs [to eat]." Author's personal information.

cosmopolitan cultural exchanges across the long walls in many periods of Chinese history.[89]

Meanwhile both Chinese and foreigners have turned their attention to more aesthetic and culturally interpretive approaches to the long walls and have arrived at alternative appraisals of their historical significance. In 2005 the art historian Minglu Gao organized an exhibition of contemporary Chinese art that opened first at the Millennium Museum in Beijing and then at the University at Buffalo and Albright-Knox Art Galleries in Buffalo. Among the pieces shown were several drawn from a larger corpus of works, including woodcuts, painting, sculpture, and behavioral (or performance) art that made it into Gao's study of the whole panoply of contemporary Chinese art.[90] Responding overtly to my book, Gao emphasized that the Japanese invasion of China in the 1930s was the crucial stimulus to contemporary Chinese interest in the long walls as a symbol of the Chinese nation.[91] As the late Professor James T. C. Liu, who lived through the period and was tortured by the Japanese, once explained to me, this was true particularly on the political left, which, although wishing to stand against Japan, had no desire to embrace the political symbolism and iconography of the Nanjing (and later Chongqing) government.[92] Chinese who mounted resistance at Xifengkou, a pass in the wall, compared it to Verdun, which had produced many heroes for France. In my work I too compared China with France and the long walls with the Maginot Line, but more recently I have been drawn to comparing China with Europe because of their similar geographic and demographic size and cultural and ethnic diversity.[93] In any case, the concept of China as a nation and

---

89   Roberts and Barmé, *Great Wall*, pp. 132, 133, 135, 136, 140, 148. See also Wang, "Material Culture," pp. 114, 116.

90   Gao, *Wall*, chapter 6.

91   Ibid., pp. 192–94, 206.

92   One reason, of course, was that Nanjing did not mount a sustained defense of the long wall line. See the entry for General Song Zheyuan, the "hero of Xifengkou," in Boorman, ed. *Biographical Dictionary*, vol. 3, pp. 190–92. See also Chapter 6 in this volume. I understand from Chinese informants that the importance of the battle of Xifengkou has been greatly inflated in the People's Republic.

93   My thinking on this was stimulated by an illustrated talk by Maurice Agulhon, author of *Marianne Into Battle,* and by my subsequent work on French nationalism, Waldron and Moran, *People in Arms.*

of the long walls as its (ineffective) defensive bulwark remains alive and
well. In 2007 the Chinese photographer Chen Changfen mounted an
exhibition of his photography of the long walls at the Museum of Fine
Arts in Houston.[94] In her introduction to the catalogue, Ann Wilkes
Tucker, the curator of the exhibition, compared China's long walls with
the Eiffel Tower, the Statue of Liberty, Big Ben, and the Sphinx, all
symbols of nation-states with international recognition.[95] In his brief
foreword to the catalogue, the historian Jonathan Spence, drawing on
Julia Lovell's book, mentions in passing that "as far as we can now tell,
for most of its existence the Wall was a failure."[96] "Failure," of course,
can be quite poignant for nationalist projects.

In the past I have made a similar argument, and pretty much continue to hold such a view today, though I am certainly willing to agree
that in certain cases, such as the defense of the capital, wall lines had
tactical value. The more basic question, however, is whether wall building and exclusion was a better *strategy* for dealing with nomadic adversaries than trade and diplomacy would have been. I still plump for
trade and diplomacy. An opposite argument can certainly be made,
however. In a recent article, Peter Hessler, alluding to my comparison
of the Ming walls to the Maginot Line, summarized my thesis as follows: the Ming was too weak to fight and too proud to talk and so came
to rely on walls that failed to prevent the fall of the dynasty. While an
exceedingly brief summary of my argument, this is not really wrong. A
young American named David Spindler, who has for the last seven
years been walking and studying the remnants of the Ming walls in the
capital region, where they were tactically most successful, qualifies that
point. He believes that the Ming response to the Mongols was more
flexible, that walls could be parts of various kinds of offensive and defensive strategies, that the Mongols' internal power struggles contributed to their need to raid, and that the walls actually held back many
attacks in the sixteenth century. In Spindler's words: "People say, was it
worth it? But I don't think that's how they thought at the time. You
don't get a nation-state saying, 'We're going to sacrifice X number of

---

94   Tucker, *Great Wall.*
95   Ibid., p. 39.
96   Ibid., p. xi.

citizens and soldiers.' That's not a calculus they used. An empire is always going to try to protect itself."[97] Spindler dislikes any symbolic use
of the Wall, especially for something as complex as Chinese culture. In
his view, the Wall represents neither national glory nor xenophobia.
He adds: "It's just one manifestation of what China has done. It's just a
way they defended themselves."[98]

Recognizing that the long walls were just one way in which China
defended itself, of course, does not solve the problem of just what that
"China" was and is. Spindler's comments are exemplary in that he refers rather indiscriminately to China as a culture, an empire, and a
nation-state, the usual alternatives in the English language. But over
the course of time and space, "China" has had many different incarnations and has adopted many different terms for itself and for others.[99]
The relationships are not at all reducible to the binaries of civilization
and barbarism, empire and colony, or nation-state among nation-
states. Efforts to describe a traditional Chinese world order, a perennial Chinese empire, or an evanescent Chinese multistate system do
not help much as they are all couched in Western terms and pay insufficient attention to the ways in which the Chinese and their neighbors
view their pasts, live their presents, and envision their futures.[100]

Instead we need to turn, as we are trying to do in this volume, to the
ways in which Chinese of various times and places have understood
and used their history to create, maintain, and change their collective
identity.[101] With regard to the visual arts, we find that in the "new period" since 1979 alone, artists have treated the long walls variously. The
walls have served as sites of ritual mourning for the dead (including
those who built the walls, suffered in the Cultural Revolution, and per-

---

97 Hessler, "Letter from China," p. 63.
98 Ibid., p. 65.
99 For example, China has been known as Huaxia, Zhongguo (the central states), or any
    one of the over two dozen dynasties, or polities, from the Zhou through the PRC. Its
    neighbors have been known to the Chinese as Yi, Di, Rong, Man, Hu, Xiongnu,
    Mongols, etc. More work is needed on what China's neighbors called themselves and
    how they referred to the Chinese over time.
100 For representative studies, see Fairbank, *Chinese World Order*; Crossley, Siu, and
    Sutton, *Empire at the Margins*; Rossabi, *China Among Equals*; Duara, *Rescuing History*;
    and Struve, *Time, Temporality*.
101 For steps in this direction, see Wang, *Inventing China*; Des Forges, *Cultural Centrality*.

ished in the streets around Tiananmen in 1989); commemoration of
humanist values (threatened by nationalist ideology and global materialism); criticism of defensive stasis (and supposed military impo-
tence); celebration of peaceful awakening (by using firepower without
military intent); ambiguous acceptance of reconstruction (using ersatz
gold bricks to mend the wall); and the airing of sexual injustice (walking nude on the wall to protest prejudice against premarital sex).[102] In
sum, in curator Gao's words, "Though the Wall is an active sign, what
it signifies is irreducibly open, and this has permitted it to be re-read as
an open space engaged in a dialogue between historical memory and
personal experience, rather than as a literal subject."[103]

   Or to put it another way, the wall in our minds and those of the
Chinese has a life of its own that is well worth our attention, but that
has only a tangential, though real, connection to the structures archaeologists examine. The photographer Chen Changfen, for example, has
devoted forty years of his life to capturing parts of the long walls,
largely in black-and white photographs of haunting starkness and contrast, which convey a powerful visual impact. In explaining his commitment to this project he has said: "There are people who praise the
Great Wall as a miracle that poor people built, and others who feel that
the Great Wall is insignificant because it has lost its functionality. Too
few people consider that the Great Wall can be a communal cultural
legacy for humanity." As a convinced Daoist who always focuses his
camera on the wall and its natural environment and consciously ex-
cludes humans from his scenes, Chen remarks: "I felt saddened when
I saw the Great Wall being destroyed and slowly disappearing. But in
another sense, after it disappeared, it returned to nature, and my mind
felt placid, because, after all, the Great Wall is a wall, and it is a wall that
divides. If the Wall no longer exists, then people can get along with
each other without obstruction."[104] This open view, from a person who
has devoted his life to capturing images of what is usually viewed as an
icon of closure or division, suggests the wide range of resonances that

---

102   Gao, *Wall*, chapter 6.
103   Ibid., p. 205.
104   Tucker, *Great Wall*, pp. x, 131.

both the idea and the reality of China's wall continue to strike, not only in China, but in today's world generally.

Works Cited

Agulhon, Maurice. *Marianne into Battle: Republican Imagery and Symbolism in France, 1789–1880.* Cambridge: Cambridge University Press, 1981.

Beijing Oriental Pearl Development Co., Ltd. *World Cultural and Natural Heritage (Chinese Section), The Great Wall.* Beijing: China Pictorial Publishing House, 1997.

Boorman, Howard L., ed. *Biographical Dictionary of Republican China.* New York and London: Columbia University Press, 1979.

Bulag, Uradyn E. "The Great Wall Embodied: Wang Zhaojun," in Roberts and Barmé, *The Great Wall of China,* pp. 214–20.

Changcheng baike quanshu [Encyclopedia of long walls]. Jilin: Jilin renmin chubanshe, 1994.

Changcheng guoji xueshu yantaohui lunwenji [Collected papers from the international conference on long walls]. Jilin: Jilin renmin chubanshe, 1995.

Chu, Godwin C., and Yanan Ju. *The Great Wall in Ruins: Communication and Cultural Change in China.* Albany: State University of New York Press, 1993.

Conner, Walker. *The National Question in Marxist-Leninist Theory and Strategy.* Princeton: Princeton University Press, 1984.

Crossley, Pamela Kyle, Helen F. Siu, and Donald S. Sutton, eds. *Empire at the Margins: Culture, Ethnicity, and Frontier in Early Modern China.* Berkeley: University of California Press, 2006.

Dao, James. "Refining an Idea as Old as Civilization Itself," *New York Times,* April 21, 2002, p. 14.

Dardess, John. "From Mongol Empire to Yüan Dynasty," *Monumenta Serica* 30 (1972–73), pp. 117–65.

Des Forges, Roger V. *Cultural Centrality and Political Change in Chinese History: Northeast Henan in the Fall of the Ming.* Stanford: Stanford University Press, 2003.

DiCosmo, Nicola. *Ancient China and Its Enemies: The Rise of Nomadic Power in East Asian History.* New York: Cambridge University Press, 2002.

Dikötter, Frank. *The Age of Openness: China before Mao.* Hong Kong: Hong Kong University Press; Berkeley: University of California Press, 2008.

Doar, Bruce Gordon. "Delimited Boundaries and Great Wall Studies," in Roberts and Barmé, eds., *The Great Wall of China*, pp. 119–27.

Dreyer, Edward. *Early Ming China: A Political History 1355–1435.* Stanford: Stanford University Press, 1982.

Duara, Prasenjit. *Rescuing History from the Nation: Questioning Narratives of Modern China.* Chicago: University of Chicago Press, 1995.

Fairbank, John K. *The Chinese World Order.* Cambridge: Harvard University Press, 1968.

Feng, Yongqian, and He Puying, eds. *Liaoning gu changcheng* [Ancient long walls of Liaoning]. Shenyang: Liaoning renmin chubanshe, 1986. (Subtitle in English: The Ancient Great Wall in Liaoning.)

Fletcher, Joseph. *Studies on Chinese and Islamic Inner Asia.* Aldershot: Variorum, 1995.

Gailuo, Weilian Aidejia (Geil, William Edgar). *Zhongguo Changcheng* [The Great Wall of China] [English edition 1909]. Shen Hong and Hui Wenjie, trans. Jinan: Shandong Huabao chubanshe, 2006.

Gao, Minglu. *The Wall: Reshaping Contemporary Chinese Art/Qiang: Zhongguo dangdai yishu de lishi yu bianjie.* Beijing and Buffalo: The Millennium Museum, University at Buffalo Art Galleries, Albright-Knox Art Gallery, 2005.

Geil, William Edgar. *The Great Wall of China.* New York: Sturgis and Walton, 1909.

Goody, Jack. *The Theft of History.* Cambridge: Cambridge University Press, 2006.

Hansen, Valerie. *The Open Empire: A History of China to 1600.* New York: W. W. Norton, 2000.

Hessler, Peter. "Letter from China: Walking the Wall, An Obsession with Mythic Structure," *New Yorker*, May 21, 2007, pp. 56–65.

Hoyt, William Graves. *Lowell and Mars.* Tucson: University of Arizona Press, 1976.

Hua Xia Zi. *Ming changcheng kaoshi* [An inquiry into the reality of the Ming long walls]. Qinhuangdao: Dang'an chubanshe, 1988.

Huang, Linshu. *Qinhuang changchengkao chugao* [Preliminary draft of an examination of the long walls of Qinhuang]. Hong Kong: Zhubai shuyuan, 1959.

———. "Shanhaiguan zhi Jiayuguan zhi wan-li changcheng fei Qin shi zhu" [The ten thousand li long wall from Shanhai pass to Jiayu pass was not built by the Qin] in *Biansai yanjiu* [*Frontier studies*] (Hong Kong: Caoyang, 1979), pp. 97–100.

Idema, Wilt L., and Haiyan Lee. *Meng Jiangnü Brings Down the Great Wall:*

Ten Versions of a Chinese Legend. Seattle: University of Washington Press, 2008.

Johnston, Alastair Iain. *Cultural Realism: Strategic Culture and Grand Strategy in Chinese History.* Princeton: Princeton University Press, 1995.

Lattimore, Owen. *Inner Asian Frontiers of China.* New York: American Geographical Society, 1940.

———. *Studies in Frontier History.* London: Oxford University Press, 1962.

Liang, Qichao. *Zhongguo lishi yanjiufa* [Methods of studying Chinese history]. Preface dated 1922; first published 1925. Reprinted edition consulted. Taipei: Taiwan Chung-hua, 1967.

Liu, Qingde et al., eds. *Zhongguo lidai changcheng shi lu* [Records of poetry on the long walls of China through the ages]. Hebei: Hebei meishu chubanshe, 1991.

Liu, Yan, and Li Yiran, comp., Luo Zhewen, advisor. *Changcheng cidian* [Dictionary of long walls]. Shanghai: Wenhui chubanshe, 1999.

Lovell, Julia. *The Great Wall: China against the World, 1000 BC–AD 2000.* New York: Grove, 2006.

Luo, Zewen, Dai Wenbao, Dick Wilson, Jean-Pierre Drège, Hubert Delalaye, and Emir Bührer. *The Great Wall.* New York: McGraw-Hill, 1981.

Luo, Zhewen. "The Great Walls of China," Bruce Doar, trans., in Roberts and Barmé, eds. *The Great Wall*, pp. 42–50.

Luo, Zhewen, and Zhao Luo. *The Great Wall of China in History and Legend.* Beijing: Foreign Languages Press, 1986.

Mann, Elizabeth. *The Great Wall.* New York: Mikaya Press, 1997.

Morgenthau, Hans J. *Politics Among Nations: The Struggle for Power and Peace.* New York: Alfred A. Knopf. 1948.

Needham, Joseph et al. *Science and Civilisation in China,* Vol. I, Introductory Orientations. Cambridge: Cambridge University Press, 1954.

———. *Science and Civilization in China,* Vol. IV. Physics and Physical Technology, Part 3, Civil Engineering and Nautics. Cambridge: Cambridge University Press, 1971.

Roberts, Claire, and Geremie R. Barmé, eds. *The Great Wall of China.* Sydney: Powerhouse Publishing, 2006.

Rodzinski, Witold. *The Walled Kingdom: A History of China from Antiquity to the Present.* New York: Free Press, 1984.

Rossabi, Morris. *China Among Equals: The Middle Kingdom and Its Neighbors, 10th–14th Centuries.* Berkeley: University of California Press, 1983.

Saussy, Haun. *Great Walls of Discourse and Other Adventures in Cultural China.* Cambridge, Mass.: Harvard University Asia Center, 2001.

Schwarzmantel, John. *Socialism and the Idea of the Nation*. London: Harvester Wheatsheaf/Prentice-Hall, 1991.

Sengupta, Somini. "With Wrath and Wire, India Builds a Great Wall," *New York Times*, 2 January 2002, A4.

Shou, Pengfei. *Lidai changcheng kao* [An investigation of the long walls through the ages], No place: No publisher, 1941.

Struve, Lynn, ed. *Time, Temporality, and Imperial Transition: East Asia from Ming to Qing*. Honolulu: Association for Asian Studies and University of Hawai'i Press, 200

Tackett, Nicolas. "The Great Wall and Conceptualizations of the Border Under the Northern Song," *Journal of Song-Yuan Studies*, no. 38 (2008), pp. 99–138.

Tucker, Anne Wilkes. *The Great Wall of China, Photographs by Chen Changfen*. Foreword by Jonathan Spence. New Haven, Connecticut: Yale University Press, 2007.

Waldron, Arthur. "The Problem of the Great Wall of China," *Harvard Journal of Asiatic Studies*, 43.1 (1983), pp. 629–49.

———. "The Great Wall Myth: Its Origins and Role in Modern China," *Yale Journal of Criticism*, 2.1 (1988), pp. 67–128.

———. *The Great Wall of China: From History to Myth*. Cambridge: Cambridge University Press, 1990; Canto edition, 1992;. Italian edition, 1993; Chinese, 2008; Korean forthcoming.

———. "Representing China: The Great Wall and Cultural Nationalism in the Twentieth Century," in *Cultural Nationalism in East Asia*, Harumi Befu, ed. Berkeley: Institute of East Asian Studies, University of California, 1993), pp. 36–60.

———. "Scholarship and Patriotic Education: The Great Wall Conference, 1994," *China Quarterly* (September 1995), pp. 192–98.

———. *From War to Nationalism: China's Turning Point, 1924–1925*. Cambridge: Cambridge University Press, 1995.

———. *The Chinese*. For the series "The Peoples of Asia," Morris Rossabi, ed. London: Blackwell, forthcoming.

Waldron, Arthur, and Daniel Moran, eds. *The People in Arms: Military Myth and National Mobilization since the French Revolution*. Cambridge, Mass.: Cambridge University Press, 2003.

Waley-Cohen, Joanna. *The Culture of War in China: Empire and the Military under the Qing Dynasty*. London: I. B. Tauris, 2006.

Waltz, Kenneth. *Theory of International Politics*. New York: McGraw-Hill, 1979.

Wang, Ch'iu-kuei. "The Transformation of the Meng Chiang-nü Story in

Chinese Popular Literature." Ph.D. dissertation, University of Cambridge, 1977.

Wang, Guoliang. *Zhongguo changcheng yange kao* [An investigation of the evolution of the long walls of China]. Shanghai: Shangwu, 1931.

Wang, Q. Edward. *Inventing China Through History: The May Fourth Approach to Historiography.* Albany: State University of New York Press, 2001.

Wang, Yueqian. "Material Culture of the Walls," Bruce Doar, trans., in Roberts and Barmé, eds., *The Great Wall of China,* pp. 112–18.

Weiner, Tim. "Walling Off Your Enemies: The Long View," *New York Times,* April 29, 2007: 14.

Woerdelun, Ase (Waldron, Arthur). *Changcheng, cong lishi dao shenhua* [The Great Wall, from History to Myth]. Nanjing: Jiangsu jiaoyu chubanshe, 2008.

Weisman, Steven R. "Walls Throughout History: Built for Security but Often Victims of Strategy," *New York Times,* May 28, 2002, A22.

Xie, Helin. *Wanli changcheng* [The 10,000 li long walls]. Shanghai: Guji chubanshe, 1996.

Xu, Pingfang. "Archaeology of the Walls," Bruce Doar, trans., in Roberts and Barmé, eds., *The Great Wall,* pp. 52–56.

———. "The Archaeology of the Great Wall of the Qin and Han Dynasties," Taotao Huang and John Moffett, trans., *Journal of East Asian Archaeology* 3.1–2 (2002), pp. 259–81.

Yang, Xiumin. "Changcheng de lishi he baohu" [The history and protection of long walls], in Zhongguo wenwuju wenwu baohusi [Cultural relics protection office of the Chinese cultural relics bureau], Jiangsu sheng wenwu guanli weiyuanhui bangong shi [Office of the Jiangsu provincial cultural relics management committee], Nanjingshi wenwu ju [Nanjing cultural relics bureau], eds., *Zhongguo gu chengqiang baohu yanjiu* [Studies of the protection of China's old city walls] (Beijing: Wenwu chubanshe, 2001), pp. 46–53.

Zhang, Liang. *Gudai changcheng: zhanzheng yu heping de niudai* [Ancient long walls: links in war and peace]. Dalian: Liaoning shifan daxue chubanshe, 1997.

Zhang, Xinbin. "Zhongyuan gu changcheng ruogan wenti de chubu yanjiu" [A preliminary study of several questions regarding the ancient long walls in the central plain], *Zhongyuan wenwu* [Cultural relics of the central plain], 2005.2, pp. 62–70.

Zhongguo changcheng xuehui [Chinese Long Walls Society], ed. *Changcheng baikequanshu* [Encyclopedia of long walls]. Changchun: Jilin renmin chubanshe, 1994.

———. *Changcheng guoji xueshu yantaohui lunwenji* [Collected papers from the international conference on long walls]. Jilin: Jilin renmin chubanshe, 1995.

Zhongguo changcheng yiji diaocha baogao ji [Collected reports on surveys of the long walls of China]. Beijing: Wenwu chubanshe, 1981.

CHAPTER TWO

Tales of Three City Walls in China's Central Plain

Roger Des Forges

The Chinese concern is with making the right *comparisons, in using the* correct *analogy, a concern that certainly does not deny, but clearly presupposes, the legitimacy of analogy and comparison when so used.*

—G. E. R. LLOYD, *DEMYSTIFYING MENTALITIES*

IT IS WELL KNOWN THAT the Chinese character *cheng* can denote a city, a wall that encompasses a settlement, and/or a more linear defensive barrier. It is widely understood that the Chinese were especially energetic from early times in building and maintaining both city walls (*chengqiang*) and long walls (*changcheng*). It is also generally recognized that the Chinese emphasized the building of walls in some periods and places more than in others.[1] To date, however, we have had no systematic explanation of the pattern of wall building over the entire course of Chinese history from early times to the present. Instead we have frequently worked within an unexamined paradigm or master narrative: the Chinese constructed and repaired walls during four millennia of a feudal, traditional, and closed empire; they then

---

1   Knapp, *China's Walled*, p. 2; Tracy, *City Walls*, p. 2; Waldron, *Great Wall*; Lovell, *Great Wall*; Roberts and Barmé, *Great Wall*. See also Chapters 1 and 3 in this volume. Recently, the term *cheng* has also been used for various clusters of shops within cities. Gao, *Wall*, p. 228.

neglected and dismantled walls after the advent of capitalist/socialist, modern, and open republics in the twentieth century.[2] In short, walls of various sorts were characteristic of an "old China" (and world); "wall-lessness" is emblematic of the "new China" (and globe).

This binary, unilinear, and teleological interpretation of the incidence of walls in Chinese history, however appealing, entrenched, and ubiquitous, does not begin to explain early episodes of not building (and even destroying) walls and recent efforts to preserve (and even to reconstruct) them. Specifically, it does not account for Deng Xiaoping's instruction in the early 1980s to "love our China (*zhonghua*) and restore our long walls (*changcheng*)," a call that inspired similar appeals to preserve city walls.[3] Indeed, it has been precisely during the recent, self-described "new age" of "reform and opening" since 1979 that the Chinese have undertaken to restore many urban enceintes and military barriers on earlier foundations and models. Ironically, given the view of walls as Chinese and traditional and "no walls" as foreign and modern, these projects of preservation and restoration are sometimes inspired by current Western practices of protecting and transmitting cultural heritages. While some economists call for a world without walls and some statesmen have dismantled walls (as in Berlin), trade barriers and material walls continue to be erected (as on the United States border with Mexico, Israel's border with the West Bank, India's border with Pakistan and—most recently—in U.S.-occupied Baghdad).[4]

This chapter seeks to discover patterns in the building and unbuilding of one kind of Chinese walls by examining the experiences of three cities located in Henan province. Long known in Chinese as the "central province" (*zhongzhou*), Henan lies at the heart of the "central plain" (*zhongyuan*), which serves as a common synecdoche for

---

2   Some authors, of course, accept only parts of the paradigm and reject others. See, for example, Hansen, *Open Empire*, pp. 13–14; Esherick, "Modernity and Nation," p. 7.

3   Sources vary on the date of Deng's pronouncement from 1980 to 1984. See for example Liu, Li, and Luo, *Changcheng*, p. 1; Waldron, *Great Wall*, p. 1. This may reflect the time it took to turn his personal aphorism into public policy. Deng's precise intention in coining the slogan remains, as we would expect, unclear, allowing others to interpret the policy in their own diverse ways, the basic value of slogans in any society and one perhaps consciously entertained by Deng in this case. For similar slogans on city walls, see below.

4   Moore, *World Without Walls*; Wiener, "Walling Off."

the "central state(s)" (*zhongguo*) or what people in the "West" (and much of the rest of the world outside East Asia) call China. The walls of the three cities of Kaifeng, Guide (also known as Shangqiu), and Zhengzhou can trace their origins back to early times and are in that sense representative of a large number of Chinese cities that have been described as "orthogenetic."[5] Kaifeng and Guide/Shangqiu have preserved more of their walls than Zhengzhou has. Taken together, however, the three represent the many Chinese cities that fall between Shanghai and Beijing, which dismantled most of their walls in the Republic and People's Republic, respectively, and Xi'an and Nanjing, which have preserved their walls remarkably well to the present.[6] By chance, these three cities in Henan also served, at one time or another, as capitals of all of the standard levels of the highly continuous (although frequently shifting) Chinese administrative hierarchy: from polity, down through province, prefecture, independent department, and department, to the county.

We begin our account with the Ming dynasty, generally recognized as a high tide of both long- and city-wall building. During this period, all three city walls were substantially reconstructed. The goals were not merely to defend the cities from floods and banditry but to order both city and countryside and to re-create the ethos of earlier epochs of cultural efflorescence.[7] The Qing, with its original base outside the long walls and its frontier administration transcending them, was less interested in wall building but it restored city walls that had been destroyed in the dynastic transition and maintained most city walls for another two and a half centuries. During the Republic and early People's Republic, the three city walls were greatly affected by concurrent or successive waves of development, militarization, destruction, and neglect. Finally, in the new era of reform and opening after 1979, both state and society have worked to protect and reconstruct these city

---

5   Farmer, " Hierarchy," p. 464.

6   For the walls of Kaifeng and Guide/Shangqiu among those of some seventeen cities in mainland China, see Zhao and Gu, *Zhongguo chengqiang*, pp. 187–220. For Beijing, see Dong, *Republican Beijing*; Wang, *Chengji*; Zhang, "From Demolition to Restoration"; for Shanghai, see Du, "Shanghai"; for Nanjing see Yang, *Nanjing*.

7   For the function of walls in ordering both city and countryside see Xu, *Chinese City*, p. 86. For the concept of efflorescence, see Goldstone, "Neither Late."

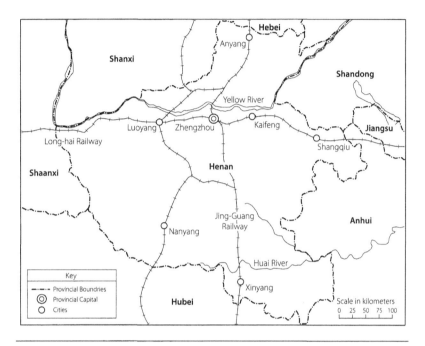

Map 1 Henan Province in the early People's Republic [based on Shanquan, *Henan*, frontispiece].

walls, leading to discussions and debates regarding their histories going back long before Ming times. From these tales we can infer a pattern of continuity and change that may approximate that of long walls. That pattern may also have implications for our understanding of the place of all Chinese city walls in time and space.

I. Ming Reconstruction

A. *Kaifeng: Song Dongjing Manqué*

The Ming founder Zhu Yuanzhang originally planned to restore Kaifeng to its former glory as the capital of the Northern Song when it had been called BianLiang or Dongjing (eastern capital). He soon decided, however, that the city was too vulnerable to the flooding of the Yellow River, and he assigned it instead the more modest status of capital of Henan province.[8] The Ming city, therefore, did not restore the original, more regular (at least as transmitted in maps) walls and the ten (or more) gates of the inner wall of the Song capital.[9] It settled instead for the somewhat more extended walls and more easily defended five gates inherited from the Jin period.

To rationalize the irregularity of Kaifeng's inner walls and to enhance confidence in its defenses, the residents were reported to have invoked geomantic principles (*fengshui*). They called Kaifeng the "city of the sleeping buffalo" (*wo niu cheng*). They visualized the animal with its head lying at the west gate and its four feet placed firmly at the other four gates, enabling it, even while asleep, to assert its earth power (*tude*) to control the water power (*shuide*) of the Yellow River. People also reassured themselves that Kaifeng was a city with "three mountains that are not apparent and five gates that are not symmetrical" (*san shan bu xian, wu men bu dui*). The three mountains were places in the city, such as the Iron Pagoda in the northeast, that were relatively elevated but became visibly so only during a flood. The five gates, like the walls, were not oriented precisely to the four directions; nor were any two directly across from each another. These cosmic infelicities were inter-

---

8   Farmer, *Early Ming Government,* pp. 43–51.
9   The regularity of BianLiang's actual walls is in question, while the number of its gates varied over time. Steinhardt, *Chinese Imperial,* pp. 137–42.

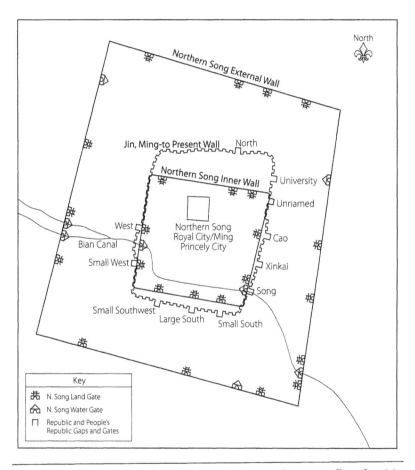

Map 2 The walls and gates of Kaifeng from the Song to the present [based on Ma, "Kaifeng chengqiang," n.p.; Liu, *Kaifeng chengqiang*, p. 22].

preted as effective geomantic means to insure that the good influences
that were thought to emanate from the West (perhaps from the ancient
capital of Luoyang) would enter the city and would remain there, unlikely to dissipate through the other gates.[10]

The Ming also adopted more material measures to strengthen the
walls and gates of Kaifeng and other such cities. Most notably it dressed
stone and baked bricks to undergird and face the walls that had previously consisted almost wholly of rammed earth. Chinese city walls,
unlike those of medieval Europe, had always been very thick as well as
high, and they were therefore relatively effective against the hot arma-
ments (e.g., cannons) invented during the Song and Yuan as well the
cold weapons (e.g., ballista) that continued to be deployed in the Ming
and Qing.[11] The Chinese, in fact, had fired bricks as early as Warring
States times. What was relatively new in the Ming period was the decision to brick the walls of major cities to protect them from erosion,
thus enhancing their durability. As time went on, the Ming state and
local society also strengthened the five gate towers, raised the height of
the wall by 50 percent, deepened the moat by 100 percent, and restored
a modest version of the external earthen wall.[12] The result was a formidable defensive structure that survived two major assaults by the rebel
Li Zicheng before succumbing in 1642 to a disastrous flood precipi-
tated by the Ming and the rebels for their respective military purposes
and greatly exacerbated by the weather.[13] Despite continuous efforts
at reconstruction, therefore, Ming Kaifeng's walls ultimately suffered
military-ecological destruction even greater than that previously visited on Song Dongjing.

10 Chang, *Rumenglu*, 1.3a; Shen and Huang, *Xinxiu Xiangfu*, 5.12; Cheng and Li, *Kaifeng chengshi*, p. 171.
11 Knapp, *China's Walled*, p. 22.
12 Li, *Bianjing*, 16: 303–306; Guan and Zhang, *Kaifeng fuzhi*, 9.6–6a; Tian, Sun, and Asiha, *Henan tongzhi*, 9.1–15b.
13 For a recent account of this well-known story, see Des Forges, *Cultural Centrality*, pp. 213–29, 254–68.

B. Guide/Shangqiu: Recovering Han Élan

The Ming founder had different plans for Guide/Shangqiu, but they too were eventually only partially realized. He demoted Guide from a prefecture to an independent department and then to a regular department.[14] After more than a century near the bottom of the urban hierarchy, the city reached its nadir in 1502 when it was destroyed by a flood of the Yellow River. Local officials and probably members of the local elite managed to prevail on the upper administration to approve abandoning the site, which had been occupied continuously since the Han dynasty. They moved the entire city to a more elevated location immediately adjacent to the north[15] (see Map 3). Two years later a local rebel led victims of the flood and the ensuing famine in an attack on the newly forming town. Those "social bandits" were driven off, but their assault, combined with the continuing danger of flooding, undoubtedly spurred interest in building a substantial wall around the new city. In 1511 the basic wall, with a modest circumference of 7.25 li and pierced by four land gates and two water gates, was completed.

During succeeding decades, Guide confronted many more challenges but was able to use them to improve its fortunes. After another rebellion in 1512 the magistrate constructed towers at the six gates. Further uprisings, floods, locusts, famines, and an epidemic resulted in the construction of an external wall in 1540. In 1545 Guide finally recovered its status as a prefectural city, now with authority over its home county of Shangqiu plus seven other counties and a department. In the same year, two members of the local elite compiled Guide's first prefectural gazetteer. After additional floods and another rebellion eight years later, the prefect reconstructed the four gate towers, erected four corner towers and thirteen watch towers, and established thirty-two guard stations. In 1558, almost certainly assisted by members of the local elite, officials began facing the walls with bricks, a project that continued under their successors.[16]

---

14   Liu and Ye, *Shangqiu xianzhi*, 1.14; Chen and Zha, *Guide fuzhi*, 11/391.
15   For evidence of local elite involvement in the planning and construction of county walls in general, see Chapter 3 in this volume.
16   *Ming Xiaozong*, 203.4b; Liu and Geng, *Henan*, I.74–76.

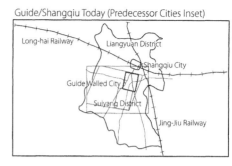

Guide/Shangqiu Today (Predecessor Cities Inset)

Predecessor Cities

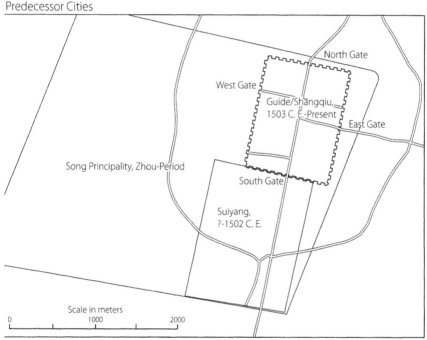

Map 3 Guide/Shangqiu in relation to predecessor and successor cities [based on Henan sheng Shangqiushi, "Dong Zhou," n.p.; Wallacker et al., *Chinese Walled*, p. 35; Shandong sheng, "Shangqiu shi," n.p.; Li et al., *Shangqiu tongshi*, frontispiece].

It is always difficult to know what was in the minds of Chinese city planners and builders. In retrospect, however, it seems clear that those who constructed the walls and gates of the new city of Guide paid closer attention to classical models and cosmic principles than might normally be expected for a city of such relatively modest size and status. The new walls constituted a highly regular rectangle, approximating the square shape associated with the earth, while the moat was more nearly circular, close to the shape associated with the heavens. Seen from above, the city thus resembled Chinese coins that were typically round with a square hole in the center. The four gates were oriented precisely to the four cardinal directions. Together with the four enceinte walls (or barbicans) that guarded passage through the gates, they provided a total of eight entrances to the city, equaling the number of trigrams in the *Book of Change(s)*. It has been argued that the orientation of the barbicans further resulted in a polarity between *yin* (or shade, the female, moon, etc.) in the northwest and *yang* (or light, the male, sun, etc.) in the southeast. During the Ming, Guide/Shangqiu was conceived of as a tortoise, the symbol of long life, whose head was said to be immersed in the southern moat, further insuring longevity.[17] All of these images may have been post facto rationalizations of Guide's walls, gates, and moat, but they all also had their roots in Han-period texts such as the "Record of Construction" (*Kao gong ji*) of the *Rites of Zhou* and *The Yellow Handbook for City Planning* (*Sanfu huang tu*) as well as in popular beliefs in "wind and water" (*Fengshui*), all closely associated with the Han dynasty.[18] Indeed, there are hints that these Han texts and beliefs were of particular interest in Henan province during the Ming.[19] It would appear that the elegant walls, gates, and moat of Guide were products of an effort on the part of local officials and literati to re-create the cultural ethos of the Liang principality that had rivaled the status of the capital city of Chang'an during the Former Han dynasty.[20]

---

17   Chen, "Shangqiu gucheng," pp. 26–28.

18   Wright, "Cosmology," pp. 43–46; Chang, "Morphology," pp. 88, 90; Mote, "Transformation," pp. 111–12; Xu, *Chinese City*, p. 234.

19   Steinhardt, *Chinese Imperial*, pp. 33–36, 141; Steinhardt, "Representations," pp. 430, 433, 449, 450.

20   Chen, *XiHan Liangguo*; for the Liang model in eastern Henan during the Ming, see Des Forges, *Cultural Centrality*, pp. 4, 75, 112, 118, 135.

Whatever the origins of the cosmic and geomantic rectitude of Guide's walls, gates, and moat, the Ming residents of the city compromised with the rebel Li Zicheng in the mid–seventeenth century in a way that allowed the city to preserve 70 percent of its infrastructure.[21]

C. Zhengzhou: Typical Ming Town

If Kaifeng and Guide/Shangqiu fluctuated considerably in official status during the Ming, Zhengzhou remained stable over the course of the dynasty as a department. In this and in other ways, it was quite representative of towns at the lower levels of the hierarchy.[22] Its walls were relatively long (9 *li*, 30 *bu*) for a department but about standard for an independent department (see Map 4). They were traced back to the Tang dynasty, when many city walls were first described in gazetteers. They were rectangular and longer east to west than north to south. They were 1.5 *zhang* (about 15 feet) wide at the top, sufficient to accommodate horse-drawn vehicles. They were therefore more defensible than the narrower walls of comparable cities in medieval Europe. The four gates were oriented to the four cardinal directions; those in the east and west faced one another while those on the north and south were offset (again, the usual arrangement). The moat was the standard 1 *zhang* deep and 2 *zhang* wide and there was no external wall, typical of cities at this level. The walls of Zhengzhou were repaired during the high tide of wall repair in the Chenghua and Zhengde reigns, and they were bricked in the Chongzhen reign, along with those of most other such towns in Henan, to strengthen defense against the armies of Li Zicheng. If Zhengzhou was distinctive among the towns of Henan in any way it was in its escape from serious damage during the

---

21 Liu and Ye, *Shangqiu xianzhi*, 1.15–16; Chen and Zha, *Guide fuzhi*, 11/391; Li et al., *Shangqiu tongshi*, pp. 159–62. The Confucian notion of the value of "yielding" may have been relevant here. For the importance of an analogous concept of "reasonable defense" in Renaissance Europe, see Tracy, *City Walls*, p. 6; Pepper, "Siege Law," p. 580.

22 Zhengzhou received a modest promotion, from a department to an independent department, in the Yongzheng reign. Tian et al., *Henan tongzhi*, 9.33b.

Ming-Qing transition, when an estimated 68 percent of such city walls in China were destroyed.[23]

II. Qing Repair and Maintenance

The Manchu bannermen, the hereditary military organization which constituted the core of the Qing state, originated outside the long walls in the northeast. They used diplomacy and warfare to bring the Mongols under their authority, rendering the long walls inherited from the Ming less significant. They nonetheless maintained a willow palisade to demarcate the frontier between their homeland and the central plain. They also adopted the Han Chinese practice of building walls around cities and they repaired and maintained the walls that had been destroyed in the dynastic transition. While the Qing used the enhanced firepower of European-style cannons to consolidate its control over the steppe, there was no need to change the technology of wall building because it continued to be effective against hot as well as cold weapons.[24]

In the first year of the Kangxi reign (1661) the governor of Henan began the process of restoring the walls of Kaifeng on their Ming base and model.[25] During the Yongzheng reign, work continued on the gates, corner towers, barbicans, and moat. Although we lack systematic financial data, the early Qianlong court provided 4,741 ounces of silver for the repair of the city's walls and moats. During the Daoguang reign in 1841, the city was devastated by another major flood. Although the Qing administration was faltering in the face of both recurrent and novel challenges, it managed to repair the city walls on the original base, using larger bricks and raising its height. The city remained the provincial capital and the head of a large prefecture through the dynasty, but its decline in the late nineteenth century was reflected in the

---

23   Zou, Li, and Zhu, *Henan tongzhi*, 13.17a; Tian, Sun, and Asiha, *Henan tongzhi*, 4.16b–18a; Zhang and Mao, *Xuxiu Zhengzhou*, 1.3b–4a; Xu, *Chinese City*, p. 128.

24   DiCosmo, "Did Guns Matter?"; Lovell, *Great Wall*, pp. 257–61; Perdue, *China Marches*, pp. 179, 184, 305. For the contrasting conditions in Europe and its colonies, see Parker, "Artillery Fortress," pp. 388, 410.

25   Gu, *Lidai zhaijing*, Kaifeng; Cheng and Li, *Kaifeng chengshi*, 249; Liu, *Kaifeng*, pp. 33–37.

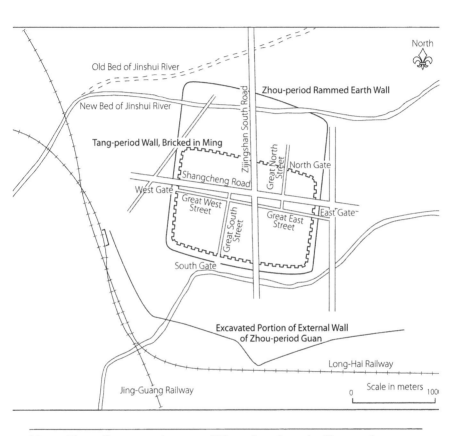

Map 4 The wall, gates, and streets of Zhengzhou from the Zhou to the present [based on Henan sheng dang'anguan, Record Group J135, 8.858:8; Zhang and Mao, *Xuxiu Zhengzhou*, 1.3b–4a; "Zhengzhou Shangdai," n.d., n.p.].

tendency to identify its wall by the name of its home county, Xiangfu, rather than the prefectural name, Kaifeng.[26]

Having suffered less than Kaifeng in the late Ming, Guide/Shangqiu recovered more quickly in the early Qing. During the Shunzhi reign officials repaired the gates, and during the Kangxi reign they repaired the towers. The early Qianlong court lavished 5,720 ounces of silver on the city walls, more than it devoted to the provincial capital. The funding, however, seems to have fallen off sharply to only 567 ounces in the twelfth year of the reign and was down to 297 ounces in Jiaqing 3 (1799).[27] Guide/Shangqiu was fortunate to avoid notable damage from flooding during the Qing. Its residents also continued the policy of reasonable defense in the face of rebellion. For example, they offered little resistance to the Taiping armies that swept through the city in 1853, leaving the walls and gates intact. Even firm resistance to the Nian rebels six years later resulted only in the burning of two city gates.[28]

Zhengzhou, too, fared well in the Qing, restoring its walls and moat during the Shunzhi and Kangxi reigns. The city was strategically located at the intersection of China's major north-south and east-west trunk roads. For this reason, perhaps, Yongzheng promoted the city to be an independent department with authority over four other counties.[29] He also supplied 1,000 ounces of silver for the repair of the city's northern and southern gates. During the Qianlong and Guangxu reigns, local magistrates made personal "contributions," "led the local elite," and mobilized "the people" to maintain the gates and their barbicans.[30]

26   Diyi lishi dang'an, 1119:59; Kong, *Rumenglu*, passim; Wei, "Tan 'Chongxiu.'" I am grate-
     ful to James Lee for alerting me to the existence of data in the Number One Historical
     Archive in Beijing on the financing of city wall construction during the high Qing and
     to Janet Chen for assisting in the mailing of transcribed data from the archive to the
     United States.

27   Liu and Ye, *Shangqiu xianzhi*, 1.16; Chen and Zha, *Guide fuzhi*, 11/391; Diyi lishi dang'an,
     1119:59; Henan sheng dang'an, Q1/83.3.

28   Shangqiu xianzhi, *Shangqiu xianzhi*, 22, 26–28; Li et al., *Shangqiu tongshi*, 159–162.

29   Tian et al., *Henan tongzhi*, 9: 33b.

30   Diyi lishi dang'an, 1119:59; Zhou, Wang, and Liu, *Zhengxian zhi*, 3.142–43.

III. Republic and Early People's Republic: Development, Militarization, Destruction, and Neglect

A. *Kaifeng: Decline*

Kaifeng retained its status as provincial capital during the Republic and the first years of the People's Republic, but its walls suffered considerable damage. During the Republic, the construction of railways near cities and the widening of streets connecting cities to suburbs resulted in the decline of city walls and gates. In 1929 the military commander Feng Yuxiang opened a passageway in the eastern part of the southern wall to facilitate traffic to and from the east-west Long-Hai railway, which passed through just south of the wall. Because it was less central than the main South Gate and lacked a barbican, it was called the Small Southern Gate.[31] In 1954 Kaifeng ceded its status as provincial capital to the transport hub Zhengzhou. It soon opened another passageway in the western wall, which became known as the Small Western Gate. In 1958, during the Great Leap Forward, another opening was made in the eastern wall. It became known as the Newly Opened Gate. All of these new passages were wider and simpler than the gates inherited from the Ming and Qing and were wholly utilitarian efforts to accommodate the growing traffic of automobiles, buses, and trucks.

While Kaifeng's walls remained generally effective against artillery and the weather, its pavilion-style gates were deemed outmoded. In 1931 the Henan governor Liu Zhi dismantled the towers and replaced them with less ornate and more solid blockhouses. After the Japanese occupied the city in 1938, they established eight large pillboxes on the walls, one of which remains on the east wall to this day.[32] The militarization of Kaifeng's walls did not prevent—and may have exacerbated—the damage they sustained during the civil war between the Nationalists and the Communists in the 1940s. Both the Large and the Small South Gates were heavily damaged during the assault by the People's Liberation Army in 1948. Bullet holes in the bricks of the interior of the western wall left from the fierce battle within the city remained visible as late as 2002.

---

31   Liu, *Kaifeng chengqiang*, p. 37.
32   Ibid.

During the Great Leap Forward and the Cultural Revolution, concerted efforts were made to dismantle Kaifeng's walls. One motive was probably to collect bricks and stones that could be used in more practical edifices; another was to destroy symbols of the "old order" such as parapets that were relatively easy to dismantle.[33] During the height of tensions with the Soviet Union in 1971 some ten thousand citizens from ninety work units were mobilized to construct a 37,000-square-meter air raid shelter in the bowels of the city wall.[34] While an ingenious and logical effort to respond to new military threats and extend the utility of the wall, this project literally undermined the wall and caused it to collapse in some places. On the plus side, the shelters were warm in winter and cool in the summer. Once the military crisis was over, they became storerooms or even homes for itinerant merchants, expanding the uses and prolonging the life of the walls.[35]

We can trace the decline of the Kaifeng city wall most clearly in the fate of two of its original gates and the nature of one new passageway, all in the eastern wall. The Cao Gate lost its pavilion and barbican in the 1950s and was completely dismantled in the Great Leap Forward. The Song Gate retained its pavilion and parapets through the 1940s and its archway and tunnel through the 1970s, but was completely eliminated during the following decade. Meanwhile a gap was made further north to permit passage along Minglun Street at the southern edge of Henan University and egress to the eastern suburbs. This break in the wall was purely utilitarian and lacked not only a gate but a name. During the 1980s, however, another passageway was made further north to permit university staff and students to get to their residences outside the wall. It was graced with a bricked archway (although no name), a modest effort to replicate earlier-style gates and a small harbinger of changes soon to take place elsewhere in the city.

---

33   Ibid., p. 38.

34   Interview with Kaifeng citizen Huang Limin, Kaifeng, November 2002.

35   Similarly, in Changzhou, near Nanjing, a short section of the city wall was preserved because it was inhabited by poor people. Interview with Changzhou citizen Su Yang-yang, July 2006.

B. Guide/Shangqiu: Persistence

During the Republic and early People's Republic, Guide/Shangqiu's walls and gates fared better than Kaifeng's. This was partly because the east-west Long-Hai railway passed through about eight kilometers north of the old Guide walled city (*Guide gucheng*), giving rise to a new, "unwalled" commercial and industrial city that took the name Shangqiu (*Shangqiu shi*). As a result, both the benefits and the costs of development accrued to the new city of Shangqiu. That left the old city of Guide with few funds for basic public amenities, such as water and sewer systems, but also allowed it to keep its inherited walls, gates, and moat largely intact.

Guide/Shangqiu survived the era relatively unscathed also because the residents maintained their practice of political flexibility or serial compromise—not to say collaboration.[36] According to local records, Nationalist troops retreated from the city in May 1938 before the Japanese troops arrived, allowing a transfer of authority with little conflict. In 1945 the Japanese forces surrendered without a fight, enabling the Nationalists to resume authority without damage to the infrastructure. In November 1948 the Nationalists once again withdrew without mounting resistance, allowing the Communist forces to take over the city without damage to its walls and gates.[37]

At some as yet undetermined time, however, the walls, gates, and moat of Guide/Shangqiu suffered the effects of entropy and neglect. By 1979 eight gate pavilions, four corner towers, thirteen watch towers, four barbicans, and some 3,600 crenels had disappeared.[38] During the later years of the Cultural Revolution, the poorer residents of the city had helped themselves to bricks from the walls to construct their own residences. During the first years of reform and opening, alcohol and textile manufacturers regularly dumped industrial waste into the moat. The population of the old city increased from 20,000 in 1949 to 40,000 in the 1980s, putting additional pressure on the walls and moat.[39]

---

36 For reflections on such terms, see Brook, *Collaboration*.

37 Shangqiu xianzhi, *Shangqiu xianzhi*, pp. 26, 27, 29, 33, 37; Li et al., *Shangqiu tongshi*, pp. 161–64, 208–10, 223–24, 235–36.

38 Wu and Liu, *Henan gudai*, pp. 214–15.

39 Interview with Chen Mouling, head of the Cultural Bureau of Suiyang District, summer 2005.

C. Zhengzhou: Rise

Zhengzhou, which had experienced great continuity in the Ming and
Qing periods, went through dramatic changes in the Republic and
early People's Republic. After 1911, despite its emergence as a major rail
hub at the intersection of the Jing-Guang and Long-Hai rail lines, the
city was suddenly and sharply demoted two ranks from an independent
department to a county. During the early People's Republic, on the
other hand, its role as a major industrial center earned it an even more
radical promotion, first to a departmental city and then, in 1954, to
capital of Henan province.

Zhengzhou's position as a major railway city had a predictably
negative effect on its inherited walls.[40] Maps of the city that highlighted
the railway terminal barely indicated the inherited city walls that were
located nearby.[41] The emphasis on transportation, including city streets,
came at the expense of the walls and the space they had once enclosed.
In 1928 the military governor Feng Yuxiang ordered the wresting of
seven million bricks from the wall to pave two streets in the city.[42] In
the People's Republic, two new thoroughfares, Zijingshan and Shangcheng, were constructed to intersect in the center of the old walled city
without regard to smaller existing streets that corresponded to the
ancient walls and gates[43] (see Map 4). In the name of "development"
and "modernization," serious damage was done to the inherited integrity of the walled city. These changes, of course, were consistent with
the standard paradigm that depicts walls as impediments to "progress."
But they also did so much violence to the cultural heritage that they
would lead to the ostensibly anomalous backlash that we shall examine
shortly.

The walls of Zhengzhou also reflected the militarization of the period. In 1912 members of the local elite floated bonds to raise five hundred ounces of silver to pay for mounting forty cannons on the walls of

---

40   Zhao, *Lao Zhengzhou*, pp. 172–73; for other such "railway cities," see Esherick, *Remak-
     ing*, chs. 2–5, 7, 10; Asher, "Delhi Walled," p. 280.
41   See, for example, Henan sheng cehuiju, "Zhengzhou shiqu."
42   Zhao, *Lao Zhengzhou*, pp. 172–73.
43   According to one later observer, Zijingshan "cut [the old Dongdajie] in half at the
     waist." Ibid., p. 178.

the city.[44] This was an ominous sign of the civil wars that would dominate the early years of the Republic. The Nanjing decade after 1927 witnessed some stabilization of the military in the central plain, but in 1937 the Japanese invaded. In 1939 the Nationalist official Sun Tongxuan responded by moving the bed of the Jinshui river south to the northern boundary of the city. He also built a dike on the south bank of the river to keep it from flooding the city and to serve as a bulwark against the invaders. This project failed to protect the city. It also unwittingly destroyed much of the northern part of an ancient city wall that was yet to be rediscovered.[45] (We shall return to this wall below.)

Zhengzhou's drive to become a major industrial city also took a toll on the city walls. According to reports in the provincial archives, by 1956, 90 percent of the existing city wall dating to the Tang was already occupied by buildings and waterways. During the Great Leap Forward, an industrial unit proposed building a fertilizer plant and an agricultural cooperative sought to construct a watercourse on the wall. Workers were accustomed to taking soil from the wall to make charcoal briquettes, which were widely used for fuel. Farmers availed themselves of earth from the wall to fertilize their fields.[46] Many residents of the city had made their homes on the wall, including a Muslim community living on the southern wall. While these people had no interest in destroying the wall (on the contrary their presence helped to preserve it), they also had no wish to vacate the wall so that it could be restored to some earlier condition.

IV. The New Era of Reform and Opening: Preservation and Reconstruction

If the Republic and early People's Republic pursued development, militarization, destruction, and neglect of the three cities' walls and gates in the name of modernization (whether capitalist or socialist), the People's Republic in the "new era" since 1979 has reshaped "mo-

---

44   Zhou et al, *Zhengxian zhi*, chengchi (walls and moats), 3.3b.

45   Zhao, *Lao Zhengzhou*, pp. 184–93.

46   Henan sheng dang'an, J 135.7.719, March 1956–October 1958, July 1959–June 1962. I am grateful to Luan Xing, senior researcher at the History Institute of the Academy of Social Sciences in Zhengzhou, for assisting me in gaining access to these records.

dernity" to include "reform" and "opening," thus authorizing the preservation and reconstruction of those walls and gates. While much of this activity is motivated by a reaction against revolution and radicalism and includes a quest for foreign investment and tourism, it has led to renewed interest in various Chinese pasts and to debates over which of those pasts should be recovered and how.

A. Kaifeng: Toward the Ming or Song?

The Henan Provincial People's Congress proclaimed Kaifeng's city walls a cultural site of the first rank in 1963, but it took a flood in 1977 and Deng Xiaoping's call for restoring walls in the early 1980s to result in concerted action. The decision was made to begin with the gates, which were the most visible parts of the wall and the easiest and cheapest to restore. It was further agreed that they should be restored in the Ming-Qing style, complete with arches and pavilions but minus the barbicans, which would unduly impede traffic.

Beginning in 1983 the Kaifeng city government made repeated requests to invest twelve million yuan in the reconstruction of the Song Gate and of the Large South Gate.[47] After the creation of a bureau, regulations, and a newspaper (the *BianLiang wanbao*) to direct and generate support for the project under such slogans as "Restore Our Walls, Love Our Kaifeng," work actually began in the 1990s on the West Gate. The west gate had long since lost its central arch, tower, and barbican, but it was still considered to be the most important entrance for favorable external influences (now featuring tourists and investors from the provincial capital of Zhengzhou). In 1998 the gate was restored to its original Ming-Qing state, minus only the barbican, at a cost of some four million yuan.[48] Work began on the North Gate in 2001 and was completed the following year; attention then turned to the Small South Gate, which was restored in 2003. Just as the long walls touted by Deng Xiaoping served as symbols of the entire polity, so the city walls cele-

---

47 "Kaifengshi renmin," Group 23, catalogue 21, no. 748 (Bianzheng 1983, no. 64), p. 5; no. 833 (Bianzeng 1985, nos. 11, 49), pp. 4–5; Liu, *Kaifeng chengqiang*, 38, pp. 119–31. The relationships among these requests and their ultimate results are unknown.

48 Interview with Liu Shun'an, June 28, 2006. Annual expenditures of the Cultural Relics Bureau were about forty million yuan.

brated by local officials reemerged as symbols of the local community working together in a new efflorescence.

The next project was supposed to have been the Large South Gate, which had lost its superstructure but, quite atypically, had retained part of its barbican. The plan was to reconstruct the entire gate in its Ming-Qing form modified only by turning the central passageway into a public park and confining traffic to the two flanking archways. This project tended to favor aesthetics and greenery over utility and transport. At the same time, it was predicated on the assumption that nongovernmental organizations in the city would provide three-quarters of the five million yuan needed to complete it. The plan therefore stimulated a lot of internal discussion. As of June 2006, it was not clear how, or even if, it would be realized. Meanwhile the Cultural Relics Bureau began the reconstruction of nine hundred meters of the city wall located east of the Southwest Gate, including land external to the wall. This is slated to be the first section of a Ring Wall Park (*huancheng gongyuan*) that should eventually encircle the entire city.[49]

The decision to reconstruct the gates of Kaifeng on the Ming-Qing base and in the Ming-Qing style (minus only the original barbicans) was popular, but the plan to restore the official Ming names (and related aphorisms) of the gates led to a lively debate.[50] Some people argued that the principal gates should continue to be identified by their common directional names: north, south, east (the Cao gate), and west.[51] They adduced some textual and cartographic evidence for their position, but they relied mainly on the popular practice that had developed in the twentieth century. A journalist suggested a compromise, putting the Ming names and aphorisms on the interior of the gates and the directional names on the exterior.

49   *BianLiang,* August 8, 2005, p. 1; June 7, 2006, p. A3. This project has cost eight million yuan so far. The contrast with Beijing, which turned almost all of its erstwhile wall into a "ring road" and has been able to save only one and a half kilometers for a public park, seems almost studied.

50   Ibid., February 26, 2004, pp. 1, 13. I am grateful to Professor Wei Qianzhi of Henan University, who played a quiet role in the debate and supplied me with copies of the relevant articles and one manuscript. Wei, "Qiewu yi dong."

51   Ibid. March 1, 2004, p. 13.

Others pointed out that Kaifeng, like China, had arguably reached its cultural, political, and economic apogee during the Northern Song period. The city had long been known as one of the great politywide capitals. Now that it had also been named a national cultural unit, it should celebrate that status by using Song-period names for its main gates.[52] One correspondent to the *BianLiang wanbao* made the same argument on more practical grounds. He pointed out that Kaifeng now had ten apertures or "gates," the same number that had existed in the Northern Song. This made it possible to use Song-period names for all of them.[53] After several weeks of debate, local officials and scholars decided to use the Ming official names (and aphorisms) because the gates were being reconstructed on the Ming base and in the Ming style. Besides, some of those Ming names actually had their origins in the Song period, making it unnecessary to choose between the Ming and the Song.[54] In other cases, the Ming model clearly prevailed over the Song and over popular custom. For example, the gate known as Cao for as long as anyone could remember would henceforth be called the Renhe Gate, the name it had in the Ming period and that had no precedent in the Song.[55] Thus the only gate in Kaifeng today with an exclusively Song name is the facsimile of the Shangshan Gate that stands by itself, innocent of any wall, in the Going up the River on the Qingming Festival Park (*Qingming Shanghe Yuan*), a theme park in the southwestern quarter of the city.[56]

---

52 Ibid., June 1, 2004, p. 12; June 22, 2004, p. 13.

53 Ibid., June 1, 2004, pp. 12, 13, 14; October 12, 2004, p. 14.

54 Ibid., February 26, 2004, pp. 1, 13; March 1, 2004, p. 13; May 25, 2004, p. 1; June 1, 2004, pp. 12, 13; June 22, 2004, p. 13; October 12, 2004, p. 14; May 17, 2006, p. 1.

55 Ibid., May 17, 2006, p. 1. The three new gaps with gates will be identified by their informal names; the two without gates will not be named.

56 Kaifeng Qing-Ming, "Qing-Ming." Advocates of Song identity must now pin their hopes on retaining or recovering some Song-period names for city streets such as the major one connecting the North (now Anyuan) Gate to the Small South (now Ximen) Gate. *BianLiang,* February 23, 2006, p. A2; March 10, 2006, p. B3; March 17, 2006, p. B3; April 17, 2006, p. A14; April 17, 2006, p. A14; Henan sheng jindi, *Zhongguo Kaifeng;* Lishi, "Kaifeng laojie," p. 2.

B. Guide/Shangqiu: Toward the Ming and the Han

In the new era, Guide/Shangqiu has been able to protect much of its cultural heritage while pursuing development. In 1986 the State Council named the old walled Guide a Famous City of History and Culture. In the same year the state constructed a new north-south trunk rail line, the Jing-Jiu, to intersect with the Long-Hai line in the new city of Shangqiu, once again leaving the Guide walled city unaffected.[57] The following year, local officials met with the City Planning Institute of Tongji University in Shanghai to discuss how to protect the city's cultural infrastructure. They noted that the walls were relatively well preserved and were especially precious because of the paucity of other historical relics in the city. The walls were useful in defending against floods and attracting tourists, and they also had historical, scientific, and spiritual value. The planners stated that "people therefore strongly hope that the wall will be protected and repaired" and that the moat will be "restored and reconstructed." At the same time, the population of the city was expected to double again, to eighty thousand, making it necessary to emphasize the people's livelihood. The planners proposed to turn the entire city into a cultural site. Housing should be in gray brick in the courtyard style; buildings along the main streets should be kept lower than seven meters so as not to block the views from the gates; heavy industry and warehouses should be moved outside the city walls; most automobiles should be parked outside the walls and bicycles should be used in the city; and the moat should become a recreational area while the external wall should serve as the basis for a tree-lined ring road.[58] The walls and moat of Guide, once designed as bulwarks against floods and rebels, were now reenvisioned as barriers against consumerism and pollution.

Ten years later Guide was designated a National Key Unit for the Protection of Cultural Relics and began to appropriate about one million yuan a year to reconstruct its walls, gates, and moat. By 2002 it had restored the North Gate, including its Ming-Qing-style tower and parapets, though not its barbican; by 2005 it had reconstructed the South Gate on the same model. The plan to exclude automobiles from the city

---

57   Shangqiu xianzhi, *Shangqiu xianzhi:* sanpian (chapter 3), dili (geography), pp. 57–58.
58   Tongji Daxue, *Shangqiu xian*, pp. 1–23.

has not yet been realized; on the contrary the number of vehicles seems to be on the increase and there appear to be no immediate plans for any great increase in public transportation. A drawbridge over the moat outside the south gate has been replaced by a permanent bridge, suggesting the continuing importance of motor vehicle traffic into and out of the city. But the moat has been cleaned up and turned into a public park and the external wall has been transformed into a ring road that is flanked by greenery according to the original plan. Most important, the idea of allowing the population to grow by 100 percent has been changed; the goal is now to stabilize it and eventually reduce it by 50 percent.[59] Guide's walls and gates, once proud containers of the dense settlement and commercial growth often associated with civilization in China as elsewhere, are now becoming markers of an effort to establish a more nearly steady-state society.

Although Guide/Shangqiu has yet to develop—let alone realize—a consistent vision of a society different from that of the "West," which seems to be on an inexorable global march, the city is well on its way to restoring a cultural infrastructure on the Ming model. Unlike in Kaifeng, there has evidently been no audible or visible controversy over the use of Ming-period names and aphorisms for the city's gates. Indeed, contemporary officials and scholars of Guide/Shangqiu take great pride in the city's Ming heritage. This includes the homes, now under reconstruction, of several leading literati families, including the Hous and the Songs, who flourished in this city during the late Ming.[60] According to local officials, such restored sites have yet to pay for themselves by attracting larger numbers of tourists, but they have served to remind the local populace of their cultural inheritance, which may in the end be a more important function.

As we have seen, the people of Guide/Shangqiu have traced the history of their city back well before the Ming and especially to the Han period. The People's Republic has recognized that heritage by naming the district subordinate to Shangqiu city the Liangyuan qu (Liang Garden District) and the district subordinate to Guide the Suiyang qu

59 Interviews with Chen Mouling and Zhang Jihong, heads of the Cultural Bureau of Suiyang District, July 2005 and June 2006.
60 For background, see Des Forges, *Cultural Centrality*, pp. 77–105; Li et al., *Shangqiu tongshi*, pp. 184–88.

(Suiyang District) (see Map 3). These names, of course, allude to the principality of Liang Xiaowang, who patronized illustrious scholars during the Former Han, and to the administrative unit of Suiyang, which existed in the Han and lasted until the creation of the new Guide walled town in the mid-Ming.[61] Local scholars are today confirming and reinforcing their identification with the Han by publishing texts on the history and literature of the Liang principality even as archaeologists are digging deeper into the even earlier origins of the ancestral Zhou city.[62]

C. Zhengzhou: Toward the Tang and the Zhou (and the Shang?)

Meanwhile archaeologists had already played an even more important role in uncovering the early foundations of the Zhengzhou city walls. In 1950 an elementary school teacher found some clay and bronze artifacts in Erligang village southeast of the extant Tang-based Ming-Qing wall. Two years later the Ministry of Culture, the Academy of Sciences, and Beijing University began extensive excavations in the area. By 1954 they were convinced that the relics in the entire site predated those of Anyang in northern Henan, generally accepted as the last capital of the Shang dynasty. In that year, as we have seen, Zhengzhou became the capital of Henan province with increased political authority, administrative influence, financial resources, and cultural prestige. In 1955 archaeologists working well to the north of the existing Ming-Qing wall discovered the deeply buried remains of a much more ancient wall. Further excavations revealed it to lie beneath the eastern, southern, and western portions of the Tang-period wall and to extend well beyond the northern edge of the Tang-period wall to enclose a space roughly twice the size of the Tang enceinte. In 1956 the Zhengzhou city

61 Shangqiu xianzhi, *Shangqiu xianzhi:* sanpian, dili, pp. 57–58.

62 Li et al., *Shangqiu tongshi*, pp. 68–78, 80–84; Xu, *Lishi wenhua*, pp. 72–75; He, *Lingting*, pp. 91–108; Wang, *XiHan Liang Guo*; Yan, *Lishi mingcheng*, 117–19, 167–69, 456–67. For the Zhou and Shang roots of Shangqiu, see Henan sheng Shangqiushi, "Dong Zhou"; Li et al., *Shangqiu tongshi*, p. 13; Xu, *Lishi wenhua*, pp. 49–53; He, *Lingting*, pp. 13–18; Yan, *Lishi mingcheng*, 5–8, 331–33, 442–46; Wang, "Shangzu."

government announced regulations to protect any and all remains of
city walls and related relics.[63]

The discovery of a massive, now subterranean, wall that was estimated to have required the labor of ten thousand men working eighteen years to construct led to a great debate among archaeologists and
historians over its likely provenance and function. In the 1950s An Jinhuai, head of the Archaeological Institute in Zhengzhou, argued that
the original wall enclosed the city of Ao to which the Shang king
Zhongding had moved his capital circa 1482 BCE.[64] In the 1960s, Zou
Heng, an archaeologist at Beijing University, proposed that the wall
encircled the city of Bo, where King Tang had founded the Shang
around 1711 BCE.[65] In the 1980s Yang Kuan, a historian from Fudan
University in Shanghai, used both archaeological and written records
to argue that the site was the city of Guan. Guan may have originally
served as a secondary capital of the Shang, but it was probably encom-
passed by the large wall only in the early Zhou. At that time the Zhou
king Wu assigned it to his younger brother Shuxian to serve as a base
from which to supervise the descendants of the erstwhile Shang royal
family.[66] In the 1990s Luan Xing, a historian at the Academy of Social
Sciences in Zhengzhou, added that the wall was most likely constructed
around Guan by Shuxian in the early Zhou and was abruptly abandoned after he joined with Shang loyalists in a rebellion that was put
down by his brother the Duke of Zhou. The Duke thereafter established
his eastern capital in Luoyang, located to the west of the now discred-
ited Guan.[67]

During the 1990s issues surrounding the ancient wall of Zhengzhou
attracted the attention of various parties. In 1991 the National Bureau
of Cultural Relics provided 2.1 million yuan to support the work of an
Office for the Protection and Management of the "Remains of the

63   Wang, Ao xu: 1; Wu and Liu, Henan gudai: 45; "Zhengzhou Shangdai."
64   An, "Shilun Zhengzhou." Guo Moruo, head of the Chinese Academy of Sciences, ac-
     cepted this view and, not coincidentally, it became the orthodoxy for many. Wang, Ao
     xu, p. 43.
65   Zou, "Zhengzhou Shangcheng." Zou's students took posts at Zhengzhou University
     where they upheld this point of view. Zheng, "Guanyu Yanshi"; Zheng, "Guanyu
     Zhengzhou"; Li, Shang wenhua. But see also Du, "ZhengBo."
66   Yang, "Shangdai"; Yang, Zhongguo, pp. 34-39.
67   Luan, "Shuo Guan," original and synopsis.

Shang City in Zhengzhou."[68] Archaeologists discovered and excavated parts of an ancient external wall that further dramatized the size and importance of the ancient city without solving the problem of the date of its walls.[69] In 1996 the central and provincial governments allocated twenty-four million yuan to engage 170 scholars to address the vexed issue of the relations among the three early dynasties of Xia, Shang, and Zhou, work that might help in the dating of Zhengzhou's walls.[70]

In the same year an artist named Wang Jin, originally from Shanxi but now living in Beijing, was commissioned by the Zhengzhou municipal government to create a sculpture to celebrate the opening of the city's first large shopping mall. The result was *Ice: Central Plain 1996* (Bing zhongyuan 1996) a thirty-meter-long wall made with six hundred blocks of ice embedded with luxury consumer goods, including jewelry, cell phones, and pharmaceuticals. Reportedly unexpectedly but ultimately without penalty, spectators soon began to dig the commodities out of the ice by whatever means they could, finally destroying the wall (see Figure 1). Wang's original goal was said to have been to "cool down" the public ardor for consumption, and even after the wall was destroyed he continued to hope that the goods "had been purified by the ice."[71] In fact, in the words of the art historian Minglu Gao referring to the people, "The ice was melted by the heat of their materialism."[72] Wang's previous work—including pouring red dye into the Red Flag Canal, painting the Beijing-Kowloon railway tracks red, painting images of U.S. dollars on bricks in the wall of the Forbidden City in Beijing, and using Coca Cola bottles to reconstruct a long-wall tower in Gansu, as well as his subsequent work on Beijing Opera costumes—suggests that he was interested in what was happening to various inherited institutions and values in the confrontation with the

68   "Zhengzhou chenghuang," interviews with Ma Yupeng, Secretary of the Zhengzhou City Temple to Walls and Moat, June 2005, June 2006.

69   Henan sheng wenwu, "Zhengzhou Shangcheng."

70   Gilley, "Digging into." For one fruit of this research, see Zhang, *Xia Shang*. In 1998 the Zhengzhou city government devoted another ten million yuan to preserving and studying the remains of the early city. Interview with Ma Yupeng, June 2006.

71   Wang, "Guanyu"; Wu, *Transience*, pp. 158–59.

72   Gao, *Wall*, pp. 150, 203, 364.

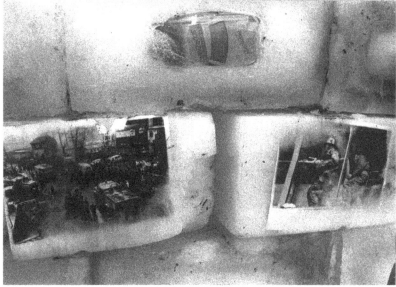

Figure 1 Wang Jin, "Ice: Central Plain 1996" [from Gao, *The Wall*, p. 203. Used with the author's permission.]

global economic system centered on the United States.[73] In the case of the ice wall, he dramatized the impact of commercialism on a wall demarcating a sub-urban social unit (the shopping mall). It is unclear whether his Zhengzhou ice wall was intended to have—or ultimately had—anything to do with the expenditure of substantial public funds to maintain and reconstruct the controversial Tang and Zhou (or Shang?) city walls made of more durable earth, stones, and bricks.

The goals and achievements of Zhang Xinbin, head of the Archaeology Institute in Zhengzhou, have been much clearer. He and his colleagues have tried to solve the problem of the dating of the wall of Zhengzhou in a way that will help earn the city greater status as one of the "great old capitals" (*dagudu*) of China.[74] In 2004 Zhang wrote that Zhengzhou qualified as such a city on the grounds of its territorial reach, administrative control, longevity as capital, general importance, and continuity with its successors. He pointed out that the city harbored archaeological sites for every stage of Shang cultural development, including those of Bo and Ao.[75] He argued that, on this basis alone, Zhengzhou had served as the Shang capital for 355 years, longer than Anyang that had been capital (for 351 years).

Perhaps concerned that this case might not be persuasive, Zhang argued further that Zhengzhou was the center of what he called an "old capital group" (*guduqun*) comprised of seven nearby archaeological sites that, taken together, pushed the story back to the earliest horizons of Chinese civilization and forward into the Eastern Zhou (see Map 5).[76] According to Zhang, Xishan in the northern suburb has Yangshao remains and a round wall that may have enclosed the capital of the Yellow Lord (*Huangdi*), the legendary common ancestor of the Chinese people. Guchengzhai in Xinmi, southwest of the city, has a rectangular wall and may have been the capital of Zhu Rong, an early ruler/official who became the fire spirit. Wangchenggang at Dengfeng has a square

73 Wu, *Transience*, pp. 86–87, 154–59. Wang's sympathy for migrant workers was evident in two other pieces of his behavioral art. Gao, *Wall*, pp. 177–78, 218–19, Plates 19, 20.

74 In the 1920s when this category first appeared it included only Xi'an, Luoyang, Beijing, Nanjing, and Kaifeng; in the 1940s it expanded to include Hangzhou; in the 1980s it took in Anyang. Chen, *Zhongguo ducheng*, pp. 1–2.

75 Zhang, "Zhengzhou dagudu," pp. 8–11.

76 Ibid.

wall that may have contained Yangcheng, the capital of the Xia founder
Yu. Xinzhai at Xinmi boasts inner and outer walls that may signify the
capital of Yu's son Qi. Dashigu in the present-day city of Zhengzhou
has a rectangular wall and moat that may be the remains of the states
of Wei and Gu. Shifo, near Zhengzhou, may have been the site of the
state of Guan, which Wu Wang assigned to Shuxian. The ancient city of
Zheng in today's Xinzheng has the remains of walls and palaces and
may have served as the capital of the Eastern Zhou for 366 years.[77] By
this count, the Zhengzhou old capital group provided "old capitals" for
another 600 years.

In sum, Zhang and his colleagues made the case that Zhengzhou
and its environs served as a great old capital (or at least as "old capitals") for a total of some 955 years, allowing it (or at least them) to
compare favorably with the longest-lasting great old capitals, Xi'an,
Luoyang, and Beijing. The case may seem problematic if only because
it does not distinguish clearly between myth and history and between
politywide capitals and lesser ones, but it was apparently strong enough
to persuade the existing members of the Great Old Capital Association
to admit Zhengzhou as their eighth member.[78] That status permits officials from Zhengzhou to attend international conferences with representatives from other ancient capitals of Eurasia including Rome,
Baghdad, Delhi, and Tokyo. Perhaps more important, the Zhengzhou
city government has committed 500 million yuan for the preservation
and reconstruction of the "Shang city" remains, including twenty-
meter-wide parks on both sides of the above-ground (Tang-based
Ming-Qing) walls, which total three kilometers in length.[79]

The Henan Archaeological Institute's theory of the "old capital
group" is remarkably consistent with the provincial government's plan
to establish the "greater city" of Zhengzhou as the center of a Central
Plains City Group (*zhongyuan chengshi qun*). Also known as the Yellow
(River) Triangle, this urban complex was first proposed in the 1990s. It
was inspired by similar projects including the Pearl (River) Triangle

---

77   For more on these sites, see Zhao, "Xinmi"; Ma, "Xinzhai"; Zhongguo gudu, *Zhongguo
      gudu*"; Ma, "Wudi shidai"; Ma, " Yu Shun."
78   Zhengzhou gudu, *Gudu Zhengzhou (2004)* provides details on the members and their
      speeches.
79   Interview with Ma Yupeng, June 2005.

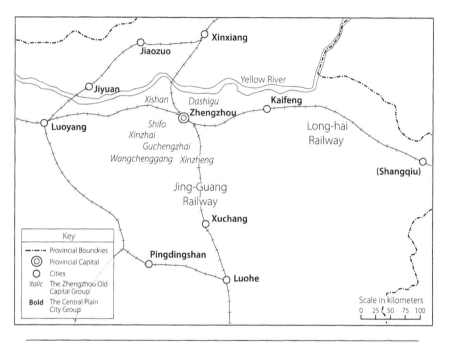

Map 5 The Zhengzhou Old Capital Group and the Central Plain City Group [based on Zhengzhou gudu, *Gudu Zhengzhou*, cover; Tian, "Henan: dazao"; Tian, "Jiedu zhongyuan"].

based on Canton, the Chang (Yangzi River) Triangle based on Shanghai, and the Bohai Bay Ring centered on Tianjin. As now envisioned,
the Central Plains City Group will include Xinxiang, Kaifeng, Xuchang,
Luohe, Pingdingshan, Luoyang, Jiyuan, and Jiaozuo (see Map 5). This
region already includes 35 percent of the provincial territory and 40
percent of its population, and it already boasts considerable agricultural, industrial, commercial, and cultural resources. The plan is to
build on this existing wealth to attain minor prosperity (*xiaokang*) by
2020. It will entail the doubling of Zhengzhou's population to five million; the increase in regional population, urban dwellers, and industrial
production to 60 percent of the provincial totals; and the quadrupling
of annual per capita gross domestic product to thirty-five thousand
yuan. Methods will include greater cooperation among the participating cities, reduction of the transaction costs of external investments,
reform of state services, development of the private economy, and an
emphasis on high technology in the eastern suburb of Zhengzhou.[80]
Many questions remain about how the center will be defined and how
it will interact with its peripheries, including cities like Shangqiu, which
have been left outside of it.[81] It would appear that Zhengzhou will follow Shangqiu in locating new industry outside the old city, thus helping to preserve the old city walls.[82] But Zhengzhou seems unlikely to
attempt to create any alternative to the developmentalism characteristic of contemporary China and the world as a whole.

Conclusions

The common view that Chinese walls were appropriate in the "old
society" but became irrelevant in the "new" was seemingly confirmed
by the decline and destruction of many walls during the Republic and
early People's Republic. This interpretation cannot, however, explain
the renewed interest in preserving and reconstructing walls in the
period of reform since 1979. The tales of three city walls in the central

---

80   Tian, "Henan: dazao," pp. 7–8; Tian, "Jiedu zhongyuan," pp. 9–13.

81   Wang, "Zhongyuan chengshi."

82   The separation of industrial activity from old cities has been dubbed the Luoyang
     model, invoking another exemplary city located in the central plain. Dan, "Cong 'yi jiu
     chen,'" p. 49.

plain, at least, suggest a more complex, recurrent, and open-ended pattern of history in which past models are invoked to maintain continuity even while effecting change.[83]

During the Ming, Kaifeng looked back to Northern Song Dongjing and served as the capital of a very large prefecture and of the province as a whole. Guide/Shangqiu was inspired by the cultural achievements in Western Han Suiyang and raised itself from a common department to a flourishing prefecture. Zhengzhou remained a common department during the Ming, but it traced its walls back to the Tang and it became an independent department in the early Qing. During the Qing, these cities restored their walls on the Ming base and model and maintained them in the face of natural and human challenges. Under the Republic and early People's Republic, the city walls were altered to accommodate traffic, militarized to prepare for and compete in warfare, dismantled in the processes of development and revolution, and left vulnerable to the ravages of time and weather. During the most recent three decades of reform and opening they have been restored and reconstructed—in Kaifeng on the model of the Ming, in Guide/Shangqiu with the inspiration of the Ming and the Han, and in Zhengzhou on the bases of the Tang and Zhou (and perhaps even the Shang). In other words, instead of simply rejecting the entire past and envisioning a wholly new future, each city has built on what it considers to be the most relevant segment or segments of its various pasts to maintain and reconstruct its walls in the present so as to shape as well as to embrace alternative societies in the future.

In line with one fundamental function of walls and moats (to defend what lies inside from threats originating outside), the three cities have sometimes competed with each other, especially in recent decades. There is no guarantee that the Central Plains City Group will promote the interest of all of its members, let alone the welfare of those who are excluded from it. Yet, consistent with the cosmic function of walls and gates (to promote harmony), these cities have also shared much in the past and they seem likely to cooperate even more closely in the future. Both Kaifeng and Shangqiu, after all, are descended from various polities named Liang and Song that flourished at different

---

83   For more on this pattern and its implications for world history, see Des Forges, *Cultural Centrality*, esp. pp.317–21; Schneewind, "Review," pp.219–20.

times and places in the past. Both Shangqiu and Zhengzhou can trace their roots to the Shang, the first fully historical dynasty the cultural influence of which extended throughout the territory that is included in present-day China.[84] According to two recent and apparently independent accounts from this region, the Shang even gave its name to the social stratum of merchants (*shangren*).[85] All three cities (as well as many others) can also identify with the Yellow Lord or Lords (perhaps a clan), the mythical common ancestor(s) of numerous groups and generations of people who have associated themselves over some four millennia with different incarnations of "China."[86]

Chinese city walls are distinguishable from Chinese long walls in their greater inclusiveness and lesser length, but the two kinds of edifices have much more in common than the simple character *cheng*.[87] In addition to their common technology of rammed earth and their shared purpose of social harmony, they may even have participated in a single pattern of historical development. They both appeared in the central plain at least by Zhou times and reappeared during the Tang and Qing despite those three polities' preferences for other tactics in dealing with their neighbors, including intermarriage, diplomacy, trade, and warfare.[88] Both city walls and long walls persisted in the central plain and on the frontiers during periods of division and/or dominion by frontier ethnic minorities, including the Spring and Autumn and Warring States; the Wei-Jin-Nanbei Chao; the Liao, Song, and Jin; and the early Republic. Despite the image of the Qin as the primordial and preeminent long-wall builder, some long walls and city

---

84 For a recent reaffirmation of the importance of the region as the principal locus of early Chinese civilization, see Allan, "Erlitou."

85 Zhao, *Lao Zhengzhou*, p. 47; Li, "Zhengzhou yongdong," p. 10; He, *Lingting gucheng*, p. 15. The point is not just antiquarian; the Chinese Communist Party has recently opened its doors wide to businessmen.

86 Anonymous, "Huangdi jisi."

87 This was recognized by earlier Western observers who also contributed to the development of the myth of a single unchanging "Great Wall." See Billings, "Great City." It is affirmed by one of China's most prolific writers on long walls. See Luo, "Great Walls," p. 42.

88 Luo and Zhao, *Great Wall*, pp. 1–2; Zhang, "Zhongyuan"; Lovell, *Great Wall*, p. 41, ch. 6; Doar, "Delimited Boundaries," p. 123.

walls were actually destroyed by that centralizing state as well as by its centralizing successors in larger worlds, the Yuan and the late Republic/early People's Republic.[89] Most clearly, both city walls and long walls reached their early apogees in the Han and Ming when they served modest offensive and more significant defensive purposes.[90] Given this rather consistent pattern, it should come as no surprise that both city and long walls are receiving renewed attention as the People's Republic, subject to the accelerating process of history, moves out of adolescence toward middle age. Both kinds of walls are serving as potentially lucrative tourist sites, to be sure, but also, and more importantly, as immediately enriching cultural capital. They are material reminders of the highly continuous but also ever changing, the very steadfast but also periodically vulnerable nature of Chinese (and, indeed, of human) civilization. As contemporary Chinese seek to restore and partially reconstruct their walls, they are eager to learn from others, including past adversaries such as the British and the Japanese, about methods of protecting cultural legacies.[91] It remains to be seen whether more recent rivals, including the erstwhile "superpower" Russia and the still expanding "hegemon" the United States, will learn anything from the recurrent Chinese practice of building, razing, and rebuilding walls as one means of maintaining cultural continuity while undergoing constant change, of retaining a core identity while remaining open to external influence. In any case, the pattern of cultural history suggested by the tales of three exemplary Chinese city walls seems likely to continue to be relevant to China—and thus to the entire world—in the increasingly integrated global civilization of the twenty-first century of the common era.

---

89 Luo and Zhao, *Great Wall*, p. 5; Liu, Li, and Luo, *Changcheng*, pp. 4–9; Wright, "Cosmology," p. 43; Chang, "Morphology," p. 75; Lovell, *Great Wall*, p. 54.

90 Lovell, *Great Wall*, p. 15, chs. 3, 8, 9; Luo, "Great Walls," p. 44; Doar, "Delimited boundaries," p. 121; the map in the front matter of Tucker, *Great Wall*. Long walls could be used to expand as well as defend territory, but the historically defensive nature of the Ming walls is demonstrated by, among other things, their modest reach in comparison with those of the antecedent Han and with the much more expansive northern borders of the subsequent Qing.

91 Qiu, "Lishi wenhua"; Li, "Wenhua Henan."

Acknowledgments

I am grateful to the Interdiscipinary Research and Creative Activities Fund of the University at Buffalo for financial support, to Luan Xing, Wei Qianzhi, Niu Jianqiang, and Ma Haitao for assistance in research, to Hu Cheng and Minglu Gao for inviting oral presentations of my preliminary findings in Nanjing and Beijing, to Qiang Fang and Minlei Ye for helping to render my talks more colloquial, and to Desmond Cheung, Liu Chiao-mei, Tobie Meyer-Fong, and Haun Saussy for comments on early versions of this chapter.

Works Cited

Allan, Sarah. "Erlitou and the Formation of Chinese Civilization: Toward a New Paradigm," *Journal of Asian Studies*, 66.2 (May 2007), pp. 461–96.

An, Jinhuai. "Shilun Zhengzhou Shangdai chengzhi—Ao du" [A discussion of the Shang dynasty remains of Zhengzhou—the capital Ao], *Wenwu* [Relics], 1961 4,5 joint issue, reprinted in Li, *Shang wenhua*, pp. 94–104.

Anonymous. "Huangdi jisi he Zhonghua chuantong wenhua xueshu yantaohui zongshu" [A Summary of the conference on the sacrifices to the yellow lord and Chinese traditional culture], *Zhongguo shi yanjiu dongtai* [Trends in Chinese historiography], 8(2005), pp. 14–15.

Asher, Catherine B. "Delhi Walled: Changing Boundaries," in Tracy, *City Walls*, pp. 247–81.

BianLiang wanbao [BianLiang Evening News]. Kaifeng: 1996–2006.

Billings, Timothy. "The Great City of China: The 'Long Wall' in Early European Texts," paper presented at the Conference "The Roles and Representations of Walls in the Reshaping of Chinese Modernity," cosponsored by the University at Buffalo Art Galleries and the Albright-Knox Art Gallery, October 20–23, 2005, Buffalo, New York. Cited with the author's permission.

Brook, Timothy. *Collaboration: Japanese Agents and Local Elites in Wartime China*. Cambridge, Massachusetts: Harvard University Press, 2005.

Chang, Moulai. *Rumenglu* [Record as from a dream]. 1 juan. Kaifeng: Henan shengli tushu guan, 1921 [1852] reprint.

Chang, Sen-dou. "The Morphology of Walled Capitals," in Skinner, *The City*, pp. 75–100.

Chen, Huaguang. "Shangqiu gucheng bianqian, qi wenhua neihan" [The evolution of the old walls of Shangqiu, its cultural significance], *Zhongzhou jingu* [The central province today and yesterday], 2(2002), pp. 26–28.

———. *Xi Han Liangguo tanwei* [A detailed investigation of the Liang principality in the Western Han]. Beijing: Zhongguo wenlian chubanshe, 2002.

Chen, Qiaoyi. *Zhongguo ducheng cidian* [Dictionary of capitals in Chinese history]. Nanchang: Jiangxi jiaoyu chubanshe, 1999.

Chen, Xilu, and Zha Changqi, eds. *Guide fuzhi* [Gazetteer of Guide prefecture]. 36 juan, one head juan (fascicle). Edited and annotated by Luan Xing, Yang Zijian, and Mo Zhenlin. Shangqiu: Shangqiu District Gazetteer Bureau, 1994 [1754] reprint.

Cheng, Ziliang, and Li Qingyin. *Kaifeng chengshi shi* [A history of Kaifeng city]. Beijing: Shehui kexue wenxian chubanshe, 1993.

Dan, Jixiang. "Cong 'yi jiu cheng wei zhongxin fazhan' dao 'fazhang xin qu, baohu jiu cheng'" [From "Take the old city as the center of development" to "Develop the new zone, protect the old city"], *Wenwu* [Cultural Relics], 5(2006), pp. 45–57.

Des Forges, Roger V. *Cultural Centrality and Political Change in Chinese History: Northeast Henan in the Fall of the Ming.* Stanford: Stanford University Press, 2003.

DiCosmo, Nicola. "Did Guns Matter? Firearms and the Qing Formation," in Lynn A. Struve, ed., *The Qing Formation in World-Historical Time.* (Cambridge, Mass.: Harvard University Asia Center, Harvard University Press, 2004), pp. 121–66.

Diyi lishi dang'an guan, junji chu, lufu, gongcheng lei [First historical archives, grand council, reference copies, construction].

Doar, Bruce Gordon, "Delimited Boundaries and Great Wall Studies," in Roberts and Barmé, eds., *The Great Wall,* pp. 119–27.

Dong, Madeleine Yue. *Republican Beijing.* Berkeley: University of California Press, 2003.

Du, Jinpeng. "'ZhengBo shuo' lilun qianti bianxi" [Disputing an assumption of the theory that "Zheng was Bo"], *Kaogu* [Archaeology], 4(2005), pp. 69–77.

Du, Zhengzhen. "Shanghai chengqiang de xingfei: yige gongneng yu xiangzheng de biaoda" [The rise and fall of Shanghai's city wall: An expression of function and symbol], *Lishi yanjiu,* 6(2004), pp. 92–104.

Esherick, Joseph W. "Modernity and Nation," in Esherick, *Remaking,* ch. 1.

———, ed. *Remaking the Chinese City: Modernity and National Identity, 1900–1950.* Honolulu: University of Hawaii Press, 2000.

Farmer, Edward L. *Early Ming Government: The Evolution of Dual Capitals.* Cambridge, Mass.: East Asian Research Center, Harvard University Press, 1976.

———. "The Hierarchy of Ming City Walls," in Tracy, *City,* pp. 461–87.

Gao, Minglu. *The Wall: Reshaping Contemporary Chinese Art/Qiang: Zhongguo dangdai yishu de lishi yu bianjie*. Beijing and Buffalo: The Millennium Museum and University at Buffalo Art Galleries, Albright-Knox Art Gallery, 2005.

Gilley, Bruce. "Digging into the Future," *Far Eastern Economic Review*, (July 2000), pp. 74–76.

Goldstone, Jack A. "Neither Late Imperial nor Early Modern: Efflorescences and the Qing Formation in World History," in *The Qing Formation in World-Historical Time*, Lynn Struve, ed. (Cambridge, Mass.: Harvard University Asia Center, Harvard University Press, 2004), pp. 242–302.

Gu, Yanwu. *Lidai zhaijing ji* [Record of capitals through the ages]. Zhonghua shuju, 1984 reprint.

Guan, Jiezhong, and Zhang Mu. *Kaifeng fuzhi* [Gazetteer of Kaifeng prefecture], 1695, 40 juan.

Hansen, Valerie. *The Open Empire: A History of China to 1600*. New York: W. W. Norton, 2000.

He, Xinnian. *Lingting gucheng* [Listening to the old city]. Beijing: Zuojia chubanshe, 2003.

Henan sheng cehuiju [Henan Province Survey Bureau]. "Zhengzhou shiqu jiaotong tu" [Traffic map of Zhengzhou city and region]. Zhengzhou: Henan renmin chubanshe, 1981–83.

Henan sheng dang'an guan [Henan Provincial archives], Zhengzhou.

Henan sheng jindi zehui jishu youxian gongse [Henan Province Map Company] et al. "Zhongguo Kaifeng jiaotong lüyou tu" [Traffic and tourist map of Kaifeng China], 2004.

Henan sheng Shangqiushi Suiyangqu wenhuaju [The cultural bureau of Suiyang district in Shangqiu city]. "Dong Zhou Songguo cheng yizhi" [Remains of the city wall of the Song state in the Eastern Zhou], unpublished report dated 1999, supplied to the author by Ma Tingfu, head of the Shangqiu Suiyang Cultural Bureau, November 2002.

Henan sheng wenwu kaogu yanjiu suo [The Henan Institute of Archaeology and Cultural Relics]. "Zhengzhou Shangcheng waiguocheng de diaocha yu shijue" [Surveys and experimental digs at the outer wall of the Shang city at Zhengzhou], *Kaogu* [archaeology], 3(2004), pp. 40–50.

Kaifeng Qing-Ming shangheyuan youxian gongsi [Kaifeng going up the river on the Qing-Ming Festival Park Company]. "Qing-Ming shang he yuan" [Going up the river on the Qing-Ming Festival Park]. Kaifeng. Undated.

"Kaifengshi renmin zhengfu wen jian" [Documents of the Kaifeng City People's Government], Group 23, catalogue 21, no. 748 (Bianzheng 1983, no. 64), p. 5, no. 833 (Bianzheng 1985, no. 11), p. 5, and no. 833 (Bianzheng 1985, no. 49, p. 4. Kaifengshi dang'an guan [Kaifeng city archives].

Knapp, Ronald G. *China's Walled Cities*. Hong Kong: Oxford University Press, 2000.

Kong, Xianyi. *Rumenglu* [Record as if of a dream]. Zhengzhou: Zhongzhou guji chubanshe, 1984.

Li, Boqian. *Shang wenhua lunji* [Collected studies of Shang culture]. Beijing: Wenwu chubanshe, 2003.

Li, Fei. "Zhengzhou yongdong gudu meng" [The emergence of an old capital dream at Zhengzhou], *Zhongzhou jingu* [Past and present in the central province] 3(2004), pp. 6–11.

Li, Gengxiang. "Wenhua Henan yu zhongyuan jueqi" [Cultural Henan and the rise of the central plain], *Zhongzhou xuekan* [Academic Journal of Zhongzhou], 1(2006), pp. 150–54.

Li, Keting, Li Huilong, Zhu Fengxiang, Song Xueqin, Jia Baomei, Li Keyu. *Shangqiu tongshi* [A comprehensive history of Shangqiu]. Kaifeng: Henan daxu chubanshe, 2000.

Li, Lian. *Bianjing yiji zhi* [Record of the historical remains of Bianjing]. Annotated by Zhou Baozhu and Cheng Minsheng. Beijing: Zhonghua shuju chubanshe, 1999 [1546] reprint.

Lishi [Strong stone]. "Kaifeng laojie ming shi lishi wenhua mingcheng de zhongyao wenhua yichan" [The old street names of Kaifeng are an important cultural legacy of the famous city of history and culture], undated and unpublished manuscript letter coauthored by Wei Qianzhi and a colleague, made available by Wei Qianzhi to the author, June 2006.

Liu, Dechang, and Ye Yun, eds. *Shangqiu xianzhi* [Gazetteer of Shangqiu county]. 20 juan. Zhengzhou: Zhongzhou guji chubanshe, 1989 [1705] reprint.

Liu, Shun'an. *Kaifeng chengqiang* [The Kaifeng city wall]. Beijing: Yanshan chubanshe, 2003.

Liu, Yan, Li Yiran, comp., and Luo Zhewen, advisor. *Changcheng cidian* [Dictionary of long walls]. Shanghai: Wenhui chubanshe, 1999.

Liu, Yongzhi, and Geng Ruiling, eds. *Henan difangzhi tiyao* [A guide to Henan gazetteers]. 2 vols. Kaifeng: Henan daxue chubanshe, 1990.

Lloyd, G. E. R. *Demystifying Mentalities*. Cambridge: Cambridge University Press, 1990.

Lovell, Julia. *The Great Wall: China against the World, 1000 BC–AD 2000*. New York: Grove, 2006.

Luan, Xing. "Shuo Guan—wei Zhengzhou gucheng zhengming" [A discussion of Guan—the proper name for the ancient city of Zhengzhou], *Zhongzhou xuekan* [Journal of the Central Province], 2(1994), pp. 117–21.

——. "Shuo Guan—wei Zhengzhou gucheng zhengming" [A discussion of Guan—the proper name for the ancient city of Zhengzhou] (synopsis) in Liang Guoying, Ding Bangyou, Sun Liying, eds., *Shixue yanjiu xin shiye, Zhongguo gudaishi fence* [New perspectives in historical studies, section of ancient Chinese history]. Ji'nan: Shandong daxue chubanshe, 1997, pp. 38–39.

Luo, Zhewen. "The Great Walls of China," Bruce Doar, trans., in Roberts and Barmé, eds., *The Great Wall*, pp. 42–50.

Luo, Zhewen, and Zhao Luo. *The Great Wall of China in History and Legend*. Beijing: Foreign Languages Press, 1986.

Ma, Haitao. "Kaifeng chengqiang yanhua shimo kao" [An investigation of the evolution of the city walls of Kaifeng from the beginning to the end]. Article manuscript used with the author's permission.

Ma, Jianhua, and Zhang Lihua. *Changcheng* [Long walls]. Lanzhou: Dunhuang wenyi chubanshe, 2004.

Ma, Shizhi. "Xinzhai yizhi yu Xiadai zaoqi ducheng" [The remains at Xinzhai and the capital of the Early Xia period], *Zhongguo wenwu* [Cultural relics of China], 4(2004), pp. 51–54.

——. "Yu Shun de wangdu yu didu" [Yu Shun's state capital and dynastic capital], *Zhongyuan wenwu* [Cultural relics of the central plain], 1(2006), pp. 24–27.

——. "Wudi shidai de chengzhi yu zhongyuan zaoqi wenming" [Walls and moats in the age of the five lords and the early civilization of the central plain], *Zhongzhou xuekan* [Academic Journal of Zhongzhou], 3(2006), pp. 167–71.

Ming Xiaozong shilu [The veritable records of Xiaozong of the Ming] in *Da Ming shilu* [Veritable records of the great Ming]. 3,045 juan. Taipei: Shiyusuo [1961–63] 1984, reprint.

Moore, Mike. *A World Without Walls: Freedom, Development, Free Trade and Global Governance*. Cambridge: Cambridge University Press, 2003.

Mote, F. W. "The Transformation of Nanking, 1350–1400," in Skinner, *The City*, pp. 101–54.

Parker, Geoffrey. "The Artillery Fortress as an Engine of European Overseas Expansion, 1480–1750," in Tracy, *City Walls*, pp. 386–416.

Pepper, Simon. "Siege Law, Siege Ritual, and the Symbolism of City Walls in Renaissance Europe," in Tracy, *City Walls*, pp. 573–604.

Perdue, Peter C. *China Marches West: The Qing Conquest of Central Eurasia*. Cambridge, Mass.: Belknap Press of Harvard University Press, 2005.

Qiu, Jingwen. "Lishi wenhua mingcheng baohu zhidu bijiao yanjiu" [A comparative study of systems to protect famous cities of history and culture], *Zhongzhou xuekan* [Academic Journal of Zhengzhou], 1(2003), pp. 166–69.

Roberts, Claire, and Geremie R. Barmé, eds., *The Great Wall of China*. Sydney: Powerhouse Publishing, 2006.

Schneewind, Sarah. Review of *Cultural Centrality and Political Change in Chinese History*, in *Harvard Journal of Asiatic Studies*, 64.1(2004), pp. 211–22.

Shandong sheng ditu chubanshe [Map publishing company of Shandong province]. Shangqiushi jiaotong lüyoutu [Tourist map of transportation in Shangqiu city], including "Shangqiu shi zheng qu tu" [Map of the cities, counties, and district of Shangqiu] and "Shangqiushi qutu" [Map of the districts of Shangqiu city]. 2005.

Shangqiu xianzhi biancuan weiyuanhui [Editorial and compilation committee of the Shangqiu county gazetteer]. *Shangqiu xianzhi* [Gazetteer of Shangqiu county]. Beijing: Sanlian shudian, 1991.

Shanquan. *Henan*. Hong Kong: Zhonghua shuju, 1977.

Shen, Zhuanyi, and Huang Shubing. *Xinxiu Xiangfu xianzhi* [New edition of the Xiangfu County Gazetteer]. 1898, 24 juan, 1 head juan.

Skinner, William, ed. *The City in Late Imperial China*. Stanford: Stanford University Press, 1977.

Steinhardt, Nancy Shatzman. *Chinese Imperial City Planning*. Honolulu: University of Hawai'i Press, 1990.

———. "Representations of Chinese Walled Cities in the Pictorial and Graphic Arts," in Tracy, *City Walls*, pp. 419–460.

Tian, Weihua. "Henan: dazao zhongyuan jingji huang san jiao" [Henan: create a yellow triangle in the central plain], *Zhongzhou jingu* [Past and present of the central province], 5, 6 combined edition (2003), pp. 7–8.

Tian, Weihua. "Jiedu zhongyuan chengshi qun" [A reading of the central plains city group], *Zhongzhou jingo* [Past and present of the central province], 5,6 combined issue (2003), pp. 9–13.

Tian, Wenjing, Sun Hao, and Asiha, eds. *Henan tongzhi, xu tongzhi* [Comprehensive gazetteer of Henan and a continuation], 80 juan. Taipei: Huawen shuju, [1735] 1969 reprint, 5 vols.

Tongji daxue jianzhu chenggui xueyuan [The architectural and city planning institute of Tongji University], Shangqiu xian renmin zhengfu [People's Government of Shangqiu county] 1987. *Shangqiu xian lishi wenhua mingcheng baohu guihua* [Plan for the protection of Shangqiu, a famous city of history and culture]. Internal document of the Cultural Bureau of

the Suiyang district of Shangqiu City, consulted courtesy of bureau head
Ma Tingfu.

Tracy, James D. *City Walls: The Urban Enceinte in Global Perspective*.
Cambridge: Cambridge University Press, 2000.

Tucker, Anne Wilkes. *The Great Wall of China, Photographs by Chen Changfen*.
Foreword by Jonathan Spence. New Haven, Conn.: Yale University Press,
2007.

Waldron, Arthur. *The Great Wall of China: From History to Myth*. Cambridge:
Cambridge University Press, 1990.

Wallacker, Benjamin E., Ronald G. Knapp, Arthur J. Van Alstyne, and Richard
J. Smith, eds. *Chinese Walled Cities: A Collection of Maps from Shina
Jokaku no Gaiyo*. Hong Kong: Chinese University Press, 1979.

Wang, Jin. "Guanyu 'Bing. 96 Zhongyuan' zuopin" [Concerning my work "Ice.
97 Central Plain], *Dangdai yishu* [Contemporary art series], 11(1996), p. 39.

Wang, Jun. *Chengji* [Record of a city]. Beijing: Shenghuo, dushu, xinzhi
Sanlian chubanshe, 2003.

Wang, Liangtian. *Xi Han Liang Guo* [The Liang principality in the Western
Han]. Beijing: Zhongguo guangbo dianshi chubanshe, 2003.

Wang, Runjie. *Ao xu* [Ruins of Ao]. Zhengzhou: Henan sheng wenwu kaogu
yanjiusuo, 1999.

Wang, Yanwu. "Zhongyuan chengshi qun jige wenti de tantao" [An inquiry
into some questions regarding the Central Plains City Group], *Zhongzhou
xuekan* [Academic Journal of Zhongzhou], 5(2004), pp. 36–40.

Wang, Zhenzhong. "Shangzu de qiyuan ji qi zaoqi qianxi" [The origins and
early migrations of the Shang clan], *Zhongguo shehui kexueyuan lishi
yanjiusuo jikan* [Journal of the history institute of the Chinese Academy of
Social Sciences], 3(2004), pp. 1–66.

Wei, Qianzhi. "Tan 'Chongxiu BianLiang chengji' bei"[A discussion of the
stele inscription "Record of the restoration of BianLiang"], *Kaifeng ribao*
[Kaifeng daily], April 30, 1993.

———. "Qiewu yi dong, nan, xi, bei mingming Kaifeng chengmen" [Be sure not
to name Kaifeng's gates east, south, west, and north], draft letter of 2004,
never sent, shown the author in July 2005.

Wiener, Tim. "Walling Off Your Enemies: The Long View," *New York Times*,
April 29, 2007, 14.

Wright, Arthur F. "The Cosmology of the Chinese City," in Skinner, *The City*,
pp. 33–74.

Wu, Hung. *Transience: Chinese Experimental Art at the End of the Twentieth
Century*. Chicago: University of Chicago Press, 2004.

Wu, Xuede, and Liu Yan, eds. *Henan gudai jianzhu shi* [A history of ancient (i.e., "traditional") architecture in Henan]. Zhengzhou: Zhongzhou guji chubanshe, 2001.

Xu, Dengwen, ed. *Lishi wenhua ming cheng: Shangqiu lansheng* [A famous city of history and culture: seeing the sights of Shangqiu]. Zhengzhou: Zhongzhou guji chubanshe, 2001.

Xu, Yinong. *The Chinese City in Space and Time: The Development of Urban Form in Suzhou*. Honolulu: University of Hawaii Press, 2000.

Yan, Genqi. *Lishi mingcheng hua: Shangqiu* [Discussing a famous historical city: Shangqiu]. Zhengzhou: Zhongzhou guji chubanshe, 2004.

Yang, Kuan. "Shangdai de biedu zhidu" [The separate capital system of the Shang dynasty], *Fudan xuebao* [Fudan University journal], 1(1984), pp. 81–86.

———. *Zhongguo gudai ducheng zhidu shi yanjiu* [A study of the history of the capital-city system of China in ancient times]. Shanghai: Renmin chubanshe, 2003.

Yang, Guoqing. *Nanjing Mingdai chengqiang* [The Ming period wall of Nanjing]. Nanjing: Nanjing chubanshe, 2002.

Zhang, Guoshuo. *Xia Shang shidai ducheng zhidu yanjiu* [A study of the capital system in the Xia and Shang periods]. Henan: Renmin chuban she, 2001.

Zhang, Xinbin. "Zhengzhou dagudu de niandai xue yanjiu" [A study of the dates of the great old capital Zhengzhou], in Zhengzhou gudu xuehui [Study society of the old capital of Zhengzhou], *Gudu Zhengzhou* [The old capital Zhengzhou]. Zhengzhou: "Gudu Zhengzhou" bianji bu, 1(2005), pp. 8–13.

———. "Zhongyuan gu changcheng ruogan wenti de chubu yanjiu" [A preliminary study of several questions regarding the ancient long walls in the central plain], *Zhongyuan wenwu* [Cultural relics of the central plain], 2(2005), pp. 82–70.

Zhang, Yue. "From Demolition to Restoration: The Story of the Old City Walls of Beijing, 1949–2005," a paper delivered at the Conference on the Roles and Representations of Walls in the Reshaping of Chinese Modernity, University at Buffalo and Albright-Knox Art Galleries, October 21, 2005. (Cited with the author's permission.)

Zhang, Yue and Mao Ruxi. *Xuxiu Zhengzhou zhi* [Supplemented gazetteer of Zhengzhou], 1748: 12 juan, 1 head juan.

Zhao, Chunqing. "Xinmi Xinzhaicheng zhi yu Xia Qi zhi ju" [The remains of Xinzhaicheng in Xinmi and the residence of Qi of the Xia], *Zhongyuan wenwu* [Cultural relics of the central plain], 3(2004), pp. 12–16.

Zhao, Fuhai. *Lao Zhengzhou—Shangdu yimeng* [Old Zhengzhou—the inherited dream of the Shang capital]. Zhengzhou: Henan renmin chubanshe, 2004.

Zhao, Suosheng, and Gu Yan'geng, eds. *Zhongguo chengqiang* [China's City Walls]. Nanjing: Jiangsu jiaoyu chubanshe, 2000.

Zheng, Jiexiang. "Guanyu Yanshi Shangcheng de niandai he xingzhi wenti" [The questions of the date and nature of the Shang city at Yanshi], *Zhongyuan wenwu* [Relics of the central plain], 1984. 4, reprinted in Li, *Shang wenhua*, pp. 146–52.

———. "Guanyu Zhengzhou Shangcheng de dingming wenti" [Regarding the problem of establishing the name of the Shang city of Zhengzhou], 4(1994), pp. 118–22.

"Zhengzhou chenghuang miao" [Temple to the Walls and Moat of Zhengzhou], tourist brochure available at the temple. Undated.

Zhengzhou gudu xuehui [Study society of the old capital of Zhengzhou]. *Gudu Zhengzhou* [The ancient capital of Zhengzhou], Zhengzhou Shangdu 3600 nian xueshu yantaohui ji Zhongguo gudu xuehui 2004 nian nianhui zhuankan [A special issue on the Conference on 3600 years of the Zhengzhou Shang Capital and the 2004 annual meeting of the Chinese old capital association]. Zhengzhou: Gudu Zhengzhou bianjibu, 2004.

"Zhengzhou Shangdai yizhi" [Zhengzhou Shang Dynasty Capital Ruins]. A tourist brochure distributed by the Office to Protect the Ruins of the Shang city in Zhengzhou located at the Temple to the Walls and Moat of Zhengzhou. Undated.

Zhongguo gudu xuehui, Xinzheng gudu xuehui (Chinese old capital study society, Xinzheng old capital study society). *Zhongguo gudu yanjiu* [A study of an old capital]. Xi'an: SanQin chubanshe, 2004.

Zhou, Bingyi, Wang Yanghan, and Liu Ruilin, eds. *Zhengxian zhi* [Gazetteer of Zheng county]. 1916, 18 juan, one head juan.

Zou, Heng. "Zhengzhou Shangcheng ji Tangdu Bo shuo" [The case for the Shang city at Zhengzhou being Tang's capital Bo], *Wenwu* [Cultural Relics], 2(1978), reprinted in Li, *Shang wenhua*, pp. 105–8.

Zou, Shouyu, Li Lian, and Zhu Mujie, eds. *Henan tongzhi* [Comprehensive gazetteer of Henan]. 1556, 45 juan.

CHAPTER THREE

Chinese County Walls between the Central State and Local Society

Evidence from Henan Province during the Ming Dynasty

Desmond Cheung

IN THE EARLY TWENTIETH CENTURY, many Chinese, seeking to rebuild and strengthen their country, deemed it necessary to destroy city walls, which they saw as emblems of the defunct "imperial" system and barriers to the "modernization" of the new nation's urban centers.[1] Yet following the hurtling pace of China's industrialization and economic reforms that have so thoroughly transformed the country's cityscapes, there have arisen contemporary concerns to recover and to re-present the past. From the late twentieth century and now into the twenty-first century, Chinese nationwide have been busy rebuilding walls and other old structures in order to reassert more "traditional" identities and to glorify different pasts for reasons that are very much bound up with the present.[2] Most famous, of course, is the "Great

---

1   For two recent collections of essays on twentieth-century Chinese cities see Esherick, *Remaking* and Cochran, Strand, and Yeh, *Cities*. Of course, China was not unique in razing its walls. Walls came tumbling down in cities all over the world—including in Europe—though perhaps more gradually and less completely than in China.

2   See Chapter 2 in this volume.

Wall," or rather more literally the "long walls," whose iconic meaning
has metamorphosed from being a symbol of imperial tyranny to being
an object of national pride. Many of these shifting meanings have little
to do with the long walls' original purpose or the context of their
construction during the Ming dynasty (especially from the 1550s
onward). As Arthur Waldron has demonstrated, the Ming long walls
were above all the products of policy decisions related to the dynasty's
military strength, border strategy, and court politics.[3]

The Ming dynasty was also a high point of the building of urban
walls. During this period walls were built around many cities and
towns where they had not existed before, giving the country "the largest constellation of walled cities on earth."[4] It is these walls that form
the subject of this chapter, specifically walls built around county towns
(*xiancheng*)—the seats of officialdom that were on the lowest rung of
the administrative hierarchy. (Here we call them towns, rather than
cities, simply because of their lesser administrative status. In Chinese,
they were all referred to as *cheng*.)

Like the long walls, urban walls have had a range of meanings built
into them; people in different times and places have read their significance variously. Walled cities symbolized the order of the realm that
was idealized in classical Chinese texts and depicted in Chinese illustrations since the first millennium BCE.[5] This enduring image of walled
cities was current in the West by at least the sixteenth century and became a prominent image representing orderly government in the European imagination. From the sixteenth to the eighteenth century,
many Europeans imagined China to be a country of walls. Enclosed by
the "Great Wall," it contained thousands of uniformly walled cities that
were as well ordered as the geometric regularity of their design
implied.[6]

This ideal of orderly rule evolved into a more sinister image that
has long influenced the historical understanding of the period, for
Chinese and European writers alike: the idea of the autocratic ruler.

3   See Waldron's *Great Wall* and Chapter 1 in this volume.
4   Mote, "Transformation of Nanking"; Farmer, "Hierarchy," pp. 467, 486. Farmer esti-
     mates the number of walled cities in Ming China to be in the thousands.
5   Steinhardt, "Representation," pp. 421–23.
6   Billings, "Visible Cities."

The Ming loyalist and political theorist Huang Zongxi (1610–1695) was probably the first to analyze the position of the Ming ruler who, according to Huang's critique, enjoyed unbridled power and put his personal fancies above the interests of the people. Ever since, many Chinese, from late-Qing reformers to Marxist historians, have examined the autocratic rule of the Chinese "emperor" at the apex of "feudal" society. Outside China, since Montesquieu (1689–1755) and Hegel (1770–1831), the idea of "oriental despotism" has been influential in the Western understanding of China, with its explanation that the political system of China's rulers was based on absolute power and the systematic use of terror.[7] Many writers have seen the Ming period as the culmination of autocratic rule, particularly in the person of the dynastic founder Zhu Yuanzhang (r. 1368–1398). Both Chinese and Western writers have compared Zhu's heightened personal and violent rule with the leadership of Mao Zedong.[8]

Without denying the brutality of the Ming founder's rule and his lasting effect on the institutions of government, we must observe that few of his successors were as able or interested in controlling the realm, and in reality no individual could direct the operations of government single-handedly. Scholars have been working to extricate themselves from the "emperor fetish,"[9] and to explore how the many institutions that together formed the Ming state worked to implement policy down to the lowest administrative level of the county and the local society around it.[10]

Following this vein of inquiry and in an attempt to get behind the welter of images of Ming rule, this chapter takes county walls as a platform to analyze the related political and symbolic connections between the central state and local society in the Ming context. We find that as defensive structures, walls both guarded the government seats they contained and contributed to the state's wider defense strategy. Just as

---

7   For different explanations of this influential view of Chinese and especially Ming state power, see Wittfogel, *Oriental Despotism*, Mote, "Growth of Chinese Despotism," and De Bary, "Chinese Despotism."

8   For historical comparisons of Zhu and Mao, see Andrew and Rapp, *Autocracy*.

9   Brook, *Chinese State*, p. 6.

10   See particularly the work of Sarah Schneewind: "Visions"; *Community Schools*; *Two Melons*; and *Long Live*.

important, walls protected local people at times of unrest. The city walls represented the central order, yet beneath this classical veneer there were also meanings that local actors inscribed on the walls, drawing from different pasts that were particular to the place and sometimes separate from those of the unifying Ming realm. While the court ordered the building of walls throughout the land, on the ground the actual construction could be a complex political process in which state agents had to win the support of local actors who had their own demands and understanding of the significance of walls in local society.

The walls studied here were all situated in Henan province, which took its name from its location straddling the unruly Yellow River and lying largely south of it.[11] Here walls were often constructed to guard against flooding as well as to ward off human assaults that grew in number and strength over the course of the dynasty. (The causes included falling temperatures and corrupt officials among other things.[12]) Henan lay in the middle of the central plain, the site of many early cultural achievements and dynastic capitals.[13] Although the center of political power shifted through the centuries along with the strategic and personal preferences of successive dynasts (e.g., the Ming capitals lay both south and north of the central plain), Henan continued to be called the "Central Province" (Zhongzhou), a term first mentioned in the *Shang shu* (Venerated Documents), a Zhou-period text.[14] Writers of this region frequently referred to the past and to the orthodox teachings upheld by the state that were so central to Chinese culture. They were inhabitants of what Edward Farmer has called "orthogenetic" cities, that is "typically inland centers, the products and bearers of indigenous cultural traditions."[15] Located in China's heartland, Henan's county towns were thus vehicles for the state's promotion of the idealized classical order. But as we shall see, the local people also identified

---

11   Henan translates literally as "south of the [Yellow] River."

12   Tong, *Disorder under Heaven*; Des Forges, *Cultural Centrality*, pp. 166ff. For a different view, emphasizing social violence from the early Ming on, see Robinson, *Bandits*.

13   See Des Forges, *Cultural Centrality*, pp. 2ff., and Chapter 2 in this volume.

14   This term was used by Ming gazetteer writers, e.g., 1555 *Zhenyang xian zhi*, 2.3a.

15   As Edward Farmer suggests, these cities represented well the purpose and hopes of the builders of the Ming order. In contrast were the "heterogenetic" cities, "typically located on the seacoast, brought about by maritime interaction between diverse cultures, home to degradation, alienation and anomie." Farmer, "Hierarchy," p. 464.

with particular pasts through their city walls that were not necessarily part of this unifying vision of the state, but had special significance to their localities.

To understand the meaning of walls in their local contexts, this chapter relies heavily on gazetteers (*difang zhi*), which are chronicles of state institutions at the local level as well as rich compendia of local historical, geographical, administrative, social, biographical, and literary knowledge. The twenty-five gazetteers used for this study date to the sixteenth century (which saw the first editions of many county gazetteers), and most were compiled during the Jiajing reign (1522–1567).[16] Ming gazetteers were in a certain sense state institutions. They were tools to enable officials to know and control localities that, by the rule of avoidance, could not be their birthplaces. Indeed, magistrates would typically serve there for only a few years. The Ming court periodically ordered the compilation of gazetteers.[17] Local magistrates were expected to read those that existed for their own and neighboring jurisdictions.[18] As official texts, gazetteers were usually compiled under the authority of the sitting magistrate, his predecessor, or another state appointee. Yet for all their official character and purpose, Ming gazetteers were also very much bound up with the identities and interests of the locality. In some ways they were only quasi-official, for their production could lie largely in the hands of local elites. In such cases, the gazetteer might not only record and celebrate local history, but also promote the interests of particular elite groups.[19]

For our purpose, gazetteers provide a wealth of information about county walls. Gazetteers typically and minimally provide data on the dimensions of the walls and moats, the number and names of the gates, and, somewhat less often, the names of the officials, local elite, and commoners (e.g., merchants) credited with their construction. Most

---

16   Brook, *Chinese State*, pp. 43–44.

17   Schneewind, *Community Schools*, pp. 139–40. The court ordered the production of gazetteers for each prefecture and county in the Hongwu reign (1368–1398) and again in 1412, 1454, 1498, and 1522.

18   Later, in the seventeenth century, Huang Liuhong explicitly endorsed such practice in his *Fuhui quan shu*. See Huang, *Complete Book*, p. 129.

19   For the roles of local families in compiling Ming gazetteers and using them to promote their own interests, see Dennis, "Writing."

accounts then go on to provide other information such as the names and dimensions of cities on the site in earlier dynasties; the purpose and import of building walls in general; and the precise circumstances (such as growing population and wealth or recent destruction or neglect) precipitating the current project.

Defensive Walls

County town walls served, perhaps most basically, as defense structures. According to one gazetteer account:

> City walls and moats are the means of defence against violence and for the protection of the people. They are the most important things established by princes and dukes. At times of great violence when bandits appear, [walls and moats] provide protection for home and family; if they do not exist because of a lack of foresight, people will face disaster.[20]

The most common motives for reconstructing and strengthening walls and moats given in the gazetteers were to respond to general decay over time, to repair the damage caused by downpours and floods, and to guard against imminent attacks by "bandits" (*fei, zei, kou,* or *dao*) or raids by "barbarians" (*yi, di, hu, or dalu*).[21] In many cases the wealth of a town was both a liability and an asset. Prosperity was a magnet for marauders of all kinds, but it also provided the resources for constructing solid walls and deep moats. For example, "bandits" attempted to take Changyuan County in 1511 because they had heard of its wealth, but they were held off by its inhabitants, who mounted a defense from behind strong walls and effective moats.[22] Larger towns and cities might suffer from leadership fractured into two or more counties, but they also benefited from their greater wealth, which could be used to maintain the defense infrastructure. Indeed, the author of one late-Ming military defense treatise explicitly stated that a prosperous city

---

20   1554 *Yancheng xian zhi*, 1.2a.

21   1542 *Gushi xian zhi*, 3.2a. Walls had been built around settlements for defense purposes since prehistoric times. Needham, *Science*, Vol. V, Part 6 p. 241.

22   1541 *Changyuan xian zhi*, 1.5a.

fortified with strong walls was especially worth defending. It was also quite capable of being defended so long as the residents were well prepared and ready to fight.[23]

From early (Neolithic) times, walls in China were constructed from rammed earth (*hangtu*) and were extremely durable.[24] The facing of earthen walls with stone and/or fired bricks, which first occurred during the Han period, became common only during the Ming dynasty, when brick-making technology reached a new level.[25] Mastery of a multistaged production process (involving the preparation of the mixture, setting it into a frame, and firing it in a carefully controlled kiln) insured a higher quality brick.[26] The Ministry of Works oversaw the collection of materials in brick yards that produced different kinds of bricks for different kinds of projects.[27] Nanjing, elevated to the primary dynastic capital by the Ming founder, set new standards for the building of city walls in China. Its bricks came from yards throughout the lower Yangzi region—as far as 1,000 km away in some cases. They were produced through the operation of the *lijia* (hundreds-and-tithings) system, through which the state registered the population and extracted corvée (unpaid labor) duty from every household. Moreover, each brick was individually dated and marked with its maker's name and provenance for quality control.[28]

County seats could not, of course, compete with the grandeur of the politywide capitals, yet the Ming-period advances in technology and production and the resultant lower costs made bricks a much more common building material than ever before. In several of our cases, walls were faced with stone or brick. A magistrate of Guangshan County, for example, restored a wall damaged by flooding and strengthened it with bricks, declaring that earth alone would not last long. The writer of another gazetteer called a project to face the town's

23   Song, *Shou cheng yao lan, juan* 1, 1b; 4, 12b–13b and elsewhere. Song had personally engaged in city defense in his years of service in the border regions of Shaanxi and Shanxi.

24   Needham, *Science*, Vol. IV, Part 3, pp. 38–40; Bagley, "Shang Archaeology," p. 160.

25   Chang, "Morphology," p. 75; Zhang, *Zhongguo*, pp. 580–81; Needham, *Science*, Vol. IV, Part 3, pp. 40-46.

26   Brook, *Confusions*, pp. 19–21.

27   Song Yingxing, *Tiangong kaiwu*, pp. 178–90; Needham, *Science*, Vol. IV, Part 3, p. 42.

28   Knapp, *China's Walled Cities*, pp. 15–20, 80ff.; Brook, *Confusions*, pp. 22–27.

walls with stone, brick, and tile "a plan for ten thousand generations."[29] Despite its recognized advantages and lower cost, brick was still an expensive burden for poorer counties. One late-sixteenth-century writer from Gaochun County, Nanzhili, estimated the cost of each brick at 0.02 tael of silver. He stated that using brick would require additional taxes that would rest heavily on a county that had only poor-quality land.[30] As we shall see, the burdens of wall building on the people could bring into question the conduct and motives of the official in charge of the project.

Builders used other materials to strengthen walls. In one county workers covered a part of the city walls with wood and tile; in another they plated the parapets atop the city gates with iron.[31] In addition to describing the construction and repair of walls and moats, gazetteers provide much information on other defense structures, including gates, towers (over gates and at the corners of walls),[32] stations (*pu*) that could be built into the wall (likely as lodging for guards),[33] para-pets, and smaller defensive walls.[34]

The gazetteer of Changyuan is unusually detailed in the informa-tion it gives for the town's walls and gates. It differentiates the outer walls (*guo*) from the inner (*cheng*) and enumerates the water gates (*shui men*) that allowed internal canals to flow out to the moat or to other bodies of water. The text provides the dimensions of additional military installations such as barbicans (*weng cheng*, literally "jar walls"), platforms (literally "enemy platforms," *ditai*), barrack walls (*ying qiang*) and related gates.[35] Barbicans, a Tang innovation, were de-signed to impede passage through city gates, which were weak spots in

29 For example, Linzhang, Xiayi, Lushan, Shangcheng, and Guangshan. 1556 *Guangshan xian zhi*, 3.1b–3.2a.

30 Fei, "Making," p. 85. A loftier wall naturally meant greater prestige. A prefect of Feng-yang, the hometown of Zhu Yuanzhang, even collected a special boat tax to raise funds to build a grander wall to honor the Ming founder. Brook, "Communications and Commerce," p. 676.

31 1548 *Xiayi xian zhi* 2.1b and 1548 *Yushi xian zhi* 1.18a.

32 Called *jiao lou* ("corner towers"), e.g., in 1555 *Zhenyang xian zhi*, 2.2b.

33 For example, 1506 *Linzhang xian zhi*; 1556 *Guangshan xian zhi*, 3.1b.

34 1548 *Yushi xian zhi*, 1.18b–19a; 1542 *Gushi xian zhi*, 3.2a; and 1548 *Xiayi xian zhi*, 2.1b.

35 1541 *Changyuan xian zhi*, 1.4b–6a.

the wall and the primary targets of assaults.[36] Platforms were fortifications built around the corners of the city wall that could house extra archers and others.[37] Defenders also erected "sheep-horse walls" (*yangma qiang*) as an additional line of fortification between the city wall and the moat.[38] Other gazetteers describe stockades, the planting of willow trees to combat erosion and impede assaults, and the building of dikes to defend against bandits.[39]

Signifying Walls

County town walls were thus the core structures within defense systems that protected administrative seats throughout the realm, and contributed to the stability and order of the idealized polity. Ming wall builders understood how county walls fit into the greater scheme, but local people also inscribed meanings on them that were rooted in the particularities of the place and its own past.

The gazetteers of Henan reveal that people saw the construction of county walls as contributing to the establishment of the central order. The author of the Lushan County gazetteer identifies strong walls and deep moats as chief bases for the welfare of the people and the authority of the state. Walls were as crucial for providing defense and establishing order as schools were necessary for educating the people and as granaries were vital for insuring the people's sustenance.[40] Wall builders recognized the political and ritual significance of walls, as emphasized in the canonical texts that they studied, which contained accounts of the origins of wall building.[41] Two accounts cite a passage

---

36 Song, *Shou cheng yao lan, juan* 1, 3a; Zhang, *Zhongguo*, pp. 342–7; Needham, *Science*, Vol. V., Part 6, pp. 307–64.

37 Song, *Shou cheng yao lan, juan* 1, 6a–6b.

38 Ibid., *juan* 1, 4a–4b; Needham, *Science*, Vol. V, Part 6, pp. 336–37.

39 For example, 1552 *Lushan xian zhi*, 4.3a–4b; *Yifeng xian zhi*, pp. 114–15; 1506 *Linzhang xian zhi*; 1537 *Neihuang xian zhi*, 4.24b. The planting of willow trees to hinder the advance of nomadic cavalry was a practice known at least as early as the Qin period. Needham, *Science*, Vol. IV, Part 3, p. 52.

40 1552 *Lushan xian zhi*, 4.1b.

41 Because the Classics reached their full form in the Han dynasty, these allusions may have been part of a larger identification of Ming-period observers with the Han period. Des Forges, *Cultural Centrality*, p. 118 and passim.

from the *Classic of Changes* (*Yijing*) that emphasizes defending the interests of the state:

> The *Changes* says: "Princes and lords set up strategic defences to protect their states. The timely use of strategic defences is important indeed!" For strategic defences let us use walls and moats. As for timely use, let us repair them at all times. Their importance is that they protect [those within them] and maintain peace.[42]

The gazetteer of Fan County cited this passage to remind the reader that wall building is always of prime importance, even in times of peace. Because of careful maintenance of their walls during 160 years of peace, the people of Fan were able to defend against assaults that occurred with the breakdown of order during the Zhengde period.[43] Other gazetteer accounts cited the *Rites of Zhou* (*Zhou Li*), likening the counties of the present to the realms of princes in the past. Both were essential for the maintenance of the proper order.

It was widely accepted that the sage kings of antiquity, including the Five Lords (*wudi*), now thought to be clans, first established walls and moats:

> The *Xuanyuan benji* (*Basic Annals of Xuanyuan* [the Yellow Lord]) states: "The Yellow Lord built towns and constructed five cities (*cheng*)." The *Han Shu* (*History of the Former Han Dynasty*) further states: "Among the instructions of the Divine Farmer there is [the building of] city walls of stone ten *ren* [about twenty meters] in height and protective moats one hundred paces [across]. Thus the construction of city walls and moats began with Divine Farmer and the Yellow Lord."[44]

---

42 1555 *Zhenyang xian zhi.* Cf. *Zhou yi zhu*, juan 3, *Siku quanshu* ed. In the *Shijing* we are told that Tanfu, the grandfather of King Wen of Zhou, built not only the first city but the first houses, the Zhou people having previously lived in loess caves. Wright, "Cosmology," p. 35.

43 1535 *Fan xian zhi*, 1.3a. Cf. 1556 *Guangshan xian zhi*, 3.2a.

44 1545 *Lanyang xian zhi*, 3.1b. The *Xuanyuan benji* seems no longer to be extant but is cited in some twenty works within the *Siku quanshu* (Complete Library of the Four Treasuries). Among those, there are two similar references to the Yellow Lord (whose name was Xuanyuan) building cities.

In the same Lanyang gazetteer, there is a statement that Gun, the father of Yu, the founder of the Xia dynasty, was the first to build outer city walls (*guo*) for protecting towns.[45] This account, which was also current in popular reference works of the Ming, notes that the outer city walls were constructed along with extended dikes to protect the people against floods.[46] In Guangshan County, the magistrate put forward another lesson from history. Advocating his own wall-building plans, he cited Mencius' advice to the ruler of the small domain of Teng to defend his city and people with high walls and deep moats—to the death if necessary.[47]

While remembering the canonical antecedents of wall building, the Ming compilers of Henan's gazetteers traced the historical origins of their own walls to various pasts that were of particular importance to the local place. Three county gazetteers placed their walls' origins in the Ming—in all three cases to the founding Hongwu reign (1368–1398). But there were other meaningful pasts beyond that of the Ming state, and they were especially numerous in Henan. In many cases, locals could draw upon those precedents to make claims for their own times—a practice that continues today.[48] In three of our gazetteers the local historians trace their walls back to "preimperial" (or pre-Qin) antiquity. One of them takes the Warring States as the period in which the city's first wall may have been built; another identifies the wall of the Ming city of Xiangcheng as having been built by King Ling of Chu (r. 540–528 BCE); the third refers to Yancheng as the former domain (*guo*) of a noble, still visible in nearby ruins.[49] Three gazetteers locate the origins of their walls in the Qin-Han period, one citing both dynasties, another specifying the Han dynasty, and the third dating the city's founding to the reign of the first Han Emperor Gaozu (r. 206–195 BCE). All three accounts then jump forward all the way to the Ming period,

45   1545 *Lanyang xian zhi*, 3.4b–5a.

46   For example, the popular late-Ming work *San cai tu hui* (Compendium of illustrations of the three powers), citing the *Wu Yue Chunqiu* (Springs and autumns of Wu and Yue) as its source. Wang and Wang, *San cai tu hui*, Vol. 2, pp. 1019–21.

47   1556 *Guangshan xian zhi*, 3.2b–3.3a. Zhu Xi, *Si shu ji zhu*, 518.

48   See Chapter 2 in this volume.

49   1548 *Xiayi xian zhi*, 2.1a; 1551 *Xiangcheng xian zhi*, 1.4b; 1554 *Yancheng xian zhi*, 1.7a–b.

a millennium and a half later.⁵⁰ The authors of the Fan County gazetteer traced the town walls back to a stockade constructed during the post-Han Jin dynasty. Xinxiang's walls were dated to the beginning of the Tang and Gushi's walls were said to have originated in the Northern Song.⁵¹ Taken together, these accounts demonstrate that local people recognized that their counties had meaningful pasts of their own that transcended those of the "classical" past and of the contemporary dynasty without being inconsistent with them.

The individual names and forms of city walls and their components were significant, too. Walls themselves were unnamed, but how people understood the word for wall is telling. As we have seen, the same graph *cheng* may be translated as "wall" or as "city"—wall and city were so closely associated that we may say that there could be no true city without a wall.⁵² As already noted, since ancient times illustrations of cities depicted them contained by a wall. Among the few images that appeared regularly in Ming gazetteers were those of city walls surrounding the administrative seat. But authors of Ming dynasty gazetteers also identified the wall closely with the people of the city: a wall contained the people too. This idea was based on an etymology that was traced back to the great Eastern Han work of philology, Xu Shen's (ca. 58–147 CE) *Shuowen jiezi* (Analyzing graphs and explaining characters). That work defined the city/wall (*cheng*) as "a settlement that contained the people," a definition echoed in two gazetteers.⁵³ This dual reading of the term underscores the need to see city walls in relation both to official structures and to local contexts.

While the walls of Chinese cities were in some respects synonymous with the cities themselves, city gates often had their own names,

50   1537 *Neihuang xian zhi*, 4.24b; 1548 *Yushi xian zhi*, 1.18a; 1542 *Gushi xian zhi*, 3.2a.

51   They were held to have been built as a base for an army of Zhuangdi (r. 923–926), a ruler of the Later Tang. *Fan xian zhi*, 1.3a–b.

52   So close is the identification between the city and its wall that one scholar has asserted that "the premodern Chinese city has no life independent of walls." Steinhardt, "Representations," p. 421. The converse, however, does not hold, for, as we have noted, there could be walls around settlements, such as towns and villages, that fell short of being cities.

53   Xu, *Shuowen jiezi zhu*, [13 *pian, xia*, 29b] 688. 1545 *Lanyang xian zhi*, 3.1a. and 1548 *Yushi xian zhi*, 1.18a.

which shed further light on the meanings—orthodox and otherwise—attached to them. The typical four principal gates normally reflected the symbolism of the four cardinal directions and the corresponding seasons, winds, and other ritual influences.[54] In Lanyang, the eastern gate was called "Spring Ploughing" (*dong zuo*) recalling the important rite performed outside the east gate by the ruler and all magistrates throughout the realm at the beginning of the year. In Lushan the western gate was called "Approaching the Sacrifice" (*lin rang*), referring to a rite performed outside the city for the expulsion of malevolent influences such as disease.[55]

City gates were often named after fundamental Confucian values—or the aspirations of Confucian-oriented governance. Changyuan's gates, for example, bore the names of "Humaneness and Harmony" (*renhe*), "Justice and Rectitude" (*yizheng*), and "Peace and Stability" (*anding*). In Yushi the eastern gate was called "Harmonious Transformation" (*dunhua*), one of the western gates was called, "Flourishing Transformation" (*xing hua*), and another western gate was named "Preserving Peace" (*baoan*).[56] Present in all these names was the ideal of the ordered state peacefully extending its influence from its seats of administration out to the surrounding countryside. Of course, the names of many larger cities, ranging from Chang'an to Nanning, and frontier towns, including those in the new Ming province of Guizhou, also evoked the ideas of peace and tranquillity.[57]

Other gates were more closely tied to the locality and were named after places, mountains, or rivers in the region. In the Henan gazetteers surveyed, more than half of the counties with recorded gate names have such toponymic associations. A prime example is Zhenyang:

> The eastern is called "Joining to Ying" (*jie Ying*). The southern is called "Passage to Chu" (*tong Chu*). The western is called "Reaching Luo" (*da Luo*). The northern is called "Going to Cai" (*shi Cai*).[58]

---

54   Knapp, *China's Walled Cities*, p. 28.
55   1545 *Lanyang xian zhi*, 3.2a; 1552 *Lushan xian zhi*, 4.2b.
56   1548 *Yushi xian zhi*, 1.18b; 1541 *Changyuan xianzhi*, 3.5a–b.
57   Woodside, *The Centre*, p. 16.
58   1555 *Zhenyang xian zhi*, 2.2b.

A look at a historical map and the geography section of the county gazetteer reveals that the names of Zhenyang's gates, all derived from old place names, fully embedded it within its surroundings.[59] The gazetteer records that "Zhenyang lies at the crossroads of Chu and Cai" and that it actually lay within what had been the realm of Chu during the Spring and Autumn period. During the Ming, the ancient land of Chu was associated with the region to the south of Henan largely within the province known as Huguang. Cai was originally the name of a feudal domain during the Zhou dynasty that lay to the north of Zhenyang. During the Song and Jin dynasties, Zhenyang was part of Cai Prefecture. In the Ming, Cai was found in the names of two nearby counties: Shangcai and Xincai to the north and east respectively. Zhenyang's eastern and western gates were named after two rivers, the Ying and the Luo, running east and northwest of Zhenyang respectively. In the Qin dynasty, Zhenyang had been part of Yingchuan Commandery, the name of a Ming garrison town to the east in Nanzhili next to Ying subprefecture. More famously, the erstwhile politywide capital city of Luoyang was situated eponymously "north of the Luo River" several hundred kilometers to the northwest of Zhenyang. One might suggest that these references to more distant places reflect an interest in linking Zhenyang with sites that had great historical—not to say classical—prestige, thus enhancing Zhenyang's own status.

The dimensions and form of city walls were also depicted and interpreted according to different registers of meaning. Gazetteers usually give measurements for walls that seem to be "real figures": they are precise and vary from one set to another. But scholars have suggested that the dimensions given for the walls of Beijing, Nanjing, and Suzhou in gazetteer accounts are highly questionable and difficult to verify against archaeological finds and remains on the ground.[60] Moreover, other statistics found in gazetteers such as population figures are often symbolic. Certainly the length of city walls, referred to as their "perimeter" (*zhou*) or "square perimeter" (*fang wei*) alluded to the ideal of the rectilinear city. One recent study based on textual and archaeological sources asserts that over 70 percent of city walls throughout China may have been approximately square or rectangular, although there

59   Ibid., 1.1a–3b; Tan, *Zhongguo lishi ditu ji*, Vol. 7, 57–58.
60   Mote, "Transformation," p. 136; Xu, *Chinese City*, pp. 103–4.

were many of irregular—even circular—form.[61] Important exceptions include Suzhou and the first Ming capital at Nanjing, but many capital cities in earlier dynasties had been largely rectilinear if only because their location— mainly in the central plain—meant that there were few obstacles to regularized city shapes.[62] City walls thus often approached the perfect square associated with the earth, as prescribed in the late Warring States work the *Kaogong ji* (Records of the study of buildings) which was incorporated into the *Zhouli* (Rites of Zhou). They were usually portrayed as such in the myriad illustrations of city walls over the course of Chinese history.[63] Many Ming city walls were irregularly shaped to varying degrees, but the rectangular ideals were still held strongly in mind by the compilers of gazetteers, as is evident from the depictions of walls in gazetteer maps.[64] Granted that the county seats we are examining here were near or at the bottom rung of the administrative hierarchy and had less symbolic and cosmic importance than did higher level prefectural, provincial, and politywide capitals, the fact that the depictions of their walls typically involved some degree of stylization in conformity with the ideal illustrates their importance in the overarching ritual and political order.

This idealized vision of city walls was by no means the only way in which their forms inspired meaning, however. The walls and gates of Henan's county towns, like those of larger cities in Henan and elsewhere in China, were sometimes constructed in line with geomantic principles, or at least were rationalized or mythologized on those grounds. Hok-lam Chan has unraveled the lore and legends around the founding and refounding of Peking (Beijing), as the capital city of the Yuan and Ming dynasties, to reveal different registers of meaning that explained the siting and shape of the city. It was centered on a most auspicious spot that drew the benefits of *qi* vital forces flowing

61   Zhang, *Zhongguo*, pp. 293–311.

62   An important exception to this was Han dynasty Chang'an. Chang, "Morphology," pp. 87–88.

63   The *Kaogong ji* gave a normative and prescriptive pattern for planning cities and their contents, including the choice and preparation of the site, its cardinal orientation, the city layout, and the disposition of its principal structures. Wright, "Cosmology," p. 47; Xu, *Chinese City*, pp. 31–39; Zhang, *Zhongguo*, pp. 57–59.

64   Farmer, "Hierarchy," p. 479.

from the heavens above and the earth below. Furthermore its eleven gates were widely held to represent the head(s) and limbs of the Buddhist-Daoist child deity Nezha (also Nazha).[65]

For county towns, the legends may have been less elaborate, but they were nonetheless important. In the gazetteer of Fan County we read,

> In ancient times Fan had been the appanage of Grand Master of Jin Kuai. Kuai's ancestor Liu Lei had once had the name of Yulong (Dragon Rider) and so the city had built six gates in order to resemble the form of a dragon. The eastern and western [gates] were its head and tail, and the southern and northern [gates] were its four feet. It lay twenty *li* southeast of the present county seat.[66]

The dragon was a common urban tutelary force that, in this case perhaps, reflected a memory of historical lore, playing a role like Nezha in Beijing, the snake in Suzhou, or the tortoise of Pingyao.[67] The dragon was also believed to be able to control water, bringing rain in times of drought and mitigating floods in times of downpours.[68] These powers were especially important for the people of Henan province.

Whatever the mix of legend and history, the link between the dragon and the fortune of the city was taken seriously by the populace of Fan. In 1511, in response to the disorders of the day, Fan's north- and southeastern gates were "temporarily blocked off" to reduce the number of entrances that had to be defended from bandits.[69] Over ten years later in 1523, the gates were still not reopened because "salt bandits" continued to wreak havoc. Yet thereafter, according to the gazet-

---

65   Chan, *Legends*. Different versions of the legend gave Nezha a different number of heads and arms.

66   1535 *Fan xian zhi*, 1.3a.

67   Xu, *Chinese City*, p. 39; Knapp, *China's Walled Cities*, p. 92. Compare the case of Quanzhou Prefecture in Fujian, where the walls were said to have been built to resemble a leaping carp. Chang, "Morphology," p. 90.

68   Chan, *Legends*, pp. 81–83.

69   Not everyone agreed with such measures. The author of a late-Ming work on city defense argued against blocking gates because it also prevented people from exiting the city. He called instead for the vigilant defense of gates by strong guards. Song, *Shou cheng yao lan, juan* 2, 1a.

teer, "The people and things [read "commerce"] deteriorated and those who succeeded in the civil service examinations were few, so popular opinion blamed [the official who had filled in the gates]." In 1534, the students in the county school sought redress and implored two officials to reopen the two gates. According to the record, when "the county magistrate Hu Laipin grudgingly restored them," scholarship in the county flourished as before.[70] That Magistrate Hu was reluctant to restore the gates of the city does not necessarily mean that he did not believe in geomancy, but it does reveal tensions between his emphasis on material defense of the town and the local literati's concern for spiritual revival of the county. As we shall see, wall-building projects could be sources of conflict as well as cooperation between state officials and local people.

State Policies of Wall Building

Wall building was a critical matter at court where the ruler and his ministers debated politywide strategy, and also in the locality where the people most immediately felt its impact. Sometimes central and local concerns were in harmony over the need for walls—such as when large-scale banditry not only brought destruction to a county but also threatened the security of the state. But when priorities did not mesh, the county magistrate and other officials had to negotiate with the local people, who had their own interests in the project.

Addressing the question of when and why the Ming state rebuilt county town walls, we find that cities that lay along the most vulnerable frontiers—particularly the northern border with Mongol lands and the coastal regions of the southeast frequented by sea raiders—were the highest priority and were rebuilt at times of increased threat. One study of city wall building in Fujian suggests that there were three waves: in the early years of the dynasty after the Ming replaced the Mongols in ruling China; in the sixteenth century following "pirate" attacks on coastal areas; and at the end of the dynasty when internal unrest combined with external attacks to threaten the very existence of

---

70   1535 *Fan xian zhi*, 1.3b–4a.

the polity.[71] A broader survey based on the court digests known as the *Veritable Records* (*shilu*) and other sources finds a similar pattern in politywide wall building.[72] The Ming court naturally focused its attention on Beijing, rebuilding its walls many times after it became the politywide capital in 1421. It also paid close attention to the walls of other cities in the capital region, including Xuanfu and Tongzhou in Shuntian prefecture, that were vulnerable to nomadic raids and had their walls rebuilt in the sixteenth century.[73] The court also paid close attention to military installations such as battalions (*qianhu suo*), forts (*bao*), and guard units (*wei*) and sections of "long walls" further north as well as to fortifications along other borderlands such as the southwest.[74]

Three entries for 1490 suggest that the court distinguished clearly between walls along the frontier under the jurisdiction of the Ministry of War and city walls under the authority of the Ministry of Works, but it also recognized that they could play similar functions in preserving politywide peace and order. In the ninth month, Ministry of War officials, citing threats from Oirat raiders along the northern border, sought and won a decree ordering all border officials to repair walls and for court officials to conduct regular inspections of walls thereafter.[75] In the tenth month the Prince of Lingchu, Shi Bian, memorialized the throne requesting the repair and rebuilding of city walls and moats, gates, waterways, roads, and forts in all places. This was approved via the Ministry of Works. Shortly after, Xiang Rong, regional inspector for Fujian province, submitted a memorial seeking to rebuild the city walls of Zhenghe County that was particularly vulnerable to bandits due to its location deep in the hills. Again the request was approved via the Ministry of Works.[76]

---

71   Fei, "Making," pp. 73–74, 78–79, 94–98. "Piracy" is another one of those terms that should be carefully defined when used.

72   Shan and Wang, *Mingdai jianzhu*. The other sources include *Ming yitong zhi* (Gazetteer of the whole Ming realm), *Ming shi* (Dynastic history of the Ming), and *Ming hui dian* (Collected statutes of the Ming).

73   Waldron, *Great Wall*, pp. 147–59.

74   Shan and Wang, *Mingdai jianzhu*, Part 3, pp. 1–163.

75   *Xiaozong shilu*, *juan* 44, 2a–2b.

76   *Xiaozong shilu*, *juan* 44, 6b–7a. Xiang also noted that the local people were willing to donate their private funds for the project, suggesting that the wall was a high priority for them.

Henan province was not located on the frontier adjacent to the steppe nor did it have a "pirate-infested" coastline. The court nonetheless paid attention to the condition of its city walls when mounting threats along the border pushed the scope of central concerns deeper into the interior, and when protracted unrest threatened more than individual counties. There was also more general attention to building the state order through the construction of county walls, although these came second to more immediate threats.

In 1448 Li Lian, an assistant administration commissioner of Shandong, reported that because Shandong and Henan were adjacent to Jiangnan[77] and had few military installations, their cities were currently largely without walls and moats, and those that existed were in disrepair. Li requested and won a decree that ordered all field administrators in the two provinces to repair the walls and moats. Later that year, however, devastating floods engulfed Shandong and resulted in a major famine. In order to alleviate the burdens on the people, the court ordered all wall-building projects in central China to be put on hold, although officials serving in border areas and places of strategic importance could repair their city walls.[78] While we are not told what happened in Henan—presumably some wall-building projects continued—this court record suggests that while city walls were important to the state order in the mid–fifteenth century, they were not to be maintained at the expense of the people, especially when and where there was no pressing threat from invaders.

Court policy changed sharply the following year, 1449, when the ruler Yingzong (r. 1436–1449, 1457–1464) was captured in the disastrous Tumu incident while campaigning against the Mongols.[79] As a result, the court's security strategy extended to building city walls even in Henan.[80] In that very year four of our Henan county towns saw the

77 Both provinces in the Ming actually bordered Nanzhili, whose northern part was not usually considered to be—as indeed it was not—"south of the Yangzi" (Jiangnan).

78 *Yingzong shilu, juan* 172, 10b–11a.

79 1526 *Yangwu xian zhi*, 836–37; 1544 *Yongcheng xian zhi*, 2.12a–b. For the Tumu incident and the political struggles around it, see Mote, "T'u-mu incident," pp. 193–257, and De Heer, *Care-Taker Emperor*. For the policy shifts at court consult Waldron, *Great Wall*, pp. 91–107.

80 *Yingzong shilu, juan* 185, 10a.

reconstruction of walls, and four other counties followed suit in the subsequent two years in response to the court order. This new policy had a lasting effect: Henan's local officials and inhabitants regularly restored (and sometimes expanded) their county walls throughout the Chenghua (1465–1487) and Hongzhi (1488–1505) reigns. Strikingly, for these four decades, the gazetteers' compilers do not attribute their wall-building efforts to any domestic unrest or banditry. Apparently, those efforts were instead a continuing reaction to the new policy that followed the crisis of 1449.

In the subsequent Zhengde reign (1506–1521), wall building continued in Henan but with a more localized concern: the predations of "bandits." In 1511 and 1512 seventeen counties engaged in wall-building projects, fourteen of which did so in response to bandit attacks. (We have already seen, in Chapter 2, the importance of this social unrest in stimulating wall building in the case of Guide/Shangqiu.) The turbulence was so severe and widespread that in 1513 the court ordered the building of walls in all administrative seats throughout the realm that did not already have them.[81]

After these tumultuous years right in the middle of the Ming, county wall construction in Henan again seems to have slowed during the relative peace and prosperity of the Jiajing reign (1522–1566). Wall building continued, but was as often in response to damage by rain and flood as to counter human threats. The two mentions of aggressors refer to bandits and northern raiders. The gazetteer does not tell us whether the raiders were a contingent of the Mongols whose increasing incursions in the northern border regions prompted the intensified building of the Ming long walls from the 1550s onward.[82] But we do know that one important factor behind the building of both city walls and long walls was the threat of external aggression. And just as court policy was arguably decisive in the building of the long walls, so local politics played an important role in the building of county town walls.

---

81   *Wuzong shilu, juan* 98, 3b.
82   Waldron, *Great Wall*, pp. 160ff.

Local Politics of Wall Building

On the ground in the county, it was the responsibility of the magistrate to carry out court instructions to build walls. But while some gazetteer accounts credit magistrates with such projects, others reveal that regional administrators and officials sent from the court as well as local residents were often involved. Evidence of interaction among all these groups allows us to reconstruct some of the localized politics of wall building.

County magistrates, known as the "mothers and fathers of the people," often took the lead in wall construction. Magistrate Jing Fang responded to the destruction of Linzhang's walls in a flood by rebuilding them and facing them with brick and stone. He also took the opportunity to add towers and other defense structures.[83] Xu Ni, the magistrate of Zhenyang County, was praised for rebuilding the city wall that withstood the assaults of Shi Shangzhao, a salt producer-merchant turned smuggler, who led an uprising in Guide prefecture in 1553.[84] Concern over (re-)building city walls was part of a larger "reorientation" of scholar-officials to practical administration during the late Ming.[85] The writing of instructional texts for administrators became an important part of this reorientation.[86] Concerning wall building, the magistrate and author of one such handbook, Wu Zun, who first served as a magistrate in the late 1540s, argued that maintaining walls and moats was so essential to the security of county towns that magistrates should take the initiative in responding to any problems without waiting for authorization from their superiors.[87] In these circumstances, concern

---

83   1506 *Linzhang xian zhi*.

84   1555 *Zhenyang xian zhi*, 2.3a. For a summary of Shi Shangzhao's uprising see Des Forges, *Cultural Centrality*, pp. 174–75.

85   See Handlin, *Action*, for this "reorientation" and the role of Lü Kun (1536–1618), who authored numerous official handbooks addressing a range of problems both in and out of office. In his hometown of Ningling, Lü participated in the rebuilding of the walls and the strengthening of its protective dike. He encountered popular protests against the project, but eventually completed it. After his death it proved effective in keeping "bandits" from entering the city. Lü, *Jiu ming shu*, preface, 1.

86   Will, *Official Handbooks*.

87   Wu, *Chushi lu*, 38b–39a.

for the welfare of the locality should trump fastidiousness in following normal bureaucratic procedures.

In practice, however, magistrates did not always take the initiative to build walls—sometimes they did not even have the capacity to do so. As a result, central and regional officials sometimes took the lead. In 1512 a provincial intendant (*jian si*) reported that the people of Gushi had allowed the moats to be filled in and had taken over the resulting land for their own use. A vice-censor-in-chief subsequently came to Gushi and reclaimed the land for the state, presumably with an eye to restoring the moat.[88] In 1511 a general surveillance administrator (*shou xun*) posted to Henan, fearing the threat of bandits, commanded the county magistrate of neighboring Lanyang County to assemble a work force to reconstruct Yifeng's wall. It is unclear why the commissioner enlisted the magistrate of a neighboring county in performing this task, sidestepping the Yifeng magistrates that regularly succeeded one another in this period. But the incident revealed the important role of higher (and nearby) officials in maintaining such public infrastructure. Twenty-three years later, another central government official, this time a superintendent, ordered Yifeng's magistrate to expand the wall after it had been damaged by a flood. On this occasion, local interests joined with central authority as two local scholar-officials holding metropolitan posts—vice-censor-in-chief and Hanlin academician—wielded their influence to prod the superintendent, and through him the local magistrate, into action.[89]

All these cases hint at Ming political processes in the locality. While magistrates often compiled the gazetteers and claimed achievements in the county, their ability to take charge of wall-building projects was limited. In reality, action often depended on central government officials such as grand coordinators and superintendents, who often possessed both the responsibility and the authority—not to speak of the political influence—that regular local officials might lack.[90] Local people, in turn, could make use of such shifting lines of authority and con-

---

88   1542 *Gushi xian zhi*, 3.2a.

89   *Jiajing Yifeng xian zhi*, pp. 97–99, 114–15, 135–36, 302–4.

90   Tang, *Bu pingheng de zhili*, pp. 61–64. Compare Hucker, "Ming Government," pp. 79–80.

nect with different levels of officials to affect what was being done in their home counties.

As Ming officials often took credit for building walls, they were naturally subject to blame when something went wrong. The authors of Lanyang's 1545 gazetteer clearly explained the opportunities and risks in building walls:

> Construction brings two good things: accomplishment for the official and benefit for the people. But there are also two ills: the blame borne by the official and the toil borne by the people. Without accomplishment, [the official's] talent is not established. And so the talented official amasses materials and gathers men for work as fits the situation. With [his] accomplishment comes benefit [for the people. . . . But without [the possibility of] blame, nothing will be achieved.[91]

When heavy rainfall damaged the walls of Lanyang in 1542, the magistrate advocated repair work with these lessons in mind. He promised the populace to undertake appropriate measures in as fair a way as possible, and swore an oath that he would be accountable for any shortcomings or irregularities. These professions revealed the political tensions that probably underlay most such projects that drew on the people's labor and resources to attain a public good.

The Lushan gazetteer contains an account that reveals more about the politics of wall building with the explicit participation of the local people. In a dialogue the likes of which was rarely recorded but may have been quite common, magistrate Yao Qing explicitly assumed personal responsibility for building the city walls to ensure the welfare of the people of the county. In an address to the local elders and elites, he stated:

> The people rely upon the city walls for their protection. If there are no city walls, there is no county, if there is no county, then there are no people. Now a magistrate is entrusted with the duty of protecting [the people]. If there are no city walls then this would be abandoning

---

91   1545 *Lanyang xian zhi*, 3.3a.

the county and abandoning the people, and the blame would surely lie with me. I will therefore put walls around the city.[92]

Wary of the magistrate's designs, the people responded that his predecessors had not carried out their duties properly, allowing irregularities in levying labor and profligacy in purchasing supplies. As a result, they said, the magistrate's immediate predecessor had refrained from building a wall lest he fall under suspicion of mismanagement.

As might be expected, Yao hastened to distance himself from such previous misconduct and irresponsibility. Apparently referring to his immediate predecessor, he declared: "That was a case of acting for private [interest] and ignoring the public [good], of serving oneself and harming the people. How can that be [permitted to persist]?" He then proceeded to expound further on the proper ways of government, drawing an analogy between an orderly office and a well-run home and echoing the model of self-cultivation and governance found in the opening section of the *Great Learning* (*Da xue*), first of the *Four Books* (*Si shu*) of Song Confucianism.[93] He also stated that proper action must be taken regardless of concern about suspicion or praise. He reiterated his resolve to carry out the construction in an exemplary manner. According to the gazetteer, he did so "using labor and materials exactly as appropriate and required, paying for them at the fair market price, and bringing as little trouble to the people as possible."[94] Although these are all clichés reflecting the ideal handling of public projects, they may have been applied appropriately in this case. At the successful completion of the project, Yao was praised on all sides and his achievements were commemorated in an inscription.[95] In the absence of any evidence of popular opposition to Yao's administration,

---

92   A literal translation of this last phrase might be "make city walls of the city walls" (*jiang cheng qi cheng*). 1552 *Lushan xian zhi*, 4.3b.

93   In the *Great Learning* the model is of the ideal ruler whose self-cultivation extends outwards from an orderly home to a well-governed state and a virtuous world. Zhu Xi, *Si shu ji zhu*, pp. 8–9.

94   For efforts to avoid suspicion by carefully calculating the cost of construction before beginning work, see the record of a magistrate in the Jiajing period. Wu, *Chushi lu*, 39a.

95   1552 *Lushan xian zhi*, 4.3b–5b.

we may accept the positive judgment passed on him and recorded in the county history.[96]

Conclusions

By investigating some two dozen county gazetteers printed in the late Ming dynasty and other primary sources such as the *Veritable Records* reflecting court policies, this chapter has attempted to reveal what the building and repair of walls and moats around as many county towns meant to the Chinese state and local populace. We have found that these modest structures were usually built to defend the residents from natural disasters such as floods and human mayhem such as banditry. They were also constructed of the same materials as the long walls that stretched across China to the north and sometimes were meant, like long walls, to protect the cities from nomadic raids. Like the long walls and enceintes around larger cities, they were constructed or refurbished in several waves during the Ming: in the early years, the mid–fifteenth century, the mid–sixteenth century, and toward the end of the dynasty.

County town walls and gates, like long walls and larger city walls and their apertures, represented far more than their earth and bricks might tell—even beyond their idealized measurements and supposed shapes. They were, above all perhaps, signs of state authority that was expected to bring peace, order, and perhaps even a modicum of justice not just to the inhabitants of the town but to the residents of the suburbs and countryside whose welfare was a prime official responsibility. Embedded in their environments, county walls and gates took on meanings that resonated with their localities and times. In this sense, city walls were not so much boundaries as multivalent sites that state and local actors could variously interpret to link the locality with the current central state and the present with various relevant pasts.

---

96 In fact, to pay for the walls, merchants were often forced to sell goods to the government at low prices that could even bankrupt them. Huang, "Ming Fiscal Administration," p. 170. Protests against wall building were not uncommon. In one case in Gaochun County, Nanjing metropolitan area, at the end of the sixteenth century, they were successful in stopping a project. Fei, "Making," pp. 73–106. For further discussion of tensions between wall-building magistrates and the local populace in Henan, see Des Forges, *Cultural Centrality*, p. 97.

Beneath representations of unifying value, local interests, both public and private, were advanced with little inhibition. The walls certainly marked the presence of the state but local society was the context in which their building and rebuilding had to be negotiated. Local officials were in charge but members of the local elite were often involved in the planning, artisans and merchants in the construction, and the general populace in the physical labor. Power was not shared equally among these groups, but the upper ranks of the hierarchy could not function without at least tacit support from the lower levels of society. Given the zealous and persistent efforts of urban reformers in some Chinese cities in the twentieth century, we might wonder whether the hold of the supposedly autocratic Ming state even came close to the control exerted over society by "modern" municipal governments.

Acknowledgments

I wish to thank Roger Des Forges for his support and encouragement for this paper, including the close reading of several versions. Tim Brook, Tim Sedo, and the members of the China Studies Group and of the graduate student group Wang She at the University of British Columbia also made useful suggestions on earlier drafts.

Works Cited

Gazetteers

All gazetteer sources for this paper are taken from the two series: *Tianyige cang Mingdai fangzhi xuan kan* (Selected Ming Gazetteers from the Tianyige Collection), Shanghai: Shanghai shudian, 1963–1965; and *Tianyige cang Mingdai fangzhi xuan kan xubian* (Selected Ming Gazetteers from the Tianyige Collection, continued), Shanghai: Shanghai shudian, 1990.

Vol. 45, *Xiangcheng xian zhi*, 1551.
Vol. 47, *Guangshan xian zhi*, 1556.
Vol. 48, *Xiayi xian zhi*, 1548.
Vol. 49, *Yushi xian zhi*, 1548.
Vol. 49, *Xinxiang xian zhi*, 1506.

Vol. 50, *Changyuan xian zhi*, 1541.
Vol. 50, *Lushan xian zhi*, 1552.
Vol. 51, *Gushi xian zhi*, 1542.
Vol. 51, *Yanling xian zhi*, 1535.
Vol. 52, *Lanyang xian zhi*, 1545.
Vol. 52, *Neihuang zhi*, 1537.
Vol. 52, *Yanshi xian zhi*, Hongzhi Period (1488–1505).
Xubian Vol. 58, *Tongxu xian zhi*, 1543.
Xubian Vol. 58, *Taikang xian zhi*, 1524.
Xubian Vol. 58, *Yangwu xian zhi*, 1526.
Xubian Vol. 58, *Shenqiu xian zhi*, 1530.
Xubian Vol. 59, *Yifeng xian zhi*, Jiajing Period (1522–1567).
Xubian Vol. 59, *Yancheng xian zhi*, 1554.
Xubian Vol. 59, *Gong xian zhi*, 1555.
Xubian Vol. 60, *Yongcheng xian zhi*, 1544.
Xubian Vol. 60, *Zhenyang xian zhi*, 1555.
Xubian Vol. 60, *Shangcheng xian zhi*, 1551.
Xubian Vol. 61, *Hui xian zhi*, 1526.
Xubian Vol. 61, *Fan xian zhi*, 1535.
Xubian Vol. 71, *Linzhang xian zhi*, 1506.

Other Sources

Andrew, Anita M., and John A. Rapp. *Autocracy and China's Rebel Founding Emperors: Comparing Chairman Mao and Ming Taizu*. New York: Rowman & Littlefield, 2000.
Bagley, Robert. "Shang Archaeology." Pp. 124–231 in Michael Loewe and Edward Shaughnessy, eds., *The Cambridge History of Ancient China: From the Origins of Civilization to 221 B.C.* Cambridge: Cambridge University Press, 1999.
Billings, Timothy. "Visible Cities: The Heterotopic Utopia of China in Early Modern European Writing," *Genre: Forms of Discourse and Culture* 30 (Fall/Winter 1997), pp. 105–34.
Brook, Timothy. "Communications and Commerce." Pp. 579–707 in Denis Twitchett and Frederick Mote, eds., *The Cambridge History of China, Volume 8: The Ming Dynasty, Part 2*. Cambridge: Cambridge University Press, 1998.
———. *The Confusions of Pleasure: Commerce and Culture in Ming China*. Berkeley: University of California Press, 1998.
———. *The Chinese State in Ming Society*. London: Routledge, 2005.

Chan Hok-lam. *Legends of the Building of Old Peking.* Hong Kong: The Chinese University Press/Seattle: University of Washington Press, 2008.

Chang Sen-dou. "The Morphology of Walled Capitals." Pp. 75–100 in G. William Skinner, ed., *The City in Late Imperial China.* Stanford: Stanford University Press, 1977.

Cochran, Sherman, and David Strand, eds. Wen-hsin Yeh, general ed., *Cities in Motion: Interior, Coast, and Diaspora in Transnational China.* Berkeley: Institute of East Asian Studies, Center for Chinese Studies, University of California, 2007.

De Bary, W. T. "Chinese Despotism and the Confucian Ideal: A Seventeenth-Century View." Pp. 163–203 in John K. Fairbank ed., *Chinese Thought and Institutions.* Chicago: University of Chicago Press, 1957.

De Heer, Ph. *The Care-Taker Emperor: Aspects of the Imperial Institution in Fifteenth-Century China as Reflected in the Political History of the Reign of Chu Ch'i-yu.* Leiden: E. J. Brill, 1986.

Dennis, Joseph Raymond. "Writing, Publishing, and Reading Local Histories in Ming China." Ph.D. dissertation, University of Minnesota, 2004.

Des Forges, Roger V. *Cultural Centrality and Political Change in Chinese History: Northeast Henan in the Fall of the Ming.* Stanford: Stanford University Press, 2003.

Esherick, Joseph W., ed. *Remaking the Chinese City, Modernity and National Identity, 1900–1950.* Honolulu: University of Hawai'i Press, 2000.

Farmer, Edward L. "The Hierarchy of Ming City Walls." Pp. 461–87 in James D. Tracy, ed., *City Walls: The Urban Enceinte in Global Perspective.* Cambridge: Cambridge University Press, 2000.

Fei Si-yen. "The Making and Remaking of the Southern Metropolis in Sixteenth- and Seventeenth-Century China." Ph.D. dissertation, Stanford University, 2004.

Handlin, Joanna F. *Action in Late Ming Thought: The Reorientation of Lü K'un and Other Scholar-Officials.* Berkeley: University of California Press, 1983.

Huang Liu-hung; Djang Chu tr. & ed. *A Complete Book Concerning Happiness and Benevolence: A Manual for Local Magistrates in Seventeenth-Century China.* Tucson: University of Arizona Press, [1699] 1984.

Huang, Ray. "The Ming Fiscal Administration." Pp. 106–71 in Denis Twitchett and Frederick Mote, eds., *The Cambridge History of China, Volume 8: The Ming Dynasty, Part 2.* Cambridge: Cambridge University Press, 1998.

Hucker, Charles O. "Ming Government." Pp. 9–105 in Denis Twitchett and Frederick Mote, eds., *The Cambridge History of China, Volume 8: The Ming Dynasty, Part 2.* Cambridge: Cambridge University Press, 1998.

Knapp, Ronald G. *China's Walled Cities*. Hong Kong: Oxford University Press, 2000.

Lü Kun (js. 1574). *Jiu ming shu* (The book for saving lives). Wang Yunwu, ed. *Congshu jicheng chu bian, Lianbing shiji ji qita yi zhong* (Collected Collectanea, 1st ed., Practical plans for training troops and one other work), vol. 3. Taipei: Commercial Press, 1936.

Ming shilu (Veritable Records of the Ming). 183 volumes. Taipei: Zhongyang yanjiu yuan, lishi yuyan yanjiusuo, 1962–1968.

Mote, F. W. "The Transformation of Nanking, 1350–1400." Pp. 101–54 in G. William Skinner, ed., *The City in Late Imperial China*. Stanford: Stanford University Press, 1977.

——. "The Growth of Chinese Despotism," *Oriens Extremus* 8(1961), pp. 1–41.

——. "The T'u-mu Incident of 1449." Pp. 243-272 in Frank A. Kierman, Jr., and John K. Fairbank, eds., *Chinese Ways in Warfare*. Cambridge, Mass.: Harvard University Press, 1974.

Needham, Joseph, et al. *Science and Civilisation in China, Volume IV: Physics and Physical Technology. Part 3: Civil Engineering and Nautics*. Cambridge: Cambridge University Press, 1971.

Needham, Joseph, et al. *Science and Civilisation in China, Volume V: Chemistry and Chemical Technology. Part 6 Military Technology: Missiles and Sieges*. Cambridge: Cambridge University Press, 1994.

Robinson, David. *Bandits, Eunuchs and the Son of Heaven: Rebellion and the Economy of Violence in Mid-Ming China*. Honolulu: University of Hawai'i Press, 2001.

Schneewind, Sarah. "Visions and Revisions: Village Policies of the Ming Founder in Seven Phases," *T'oung Pao* 87 (2002): 1–43.

——. *Community Schools and the State in Ming China*. Stanford: Stanford University Press, 2006.

——. *A Tale of Two Melons: Emperor and Subject in Ming China*. Indianapolis/Cambridge: Hackett Publishing Company, Inc., 2006.

——, ed. *Long Live the Emperor! Uses of the Ming Founder across Six Centuries of East Asian History*. Minneapolis: Society for Ming Studies, No. 4, 2008.

Shan Shiyuan, and Wang Biwen, comps. *Mingdai jianzhu da shi nianbiao* (Chronological tables of major building projects of the Ming Period). Taipei: Zhongguo yingzao xueshe, 1976.

Song Yingxing, Zhong Guangyan, annot. *Tiangong kaiwu* (The exploitation of the works of nature). Hong Kong: Zhonghua shuju, [1637] 1978.

Song Zushun. *Shou cheng yao lan* (Survey on the essentials of city defense). Shanghai Library, Guji #555691–94, [1635] 1829.

Steinhardt, Nancy Shatzman. "Representations of Chinese Walled Cities in the Pictorial and Graphic Arts." Pp. 419–60 in James D. Tracy, ed. *City Walls: The Urban Enceinte in Global Perspective*. Cambridge: Cambridge University Press, 2000.

Tan Qixiang, ed. *Zhongguo lishi ditu ji. Di qi ce: Yuan, Ming shiqi* (Historical atlas of China, Volume 7: The Yuan and Ming periods). Taipei: Hsiao Yuan Publication Co., 1991. [Taiwan reprint of 1980 edition published by Zhongguo ditu chubanshe.]

Tang Kejun. *Bu pingheng de zhili: Mingdai zhengfu yunxing yanjiu* (Uneven governance: studies in the operations of Ming government). Wuhan: Wuhan chubanshe, 2004.

Tong, James W. *Disorder under Heaven: Collective Violence in the Ming Dynasty*. Stanford: Stanford University Press, 1991.

Tracy, James D., ed. *City Walls: The Urban Enceinte in Global Perspective*. Cambridge: Cambridge University Press, 2000.

Waldron, Arthur. *The Great Wall of China: From History to Myth*. Cambridge: Cambridge University Press, 1990.

Wang Qi, and Wang Siyi, comp. eds. *San cai tu hui* (Compendium of illustrations of the three powers), 106 *juan*. Prefaces of 1607 and 1609. Reprinted in three volumes, Shanghai: Shanghai guji chubanshe, 1988.

Will, Pierre-Étienne. *Official Handbooks and Anthologies of Imperial China: A Descriptive and Critical Bibliography*. Work in progress obtained from author, electronic version as of 10 September 2005; hard copy in press.

Wittfogel, Karl A. *Oriental Despotism: A Comparative Study of Total Power*. New Haven, Connecticut: Yale University Press, 1957.

Woodside, Alexander. "The Centre and the Borderlands in Chinese Political Theory." Pp. 11–28 in Diana Lary, ed., *The Chinese State at the Borders*. Vancouver, BC: University of British Columbia Press, 2007.

Wright, Arthur W. "The Cosmology of the Chinese City." Pp. 33–74 in G. William Skinner, ed., *The City in Late Imperial China*. Stanford: Stanford University Press, 1977.

Wu, Zun (js. 1547). *Chushi lu* (Records of a beginner official). *Guanzhen shu jicheng* [Collected Official Handbooks]. Hefei: Huangshan shushe, 1998, pp. 35–55.

Xu Shen, comp. (100 CE), Duan Yucai annot., *Shuowen jiezi zhu* (Analyzing graphs and explaining characters, annotated). Taipei: Liming, 1974.

Xu, Yinong. *The Chinese City in Space and Time: The Development of Urban Form in Suzhou*. Honolulu: University of Hawai'i Press, 2000.

Zhang Yuhuan. *Zhongguo chengchi shi* (A history of China's walls and moats). Tianjin: Baihua Literature and Art Publishing House, 2003.

Zhu Xi. *Si shu ji zhu* (Collected commentaries on the Four Books). Reprinted, Taipei: Yiwen yinshuguan, 1996.

PART TWO

Walls within Cities

CHINA IS FAMOUS FOR ITS walls not only because of the somewhat overblown image of long walls and the undoubted ubiquity of its city walls but also because of the importance of walls within cities, including those around palaces in capital cities and those around other domiciles in all cities. These latter enclosures lie largely outside the scope of this book, but there were other intra-urban walls that merit our attention. There were, first, the material walls and gates of the many wards (*fangli*) of Chang'an, the major city in the northwest that served as the capital of several early dynasties, including especially the Tang. Tang Chang'an also served as a model for other capital cities of East Asia such as Nara and Kyoto in Japan. Then there were the virtual "walls" and "gates" separating and connecting the multiple judicial jurisdictions erected by the Chinese in the late Qing in the southeastern metropolis of Shanghai. They were designed to accommodate and contain the numerous foreign powers (mainly Euro-American) that exacted and defended extraterritorial privileges for their nationals resident there.

In addition to being, respectively, material and virtual and located in a political capital and in a metropolitan city, these two sets of walls were different in other ways. The ward walls of eighth-century Tang Chang'an resulted from an effort to establish a well-ordered society based on models projected back into the Zhou dynasty and approximated during the Han dynasty and its epigones. The juridical walls in late nineteenth- and early-twentieth-century Shanghai represented a Chinese strategy of incorporating practices from abroad, and especially from the "West." The ward walls of Tang Chang'an were part of an effort to establish a ideal society while the jurisdictional walls of Qing and

Republican Shanghai were designed to mitigate a loss of sovereignty
and to regain it as quickly as possible. Some might even go so far as to
suggest that the ward walls of Chang'an were designed to maintain a
"traditional" or "feudal" social order while the jurisdictional walls of
Shanghai were intended to establish a "modern" or "capitalist" society.

In other ways, however, the two cases are remarkably similar. The
ward walls and gates of mid-Tang Chang'an, although designed to
separate and thereby harmonize various social strata, ethnic groups,
and familial domiciles, could, under certain circumstances, be casually
penetrated or purposely manipulated to achieve social mobility, ethnic
hybridity, and individual freedom. The juridical "walls" of late Qing
Shanghai were intended to insure distinctions between different kinds
of laws, different communities, and different concepts of justice, but
they also could be used on some occasions to facilitate hybrid forms of
legal procedure, cultural practice, and professional development. Over
time, both kinds of edifices may have helped to yield—or at least
permit—the evolution of different forms of society. But those forms,
like the "walls" themselves, arguably also had antecedents in the past as
well as analogues elsewhere in the world.

CHAPTER FOUR

The Ward Walls and Gates of Tang Chang'an as Seen in "The Tale of Li Wa"

Keyang Tang

"The Wall was a masterpiece."

—REM KOOLHAAS, "EXODUS, OR
THE VOLUNTARY PRISONERS OF ARCHITECTURE"[1]

CHANG'AN IN THE TANG DYNASTY, like all other Chinese dynastic capitals except perhaps Anyang in the Shang dynasty, was circumscribed by an imposing wall and had within it substantial palaces that were themselves surrounded by walls. Tang Chang'an was more distinctive in following the supposed Zhou model, probably invented in the Han and practiced in the Northern Wei and Sui, dividing the rest of the city into strictly ordered walled wards (*li-fang* or *fang-li*). We know something about the wards of Tang Chang'an, such as their names, shapes, and approximate locations and sizes, but there is much that we do not know, including details regarding the supposedly diverse

---

1 Page 16. The reference, in 1972, was to the Berlin Wall, which increased the isolation of West Berlin from East Berlin and from the surrounding territory of the German Democratic Republic, "imprisoning" the half-city even as it considered itself to be "free" and a Mecca for refugees. Conversely, I shall suggest, the ward walls and gates of Tang Chang'an may have provided refuges for some of its residents even as they supposedly fixed them within an ideal political and social structure.

identities of their residents and their tangible impact on the lives of the
common people who constituted the vast majority of the populace in
the city. Some of what we know we have learned not just from fragments
of maps, statutes, and formal histories but also from art and literature,
including a form of fiction known as romantic tales (*chuanqi*, lit.,
"transmissions of the strange").

In this chapter we explore the ways in which the walls and gates of
Chang'an's wards actually functioned during the height of the Tang dynasty in the early eighth century as seen in "The Tale of Li Wa" (*Li Wa
zhuan*), said to have been written by Bai Xingjian (776–826 CE),
younger brother of the famous poet Bai Juyi (772–846 CE).[2] In this
story we shall see how the system of ward walls and gates, and the accompanying institutions of guards and curfews, shaped the fortunes of
a young man who deviated for a time from the path of becoming a
scholar-official and a young woman who first lured him away from and
then helped lead him back to his expected role in society.

The Wards of Chang'an

Tang Chang'an, like Sui Daxing (lit., Great Prosperity), which preceded
it on the same site, was based on the Zhou model as canonized in Han-
period texts and as approximated in the capital designs of the Northern
and Southern Dynasties. Like its antecedents such as Northern Wei
Luoyang, however, Chang'an actually diverged considerably from the
Zhou model from the beginning. For example, in the Zhou model, the
royal palaces were to be located in the center of the city facing south
and the markets were to be established behind the palaces. In both
Northern Wei Luoyang and Tang Chang'an, however, the palaces were
actually placed against the northern wall of the city and the markets
were set up southwest and southeast of the palaces (see Figure 1).[3]

The ideal of dividing the city into wards, nevertheless, was given
full expression in all of these early capital cities. Tang Chang'an, which
was square, was divided symmetrically by fourteen longitudinal and

---

2   For Bai Juyi, see Waley, *Life*.
3   Wright, "Cosmology," pp. 55-60.

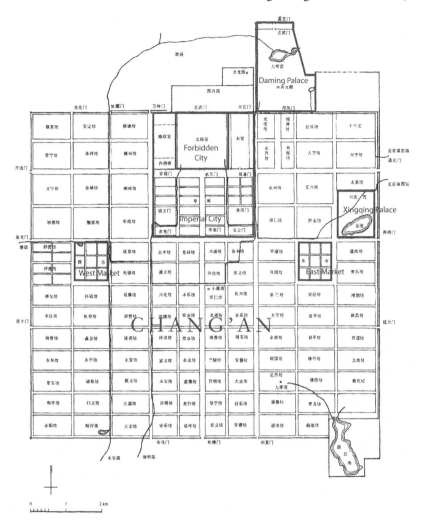

Figure 1 The Walls of Tang Chang'an. Based on Fu, *Zhongguo*, p. 318.

eleven latitudinal streets that yielded 108 wards and two markets.[4] The wards were rectangular, longer east to west than north to south, and of varying sizes, and they each had four gates, one in each wall, that were connected by streets, dividing the ward into four square subsections.[5] In some cases, the four subsections, in turn, were each further divided into four parts.[6] A principal purpose of the layout was to order various groups defined by origins, ethnicity, class, or occupation into specific wards and to monitor relations among them so as to minimize illegitimate contacts including sexual promiscuity. To insure compliance, guards closed and locked the ward gates at night and opened them in the morning.

The system of walled wards may have developed in accord with the writings of Guan Zhong (?–645 BCE), an influential administrative theorist and practitioner of the late Zhou (i.e., the Chunqiu or Spring and Autumn) period. The system was associated with the collective responsibility system, also dating from the Zhou period, in which groups of families took responsibility for maintaining order in local communities, and, by extension, collected taxes and recruited troops.[7] While these systems were designed to extend close state control over the affected (in this case urban) population, they could also be used by the populace to preserve elements of local autonomy or even to assert their private interests. Local autonomy was possible in part because of the relatively small bureaucracy of the Tang state as compared with the large population and territory it governed. In the case of eighth-century Chang'an, the residents rose to about one million people while the territory within the walls totaled some eighty-four square kilometers.[8] (In another estimate, apparently assuming only half that population, it has been suggested that the population of the city was roughly 5,700

4   Steinhardt, *Chinese Imperial*, pp. 94–95; for the 160 wards of Han Chang'an, see ibid., p. 67.
5   Some wards, such as Fengle and Anye, two of the smallest in the center city, did not have crossed central streets but only two parallel central streets running east and west. Some wards, such as Fengle and Anren, might have had an irregular number of gates, reflecting their various political and administrative roles.
6   Steinhardt, *Chinese Imperial*, p. 117.
7   Ibid., p. 67; Bray, *Social Space*, pp. 24–25.
8   Fu, *Zhongguo*, p. 318.

persons per ward.[9]) In any case, the wards of Tang Chang'an were quite large, measuring one li (about half a kilometer) or more on each side.[10]

While Tang Chang'an shared a basic grid pattern with other cities of Europe, North America, and Ming-Qing China, therefore, each of the four sections of its wards was many times larger than the block and other comparable subdivision of those "Western" or more recent Chinese cities (see Figure 2).[11]

The basic infrastructure of Sui-Tang Chang'an, including the external walls, the palaces and administrative buildings, and the grid of ward walls, had been constructed very quickly in 582–583 CE, but the external walls were extensively rebuilt in 613, 654, and 730. The 108 wards were probably populated rather slowly over the same century and they were apparently more subject to change than the exterior city walls over the course of the dynasty.[12] According to one source, the city planners adopted a pragmatic strategy in the large residential areas, "letting people claim the land and build on their own."[13] Scholars such as Su Bai believe that, as the wards filled up during the Tianbao era (742–756), narrow alleys and serpentine lanes (*xiang, qu*) appeared within the wards and their subsections. These lanes, which never appeared on any official maps, allowed residents to get around the city and its wards in less regulated ways. Contrary to one goal of the original ward system (control), they also allowed people to hide away from the better known and more carefully monitored ward streets and city avenues and boulevards.[14] Archaeologists are uncovering remnants of the palaces of Chang'an but they have so far found little detailed evidence of the walls and gates that shaped the daily life of the ward inhabitants. We must therefore turn to works of "fiction" such as "The Tale of Li Wa" to find out more about the actual functions of the walls and gates in those parts of the city.

---

9   Sun and Liang, "Tang Chang'an," p. 80.
10 Xiong, *Sui-Tang Chang'an*, pp. 195–96.
11 Dong, *Zhongguo gudai chengshi jiansheshi*, p. 41
12 Steinhardt, *Chinese Imperial*, pp. 101–8; Bray, *Social Space*, p. 19.
13 Fu, *History*, p. 315. It was believed that in the initial period of *fang-li* planning, walls were erected to allow residents to claim land but some houses were in fact never built.
14 Su, "Sui Tang Chang'an," p. 410; Yang, "Fang nei qü," pp. 242–47.

External and Internal Walls of a Single Chang'an Ward

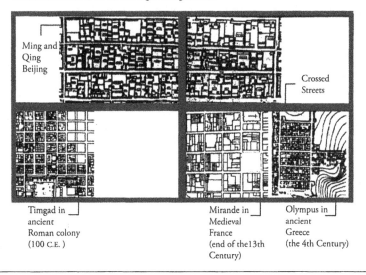

Figure 2 The Large Size of the Wards of Chang'an as Compared with Comparable Subdivisions of some other "Grid" Cities. Based on Sun and Liang, "Tang Chang'an," p. 78.

"The Tale of Li Wa"

The scholar Bai Xingjian seems to have written "The Tale of Li Wa" in 795 CE as a kind of allegory with a composite "hero" based on the actual experiences of three members of a contemporary aristocratic family named Zheng.[15] In writing the story, Bai may have drawn on oral tales recounted among friends or in public places. He may have used his own account as "a 'warming' exercise to impress his examiner with his literary talents."[16]

The main protagonist in the story is a "young scholar" who, like many examination candidates in the era, was the son of an aristocratic, wealthy, and powerful high official. Armed with extensive resources, including books, money, and a larger retinue, the young scholar leaves his home in the provincial town of Yingyang and arrives in Chang'an to prepare for the examinations that are becoming an important path to office in this period. One day, on his way home from visit to a market, he catches a glimpse of a beautiful young woman and is completely smitten by her. He does not approach her but asks about her among his friends and finds out that she is a famous courtesan, the kind of woman whose talents in singing and poetry permit her to be highly selective in offering her sexual services. When he returns to her residence and seeks entry, the girl's "mother," the madam of the house, at first refuses, but she is soon bought off with promises of many bolts of silk and other valuable gifts. The young man not only spends the night with Li Wa but extends his stay for a whole year, abandoning his studies and spending his money on his newfound love.

When the young scholar's funds are exhausted he is apparently reluctant to leave his mistress. The madam therefore persuades Li Wa to join her in tricking him into leaving the compound and then preventing him from returning. Locked out of what had become his home and a refuge from the intense study of the examination life, he first pawns his clothes to pay for lodging but soon falls ill from hunger, cold, and disappointment and is eventually left for dead at a shop selling funeral services. Sympathetic workers at the shop nurse him back to life; he in turn studies their trade and soon becomes a talented singer of funeral

---

15 Dudbridge, *Tale*, p. 52.
16 Hansen, *Open*, p. 211.

dirges. He is so successful at his new trade that he is selected by his boss to enter a singing contest, which he wins handily. Unfortunately his father the governor happens to be in town and catches sight of his wayward son. Angry at his son's having frittered away the family's wealth, cut his ties with relatives in favor of a prostitute, and survived only by recourse to a low-class profession associated with death, the governor beats him severely and leaves him for dead. The young scholar survives by becoming a mendicant who sleeps outside at night wherever he can and begs for food at the market during the day. One snowy day, begging in the street, he cries out and his voice reaches the ears of Li Wa, now living in a new place. Apparently having regretted her earlier role in helping to expel the young scholar from her house when his money ran out, Li Wa now takes him in and nurses him back to health. She uses her considerable resources to buy herself out of the brothel and to support him as he prepares for the civil service examinations. A year later her lover not only passes the examinations but does so brilliantly and becomes an official. He reconciles with his father, gets his permission to marry Li Wa, and produces four sons with her.[17]

Like any such story, "The Tale of Li Wa" is subject to many different interpretations and uses. Glen Dudbridge, who offers a very useful line-by-line translation along with the Chinese text, argues that it was above all a literary construct, likely based on some actual people and experiences, but above all fictional. In his careful commentaries, Dudbridge shows how the story relates to numerous historical and literary antecedents going back to early times.[18] He thus places the story quite effectively in time. More recently Seo Tatsuhiko has surveyed several tales from the Tang period and has shown how this one pays particularly close attention to the detailed anatomy of the city of Chang'an in which it largely took place.[19] He thus carefully contextualizes the story in space. Most recently in a brief analysis, Valerie Hansen observes that the story "vividly captures the degree of surveillance under which the

---

17 Summary based on Dudbridge, *Tale*, pp. 104–86, translating the *Taiping guangji* edition of the story; see also Hansen, *Open*, pp. 211–13.

18 Dudbridge, *Tale*, pp. 39–57.

19 Seo, "Tangdai houqi," pp. 543–44; see also Zhu, "Characters," pp. 117–18, for a Five Dynasties tale that is set in Chang'an but pays less attention to the city's precise layout.

people of Chang'an lived." She argues that despite previous commentaries emphasizing social change in the story, the tale "is really about the lack of social change in Tang society." She concludes that "Tang China was no different from other traditional societies" in, on occasion, allowing beautiful women "to marry outside their social class."[20] Despite evidence of social tensions in the story, Hansen considers it to be ultimately a reaffirmation of the Confucian ideal of the scholar-official in the face of the possibility of alternative careers.

Any interpretation of "The Tale of Li Wa" needs to take full account of the way it depicts the ward walls and gates of Chang'an and the roles they play in influencing the two main protagonists' fate. When the young scholar arrives in Chang'an to prepare for the examinations, he first lodges in Buzheng ward, just west of the forbidden city and just northeast of the western market (see Figure 3).

Buzheng ward is in the part of the city inhabited by commoners and foreigners, suitable for a student from out of town who has yet to pass the examinations. Wandering one day in Pingkang ward, located to the east between the forbidden city and the eastern market, the young scholar chances to encounter Li Wa. This is the part of the city inhabited by the nobility and courtesans, not so appropriate for the young scholar who, although the scion of an aristocratic family, is seemingly prepared to make his way in society on the basis of his own merits (i.e., through the budding civil service examination system).

As if to explain the young man's errantry, the text reads:

> Once, on his way home from a visit to the East Market, he entered the east gate of Pingkang ward, meaning to call on a friend in the southwest part. When he came to Jingling Harness Lane he saw a residence with a modestly proportioned entrance courtyard, but with buildings that were deep and impressive. One of the double gates was closed. Standing there, supported by a maid with hair in double coils was a woman whose bewitching looks were exquisite beyond compare.[21]

---

20   Hansen, *Open,* p. 213.
21   Dudbridge, *Tale,* pp. 109, 111.

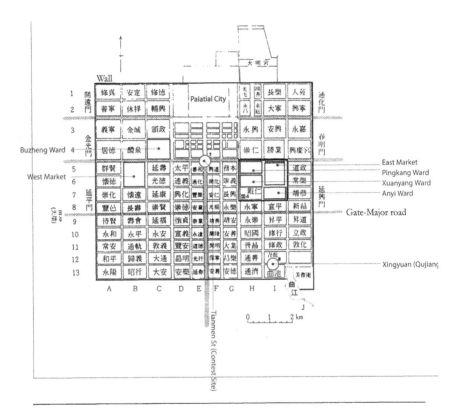

Figure 3   Sites in Chang'an Particularly Relevant to "The Tale of Li Wa." Adapted from Seo, "Tangdai houqi," p. 511.

Given the young gentleman's residence in Buzheng ward near the West Market, his visit to the East Market seems unnecessary, but his desire to "call on a friend" in southwest Pingkang ward seems quite legitimate. His chance encounter with the courtesan Li Wa in Jingling Harness Lane was perhaps not completely his fault, for she made herself visible through the half-open gate of her unmarked compound and she seemed to reciprocate his fascination. After learning about Li Wa's status as a famous courtesan, however, the young scholar's decision to return to Jingling Harness Lane with "a man about town" was apparently his alone. In the eyes of the author, it was perhaps the beginning of his "downfall" or at least his deviation from the increasingly accepted and admired path to wealth, power, and fame.

When the infatuated young man returns to Li Wa's residence he is greeted by her and decides that the attraction is mutual. The madam, for her part, arranges for Li Wa to engage her guest in pleasantries so as to keep him until after the evening curfew, forcing him to stay the night and make a significant commitment of gifts to do so. Here we see the older businesswoman using the curfew designed in part to impede such assignations as a tool to abet this match, all for the purpose of enhancing the profits of her establishment.

When the young man stays on for a year and spends lavishly in the process, the madam and Li Wa are undoubtedly greatly enriched, but after he empties his purse he is no longer welcome in the pleasure quarters. Since the young scholar has given up his ambition to take the examination and remains very attached to Li Wa, he apparently wishes to stay with her without even paying rent. When he refuses to leave, we may infer, the madam hatches a scheme to lure him out of the pleasure quarters on the pretext of visiting a public shrine to the Spirit of the Bamboo Grove, ostensibly to pray for a child. Whether willingly or under duress, Li Wa agrees to join in the scheme. In the words of the text,

After two nights [at the shrine] they returned. On the way [to Pingkang ward] they came out through Xuanyang ward. [Li Wa led the way and the young scholar] followed behind, whipping his donkey. As they arrived at the north gate of the ward Li Wa said to the young man: "In a little lane turning off east from here is my aunt's house.

May we interrupt our journey to call on her?" The young man did as she suggested. Sure enough, before they had advanced more than a hundred paces, he saw a carriage-gate and glimpsed the extent [of the courtyard inside it], which was wide and spacious.[22]

Li Wa's "aunt" then contributes to the scheme by keeping the young scholar at her place after Li Wa and the madam leaves. Indeed, she keeps him there until just before the curfew so that he will not be able to return to the Xuanyang ward after learning, as he soon will, that the madam and Li Wa are no longer at the establishment in Jingling Harness Lane in Pingkang ward and have moved to some unspecified place. In this case the curfew is used to attain a goal consistent with its original purpose, to detach a young man from the object of his infatuation. The institution is used by commoners in pursuit of profit, however, not by aristocrats to preserve some sort of Confucian morality.

After the young scholar nearly dies of hunger and illness and survives only by becoming a dirge singer, he gets a chance at almost full recovery in a different profession by winning a singing contest. The contest is held in a public location on Tianmen street located just south of the palaces and administration and halfway between the East and West markets. The public nature of this site enables a large crowd to assemble, thus offering the young man an opportunity to gain wealth and fame. But the site and the crowd also bring the event to his father's attention and allow his father to wreak vengeance on him. Here again, as at the shrine, we see both the opportunities and the risks of entry into an unwalled, public space, in which people of all origins and kinds may mix but where acts deemed unworthy of fame and fortune can also be sighted and punished. The young scholar's father beats his son nearly to death in Xingyuan, on Qujiang pond, a quiet, less populated site at the far southeastern corner of the city. Reduced once again to penury and forced to become a beggar, the young man again recovers with the help of an open gate. For it is on one wintry day while begging in the An'yi ward, adjacent to the southern border of the East market and near his old haunts, that the young scholar once again is saved. In the words of the text,

---

22   Ibid. p. 131.

Coming to the east gate of An'yi ward, he [entered it and] followed [the interior side of its] wall round to the north. In the seventh or eighth house along there was an entrance in which just the left-hand gate was open. This was where Li Wa lived.[23]

Although the young scholar has no way of knowing that Li Wa is living there, as it happens the gate is partially open, enhancing the chances that the man's pitiful cries will reach Li Wa's ears and finally win her active sympathy. We do not learn where Li Wa nurses her lover back to health and assists him in preparing for the examinations, but wherever they reside, they are finally successful in freely consummating their romance and entering elite society. The story ends with them happily living in the provincial city of Chengdu in the neighboring province of Sichuan.

Interpreting the Tale

Dudbridge has suggested that despite the fact that it is based upon a series of real events, the essential tale is "a formal, not a historical construct."[24] In his words, the elaborate Confucian fable contains an "independent narrative core, perfectly viable in its own right." And the core-story has "its own distinctive focus of attention." As Dudbridge's arguments imply, the thematic structure of the story is symmetrical and underlines a spatial order on its own which forms itself first of all upon the career of Li Wa's lover:

A young man falls from the height of social and academic distinction into moral turpitude, poverty and social disgrace; he then rises to recover step by step the academic success, public recognition and family fulfillment for which he was originally destined. The center-point is the lowest depth of the young man's fortunes: the scene in which he wanders begging through a snow-bound city of closed doors. From here on the story reverses its movement. The girl who consumed the young scholar's fortune and divided him from his father now cares and provides for him; the young man who sacrificed

---

23   Ibid. p. 161.
24   Dudbridge, *Tale*, p. 60.

orthodox success for a bohemian life with his mistress in the great city now studies and succeeds under her stern direction; the father who rejected and would have killed his son for a shameful failure in family duty now welcomes him back with the woman who first led him astray. These reversals are the very stuff of the story.[25]

Dudbridge also argues that "expressed in the simplest schematic terms, they are the movements in a formal dance between two sets of balanced and complementary characters: male and female, young and old. The gentleman of Yingyang and his father face the courtesan Li Wa and her mother." However, what Dudbridge does not explore is that, by the relative position of these characters in the world defined by the walls, the relationship between them also suggests another movement that has more to do with Chang'an, the primary story setting. Dudbridge is right to see that the movement between these characters is interpreted as a *spatial* movement—but in saying that "it begins when the son leaves his father's side to join the women; it ends when Li Wa joins him to end on the side of the men," he takes too little account of the intervening steps in the story. In fact, by the time of what he considers to be the "center-point" of the story, i.e., "the lowest depth of the young man's fortunes" or shortly before Li Wa "joins him to end on the side of the men," the most significant three-fourths of the story has unfolded. In an alternative interpretation of such a movement among characters, there is no midpoint but only a series of unbalanced relationships between the young scholar and the courtesan. Tensions are created by their separation and reseparation and released by their temporary union and reunion. The final union of the couple ends the story in an arbitrary way, but there is no guarantee that the lives of the protagonists will not continue to unfold and change.

Walls thus play a particular role in this literarily constructed space, dividing the city into two basic categories, inside and outside (see Figure 4).

On the one hand, the wall serves as a solid (yet simultaneously alluring) boundary and indicates the obvious difference between being on the inside or the outside. Once admitted into the realm behind the

---

25 Ibid.

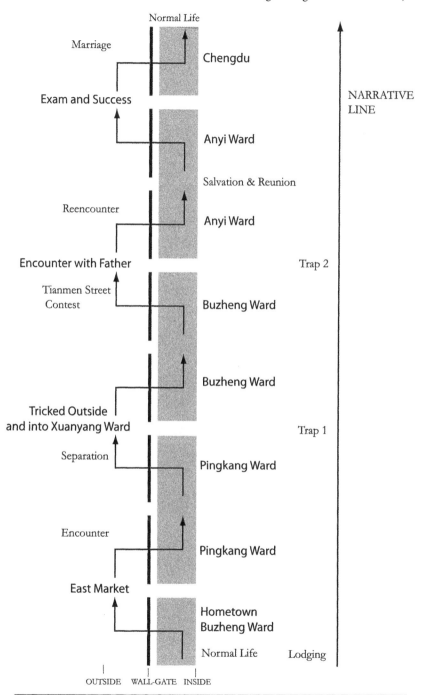

Normal Life

Marriage

Chengdu

Exam and Success   NARRATIVE
                                                             LINE

Anyi Ward

Salvation & Reunion

Reencounter

Anyi Ward

Encounter with Father   Trap 2

Tianmen Street
Contest   Buzheng Ward

Buzheng Ward

Tricked Outside
and into Xuanyang Ward   Trap 1

Separation   Pingkang Ward

Encounter   Pingkang Ward

East Market

Hometown
Buzheng Ward

Normal Life   Lodging

OUTSIDE   WALL-GATE INSIDE

Figure 4 The Pattern of the Narrative. Author's diagram.

wall of Pingkang ward and Li Was establishment and making them his "home," the young man voluntarily gave up the "normative" life: the world of civil service exams, government office, family prestige, etc. On the other hand, for that curious outsider/insider, the presence of the wall also embodied a liminal and indecisive moment that could arrive at *any* potential gateway that he might find in the residential wards. At such a moment, he may walk in or out but may thereafter find himself unable to return to where he had been. In the narrative, the still spatial relationship with a definite *interface* established between the outside and the inside is therefore replaced with a dynamic and flexible institution of *interfacing*, which emphasizes the interchangeability of life on the two sides of the wall. The two-sided, freestanding wall that presents an uninviting image is replaced by the gateways that convey an enticing message. The gateways tempt the visitor to enter into a series of adventures, in which the ordered and dull reality collapses into a fragmented, exciting dream.

In the tale and, presumably, in the lives of some residents of Chang'an, walls both separate people from different walks of life and attract some of them to cross over from one path to another. Similarly, gates enable them to move from one side of a wall to the other, but they may also be closed to keep them from moving. Such a double role of walls and gates may be easily associated with the literary versus the physical or the verbal versus the spatial. Literary works encourage imagination that "transcends" physical limits. Verbal representations tend to follow a linear movement while spatial representations (such as the carnival scenes depicted by Pieter Bruegel the Elder) may point to a commotion that is not restricted to moving in a single direction.[26] The main issue is how the literary construct which was inspired by personal adventures became tangible to contemporary readers and resonated with their spatial experience in a collective practice. If the literary must be different from the architectonic, the linear literary movement as sensed in the story must have been "translated" from a newly emerging spatial mobility that increasingly challenged the rigid order as embodied in the initial design of Chang'an.

---

26 See Sellink, *Pieter Bruegel.*

Wu Hung argues that in approaching "ancient" Chinese cities, there are usually two alternative perspectives or positions. In one view, the city is "a changing historical entity with specific causes for its birth, growth and decay. The purpose of a reconstruction is to trace this process throughout the course of its development." In the other view, the city is "the sum of all its historical fragments and is often represented by its culminating stage." In this case the observer tries to depict such an image and to interpret it according to some general cultural and ideological principles.[27]

In accord with these two views, we may find two different spatial constructs of Chang'an. The first one, embraced by the protagonists of the story, is difficult to summarize in a map or plan but relies heavily on a collage of chronological and individual experience. The second one, identified by Hansen in Bai's tale, looks more canonical; it presents a definite, overall design of the city. It reveals the ideal spatial order of the capital and is therefore frequently used as a substitute for the real city as a timeless "standard image" of Chang'an.

These two constructs intersect at particular historical moments for good reasons. The Chang'an in Seo's understanding is already a historical construct, an embodiment of a *transformed* political space at a particular historical moment: the late Tang dynasty.[28] During the city's history of 321 years, important structural changes were made in its design. For example, the symmetry of the city was broken by the construction of Daming Palace in the northeast corner in Gaozong's reign (649–683), almost a century after the initial symmetrical design of the city was drawn up by Yuwen Kai.[29] Another change occurred in 714 CE with the choice of Xingqing Ward as the location for the new Xingqing Palace, and so on.[30] Seo convinces us of the consequences of this his-

---

27 Wu Hung, *Monumentality*, p. 144. Of course, these two perspectives can coexist as in the chapters in Part I of this volume.

28 Actually the events in the tale preceded the An Lushan uprising of 755, the usual breaking point between high Tang and late Tang, but the story followed that uprising in 795 and therefore might be considered late Tang, although just barely.

29 Daxing Chang'an was designed in 582 CE. Daming Palace was formally constructed in 663 CE.

30 Steinhardt, *Chinese Imperial*, p. 102

torical process: the political pivot of Chang'an moved to the east; urban population dramatically increased and diversified (see Figure 5).

In fact, this process is reflected in the narrative of "The Tale of Li Wa," which offers an altered personal experience of urbanity. The changes in the late Tang were confirmed post facto. Tang Chang'an was the last politywide capital city with walled residential wards that were locked at night.[31]

In my view, the most important message that the walls in "The Tale of Li Wa" convey is that a structural change occurred in Chang'an in the late Tang. The profound change was embodied first of all in an enriched and personified vision of urbanity that was no longer dominated by the aristocracy.[32] Instead it was increasingly shaped by a newly rising class of scholar-bureaucrats. The creation of such a vision has long been thought, especially by Japanese scholars, to reflect a more general historical phenomenon: the movement from "ancient" to "medieval" or even from "medieval" to "modern" China.[33] Meanwhile the change is also closely linked to a contradiction between the ideal design of the city and the actual functioning of its infrastructure. The short and narrow lanes (*qu*), demarcated by the walls flanking them, were characteristic of the developing urban infrastructure of Chang'an in the eighth to ninth centuries. Many critical moments in other Tang tales, which appeared during and after the middle-Tang period, start with scenes in these lanes. For example,

> "She lives in Old Temple Lane (Gusi qu) in the Shengye Quarter, in the house just beyond the carriage gate." (*Huo Xiaoyu*)[34]

---

31 Sun and Liang, "Reading," pp. 77–82. Perhaps because the Tang was followed by a period of division in which there was no single politywide capital, the shift is sometimes dated to the Northern Song, the first dynasty with a capital (Kaifeng) that did not have ward walls, guards, and curfews. Bray, *Social Space*, p. 24.

32 To be sure, some scholars are no longer as convinced of the extent and significance of this change as they once were. See, for example, Twitchett, "Composition."

33 For an English-language introduction to the enormous Japanese scholarly literature on "medieval" or "modern" China, representing the Tokyo and Kyoto schools respectively, see Zurndorfer, *China Bibliography*, pp. 16–22.

34 Owen, *End*, p. 179.

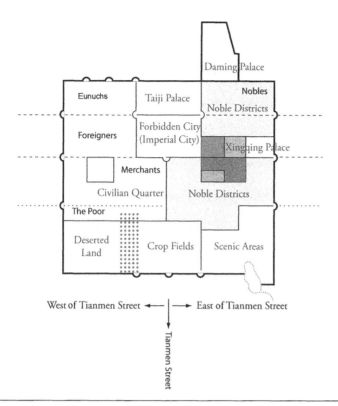

Figure 5 The Social Map of Tang Chang'an. Adapted from Seo, "Tangdai houqi,"
p. 510.

Liu Biejia from Hejian . . . arrives at the Tonghua Gate in the West
Capital [Chang'an] and sees a beautiful woman in the carriage. . . .
He thereafter follows her to her residence in the lane behind the
Zisheng Temple (Zisheng si hou qu). (*Hejian Liu Biejia*).[35]

In this sense, although Chang'an and other early Chinese cities are
often thought to have been definitively "planned," the planning actually

35   Li, *Taiping Guangji*, ch. 334.

ended at a very initial point. Addresses in Chang'an's residential wards referred only to places in relationship to gates and main streets. In the case of residential wards, "main streets" usually meant the eight streets immediately inside and outside the walls as well as the two streets that crossed in the center of the ward. It was likely that these elements, which were shared by most wards, were no more than part of the roughly "planned" city infrastructures. The remaining spaces that were extremely large, however, were unspecified and unplanned.

Smaller and shorter walls flanking the lanes within the residential wards and their subdivisions were different from the ward walls. First, with varied sizes and shapes, these walls were not the results of systematic city planning but merely by-products of more or less spontaneous construction.[36] Second, these walls were less visible than city and ward walls because the former were commonly attached to larger architectonic complexes on two sides of the lane as firewalls or sidewalls, while the ward walls were often freestanding (i.e., there were spaces between them and the four ward sections] Walls that demarcated *qu* were hidden in cramped neighborhoods, while city and ward walls boasted ample public edges that allowed people to see them from a distance. *Qu* walls therefore allowed people to live in them relatively quietly and privately, without significant outside or public interference.

The development of Chang'an after the Tianbao era (742–756) created an ambiguous individual sphere at the lowest level of the city. In the absence of a powerful ruler, control over an individual space, such as those insider-exclusive pleasure houses hidden in the lanes, became more closely tied to nuclear-family-based property rights than to government-level planning.[37] The walls flanking small streets and lanes failed to clearly define a place as an orderly space. But they well concealed private spheres from public view. The spaces within the walls were thus shielded from outsiders. The same was true of the privileged access and favored "vantage points," when visual privacy be-

---

36 Excavation of Yongning Ward revealed that a lane could be as narrow as two meters. Ma, "Tang Chang'an Cheng Anding," p. 323.

37 There is evidence that, in the late Tang period, residential wards tended to be divided into smaller lots. For example, in the early Tang individual lords who did not live in the palace commonly occupied whole wards. By the middle Tang period, many lords shared residences in the same ward. See Sun, "Sui-Tang Chang'an," pp. 185–204.

came a symbol of social dominance, and social dominance permitted visual privacy.[38]

The tale reveals that, at the time, the insider experience was purchasable—though only in an implicit and indirect way. Residence was not tightly tied to ownership any more. In the tale, even the residence of a *shang shu* (the third highest of the nine ranks among the Tang officials) was rentable (e.g., by Li Wa's "aunt"). Chang'an in the late Tang period thus harbored more mixed social identities and diversified life experiences than before. The relocation of the young scholar's and even Li Wa's domiciles to various wards suggests the general trend toward more mobility, both social and spatial. The tale thus constituted an alluring narrative that reflected the transformation of an apparently seamless and sacred city order into a labyrinthine and sybaritic maze. In turn, it offered a vision that would become a key factor in the unfolding of fresh forms of time and space. The young scholar could transcend walls both material and occupational. In another short story, "The Curly-Bearded Stranger" *(Qiuran ke zhuan)*, the talented hero could turn any part of a wall into an opening. In that case, given the hero's acrobatic skills, the point of entry was not confined to the gateway but could be almost anywhere on the wall.[39]

With problematic moral legitimacy, the "space for escape" contains an uncertainty, an ambiguous message that swings between the forbidden and the alluring. On the one hand, the secret, immoral, and excessive passion is doomed to be brief and has ultimately to be legitimized by marriage, as the end of the story reminds us. Otherwise the young scholar would have simply fallen "from the height of social and academic distinction into moral turpitude, poverty and social disgrace"— and stayed there.[40] Even when the young man is stuck by his desires at the pleasure house, his bohemian life with his mistress has to be disguised by focusing on the refined manners one expects to find only

---

38   When selecting the new site for Daming Palace, control of visibility had become a primary concern for imperial planners. See Wei Shu, *Liangjing xinji*, vol. 1, ch. 73. In the late Tang period, the restriction of building heights, which was associated with the privacy of neighborhoods, was formalized as part of the building codes. See Wang, *Tang huiyao*, p. 575.

39   Edwards, *Chinese Prose,* vol. 2,: pp. 35–44; Swatek, "Self."

40   Dudbridge, *Tale,* p. 38.

between husbands and wives. On the other hand, although the tale may not be a political fable simply "portraying contemporary society's most conspicuous new direction of development,"[41] it does reflect a general change in Chinese urban life at the time. Throughout the Tang period, the government prohibited any "removal of" or "opening on" the walls of the wards, an effort to maintain the order of society based on the integrity of the family.[42] But right after the Tang dynasty fell, the walled *fang-li* system collapsed and opened a new economic panorama in China. It was exactly in that transitional historical extended "moment," i.e., middle-to-late Tang, a time of uncertainty, that an unexpected, exotic urban experience was born.[43] This experience is also what the *chuan qi*, "transmission of the strange," a new literary genre, embodied. As Stephen Owen has written:

> The Mid-Tang saw the rise of a culture of romance, with the representation of individually chosen and socially unauthorized relationships between men and women. The rise of romance is closely related to the development of individual acts of interpretation or valuation and the demarcation of private space.[44]

At the same time, "The Tale of Li Wa" may also be said to have appeared at one of those many times and places that celebrated romantic love long before its commonly supposed origin in medieval Europe.[45]

---

41 Ibid. p. 78, disagreeing with Liu, *Tangdai xiaoshuo*, p. 105.

42 With few exceptions, no residential door was allowed to open directly to the main streets, see Wang, *Tang huiyao*, p. 1575.

43 One might say "reborn," reenacting a process seen in the Spring and Autumn and Warring States period, but the Tang order is much better documented and therefore perhaps more real than the Zhou order that served as its sometime model. Of course, by this standard, changes in the late Qing dynasty along the same lines would be even more "real" than—but not necessarily structurally different from—those of the late Zhou and late Tang.

44 Stephen Owen, "The End," p. 130. For important differences between Chinese and European "romanticism," see Chaves, "The Expression."

45 For other cases elsewhere in the world, see Goody, *Theft*, ch. 10. For later development of the theme in China well before extensive "Western" influence, see Hanan, *Falling in Love*.

Conclusion

As Ma Yau-woon put it, "the fantasy world in Tang tales, in spite of all its factual claims, is only a product of the imagination patterned after its own laws of reality."

> It offers the reader the satisfying experience of a carefully wrought mythological perception of wish-fulfillment and redeemed settlement. In this regard, fantasy comes close to the level of myth. This particular area of imagination is a challenge to the celebrated Coleridgian conception of "willing suspension of disbelief" (*Biographia Literaria* 14), as the reader is invited to share the world of sub-creation in which everything the storymaker relates is true to the laws of the sub-created cosmos and made credible with the audacity of that sub-creation.[46]

Certainly, one may argue that the literary perception of the spatial order has its own logic and thus cannot be accepted at face value as an accurate representation of actual space without further careful examination. However, this essay presumes that there is not a *given* order to space. Instead, the representation of space makes up part of the reality that will accordingly exert its influence on the development and reception of socially viable spaces. In our case, the literary interpretations of Tang ward life in tales have in fact been taken as quasi-historical representations that correspondingly helped to reshape ninth-century visions of the urban spaces of Chang'an.[47] Scholars may still have good reasons to question the accuracy and importance of these sources. However different from the intended but never tangibly rendered meanings of Chinese spatial order, the "nonfactual" reproduction of urban spaces in their pictorial or literary representation, as seen in

---

46 Ma Yau-Woon, "Fact and Fantasy," vol. 2, pp. 180–81.

47 Modern Chinese scholars generally believe that these narratives are of quasi-historical value to us today. For example, in Yang Hongnian's monograph on Chang'an and Luoyang, many references are to sources that are generally thought of as fiction, including *Taiping guangji* [Extensive records of the Taiping era], *Chaoye qianzai* [Commentary on events at court and in society), and *Youyang zazu* [Miscellaneous morsels from Youyang).

"The Tale of Li Wa," may deliver a more convincing message about how the space should be interpreted.

As Ma also concedes, such a reproduction is more than a fantasy created solely by and for the author himself. The realistic commentary at the end of the tale by the author must have been directed at intended readers, whose favor would bring the author accolades and professional advancement.[48] The tale is thus not just a passive reflection of the political or economic history of the late Tang dynasty but rather represents an emerging private view of city life, a pervasive vision of Chang'an in the eyes of its contemporaries and later generations. In the "secondary world"—to borrow from John R. R. Tolkien—that the writer and the readers nurture together, the wall thus also implies a sociological function that brought together in reality their mutual interests in a playful way.[49] The representation of space, therefore, cannot be entirely separated from the behaviors and attitudes of the people who actually inhabit it.

Works Cited

Bray, David. *Social Space and Governance in Urban China: The Danwei System from Origins to Reform.* Stanford: Stanford University Press, 2005.

Chaves, Jonathan. "The Expression of Self in the Kung-an School: Non-Romantic Individualism." Pp. 123–52 in *Expressions of Self in Chinese Literature,* Robert E. Hegel and Richard C. Hessney, eds. New York: Columbia University Press, 1985.

Dong, Jianhong. *Zhongguo gudai chengshi jiansheshi* (A History of ancient Chinese urban development). Beijing: Zhongguo jianzhu gongye chubanshe, 1986.

Dudbridge, Glen. *The Tale of Li Wa: Study and Critical Editions of a Chinese Story from the Ninth Century.* London: Ithaca, 1983.

Edwards, E. D. *Chinese Prose Literature of the T'ang Period, AD 618–906,* 2 vols. London, 1938.

Fu, Xinian, ed. *Zhongguo gudai jianzhu shi* (The history of Chinese architecture). Beijing: Zhongguo jianzhu gongye chubanshe, 2001.

---

48 Ma Yau-Woon, "Fact and Fantasy," p. 179.

49 "Secondary world" is a concept that Tolkien first articulated in his 1939 lecture and expanded upon in his *Essays Presented to Charles Williams.*

Goody, Jack. *The Theft of History.* Cambridge: Cambridge University Press, 2006.

Hanan, Patrick, trans. *Falling in Love: Stories from Ming China.* Honolulu: University of Hawai'i Press, 2006.

Hansen, Valerie. *The Open Empire: A History of China to 1600.* New York: W. W. Norton, 2000.

Koolhaas, Rem. "Exodus, or the Voluntary Prisoners of Architecture." Pp. 14–33 in *Perfect Acts of Architecture,* Terence Riley, ed. New York: Museum of Modern Art, 2001.

Li, Fang. *Taiping Guangji* (Extensive records of the Taiping era). Beijing: Zhonghua shuju, 1962.

Liu, Kairong. *Tangdai xiaoshuo yanjiu* (A study of Tang period novels), 2nd ed. Shanghai: Shangwu yinshuguan, 1955.

Ma, Dezhi. "Tang Chang'an cheng Anding fang fajue ji" (The excavation of Anding Ward, Chang'an), *Kaogu* (Archaeology), 4(1989), pp. 319–23.

Ma, Yau-Woon. "Fact and Fantasy in T'ang Tales," *Chinese Literature: Essays, Articles, Reviews (CLEAR)*, 2(1980), pp. 180–81.

Owen, Stephen. *The End of the Chinese "Middle Ages": Essays in Mid-Tang Literary Culture.* Stanford: Stanford University Press, 1996.

Sellink, Manfred, ed. *Pieter Bruegel the Elder.* Amsterdam: Sound & Vision, 2006.

Seo, Tatsuhiko. "Tangdai houqi de Chang'an yu chuanqi xiaoshuo" (Chang'an and chuanqi fictions in the late Tang period)." Pp. 509–53 in *Riben zhongqingnian xuezhe lun Zhongguo shi* (Young Japanese scholars on Chinese history), Liu Junwen, ed. Shanghai: Shanghai guji chubanshe, 1995.

Shi, Nianhai. "Tangdai Chang'an waiguocheng ji lifang de bianqiang" (The transformation of the outer city and residential wards of Chang'an), in Shi Nianhai, *Tangdai lishi dili yanjiu* (Studies of Tang historical geography). Beijing: Zhongguo shehui kexue chubanshe, 1998.

Steinhardt, Nancy Shatzman. *Chinese Imperial City Planning.* Honolulu: University of Hawai'i Press, 1990.

Su, Bai. "Sui Tang Chang'an cheng he Luoyang cheng" (Chang'an and Luoyang in the Sui-Tang periods), *Kaogu* (Archaeology), 6(1978), pp. 408–25.

Sun, Hui, and Liang Jiang. "Tang Chang'an chengshi buju yu fangli xingtai de xinjie" (Reading the urban form and layout of fang-li units of Tang Chang'an), *Chengshi guihua* (City planning review), 1(2003), pp. 77–82.

Sun, Yingang. "Sui-Tang Chang'an de wangfu yu wangzhai" (The royal highnesses' governmental offices and residences in Chang'an during the Sui-Tang periods), *Tang yanjiu* (Tang Studies), 2003, pp. 185–204.

Swatek, Catherine. "The Self in Conflict: Paradigms of Change in a T'ang Legend." Pp. 153–88 in *Expressions of Self in Chinese Literature*, Robert E. Hegel and Richard C. Hessney, eds. New York: Columbia University Press, 1985.

Tolkien, John R. R. *Essays Presented to Charles Williams*. Oxford: Oxford University Press, 1947.

Twitchett, D. C. "The Composition of the T'ang Ruling Class: New Evidence from Tunhuang." In *Perspectives on the T'ang*, Arthur Wright and Dennis Twitchett, eds., New Haven, Connecticut: Yale University Press, 1973.

Waley, Arthur. *The Life and Times of Po Chü-i*. London: George Allen and Unwin, 1949.

Wang, Fu, et al. *Tang huiyao* (Collection of Tang historical materials). Beijing: Zhonghua shuju, 1985.

Wei, Shu. *Liangjing xinji* (New accounts of two capitals). Taipei: Shijie shuju, 1963.

Wright, Arthur F. "The Cosmology of the Chinese City." Pp. 33–73 in G. William Skinner, ed., *The City in Late Imperial China*, Stanford: Stanford University Press, 1977.

Wu, Hung. *Monumentality in Early Chinese Art and Architecture*. Stanford: Stanford University Press, 1995.

———. *Transience: Chinese Experimental Art at the End of the Twentieth Century*. Chicago: University of Chicago Press, 2004.

Xiong, Victor Cunrui. *Sui-Tang Chang'an: A Study in the Urban History of Medieval China*. Ann Arbor: Center for Chinese Studies, University of Michigan, 2000.

Yang, Hongnian, "Fang nei qu" (*Qu* within the residential wards), *Sui-tang liangjing kao* (On two capitals of the Sui-Tang periods). Wuhan: Wuhan daxue chubanshe, 2000.

Zhu, Yuqi. "Sui-Tang wenxue renwu yu Chang'an fangli kongjian" (Characters in the literature of the Sui and Tang and the warded space in Chang'an city), *Tang yanjiu* (Tang Studies) 2003, pp. 85–128.

Zurndorfer, Harriet T. *China Bibliography*. Leiden: E. J. Brill, 1995.

CHAPTER FIVE

A Maze of Jurisdictional Walls

Conflict and Cooperation Among the Courts in Republican-Era Shanghai

*Tahirih V. Lee**

THE CHINESE CITY OF SHANGHAI from the mid–nineteenth century through the Japanese invasion of 1941 housed several different legal systems dominated by representatives from the several dozen foreign nationalities living there.[1] Three different municipal governments operated independently of each other in separate areas of the city. They enacted their own regulations and ran their own police forces and

---

* This chapter is part of a larger study of Shanghai's legal system during the late imperial and Republican periods. It draws from material in my book manuscript *Benchmarks* and my Ph.D. dissertation, "Law and Local Autonomy." Some of the material in this article appeared in my "Risky Business" and "The United States Court for China." For studies of the International Mixed Court, see Stephens *Order and Discipline,* Kotenev's *Shanghai: Its Mixed Court,* and *Shanghai: Its Municipality.* In Chinese see Xue, *BaFuLi* based on materials I obtained from the Shanghai Municipal Archives and made available to him. None of these studies provides a comprehensive description or analysis of the International Mixed Court let alone all of the courts in Shanghai.

---

1   For the origins of the system, see Johnson, *Shanghai.* There were members of forty-one different nationalities living in Shanghai in 1925. Zou, *Jiu Shanghai,* 81; Census Tables in *Shanghai Municipal Council Annual Report 1925.*

courts. In addition, fourteen foreign consulates operated their own courts. The jurisdictional contours of all of these courts formed a patchwork of extraordinary complexity. Looked at from another perspective, over a dozen separate court systems consisting of a total of twenty-eight courts heard criminal and civil cases. Only one of them, the United States Court for China, allowed appeals to a court outside the city. Before 1930, only two British courts, two American courts, and seven Chinese courts (known as *shenpanting*) were part of the same court system. The territorial jurisdictions of several courts actually stretched far beyond the city's boundaries,[2] but at the same time they were formally restricted to certain districts within the city and, within those districts, to litigants of certain nationalities.[3]

My aim in exploring this city's legal landscape is to determine how these multiple legal systems interacted both in theory and in fact. Did they compete with and undermine one another as one might reasonably expect they would, or did they on balance collaborate with and strengthen one another? To answer this question, I will look at several kinds of borders among these legal systems (geographical, legal, national, and cultural) and examine how they were managed.

In describing the courts that operated in Shanghai in the late nineteenth and early twentieth centuries, I shall begin with the class of mixed courts. They were the most controversial and, taken together, they tried the largest number of cases. They were the International Mixed Court, founded in 1864, the French Mixed Court, founded in 1869, and the Chinese, British, and French police courts. I shall then turn to the purely foreign courts that were run principally by the consulates stationed in the city. Finally, I shall describe the Chinese courts that operated in Shanghai. Having laid out the three types of courts separately, I will then focus on their interrelationships, looking at the major barriers to cooperation and then at the most common forms of cooperation. My conclusion is that the borders, or putative "walls,"

---

2   FO 656/131, Memorandum on the rendition of parties to a case as between the Courts inside and outside the International Settlement, Shanghai, by Handley-Derry, copy to British Assessor Garstin, May 1913, 2.

3   Only the "Chinese Chief Authority" could punish unrepresented foreigners for breach of the Land Regulations. See the 1845 version of the Land Regulations (*tudi zhangcheng*), text in *Shanghai gonggong zujie zhidu*, pp. 200–13, article 8.

among the polyglot courts of Shanghai produced not only complexity and tensions but also, and on balance more importantly, cooperation and efficiency in the administration of the law. Once again, walls, in this case virtual ones, erected to attain certain purposes, including the protection of foreign interests and an evolving social order in China, actually served other purposes as well, including the mixing of Chinese and foreign concepts and practices of jurisprudence and the conduct of revolutionary politics oriented toward making radical changes in the social order. Whether those walls resulted in equal justice for the Chinese and foreign residents of the city is another and larger question requiring further research.[4]

The Mixed Courts

Where for two centuries there had been but one court, the Qing county magistrate sitting in his official quarters (*yamen*), twenty-seven more courts sprang up in Shanghai over a period of seventy years, from 1843 to 1913. It happened in two waves. First, foreigners set up sixteen courts, including fourteen consular courts and two "mixed" courts, in the 1840s through the 1880s. Then the Chinese established ten other courts from 1905 through 1913 (when the United States also established its court, making the total eleven). Though the courts in the first wave were dominated by foreigners, and those in the second wave—with the exception of the United States Court for China—were more under Chinese control, the foreigners in the first wave and the Chinese in the second shared a common approach to defining the courts' procedures and jurisdictions. This approach was a hybrid that combined foreign and Chinese legal traits in a strikingly local way.

At that time, "local" meant that all of these courts bore the stamp of a political system, extraterritoriality, that was uniquely adapted to polyglot Shanghai. The century between 1844 and 1943 was known in English as the period of "extraterritoriality" and in Chinese it became known as the age of "unequal treaties." The term "extraterritoriality" was drawn from Britain's legal lexicon and fittingly so. The system was imposed by the British, the most powerful empire in the nineteenth

---

4   For studies of justice in the Nanjing decade, see Wakeman, *Policing*; Kirby, "Chinese Party-State."

century, and resulted both from and in conflicts over jurisdiction between the British and Chinese that persisted throughout the century.[5]
Chinese efforts to block the British import of opium into China had
led to a military crisis in the 1840s. In the wake of the British victory,
representatives of fourteen foreign governments extracted the Qing
state's permission to move to Shanghai and set up their own settlements and their own courts. In 1841 Lord Palmerston's gunboats, followed two decades later by British, French, and American forces defending Shanghai from attack by the Taipings,[6] paved the way for Consul G. Balfour in 1864 to conclude an agreement with the Qing that
established a tribunal in which foreign consuls would join with Chinese judges in cases involving foreign interests. The International
Mixed Court of Shanghai was thus born. Along with the French Mixed
Court established five years later, it served as a linchpin of the whole
system of extraterritoriality. Although envisioned as a compromise between Chinese and Western legal systems, these two courts actually
allowed foreigners to apply their own laws to Chinese subjects so long
as a Chinese judge could be cajoled into agreement.[7]

The Chinese authorities in Beijing had agreed to the plan during a
period of weakness while confronting the Taiping rebellion. In an effort to win foreign support or at least neutrality, the Qing accepted the
need for innovation and expressed willingness to experiment with
mechanisms for cooperation with foreign governments. They even
agreed to name the International Mixed Court the "joint investigation
bureau (*Huishen yamen*), using the same term (*yamen*) as that for

---

5   Li, *Abolition*, pp. 1–2. For the rather complex cultural and political background of this
    system, see Edwards, "Ch'ing Legal Jurisdiction."

6   For a British view of this process, see Selby, *Paper Dragon*, pp. 11–87, 109–44, 146. For
    an account in English depicting the first stage of this conflict from a Chinese perspec-
    tive, see Waley, *Opium War*. For a recent, critical view of British imperialism, see Hevia,
    English Lessons, esp. ch. 3.

7   For an early discussion of tensions in the system, see "Zongli Yamen Document"; for
    further information on the functioning of the system, see "Sifabu duiyi"; *Shanghai xian-
    hua*, p. 8, Memorandum, Appendix A; *Yangkingpang* rules, p. 1. For a general analysis
    of Qing and British views of sovereignty in the nineteenth century, see Liu, *Clash of
    Empires*, chs. 3–4.

other Qing offices, including the county magistrate."[8] While the institution reflected local conditions, it involved a practice that recurred elsewhere in the British-dominated world. For example, a decade later a similar kind of court was established by the British in Egypt.[9]

The court was "joint" in the sense that in each trial, a Chinese judge presided alongside a judge of one of the nationalities whose government had secured extraterritorial privileges in China.[10] Chinese and British judges and litigants all made selective use of various Chinese and British legal procedures. Chinese procedures included the use of the same summonses and warrants used by county magistrates and their delivery, at least until 1905, by the existing Chinese yamen runners. Anglo-American procedures included the use by litigants of lawyers to argue their cases (but not the empanelling of juries that only the British practiced in China).[11] Another mixed feature of the court was that attorneys from fourteen different countries represented clients there of over forty different nationalities.

Although there was a Qing tradition of allowing foreigners to manage their own legal affairs in China, it had arguably been hundreds of years (back to the Yuan dynasty) since true foreigners had been allowed to apply their own laws to the Chinese population.[12] What began in the nineteenth-century treaties as a Chinese imperial delegation of authority over their own subjects to foreign ministers, resulted in something quite different: the International Mixed Court in which those foreign officials exercised authority over hundreds of thousands of Chinese.[13] Much of this expansion of the foreigners' juridical authority under the treaties was accomplished by keeping the mixed courts independent from Chinese review and by introducing foreign con-

---

8   See definitions in Giles, *Chinese-English*, pp. 644, 829. The bureau was also called the *Huishen gongtang*, "joint investigation room."

9   See Hoyle, *Mixed Courts*.

10 Gundry, "Status," p. 53.

11 *Shen bao*, Jan. 11, 1874, pp. 2–3; Feb. 15, 1874, p. 2; Feb. 20, 1874, p. 2; *Huayang susong lian huibian*, pp. 710–19.

12 For the Qing, see Fletcher, "Heyday"; for the Yuan, see Fang and Des Forges, "Were Chinese Rulers," pp. 124–26.

13 See Shanghai Municipal Police files, file 7245, July 19, 1926; Keeton, *Development*, Vol. I, pp. 370, 379; Kotenev, *Mixed*, pp. 118, 122, 125, 157–58, 162–63. See also Edwards, "Ch'ing Legal Jurisdiction," for a general discussion.

cepts of law, such as the category of "civil" cases, which were not explicitly recognized as such in Chinese law. Instead they were generally considered "minor" cases not subject to appeal to higher levels of the judicial system.[14]

The foreign judges at the International Mixed Court also did what they could to maximize the independence of the court from the Chinese administration. One way was to take advantage of the Qing conception of jurisdiction based on the level of severity of punishments.[15] This approach, which could be termed "penal jurisdiction," divided lower courts from higher-level courts by appraising the seriousness of the case before trial. If the defendant was accused of an act that, under the Qing Code, warranted anything less than the most severe degrees of banishment or death, the case was considered "minor" and could be handled in the first instance by the lowest level court.[16] If the case involved a charge or allegation that, if proved, would warrant the least severe punishments, such as time in the cangue—a local version of the stocks—or working off a debt through hard labor, then the case was considered too minor for appeal. Such cases concerned mainly disputes over property and inheritances, thus approaching what in the West were called "civil cases."[17]

The Chinese authorities in Shanghai, including the Shanghai district magistrate who ran the lowest-level Chinese official court in Shanghai, considered the International Mixed Court to be lower than their own courts, and therefore restricted to trying only "minor" cases. This Chinese view of the International Mixed Court's status, ironically,

---

14   See Huang, "Codified Law," pp. 142–86; Allee, "Code," pp. 122–41; and Jin, "Qing Civil," p. 82.

15   For an English translation of the text of Article 1 of the Qing Code, specifying twenty degrees of punishment, see Jones, *Great Qing Code*, pp. 33–34. For a condensed discussion of the provisions for these punishments, see MacCormack, *Traditional*. Mark Allee found in his study of yamen records in nineteenth-century Taiwan that, in theory, appeal was to be permitted only for "serious" cases, but, in practice, appeals were accepted as well in minor cases. Review, however, was limited to matters of procedure. See Allee, *Law*, pp. 63, 107, 142–44. For an argument emphasizing the difference between Chinese "small matters" and Western "civil matters," see Bourgon, "Rights," pp. 91–93.

16   FO 656/116, letter from Joseph Hertz, Apr. 30, 1908; FO 656/131, Memorandum, May 1913, p. 13, Appendix A, pp. 1–3.

17   See, for example, the case of Mrs. Zhou née Xu, Allee, *Law*, pp. 137–44.

helped to free it from the district magistrate's review, by excluding it from the national appeals system.[18] Foreign judges at the International Mixed Court no doubt also actively discouraged the county magistrate from taking the initiative in pressing for review of the Mixed Court's cases by cultivating good relations with him and with the Shanghai prefect, the magistrate's immediate superior.

Further reinforcing its freedom from appellate review was the Mixed Court's openness to handling cases involving matters that did not call for severe punishments under the Qing Code, such as commercial disputes, traffic violations, and a panoply of municipal regulations enacted by the Shanghai Municipal Council. The International Mixed Court used the European term "civil cases" to categorize these lawsuits,[19] a term with no precise counterpart in the Qing judicial system. Applying the foreign term to some of the court's cases only strengthened the impression that the court's work was separate from that of Chinese courts.

Although civil cases made up only a small fraction of the International Mixed Court's caseload, the court adopted several measures to encourage the bringing of these cases. In the 1900s and 1910s it lowered the fees required of litigants and agreed to consider cases of all sizes involving almost all subjects. Such flexibility and economy resulted in increased numbers of lawsuits. The International Mixed Court also favored plaintiffs by disposing quickly of cases in general and by adopting summary processes for landlord-tenant disputes. As a consequence, this court managed the largest number of civil cases of any Shanghai court and proved unable to handle all the commercial disputes that were brought to its attention. A comparison of the yearly figures of "Chinese civil suits awaiting first hearing" with the growing number of cases actually tried reveals a rising backlog of Chinese cases at the court over time.[20] The court hired more judges to hear these

---

18   FO 656/116, letter from Joseph Hertz, Apr. 30, 1908; FO 656/131, Memorandum, May 1913, p. 13, Appendix A, pp. 1–3.

19   Keeton, *Development*, Vol. I, p. 348; Kotenev, *Mixed*, pp. 56, 78–79.

20   Between 1913 and 1926, Chinese litigation at the court held steady at about 1,700 cases filed per month, for an annual total of about 20,400 lawsuits. More Chinese than foreigners sued at the International Mixed Court, but as a percentage of their respective populations in the International Settlement, or in Shanghai as a whole, fewer Chinese

cases, extended its Chinese civil sessions into the wee hours of the morning and into Saturdays, and appealed to the public to support funding for more courtrooms.[21] The International Mixed Court was a large court that had a big impact on the city. During its lifetime, it processed about a million cases, making it Shanghai's—perhaps the world's—busiest court.[22] It had a broad jurisdiction, covering all residents of the International Settlement, including foreigners without consular representation in Shanghai. Thus it was able to exercise authority over about 98 percent of the International Settlement's diverse population. According to the census, between 1860 and 1940, this population hailed from twenty-one different provinces of China and fifty-eight foreign countries.[23]

Although the International Mixed Court had broad jurisdiction over persons, it was supposed to have restricted jurisdiction over territory, confined as it was by law to the International Settlement (see Map 1).[24] The Settlement constituted, during much of this period, only about one-quarter of Shanghai's urban space and roughly one-third of its population[25] (see Map 2). As we have seen, the court was supposed to hear only cases that, when guilt was proven, would incur only minor punishments (such as imprisonment, light beatings, and fines) under the Qing Code. It was forbidden to entertain cases that might result in heavy physical punishment and the death penalty.[26]

Despite these restrictions, the foreign judges of the court worked to expand the jurisdiction of the court beyond its original boundaries. In addition to exercising the raw political, economic, and military power

---

brought suit. The total annual criminal caseload for the court in this period ranged from 38,307 cases in 1919 to 103,932 in 1926. These figures are taken from *Shanghai Municipal Council Annual Report* (1912–1926), "Mixed Court" sections.

21   See *Annual Report*, "Mixed Court" sections, 1921–1925.

22   For data concerning the Mixed Court's caseload, see *Municipal Gazette*; *Annual Reports 1921; 1918–1919*, pp. 57A–58A, pp. 67A–68A; *1922*, p. 70A; *1923*, p. 39; *1924*, pp. 45, 47; *1925*, pp. 39–41; Johnstone, *Administration* p. 135.

23   Zou, *Jiu Shanghai*, p. 81.

24   *Yangkingpang huishen zhangcheng* rules in *Shanghai gonggong zujie zhidu*, pp. 215–16, and Memorandum, p. 1.

25   See Zou, *Jiu Shanghai*, Tables 1 and 22.

26   See FO 656/116, letter from Joseph Herz, Apr. 30, 1908; see also FO 656/131, Memorandum, May 1913, p. 13, Appendix A, pp. 1–3.

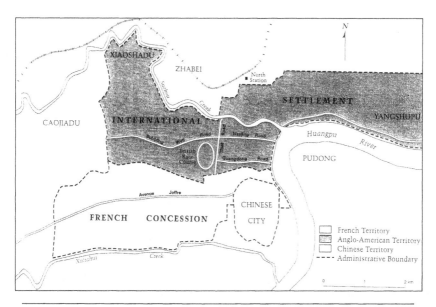

Map 1 Treaty port Shanghai, 1919. Adapted from Emily Honig, *Sisters and Strangers.*

they possessed, they found ingenious ways to expand the court's territorial and penal jurisdictions. They extended its reach beyond the International Settlement by maintaining close ties with the Shanghai intendant (*daotai*) for Jiangsu province, his immediate inferior the Shanghai county magistrate, and the Chinese commissioner for foreign affairs in Shanghai, all of whom presided in the older, Chinese-run section of the city, known as Nanshi (lit., South Market). Many of the people who used the court and whose lives and fortunes were influenced by its decisions actually lived outside the International Settlement. Litigants, third parties, and Chinese officials in East China and from as far away as the southwestern province of Yunnan,[27] and the southern ports of Macao and Hong Kong recognized or obeyed its judgments.[28] The judges did not let the court's officially small penal jurisdiction, covering only "minor" cases, deter them from accepting every imaginable claim or charge, including homicide cases.

In 1869, five years after the International Mixed Court was established, and in the very year in which a new Qing Foreign Office (the *Zongli yamen*) approved a code of rules for the court, the French Consul in Shanghai signed an agreement with the Chinese mayor of Shanghai that established a French Mixed Court, in a separate section of the city known as the French Concession. This section was adjacent to the International Settlement and because of its lovely, winding tree-lined roads and gracious houses, was considered a highly desirable place to live. The French authorities there set up a small government and police force to run the Concession, but the reputation of these forces, in contrast to those of the International Settlement, was one of laxity.[29] Because of this, the Chinese Communist Party found the French Conces-

27   FO 656/137, letter from Brunner, Mond & Co, Mar. 1, 1916.
28   See FO 656/118, letter from Ne Shu Yuen native bank, Oct. 12, 1909; FO 656/154, petition of several Hong Kong creditors, May 1910. The accountant of Chun Shing Cheong had fled to Shanghai with a large fraction of the firm's assets.
29   A French court of appeals declared that the French Settlement was not precisely the same as French territory, and therefore French law could not be strictly imposed even on French citizens there, see Chan, *Merchants, Mandarins*, pp. 119–32; and Citizens' League, *Syllabus, in toto*.

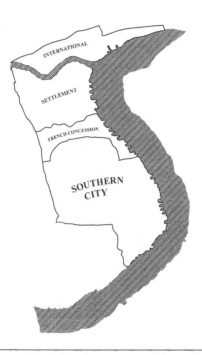

Map 2 Schematic Map of Shanghai Showing Actual Size of the Chinese City in 1895. Photograph courtesy of Wei Shaochang. Taken from "Xinzeng." Source: Des Forges, *Mediasphere*, p. 53.

sion safe enough to hold their first plenary meeting there in July 1921,[30] and the outlawed Green Gang operated freely there in the late 1920s.[31]

With a Chinese judge and a French consular official presiding together on its bench, the French Mixed Court tried roughly two-fifths of the number of civil cases tried by the International Mixed Court.[32] The French Mixed Court's jurisdiction was similar to that of its counterpart in the International Settlement, providing for adjudication of any cases that arose in the French Concession, including those involving Chinese residents. The court relied on the French Concession's own police force, and it enforced the laws of the French Municipal Council. It remained independent from the International Mixed Court, just as the French Municipal Council and police remained independent from their equivalents in the International Settlement. So distinct were the neighboring International Settlement and French Concession that they kept separate population statistics. For example, they reported in 1932 that foreigners of forty-four nationalities were residing in the International Settlement while members of thirty-three nationalities were living in the French Concession.[33]

In 1914, the court moved to a new building in the French consular compound. It remained there until 1931 when it was taken over by the Guomindang-led Republic based in Nanjing and was renamed the Second Special District Court.[34] During both its French and Chinese phases, its civil division tried a rich variety of debt and contract disputes among Chinese parties.[35]

A third type of hybrid court in Shanghai was the police courts. The Chinese police, the British police, and the French police each operated their own courts somewhat independently of the city's various governments. Chinese judges presided alongside foreign judges at these purely criminal courts. The accused were of various nationalities, but

---

30 See the reference in Spence, *Search*, p. 322.

31 See Martin, "Pact," pp. 240–66.

32 This number is my estimate based on the ratios of reported cases in the *Shen bao* and on published caseload statistics from the two courts after 1930. See reports of court sessions, *Shen bao*, Jan.–Dec. 1914.

33 Census Tables in *Annual Report 1925*.

34 See *Shanghai Shi Nianjian* [Annual of Shanghai], "Sifa" [judicial] section at 12.

35 Ibid.

most were Chinese. The police forces that served these courts were also multinational. The largest police force in Shanghai, the Shanghai Municipal Police, employed British and Americans in clerical, intelligence, and leadership positions, and recruited Chinese, Japanese, White Russians, and Sikhs into its rank and file.[36] Through these courts, the British and American municipal government in the International Settlement, the principal foreign district of Shanghai, took the initiative in the incarceration or deportation of "troublemakers." The Shanghai Municipal Council, comprised of Britons and Americans,[37] and its strong arm, the British-dominated Municipal Police, established a monopoly over the prosecution of both Chinese and foreigners in the International Settlement.[38]

The establishment of the two mixed courts and the police courts showed innovation and adaptation to the rapid growth of a multinational population in Shanghai and a local economy rooted in international trade and finance. To be sure, these courts had been forced on Shanghai by foreigners. Foreigners established them and operated them, and even though Chinese collaborated in both their establishment and operation,[39] the courts clearly allowed foreigners to exercise a degree of control over parts of Shanghai, especially its Chinese population, that they could not otherwise have maintained for as long as they did. But regardless of whose interests predominated among the complex collection of interests they served, these courts arose to meet a unique set of local needs, stemming from rapid economic development and a highly multinational population. They reflected in their own composition, jurisdiction, and procedures the multinational

---

36 For data on the growth of the Municipal Police, see Monthly Police Reports in *Municipal Gazette*. For a comprehensive study of the Shanghai Municipal Police, see Wakeman, *Policing Shanghai*.

37 See Henriot, *Shanghai*.

38 For an illustration of the power exercised by the Council, see *Municipal Gazette*, 7/5/19, p. 216, in which the Municipal Council reportedly urged the Consular Body to agree that "no power is more essential than the power of immediate action by the Council, without recourse to any other Authority." See also *Municipal Gazette*, 9/20/23, p. 334 and 11/22/23, p. 400, stating that the Municipal Police was the entity providing evidence essential to criminal convictions to the Mixed Court.

39 For the complexity of collaboration in the related context of Sino-Japanese relations, see Brook, *Collaboration*.

character of the city, and this hybrid form was mirrored to some extent even in the purely foreign courts by the turn of the twentieth century. Their prodigious caseloads—five million cases by my best estimate for the International Mixed Court alone, including its years between 1927 and 1941 when it served as the First Special District Court under Chinese control—provide further evidence of their ability to function effectively, not just for the police, who prosecuted cases there, but also for the Chinese civil litigants who initiated lawsuits there.

As further evidence of their high status and appeal in Chinese eyes, they introduced to Shanghai three characteristics of courts that were adopted by each of the Chinese courts founded in the second wave. These characteristics were the civil-criminal distinction, the use of lawyers in the courtroom, and the reliance on a professional police force. Their influence on the foreign and Chinese courts, described below, suggests that the mixed courts served the interests of and received cooperation from a wide range of the populace.

Wholly Foreign Courts

In the consular courts, consuls-general presided as judges in their consulates over cases in which at least the defendants were their own nationals. Their home governments expected them to apply the laws of their respective countries.[40] The consular court system never became very large or well organized. From 1921 to 1925, for example, the consular courts altogether tried only about 0.5 percent of the cases that the International Mixed Court did.[41] Although sixteen countries (Belgium, Brazil, Britain, Denmark, France, Italy, Japan, Mexico, the Netherlands, Norway, Peru, Portugal, Spain, Sweden, Switzerland, and the United States) signed treaties with China obtaining immunity for their nationals from prosecution in Chinese courts according to Chinese law,[42] only the British, American, Japanese, and French appear

---

40   See Piggot, *Extraterritoriality*, p. 61 (stating that British citizens were subject first to British law applied in the form of consular jurisdiction).

41   See statistics in Annual Report, pp. 55A, 66A (1921), pp. 68A, 73A (1922), pp. 37, 42 (1923), pp. 59–60 (1924), p. 55 (125), p. 54 (1926); Monthly Police Reports in the *Municipal Gazette*, 1924–1925.

42   Li, *Abolition*, p. 2.

to have heard cases in their consulates on a regular basis,[43] and only the British and American consular courts did not use the International Mixed Court to try cases involving their nationals. The other consular courts that did use the Mixed Court in this way violated the rules in the 1920s by sending vice-consuls to preside in the Mixed Court courtroom as sole judges over cases involving their nationals.

The British system of extraterritorial courts was the most developed of its kind in Shanghai. The British government set up over its consular court a British Supreme Court in the city with its own code of regulations. It empanelled juries for both criminal and civil trials.[44]

In 1906 the U.S. Congress founded a federal court in Shanghai called "The United States Court for China."[45] It was modeled on the British Supreme Court but, unlike that court, it never adopted the jury system.[46] Congress gave it appellate jurisdiction over the American consular court and original jurisdiction over all of the most serious types of cases that arose in Shanghai involving American defendants. The Philippines also came to be included in its jurisdiction as well.[47] This court was part of the Ninth Circuit of the United States Federal Court of Appeals, and it submitted several cases originating in China to the U.S. Supreme Court.[48]

One final legal tribunal that was purely foreign was the Court of Consuls, which was organized by all the consuls-general posted in Shanghai when the International Mixed Court was dismantled in 1927. It operated well into 1940, on the eve of the Japanese takeover of the city. In this court, a bench of three consuls tried all cases in which for-

---

43 All three maintained their own prison facilities. *Gazette*, 11/21/18, p. 366. For prisons in general, see Dikotter, *Crime*.

44 For the rules of the court that provided for juries, see British Jurisdiction in China, "China Rules, 1905," Rules 26–30, pp. 17–18.

45 Act of June 30, 1906, c. 3934, 34 Stat. pt. I, p. 814 (U.S. Comp. St. Supp. 1907, 797).

46 See "United States Court for China," 65th Cong. 55 (1917), pp. 7–12, 16.

47 For a case brought in the United States Court for China against a Filipino, see "United States v. Juvenile Offender," p. 380. The American consular court also exercised jurisdiction over Filipino defendants. See, e.g., letter of complaint for uncollected rent, E. D. Sassoon & Co.

48 For the intention of Congress that the United States Court for China be a part of the Ninth Circuit, see Act of June 30, 1906, ch. 3934, Section 3, 34 Stat. pp. 814, 815. Lee, "United States Court."

eigners sued the Municipal Council.[49] The proceedings could be quite formal, with attorneys on both sides filing briefs of dozens of pages citing local ordinances and the court's own precedents,[50] and with a special master appointed by the court to hear the evidence, which might be presented in several hearings for just that purpose.[51] The court issued written judgments that included the basic facts, the court's decision, and a lengthy exposition of the reasoning behind it.[52]

Despite their relatively small caseloads, the consular courts and the two appellate courts, the British Supreme Court and the United States Court for China, played crucial roles in further insuring foreign privileges in China. They permitted British subjects to sue Chinese before a British judge, and prevented Chinese plaintiffs from suing British subjects before a Chinese judge. That is, all foreigners had to be sued in their consular courts before a judge of their nationality, while Chinese who lived in the International Settlement or the French Concession had to be sued in the mixed courts, where a judge of the foreign plaintiff's nationality was allowed to decide the case alongside his Chinese counterpart, who was constrained to be compliant.

By requiring foreigners to be tried before foreign judges and Chinese before a mixed bench of both Chinese and foreign judges, the foreign courts of Shanghai, in tandem with the mixed courts, delivered a greater advantage to non-Chinese than to Chinese even on Chinese soil. And yet this obvious inequality was qualified by an important irony. Over time, at least some of the foreign courts became less foreign by taking on some of the characteristics of the local Chinese system of justice. Judges came to mediate cases instead of deciding them outright on the basis of legal statutes. Unlike in Britain and in the United States, juries generally played no role in the foreign courts (the British Supreme Court in Shanghai remained an exception). Judges in the foreign courts, like those in the mixed courts, sometimes paid little

---

49 See Feetham, *Great Britain*, p. 15. For a comprehensive and path-breaking study of the Shanghai Municipal Council, see Henriot, *Shanghai*.

50 Michael Storchilo vs. Shanghai Municipal Council, in the Court of Consuls at Shanghai, (1940), microformed on Microcopy F167, Record Group 84, Roll No. 3, frames 221–83. See Shanghai Municipal Council. "Letter."

51 Ibid., frame 210.

52 Ibid., frames 213–20.

heed to substantive law when reaching their decisions, instead applying local norms. Jurisdictional boundaries in Shanghai conformed completely to those set by the system of extraterritoriality, rather than those stipulated by the court systems in the foreign judges' and litigants' home countries. From this we can suggest that the Shanghai legal environment exerted an influence upon its foreign courts and helped to shape them, along with courts where only Chinese judges presided, into a workable and cohesive whole.

Chinese Courts

Between 1905 and 1933 the Chinese in Shanghai initiated a second wave of courts modeled in part on the foreign and mixed courts in the city.[53] The new Chinese courts adopted three characteristics of the International Mixed Court that had been borrowed from the West: the distinction between criminal and civil cases, the use of lawyers in the courtroom,[54] and the reliance on a professional police force.[55]

In 1905 a new style of Chinese local government called the Shanghai City Council[56] set up a court called the *caipansuo* to try both criminal and civil cases arising in the Chinese sections of the city. The council funded the court and staffed its six branches with locally elected judges. The court heard a little over 1,700 cases a year until it was dissolved in 1912 along with the Qing dynasty.

In 1912, under the Republic, yet another form of Chinese municipal government set up new-style courts in the same section of the city as

---

53   See, e.g., *Municipal Gazette*, 4/9/20, p. 160, documenting a proposal, backed by Chinese and foreigners in the Settlement in April 1920, calling for the replacement of the Mixed Court by a Shanghai subdistrict court. See also, e.g., file 179.4.2, "Qian Jiangsu jiaosheshu shouhui gongxie gexiang wenjian," pp. 1–41, Shanghai Municipal Archives, documenting dozens of letters and telegrams from the Shanghai General Chamber of Commerce to the Commissioner for Foreign Affairs, urging him to pressure the Shanghai consuls into surrendering control over the Mixed Court's operations.

54   "Faquan taolun," *Falu zhoukan*.

55   Shanghai Municipal Police files, IO Dossiers, file 7245, May 14, 1935 (documenting the Municipal Police's participation in the Chinese courts, which lasted until 1936).

56   For the new Shanghai City Council, see Elvin, "Administration," pp. 239–62, especially p. 246.

the magistrate's *yamen.* This type of court was called the *shenpanting,*[57] after the Japanese name for a German-style judicial body. The jurisdictional boundary between the *yamen* and the *shenpanting* was unclear.[58] The *shenpanting* performed the same judicial functions as the yamen court, and, like it, was under the authority of the Ministry of Justice and bound to follow Chinese national substantive and procedural laws.[59] But the *shenpanting* was more specialized and foreign in style. For example, it had both a civil and a criminal section. Local officials operated seven *shenpanting,* including one in the Chinese "old city" in the southern part of Shanghai, until 1914 when they merged the seven into one. In 1927, the Guomindang government established in Nanjing renamed this court the "District Court" and reorganized it to include three civil courts and three criminal courts.[60] It gave to it the same status as other basic-level courts across China at the *xian* or county level.[61]

The Chinese of Shanghai who used the mixed courts, including lawyers who represented clients there, backed efforts to transfer the court into local Chinese hands.[62] Their hopes for a Chinese local court that continued the proplaintiff (i.e., swift) procedure of the International Mixed Court came to fruition between 1927 and 1930 with the reincarnation of the court in the form of the Shanghai Provisional Court.[63] The court was further reconstituted in 1930 to fit within the new Guomindang court system and it was renamed the "First Special District Court." Under the new name, the court continued to inspire

---

57 Ibid., pp. 252–53.
58 For information regarding the variety of cases the central government allowed the *yamen* to try, see *China Yearbook,* pp. 760–61.
59 Interviews with members of the Shanghai *faxueyuan* and the Shanghai *fazhengxueyuan* alumni associations, Aug. 11–12, 1990, Shanghai.
60 *Shanghai shi tongji,* sifa section, pp. 3–5.
61 See "Zanzhuben Tongji Zhige Renji Jiguan Yilan Biao," in *Shanghai shi tongji,* unnumbered page at front, and tables 1, 5, 6, 19 in Sifa (Judicial Administration) section, 1, 3, 4, 13; Bhatia and Tan, eds, *Legal,* p. 146. Trial-level courts typically are those that receive lawsuits that have yet to be tried and that perform, or assist in performing, the gathering and evaluating of evidence.
62 See, for example, "Ex-Minister Tung Kang's Opinion," pp. 1–3; Chan, *Concessions.*
63 See Johnstone, *Administration,* p. 138. See also FO 656/205, Shanghai Bar Association Report, Mar. 24, 1930.

the melding of Chinese and foreign procedure in Shanghai, serving as the model for the new Shanghai District Court, which had replaced the *shenpanting* in 1927. At about the same time, the French Mixed Court was renamed the Second Special District Court (*difang fayuan*).[64] Both mixed courts were thus drawn into the national Chinese court system, where they continued to operate until 1943. In that year, Wang Jingwei, head of the Reformed Republic of China based in Nanjing that collaborated with the Japanese, abolished them, along with the foreign courts in Shanghai. It was left to the national governments who had signed the "unequal treaties" with China, however, officially to disband the entire system in which all of the new courts of Shanghai in the last century had originated. This they did on January 11, 1943, a belated foreign acceptance of the Republic of China's effort to abolish extraterritorial rights more than thirteen years earlier and a pragmatic recognition of the loss of Euro-American control over the China coast.[65]

Competition or Cooperation?

Competition

Distinctions among the various courts in Shanghai impeded the achievement of a fully integrated, smooth-running system. Conflict arose from competition among the many officials stationed in Shanghai from various parts of the world, and from the juxtaposition of so many different jurisdictions and approaches to law in such a small territory. Authority in Shanghai was splintered, and so it was too in the International Mixed Court. Various foreign judges competed for control of the court's finances, record-keeping, and police force. They jockeyed for positions of power at the court, trying to exercise greater authority than their colleagues over decisions such as who would hear which cases.[66] They cooperated mainly to try to find ways to minimize the power of the Chinese judge.[67] For example, aided by the Municipal Council, the foreign judges at the International Mixed Court used an

---

64 Shanghai Dengyi.
65 Fishel, *End of Extraterritoriality*, pp. 1–2.
66 See *Municipal Gazette*, 1/10/18, p. 16; 1/24/18, 31; 2/28/18, p. 56.
67 See, e.g., FO 656/131, Apr. 1, 1913; FO 656/131, May 19, 1913; FO 656/126, Aug. 19, 1912.

imperial edict issued in 1905 that they interpreted as a threat to the
existence of the court as a pretext to replace the existing Chinese judge
with one more acceptable to them and to replace Chinese runners with
the Shanghai Municipal Police.[68]

Conflict among foreigners for authority at the court stemmed in
part from a tension between those who were employed by their home
governments and those who were employed by the Shanghai Municipal Council. Another fault line among the foreigners at the court was
the rift between the "major" and "minor" treaty powers. Prior to World
War I, the "major powers" were Britain, the United States, and Germany, and all the others were considered by them to fall in the "minor"
category.[69] The British, American, and German judges at the International Mixed Court accorded themselves privileges and power that
they denied to judges of other nationalities, such as the right to sit in
cases involving nationalities other than their own, or nationalities not
represented by one of the treaty signatories.[70] Consular officials from
"minor powers" produced the most protests against the performance
of the Municipal Police and the International Mixed Court.

Representatives from the "major powers" also competed among
themselves.[71] After World War I, when Germany lost its extraterritorial
privileges, it also lost its right to send a judge to preside over cases at
the International Mixed Court. British and Americans thereafter consolidated their control over the court. More precisely, British subjects,
with the help of Americans, Germans, Japanese, and Chinese, effectively ran the Court.[72]

One dimension of the competition was over legal models across the
courts of Shanghai. The British and Americans touted their model,
which was adversarial, decentralized, and relied on judge or jury-made

68   Shanghai Municipal Council, "Letter."
69   *Huayang susong li'an huibian*, p. 713; FO 656/131, Nov. 13, 1913.
70   Ibid., p. 713; FO 656/131, resolution signed by British, American, and German Assessors,
     Nov. 13, 1913.
71   See, e.g., FO 656/118, reporting the disproportionate hours assessors from different na-
     tionalities spent on the bench.
72   Mixed Court Monthly Reports in the *Municipal Gazette*, 1/10/18, p. 16; 1/24/18, 31;
     2/28/18, 56. See also *Huayang susong li'an huibian*, p. 713; FO 656/131, resolution signed
     by British, American, and German Assessors, Nov. 13, 1913. See also FO 656/118, M.O.
     Springfield's report.

law. The Germans and Japanese touted theirs, which was inquisitorial, centralized, and relied on legislated law. Some Chinese took sides in this clash. Some young men and women in Shanghai consciously or unconsciously chose the Anglo-American path when they enrolled in the Soochow [Suzhou] School of Comparative Law, and others effectively chose the German-Japanese when they enrolled in the Shanghai College of Law and Politics.

The clash peaked in the mid 1920s when Chinese nationalists of various stripes protested the Anglo-American judicial model associated with British and American domination and exploitation.[73] The International Mixed Court became the most controversial aspect of the system of extraterritoriality. Its hybrid nature, once a source of its acceptability, became the main cause of its unpopularity.[74] The court itself became an irritant in China's relations with foreign countries. Chinese critics, including ex-officials, considered the court insufficiently Chinese.[75] British subjects deemed the court insufficiently British and some pushed for its reform while others ignored it.[76] Some among both Chinese and British alike regarded the Court at best as a legal failure and at worst as a political tool of foreign imperialists. British Minister Miles Lampson's willingness to negotiate for the return of the Court to the Chinese in the wake of the May 30 movement revealed his government's diminished ability to determine and enforce its interpretation of international legal norms.

There were also tensions within individual courts in Shanghai. The judges of various nationalities manifested different modes of presiding over the International Mixed Court. Litigants before the Mixed Court held different views on the nature of justice and the methods of obtaining it. For example, Chinese judges tended to assume that all parties involved in a criminal case, defendants, plaintiffs, and even, in some

---

73 See Kotenev, *Mixed*, 10. This topic is treated in depth in Clifford's *Shanghai 1925* and *Spoilt Children*.
74 Ibid., p. 279; Johnstone, p. 175.
75 For a sharp Chinese criticism of the court that actually preceded the 1925 May 30th Movement, see "Ex-Minister Tung Kang's Opinion," pp. 1–3.
76 Johnstone, "Administration," p. 173; Keeton, *Development*, Vol. I, pp. 354–55, 360–61, Vol. II, pp. 365, 368–69; Latter, "Extraterritorial," pp. 67, 69; Packer, "Extraterritoriality," p. 305; Piggot, *Extraterritoriality*, pp. 182–83.

cases witnesses, were potentially subject to punishment, while the British judges tended to focus on the guilt or innocence of individual defendants.

Surprisingly enough, although perhaps predictably in an age of nationalism, both Chinese and foreigners were more likely to call into question the legitimacy of the mixed courts of Shanghai than they were to challenge the more purely foreign courts. To be sure, the fledgling size and ad hoc nature of most of the consular courts,[77] and their purely foreign control and foreign procedure,[78] made them easy targets for critics of foreign domination of China. At the same time, however, consular courts rested on a firmer constitutional footing than did the mixed courts, provided for as they were by international treaties (however unequal) rather than by a mere set of agreed-upon (but often violated) rules. The treaties explicitly accorded the foreign powers "most favored nation" rights that included independent jurisdiction over their own nationals, but it did not mention anything about foreign jurisdiction over Chinese, the authority that had been assumed by the mixed courts.[79] Despite—but also because of—its hybrid nature, the International Mixed Court could be seen by Chinese nationalists as essentially a foreign court,[80] while at the same time being viewed by the British imperialists as too much a Chinese court.[81]

Tensions outside the International Mixed Court aggravated the tensions within. World War I inflamed conflicts at the court because it prompted a redrawing of the jurisdictional lines. The court enlarged its subject matter jurisdiction to include cases involving the confiscation of the property of enemy subjects, the forced registration of enemy

---

77 The consular court system never became very large or well organized. From 1921 to 1925, it tried about 0.5 percent of the quantity of cases that the Mixed Court did. Johnstone, "Administration," p. 141. This percentage is calculated from figures in Shanghai Municipal Council, *Annual Report 1921*, pp. 55A, 66A; *1922*, pp. 68A, 73A; *1923*, pp. 37, 42; *1924*, pp. 59–60; *1925*, p. 55; and monthly Police Reports, *Municipal Gazette*, 1924–1925.

78 Keeton, *Development* Vol. II, p. 146.

79 For pre-Mixed Court mixed cases in consular courts, see Fishel, *End of Extraterritoriality*, p. 23.

80 Chan, *Merchants, Mandarins*, pp. 111–16; Kotenev, *Mixed*, pp. 274, 276.

81 Johnstone, "Administration," p. 123; Keeton, *Development*, Vol. I, pp. 354–55, 360–61; Vol. II, pp. 368–69.

subjects in the Settlement, and their eventual deportation.[82] Germans and Chinese protested that the court's personal jurisdiction should no longer include German cases, yet the court continued to take such cases despite the resistance of the German subjects brought before it.[83]

Some of the strongest tensions at the International Mixed Court were between the Consular Body and the Municipal Council. The consuls tended to side with local business interests, while the council was more concerned with public order. The consuls generally tried to limit municipal police power,[84] while the council tried to expand it.[85] The two bodies disagreed over matters involving Chinese politics. Despite its wholly foreign personnel, the Consular Body's role as intermediary between both local and provincial Chinese authorities and the Municipal Council made it more sympathetic to the agendas of the Chinese authorities than was the council.[86]

Rules designed to deter competition among legal jurisdictions often broke down. As we have seen, different courts had authority over different defendants according to their nationalities. Complications arose because nationality was a highly fluid status in China—and particularly in Shanghai—at this time. As is well known, no passport was required for entry into Shanghai.[87] Moreover, China's Republican government frequently shifted alliances with other states. Efforts at the courts to make nationality contingent on place of birth were handicapped in a city where most residents were born elsewhere, making proof of birthplace often unavailable or suspect. Further complicating the concept of nationality as a way to distinguish among Shanghai's courts was the promiscuity with which foreign consuls in Shanghai sold citizenship to Chinese and to foreigners who had minimal—or

---

82 See *Municipal Gazette*, 2/21/18, p. 50; 3/14/18, p. 77.

83 Ibid., 12/1/21, p. 400; Kotenev, *Mixed*, p. 222.

84 See, e.g., Kotenev, *Municipality*, p. 216. The Consular Body tried to block the Municipal Police's control of the Court by declaring that the Court could not grant petitions for extradition without the approval of the petitioner's consul.

85 See, e.g., *Annual Reports 1925*, p. 80A, indicating that from 1921 to 1925, Police force expenditures constituted from 25 to 28 percent of the Municipal Council budget.

86 See Chao Shi'en, untitled essay. Chao Shi'en was a delegate of the Shanghai General Chamber of Commerce to the Diplomatic Body in Beijing, 1924.

87 Zou, *Jiu Shanghai*, p. 37.

even no—contacts with the country in question.[88] Yet another problem arose when courts in Shanghai allowed foreign employers to extend their nationality to their employees for limited purposes.[89]

Foreigners without consular representation presented a further complication because they had no court of their own in all of Shanghai in which they could be tried. They were accorded a legal status similar to that of the Chinese, meaning that they were all subject to the jurisdiction of the International Mixed Court.[90] The actual content of this category of diplomatically unrepresented persons changed as China's relations with foreign powers shifted in the wake of World War I and the Russian Revolution of 1917.[91]

Cooperation

Despite the conflicts within and among the courts, members of the Shanghai legal community often worked together across jurisdictions. British vice-consuls and Chinese bureaucrats closely cooperated to resolve cases at the International Mixed Court.[92] Judges cultivated harmonious relations across courts by letters that were more formal between Chinese and foreign judges and less formal among the foreign judges. Their goals were often pragmatic, such as securing assets, witnesses, or defendants that lay beyond their control, or smoothing over rifts that threatened to undermine the independence of a court by

88 See, e.g., the case of Whang Tung Ling v. Yen Yoong Sung, FO 656/175, Nov. 20, 1924; the case of Tung Hua v. Jui Liao Sse, FO 656/137, Jul. 9, 1915; and Foh Hsing Chong Hong v. Yue Hsing Co. and Tsu Wong Sz, FO 656/175, May 6, 1924.

89 See, e.g., FO 656/164, Oct. 17, 1921, documenting the dropping of a suit against a Chinese language newspaper when it was discovered that a nominal owner of the newspaper claimed American nationality.

90 Keeton, *Development*, Vol. I, p. 348; Kotenev, *Mixed*, pp. 56, 78–79. See, e.g., *Municipal Gazette*, 3/22/19, p. 80.

91 See FO 656/175, Jan. 7, 1923 and Jan. 12, 1923; FO 656/141; FO 656/160, Oct. 18, 1920; FO 656/175, Apr. 21–25, 1925.

92 See, e.g., F/O 656/116, letter from Joseph Hertz, Apr. 30, 1908, describing the intended system that the Mixed Court's trial and punishment for all cases calling for punishment above the *tu* and *liu* degrees of punishment be passed up to the Shanghai district magistrate. In serious cases, the district magistrate's decisions in turn were reviewed by his superiors, up to the emperor himself. See also Alford, "Arsenic," for a description of the appellate system in theory and practice.

causing a diplomatic scandal. But the pragmatism yielded mutual benefit and was widely shared.

A main purpose of the Court of Consuls appears to have been to shield the Municipal Council from legal liability, and in this the diplomatic representatives of various nations stationed in Shanghai were of course united. The process of drafting the judgments was shared among all three judges. Typically one of the judges drafted a judgment and circulated it to the other members of the judicial panel for their comments. Input was given in writing by way of confidential diplomatic letters sent from one consulate to another, and their tone was generally constructive and respectful. Even the political tensions between Allies and Axis powers leading up to World War II did not diminish the ability of the Japanese, British, and American consuls to work together at times. For example, they were able to agree on the result and the wording of the judgment in a case decided in February, 1940, on the eve of the United States' declaration of war against Japan. In this case, the consul-judges' communications showed no trace of rancor, no obvious intrusion of anything other than their effort to deny compensation from the Municipal Council to a former member of an arm of the council, the Russian Regiment of the Shanghai Volunteer Corps, for injuries he sustained while in its service.[93]

Cooperation within the Court of Consuls was often accompanied by cooperation of that court with other courts in the city. Another purpose of the Court of Councils was to assist the successors to the mixed courts, run by Chinese officials in the city, in the enforcement of their judgments. For example, when a plaintiff received a judgment from the District Court of the First Special Area at Shanghai, the International Mixed Court's successor, he brought it to the Court of Consuls to enforce the judgment in what was known as an "attachment or garnishee proceeding." The plaintiff merely asked the Court of Consuls to order the defendant's employer to reroute to him, the plaintiff, enough of the defendants' wages to satisfy the judgment. This was particularly effective when the employer was the Shanghai Metropolitan Council or

93   Michael Storchilo vs. Shanghai Municipal Council, in the Court of Consuls at Shanghai, (1940), microformed on Microcopy F167, Record Group 84, Roll No. 3, frames 209–92 (National Archives). Of course, the Russian nationality of the plaintiff and possibly his social status may not have been irrelevant in this case.

some branch thereof. The Court of Consuls granted the order, after
satisfying itself that the plaintiff had waived his right to sue the Shanghai Municipal Council for damages related to the lawsuit.[94]

The jurisdictional rules deterred competition among the courts of
Shanghai by resolving in advance many arguments about which
cases went to which courts. These rules functioned like a compromise
among the courts, a power-sharing agreement. The rules also proved
troublesome to apply in some instances, with requirements as to defendants' identity, residence, location at the time of arrest or other relevant act, and the seriousness of the offense all needing to be determined and possibly proved with evidence. In particular, judges at the
International Mixed Court, the United States Court for China, and
the American Consular Court carefully screened defendants' nationalities to ensure that the personal jurisdiction rules were complied
with. Their efforts to respect jurisdictional "walls" and deal only with
cases under their purview suggest their emphasis on cooperation over
competition.

Foreign judges at the International Mixed Court did sometimes
transgress the limits of their territorial jurisdiction by trying Chinese
who resided outside the International Settlement. But their motives
involved defense of the status quo as much as any ambition to change
it. They argued in some cases that they had either to ignore where the
Chinese defendant resided or give up altogether the long standing
practice of trying Chinese. This was because the jurisdictional divi-
sions within the city were not separated by material walls and gates so
it was relatively easy for suspects to abscond across jurisdictional borders in their efforts to avoid arrest and prosecution.

These same judges also applied the principle of penal jurisdiction
not only to prevent review by the Shanghai county magistrate but also
to forestall clashes between Chinese and foreign officials. The International Mixed Court broadened its subject matter jurisdiction to include even the grave offense of homicide, thus defying the legal restriction of the mixed courts to "minor" cases, but it did so quietly and

---

94 For example, Hazara Singh vs. Shanghai Municipal Council, V. M. Maximoff, G. N.
    Milutin, in the Court of Consuls (1938), microformed on Microcopy F167, Record
    Group 84, Roll No. 2, frames 469–77 (National Archives).

unofficially. It thereby generally avoided confrontation with the Chinese courts about this, with the occasional exception of hard negotiations between the Chinese city (Nanshi) and the International Settlement over a prisoner wanted for capital crimes.

For all their faults, the mixed courts were truly hybrid institutions, reflecting an overarching effort to accommodate differences. This enhanced their usefulness for litigants who lived in the highly heterogeneous city. It also improved their value as models for new Chinese courts in Shanghai. British legal procedure coexisted there with inherited Chinese elements. Even the jurisdictions of the Mixed Court were defined by mixtures of foreign and Chinese notions. One of the written sources of law issued by foreigners, the Municipal Council proclamations, assumed an "imperial" Chinese form.[95]

The self-serving nature of the cooperation should not obscure its social benefits. Despite years of political campaigns against it, the hybrid model was generally popular because it pleased plaintiffs and offered something familiar to everyone involved. The procedure that evolved at the mixed courts was attuned to the locality and it served the needs of Chinese merchants.[96] It offered speedy dispositions and delivery of summonses and orders, and allowed a wide range of functions for legal counsel hired by the parties. Chinese judges and lawyers in Shanghai sought to graft elements of foreign law onto Chinese law out of a need to accommodate new participants in the Chinese world.

The principal proof of the perceived utility of this hybrid approach was the number of its imitators, including the local Chinese court created in 1905 to try civil cases, and the *Shenpanting*, discussed above. The *Shenpanting's* reincarnation—the Shanghai District Court—and the Mixed Court's reincarnations—the Provisional Court, the Special District Court, and the First District Court—all possessed jurisdictional and procedural features similar to those of the International Mixed Court, such as the division between the civil and criminal dock-

---

95 Keeton, *Development*, Vol. I, pp. 350–51, 363; Kotenev, *Mixed*, p. 211.

96 See, e.g., communiqué from the Shanghai gelu shangjie zonglianhehui [United Street Merchants Association] to Shanghai jiaoshe shixu [Shanghai Commissioner for Foreign Affairs], Aug. 10, 1926, pp. 87–89, consisting of merchant requests to preserve the independence of the court after its reorganization following the Chinese takeover.

ets and the use of lawyers in the courtroom to present and argue evidence.

Conclusion

In this tally of competition and cooperation among the courts of late-nineteenth- and early-twentieth-century Shanghai, it is easy to focus upon the examples of competition, perhaps because they are more dramatic. And yet, the cooperative factors should carry more weight than the competitive factors. For one thing, they are more surprising. Tensions riddle all court systems, even purely domestic and culturally homogeneous ones. So one should expect a collection of multinational courts all within the same city to experience many of them. More remarkable is the degree to which these courts collaborated with one another, as part of a system in which each agreed to play its assigned role. It is no small measure of the effectiveness of the cooperation that this system endured, in some form or other, for nearly eighty years. Cooperation within and among the courts of Shanghai between the 1840s and 1940s more often than not overcame the barriers posed by the complexity and rivalries of that system. The multiple systems within that city strengthened one another more than they undermined one another. Perhaps this was a case where legal "walls," or more precisely virtual walls among various legal jurisdictions, carefully constructed and properly tended, contributed to some degree of social order and even to some modicum of justice.

Works Cited

Alford, William P. "Of Arsenic and Old Laws: Looking Anew at Criminal Justice in Late Imperial China," *California Law Review*, 72 (1984), pp. 1180–1249.

Allee, Mark A. "Code, Culture, and Custom: Foundations of Civil Case Verdicts in a Nineteenth-Century County Court." Pp. 122–41 in Huang, Philip C. C., and Kathryn Bernhardt, eds. *Civil Law in Qing and Republican China*. Stanford: Stanford University Press, 1994.

———. *Law and Local Society in Late Imperial China*. Stanford: Stanford University Press, 1994.

Bhatia, H. S., and Tan Chung, eds. *Legal and Political System in China*, Vol. 1. New Delhi: Deep & Deep, 1974.

Bourgon, Jérome. "Rights, Freedoms, and Customs in the Making of Chinese Civil Law, 1900–1936." Pp. 84–112 in Kirby, *Realms of Freedom*.

British Jurisdiction in China: Rules of Court, 1905–1916. W. B. Kennett, ed. Shanghai: Printed and Published for the Committee of the Bar of H. B. M. Supreme Court for China by *The North-China Daily News & Herald, Ltd.*, 1918.

Brook, Timothy. *Collaboration: Japanese Agents and Local Elites in Wartime China.* Cambridge, Mass.: Harvard University Press, 2005.

Chan, Chung-sing. *Les Concessions en Chine.* Paris: Les Presses Universitaires de France, 1925.

Chan, Wellington K. K. *Merchants, Mandarins, and Modern Enterprise in Late Ch'ing China.* Cambridge, Mass.: East Asian Research Center, Harvard University, 1977.

Chao Shi'en. Untitled essay. *Falü pinglun* [Legal review], 52 (June 22, 1924), p. 3.

"China Rules of Court, 1905." Rules 26–30, in *British Jurisdiction in China: Rules of Court 1905–1916*, W. B. Kennett ed. (1918), pp. 17–18.

China Yearbook. Tientsin: Tientsin Press, 1926–1927.

Citizens' League. *Syllabus on Extraterritoriality in China.* Nanking, no publisher, ca. 1930.

Clifford, Nicholas. *Shanghai 1925: Urbanization and the Defense of Foreign Privilege.* Ann Arbor: University of Michigan Papers in Chinese Studies, 1979.

———. *Spoilt Children of Empire: Westerners in Shanghai and the Chinese Revolution of the 1920s.* Middlebury, Vt. Middlebury College Press, 1991.

Cohen, Jerome, R. Randle Edwards, and Fu-mei Chang Chen, eds., *Essays on China's Legal Tradition.* Princeton: Princeton University Press, 1980.

Des Forges, Alexander. *Mediasphere Shanghai: The Aesthetics of Cultural Production.* Honolulu: University of Hawai'i Press, 2007.

Dikotter, Frank. *Crime, Punishment and the Prison in Modern China.* New York: Columbia University Press, 2002.

E. D. Sassoon & Co. "Letter to J. L. Rodgers, Consul General for America" (May 31, 1905), microformed on Microcopy F167, Record Group 84, Roll No. 1, Frame 672 (National Archives).

Edwards, R. Randle. "Ch'ing Legal Jurisdiction Over Foreigners." Pp. 222–69 in *Essays on China's Legal Tradition,* Jerome Alan Cohen, R. Randle Edwards, and Fu-mei Chang Chen, eds. Princeton: Princeton University Press, 1980.

Elvin, Mark. "The Administration of Shanghai, 1905–1914." Pp. 239–62 in *The*

Chinese City Between Two Worlds. M. Elvin and G. W. Skinner, eds. Stanford: Stanford University Press, 1974.

"Ex-Minister Tung Kang's Opinion Concerning the Mixed Court of Shanghai." *Falü pinglun* [Legal review] 50(June 8, 1924), pp. 1–3.

Fang, Qiang, and Roger Des Forges, "Were Chinese Rulers Above the Law? Toward a Theory of the Rule of Law in Chinese History from Early Times to 1949," *Stanford Journal of International Law*, 101(2008), pp. 101–46.

"Faquan taolun." *Falü zhoukan* [Legal weekly] 10(Sept. 9, 1923), pp. 19–20.

Feetham, Justice. *Great Britain and China: The Future of Shanghai: The Hon. Mr. Justice Feetham's Report.* No place, no publisher, ca. 1930.

Fishel, Wesley R. *The End of Extraterritoriality in China.* Berkeley: University of California Press, 1952.

Fletcher, Joseph. "The Heyday of the Ch'ing Order in Mongolia, Sinkiang and Tibet." Pp. 377–83 in *The Cambridge History of China*, Vol. 10. John Fairbank, ed. Cambridge: Cambridge University Press, 1978.

Foreign Office records. Public Records Office, Surrey, England. 656 series, 1905–1930.

Giles, Herbert A. *A Chinese-English Dictionary*, 1st ed. Shanghai: 1892, 2nd ed. Shanghai and London: 1912; reprinted Taipei: Ch'eng Wen Publishing Co., 1972.

Gundry, R. S. "The Status of the Shanghai Municipality." *Journal of Comparative Legislation and International Law*, 2(1920), p. 53.

Henriot, Christian. *Shanghai 1927–1937: Municipal Power, Locality, and Modernization.* Noel Castelino, trans. Berkeley: University of California Press, 1993.

Hevia, James L. *English Lessons: The Pedagogy of Imperialism in Nineteenth-Century China.* Durham, North Carolina: Duke University Press, 2004.

Honig, Emily. *Sisters and Strangers: Women in the Shanghai Cotton Mills, 1919-1949.* Stanford: Stanford University Press, 1986.

Hoyle, Mark. *Mixed Courts of Egypt.* London: Graham & Trotman, 1991.

Huang, Philip C. C. "Codified Law and Magisterial Adjudication in the Qing." Pp. 142–86 in *Civil Law in Qing and Republican China*, Philip C. C. Huang and Kathryn Bernhardt, eds. Stanford: Stanford University Press, 1994.

Huayang susong li'an huibian [Collection of foreign lawsuits], 2 vols. Shanghai: Shanghai shangwu yinshuguan chuban, 1915.

Jin Junjian, "Qing Civil Economic Legislation." P. 42–84, 82 in *Civil Law in Qing and Republican China*, Philip Huang and Kathryn Bernhardt, eds. Stanford: Stanford University Press, 1994.

Jingxie shiyong fa [Law relating to police use of arms]. No place, no publisher, March 2, 1914.

Johnson, Linda Cooke. *Shanghai: From Market-town to Treaty Port, 1274–1858.* Stanford: Stanford University Press, 1995.

Johnstone, William Crane. "The Administration of the International Settlement at Shanghai, China." Unpublished Ph.D. dissertation, Stanford University, 1931.

Jones, William, trans., *The Great Qing Code.* Oxford: Clarendon Press, 1994.

Keeton, G. W. *The Development of Extraterritoriality in China*, Vols. I and II. London: Longmans Green, 1928.

Kirby, William C. "The Chinese Party-State under Dictatorship and Democracy on the Mainland and in Taiwan." Pp. 113–38 in Kirby, *Realms of Freedom.*

———, ed. *Realms of Freedom in Modern China.* Stanford: Stanford University Press, 2004.

Kotenev, Anatol M. *Shanghai: Its Mixed Court and Council.* Taipei: Ch'eng-wen Publishing Company, 1968. Reprint of original edition. Shanghai: North-China Daily News & Herald, Limited, 1925.

———. *Shanghai: Its Municipality and the Chinese.* Shanghai: North-China Daily News & Herald, Limited, 1927.

Latter, A. M. "Extraterritorial Jurisdiction in Hong-Kong." *Journal of the Society of Comparative Legislation*, 4(1902), pp. 67–70.

Lee, Tahirih V. "Law and Local Autonomy at the International Mixed Court of Shanghai." Ph.D. dissertation, Yale University, 1990.

———. "Risky Business: Courts, Culture, and the Marketplace." *University of Miami Law Review*, 47(May 1993), pp. 923–1075.

———. "The United States Court for China: A Triumph of Local Law." *Buffalo Law Review*, 52(Dec. 2004), pp. 923–1075.

———. *Benchmarks: The Courts of Shanghai, 1900–1950.* A monograph manuscript on file with the author.

Li, Tz-hyung. *Abolition of Extraterritoriality in China.* N.p.: Published under the Auspices of the International Relations Committee, 1929.

Liu, Lydia He. *The Clash of Empires: The Invention of China in Modern World Making.* Cambridge, Mass.: Harvard University Press, 2004.

MacCormack, Geoffrey. *Traditional Chinese Penal Law.* Aberdeen University Press, 1990.

Martin, Brian G. "The Pact with the Devil. The Relationships between the Green Gang and the French Concession Authorities, 1925–1935." Pp. 240–66 in *Shanghai Sojourners.* Frederic Wakeman and Yeh Wen-hsin, eds. Berkeley: University of California Press, 1992.

Municipal Gazette. Shanghai Evening Post and Mercury, 1908–1930.

Packer, Launcelot. "Extraterritoriality in China." *Journal of Comparative Legislation and International Law*, 3(1921), p. 305.

Piggot, Frances. *Extraterritoriality*. London: Butterworth, 1907.

Selby, John. *The Paper Dragon: An Account of the China Wars, 1840–1900*. New York: Praeger, 1968.

Shanghai Dengyi tequ difang fayuan (Third District Court for the Second Special Area in Shanghai).

Shanghai gelu shangjie zong lianhehui [United Street Merchants Association]. Letter to Shanghai jiaoshe shixu [Shanghai commissioner for foreign affairs], Aug. 10, 1926, 87–89, file 179.4.4, Shanghai Municipal Archives.

Shanghai gonggong zujie zhidu [The system of Shanghai's international settlement]. N.p.: Zhongguo kexue gongsi chengyin, 1931.

Shanghai Municipal Council. *Annual Reports*, 1912–1926.

———. "Letter to American Consul-General in Shanghai, James L. Rodgers." Dec. 12, 1905, microformed on Microcopy F167, Record Group 84, Roll No. 1, Frames 456–58. United States National Archives, Washington, D.C.

Shanghai Municipal Police Files. IO Dossiers, 1926–1935. United States National Archives, Washington, D.C.

Shanghai xianhua [Shanghai memories]. Shanghai: Shanghai guji chubanshe, 1988.

Shanghai shi nianjian [Annals of Shanghai City], 1937.

Shanghai shi tongji [Statistics of Shanghai]. Shanghai: Shanghaishi difang xiehui, 1933.

Shen bao. Shanghai: Shen bao guan, 1874–1928.

"Sifabu duiyi Shanghai zujie huishen gongtang" [The Ministry of Justice on the International Mixed Court of the Shanghai International Settlement], *Falü zhoukan* [Law Weekly], 11(1923), p. 17.

Spence, Jonathan D. *The Search for Modern China*. New York: W. W. Norton, 1990.

Stephens, Thomas B. *Order and Discipline in China: The Shanghai Mixed Court, 1911–1927*. Seattle: University of Washington Press, 1992.

United States Act of June 30, 1906, ch. 3934, Section 3, 34 Statutes-at-Large, 814, 815. Washington, D.C.

United States Court for China: Hearings Before the House Foreign Affairs Committee on the United States Court for China. 65th Congress, 7, 12, 16 (1917).

"United States v. Juvenile Offender." *Millard's Review of the Far East* (Feb. 16, 1918), p. 380.

Wakeman, Jr., Frederic E. *Policing Shanghai, 1927–1937*. Berkeley: University of California Press, 1995.

Waley, Arthur. *The Opium War Through Chinese Eyes*. New York: Macmillan, 1958.

"Zongli Yamen Document on the Unequal Treaties, 1878." Pp. 157–59 in *The Search for Modern China: A Documentary Collection*. Pei-kai Cheng and Michael Lestz with Jonathan D. Spence, eds. New York: W. W. Norton, 1999.

Zou Yiren. *Jiu Shanghai renkou bianqian de yanjiu* [Research on demographic change in old Shanghai]. Shanghai: Renmin chubanshe, 1980.

PART THREE

Containment and Breaches

AS WE HAVE SEEN, THE People's Republic of China (PRC), for all its vaunted break with "feudal tradition," has recently begun to preserve and even selectively reconstruct its material long walls, city walls, and town walls, in part, ironically, to attract more foreign tourists. It has even used, perhaps quite unconsciously, the cultural foundations of urban wards and collective institutions to construct sub-urban control mechanisms such as units (*danwei*) and street committees, although these social formations are now being replaced by the quite different— but not wholly unrelated—institutions of gated communities and people's armed police. The People's Republic is also returning to the late Qing and Republican effort to incorporate foreign, mainly "Western," institutions and practices in a renewed quest to enhance "the rule of law." It is attempting to erect virtual walls between state and party, between civil and criminal law, and among executive, legislative, and judicial powers to enhance the possibility of justice. From the beginning, the PRC has also deployed other kinds of virtual walls, including artistic depictions of material walls, administrative measures of public health, and state surveillance of mass media, all in pursuit of national security and global responsibility.

The early People's Republic seized on the images of long walls, city walls, and palace walls to discredit political rivals, symbolize national unity, defend territorial borders from a threatening distant power, celebrate an alliance with a supportive neighbor, and develop the charisma of its primary leader. The PRC relied on social mobilization to wipe out longstanding practices, such as drug abuse and prostitution; control endemic diseases, such as malaria and smallpox; and, most recently, combat new viruses, such as Severe Acute Respiratory Syndrome (SARS) and H5N1 Avian Influenza. Operating on the long-standing Chinese cultural assumption that states are responsible for helping to shape how people think, the new government conducted propaganda through the existing media, such as the press, radio, and television. More recently it has pushed publicity through the new digital media of the Internet, mobile phones, and text messaging. Just as earlier Chinese polities recurrently mobilized scholar-officials to censor unorthodox publications, so the PRC has recently constructed a "great firewall" to control "unhealthful" communications on the worldwide web.

Since we are unable to predict the fate of the People's Republic, we cannot fully assess the efficacy of its multiple efforts to use virtual walls to establish and maintain its political legitimacy. In historical and comparative perspective, however, we may suggest some differences as well as similarities among efforts in the three areas of political cartoons, public health, and electronic communication. The first strategy of using political cartoons featuring walls to establish and consolidate the authority of the new government seems to have been quite effective in the short run but perhaps less successful in the long run, depending, of course, upon our standards of "success" and our definition of the "long run." The second policy of suppressing and even denying information about the appearance of a new pathogen that had jumped the usual walls between wild animals, domesticates, and humans was quite harmful in the short run, but the determination to use state authority to enforce a strict quarantine of all suspected carriers seems to have been more positive in the long run. The third strategy of forming a substantial cadre of Internet police to control the diffusion of information on the Internet, especially that relating to politics and sex, is probably too recent to appraise. But China's long experience in attempting to control the dissemination of information and current efforts elsewhere in the world to do the same suggest that the Chinese state may be as successful in this effort as any regime has ever been. The consequences, of course, remain to be seen, and the interpretations of them will probably be as numerous and various as those of other such efforts in the past and around the world.

CHAPTER SIX

Walls as Multivalent Icons in Early People's Republican Political Cartoons, 1946–1951

Adam Cathcart

AS THE ULTIMATE INHERITORS OF the whirlwind of the Sino-Japanese war, during which the long walls of China reached their apotheosis as symbols of Chinese defense against external aggression, the Chinese Communist Party (CCP) quite naturally considered the utility of walls as political symbols in the effort to consolidate the authority of their new state. In this chapter we tap a rare collection of Chinese propaganda cartoons to analyze how the new government used various images of walls and gates to discredit political rivals, symbolize national unity, rally support for defense against a distant foreign power, celebrate an alliance with a neighboring state, and identify themselves as the legitimate successors of the Qing dynasts.[1] In the short term, the efforts appear to have been quite successful as the People's Republic warded off domestic and foreign challenges to its rule. In the longer term, however, the arguably related Maoist policies

---

1 Hunter Collection. The collection is named after Edward Hunter, an American journalist who lived in China from 1949 to 1951 and collected nearly three hundred pamphlets. It is housed at the Center for Research Libraries in Chicago. Some of the material may also be found at the Shanghai Municipal Library. For more on the collection, see Reilly et al., "Political Communication"; for background on the collector, see Hunter, *Brainwashing*.

of self-reliance and permanent revolution had mixed consequences for China's capacity to compete with other major powers in the world.

Walls as Negative Symbols of "Feudal Tradition" and "National Weakness"

The Chinese Communists' views of walls were ambivalent from the beginning. As children of the New Culture and May Fourth Movements of the 1910s and as recent denizens of the hills of Yan'an, the revolutionaries had long criticized China's "feudal culture," including Confucian dogma, gender inequality, national weakness, and social stratification. The party's jaundiced view of Chinese "feudalism" would eventually propel it to try to destroy what it would come to call "the four olds" (old culture, ideas, habits, and customs) during the Cultural Revolution. As we have seen in Chapter 2 of this volume, the targets included city walls and gates.

The CCP's critique of China's "feudal" past pervades officially sanctioned cartoons dating from the pivotal years of 1949–1951. The theme was consistent with the party's need to repudiate the old regime and root out lingering opposition, goals that, ironically, placed the CCP squarely in line with the previous polities we generally call "dynasties."[2] During the initial years of the People's Republic, the image frequently appeared of uprooting, or "turning over" (*fanshen*) in one common phrase of the day.[3] Some woodcut cartoons depicted enormous human hands digging out deep roots representing "the old society," while others advocated "storming the citadel" to destroy China's sedimentary past.[4] Walls were used to symbolize the supposedly monolithic force of "tradition" and the confining aspects of Chinese culture.[5]

---

2   For an early interpretation of the Communist takeover within the framework of dynastic history, see Fitzgerald, *Birth*. For recognition of a more particular parallel between the Ming founding and that of the PRC, see Andrew and Rapp, *Autocracy*; Schneewind, *Long Live*.

3   For an example, see Hinton, *Fanshen*.

4   Li, "Pulling Up"; Li, "Storming the Citadel."

5   Walls were also symbols of "tradition" and targets of "reformists" in the 1988 television series *He Shang* (*River Elegy*). See Su, *Deathsong*.

City walls were not only viewed as old, they were also thought to have been ineffective in resisting the Japanese. At the conclusion of the War of Resistance in 1945, the Chinese Communists juxtaposed their own unflinching resistance to Japan in the rural north with the alleged laxity of the Nationalists' defense of urban areas in the south. The Communists hoped to show that they, rather than the rival government and army led by Chiang Kai-shek, were the true carriers of the banner of nationalism. The CCP inspired political cartoons showing images of walls being transgressed to discredit a wide range of Guomindang policies toward Japan.

During the ensuing civil war, the *Northeastern Illustrated Gazette* (*Dongbei Huabao*), published in the party's urban redoubt of Harbin, served as the preeminent forum for the dissemination of political cartoons. Through the efforts of two skilled artists, Hua Junwu and Zhang Ding, the paper printed even more satirical cartoons than emanated from the Communist headquarters in Yan'an.[6] The young Zhang Ding was among the most prolific and influential propagandists for the CCP in the late 1940s.[7] In Figure 1, Zhang uses images of walls to illustrate Chiang Kai-shek's inability to protect China from successive foreign threats.

In the left panel, depicting the year 1931, Chiang allows the Japanese to raise their flag on the wall; in the right panel dated 1946 he permits the Americans to do the same. By placing the blue portion of the American flag outside the 1946 picture frame, leaving only the red and white, the artist cleverly evokes the similarity between the "rising sun" standard of the Japanese empire and the "stars and stripes" of the American imperialists. Given Chiang's apparent willingness to cede sovereignty to stay in power, the walls fall into foreign hands and become merely sites for outsiders to demonstrate and celebrate their domination of China. The walls' onetime function as effective bulwarks against foreign rule has been inverted. Linking the more recent past and the present, the artist depicts Chiang using the radio microphone in 1931 to "encourage cooperation" (*dunmu bangjiao*) with the Japanese and the same instrument in 1946 to trumpet the benefit of a

---

6   Zhang et al., *Dongbei.*
7   Zhang Ding gained fame as a cartoonist in the "Anti-Japanese Cartoon Brigades" formed during the War of Resistance. See Hung, "Fuming," p. 130.

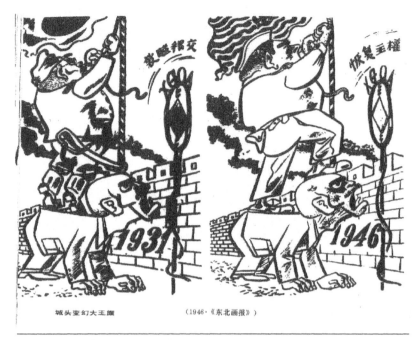

城头变幻大王旗　　　　　（1946・《东北画报》）

Figure 1 "Switching the Flags of the Rulers at the City Wall"(Zhang Ding, *Dongbei Huabao*, September 1946).

mythical "resumption of sovereignty" (*huifu zhuquan*) under American dominion.[8] The reference to radio broadcasting tacitly reinforced Mao's axiom that technology would never be decisive in warfare and it indirectly suggested Chiang's inability to reach rural areas where radios were in short supply during the civil war.[9] Implied also in the image is China's need for a ruler strong enough to stand up to foreigners—now chiefly the Americans.

Zhang's cartoon was an example of the CCP's adoption of a strategy of substitution begun during their first united front with the Nation-

8   For a critique of the myth of strong Chinese resistance to Japanese control in the northeast, see Mitter, *Manchurian*. For other literature on this question, see Israel, *Lianda*; Wasserstrom, *Student Protests*; Johnson, *Peasant Nationalism*.

9   For radio communication in China see Chu and Tu, *Great Wall*; Chang, *Mass Media*.

alists.[10] In the 1920s, propagandists on the Northern Expedition had depicted their warlord opponents as pawns of China's foreign enemies, and the Japanese were successors to British imperialism. Now, in the 1940s, Figure 1 explicitly juxtaposes the Japanese past and the American present, ignoring a reality of which Zhang Ding's northeastern audience would have been well aware. In 1946, the foreign army of occupation in northeast China was Soviet, not American.[11] To be sure, there were also 54,000 American troops in Qingdao and Beijing, some of whom committed abuses, but they did not cart off much of the region's industrial plant as the Russians had done in the northeast.[12] By suggesting a parallel between the Japanese and American roles, the CCP attempted to discredit the United States and to sidestep the difficult issue of whether the Soviet Union's role in the northeast was consistent with China's best interests.

In the same month of September 1946, Zhang Ding again invoked historical events to illustrate Chiang Kai-shek's supposed lack of interest in protecting the sovereignty of the northeast. In Figure 2, Zhang depicted an immense soldier of the northeastern army staring north, his attention fixed on a plume of smoke marked with the cipher "9–18," a well-known reference to the Japanese annexation of China's northeastern provinces (also called Manchuria) on September 18, 1931. Japanese flags dot a wall extending to the horizon. Mockingly, Chiang's face appears on a ball and chain attached to the soldier's leg, labeled Don't Resist (*bu di kang*).

---

10 For discussion of the effectiveness of Nationalist propaganda in associating foreign imperialism with domestic enemies, see Jordan, *Northern Expedition*, p. 9. For the CCP's postwar strategy of substituting the United States for imperial Japan and Chiang Kaishek for Pu Yi and Wang Jingwei, see Cathcart, "Chinese Nationalism."

11 Several hundred thousand Soviet troops pulled out of Manchuria in May 1946, but about 50,000 remained in Dalian until 1949, thereafter moving to Lüshun until 1955. See Wang, *Dalian*.

12 American troop levels peaked in China at about 54,000 in late 1945; the number was drawn down to 34,000 by late March 1946, and further reduced to 22,000 by September 1946. U.S. troops remained in Qingdao until April 1949. See Memorandum by General Marshall to the Secretary of State, March 26, 1946, *Foreign Relations*, Vol. X, p. 859, and General Marshall to the Acting Secretary of State, Sept. 25 1946, *Foreign Relations*, Vol. X, pp. 875–76. For figures on Qingdao, see Yang, "U.S. Marines."

东北军脚上的镣铐   (1946·《东北漫画》)

Figure 2 "The Ball and Chain on the Legs of the Northeastern Army" (Zhang Ding, *Dongbei Huabao*, September 1946)

In this cartoon, Zhang Ding encouraged Chinese viewers to recall the Guomindang's appeasement of Japan in 1931, which demonstrated that Chiang's party did not care about the people.[13] Having left the people to Japanese imperialism in 1937, the reasoning went, the Guomindang would not hesitate to accept similar American domination of the northeast. This line of argument strongly appealed to many people's sense of recent history, widely evoking the welter of nationalistic arguments first put forth by both moderates and radicals in the 1930s.[14] Referring time and again to the loss of Manchuria in 1931, the CCP

13   For a balanced assessment, see Jordan, *Chinese Boycotts,* ch. 2.
14   Coble, *Facing Japan.*

used history as a weapon to lash out at its opposition.[15] In 1946, images of Japanese flags raised along the length of the Great Wall were an alarming reminder of China's recent domination at foreign hands, effective spurs to Chinese of all political persuasions to work together for the nation's defense.

The CCP used political cartoons to reinforce radio broadcasts and street theatre that were becoming vital conduits of mass communication. Centrally approved and professionally produced cartoons served as models for local amateur artists in the new areas coming under the control of the CCP.[16] Cartoons published in *People's Daily* were widely copied onto posters and chalkboards in outlying villages, schools, factories, and army units. The party center created guidebooks, called "Propaganda Source Materials," to assist legions of both amateur and professional cartoonists across China. Thus the new People's Republic of China, which possessed limited amounts of capital-intensive technology such as radio and television, used longstanding labor-intensive methods to spread its message quite effectively over the entire polity.

In addition to images reproduced on chalkboards and posters and mounted on walls for public inspection, the government encouraged authors to include illustrations of walls in comic books designed for young people.[17] In one postwar narrative of victimization and heroism, an illustration (Figure 3) featured a city wall being defended against the Japanese. During the war with Japan, many Chinese had viewed film footage of the Japanese claiming victory in 1937 at Nanjing, the Nationalist capital. In the clips, Japanese soldiers were depicted standing triumphantly atop the city's formidable walls. The vertical caption on Figure 3 reads: "Chiang's regime believes that American imperialism should be allowed to come to destroy the country and enslave the people, relinquishing our country's sovereignty; but this will result in

---

15 For Zhou Enlai's views on the Guomindang policy of "nonresistance" after the September 18, 1931, incident, see Zhou Enlai, "Speech in Yan'an Commemorating the 'Double Twelve,'" December 12, 1946, *Jiefang Ribao*, Dec. 13, 1946 [reprinted in Zhou, *Zhou Enlai xuanji*, Vol. 2, pp. 247–50]. For discussion of CCP party history, see Weigelin-Schwiedrzik, "Party Historiography," pp. 149–73.

16 Cathcart, "Cruel Resurrection."

17 Shen, "Lianhuanhua."

Figure 3 "The Japanese pirates (or bandits) gathered several tens of thousands of soldiers, but after a few days and nights of bombing, they were defeated" (*Xie Shou Lianhuanhua [Bloody Hands]*) (Shanghai: Meishu Chubanshe, June 1951), p. 157.

his self-destruction!" The artists thus effectively melded the lessons of the past and the imperatives of the present.

During the civil war, the Chinese Communists ridiculed Chiang's urban strategy of emphasizing the control of cities and depicted him as weak, passive, and dependent on ineffective city walls for his defenses. Indeed, they suggested, such walls actually weighed him down, acting as virtual gravestones. The success of commander Lin Biao of the People's Liberation Army in using mobile warfare against the Guomindang seemed to confirm as much.[18] In fact, the Communists had actually tried to take cities in the early years of the civil war, but had been unable to do so. They therefore rationalized their own lack of influence in urban areas by using city walls as symbols of Chiang's isolation.[19] Still, Communist reservations about trying to take China's urban areas did not simply result from military weakness. The CCP regarded ur-

---

18   Li, "Under the Direction," p. 11.
19   Peng, "Zhangwo, p. 111; Zhang, *Xue Bai*, pp. 77, 111–16; Potter, *From Leninist*, p. 54.

刘伯承将军说: "我们把这些包
袱一个个给蒋介石加到背上了，他背
得愈多，就愈重，就愈走不动。"

(1946·《东北画报》)

59

Figure 4 " General Liu Bocheng . . ." (Zhang Ding, *Dongbei Ribao* 1946)

ban society with ambivalence because they had been roundly defeated there in 1927 and because cities were bastions of feudal/bourgeois power. It would take victory in the countryside to enable the party to once again attempt to take cities like Shanghai that were important hubs of cultural, economic, and political activity.[20] Another cartoon (Figure 4) further dramatized the idea that cities would become deadweight in Chiang Kai-shek's effort to maintain his authority in China.

The caption in Figure 4 reads: "General Liu Bocheng [an important CCP general in north China] said: 'With regard to Chiang's armies, we will take them one by one. Let him take city after city, for soon the weight will overtake him and he will become immobile.'" The charac-

---

20 For an example of CCP artists' efforts to transform urban culture in line with rural socialist models just after liberation, see Shen, *Jiefang*.

Figure 5 Ah Yang, "At Ease," *Zheshi yige manhua de shidai*, [This is an age of cartoons] (Hong Kong, 1948), p. 6.

ters underneath Chiang's leg read, "Destruction of forty brigades of Chiang's troops," while the citadel in the giant hand is emblazoned with the words, "Take our troops out of the cities on our own."

While Figure 4 suggested that Chiang Kai-shek's reliance on walled cities was anachronistic, such cities still served as important military bastions in the late 1940s. The Chinese civil war was only the most recent of a long line of Chinese military contests over political authority that had as their target walled cities. In the years just prior to the Communist accession to power, city fortifications across China had reached, in many cases, their maximum capability as a means of defense against bandits, militarists, Japanese armies, and then attacks by Nationalists and Communists.[21]

This militarization of the Republican-period city can be seen in Figure 5, a parody of the Guomindang occupation of Chinese cities during the civil war. The cartoon by Ah Yang, labeled "At Ease," which appeared in an influential left-leaning collection of cartoons in Hong Kong, does not depict the Communist armies in the countryside, but focuses on the Guomindang army, which is shown filling every corner of the city, pushing aside the civilian populace.[22]

Here the walls are used to illustrate the Guomindang's isolation in the cities, which allegedly led to its ultimate defeat. However, with the victory of 1949, the CCP turned to preserving much of what they had discounted and even in some cases had helped to destroy: the cities and their walls and gates.[23]

Walls as Positive Symbols of a New China

With the retreat of the Guomindang to offshore islands, including principally Taiwan, and with the ascendance of the CCP on most of the mainland, images of walls proliferated and took on more positive connotations. They suddenly became icons of the PRC's own achievement in reunifying China and ending foreign domination over most of Chinese territory. In a decisive break with a "Century of Humiliation," the Chinese people had, in Mao Zedong's forceful if somewhat hyperbolic words, "stood up." In this view, China would henceforth be strong enough to repel any assault from outside. Having failed for a variety of reasons to establish capitalism, China would now seek wealth and power by establishing socialism.

In Figure 6, artist Dun Xin's simple ink drawing depicts the People's Republic of China as an agricultural and industrial utopia. At the center of the frame, the worker raises his arms to celebrate the new order, emphasizing how economic production will now benefit the people.

---

21 See Chapter 2 in this volume.

22 For a critical first-hand account of the problems caused by Guomindang soldiers inside a besieged city, see Bodde, *Peking Diary*.

23 For discussions of the CCP's changing attitude toward cities in 1949, see Gao, *Communist*; Lieberthal, *Revolution*; Yick, *Making Urban*.

Figure 6 Dun Xin, "Building Up New China," *Jiefang Manhua Xuan* [Selection of Cartoons of Liberation] (Shanghai, 1950), p. 36. (Hunter Collection)

The smokestack offered an implicit criticism of the Guomindang, under which industry had allegedly lain dormant.[24] The image suggests that China, if left to its own devices, will prosper, bringing a smile to the face of its representative worker. Around the country runs a high and stout wall denoting an effective defense of the national borders.

As the party gained control over the artistic production of the entire country, it promoted a wealth of images of menacing foreigners lurking at the gates. However, such dangers were mitigated by representations of China's host of friends from other new "people's democracies." A private artist known as Mengzi drew a series of cartoons, featuring China's friends and foes, that he featured on patriotic postcards sold to PRC sympathizers in Hong Kong. In Figure 7, Mengzi places the entire socialist bloc, with the Chinese in the vanguard, inside a high wall. They are all united against two hapless reactionary leaders: Winston Churchill and a composite figure of Douglas MacArthur and Harry Truman. Both of the imperialists appear terrified by

24 Westad, *Decisive*, preface to ch. 2.

世 界 和 平 人 民
大 团 结 !

32.世界和平人民大團結,勝利萬歲!

Figure 7 Mengzi, "Long Live the Victory of the Unity of the World's Peaceful People!" *Postcards to Prevent American Revival of Japanese Militarism*, No. 32.

the slogan on the wall reading, Peaceful People of the World Unite. Apparently most fearsome to the imperialists were the two characters *he* (as in peace) and *tuan* (as in militia) that could be read vertically, thus evoking the *Yi he tuan* (lit., militia of justice and peace), the Chinese name of the Boxers who had famously erupted in violent reaction against foreign missionaries, merchants, and troops in north China in 1900.[25] The power of the graphs evoking the Boxers was emphasized by their central placement and by Churchill's cigar smoke, which rises away from the wall and its inscription.

The depiction of outsized Chinese workers behind a stalwart wall was not coincidental, as party propaganda guidebooks repeatedly recommended the trope. One such guidebook, printed in December 1950, depicts the building of a wall marked "Peaceful Construction" against the "Chiang Bandits" (*Jiang fei*) and "American Imperialists" (*Mei di-*

25   For Chinese praise of the Boxers as a patriotic movement, a view that would peak in the
      Cultural Revolution, see Cohen, *History*, ch. 9.

guozhuyizhe). A brawny Chinese construction worker towers over a bomb-throwing and unshaven Douglas MacArthur and a squinting Uncle Sam who, like Chiang Kai-shek in Figure 1, uses a radio to project his voice over the city gates. The defensive wall, like the nation, is bright red, an auspicious color in China long before—as well as after—the revolution.[26]

The theme of national defense was picked up in *Manhua* (Cartoon), a graphic publication the importance of which was evident in its relatively lavish production—including colored and glossy covers—in the early People's Republic, a period marked by material shortages. One cartoon shows a sea wall under construction, effectively warding off the surf bearing the visages of the likes of Truman, Churchill, and other "reactionary" and even "fascist" enemies of the New China. The surf may continue to pound the wall, but the wall, symbol of China's defenses, will stand firm.[27]

In another variation on the theme of national defense versus bloodthirsty imperialists, Figure 8 depicts a specific interpretation of Chinese involvement in the Korean War.

In this visual, a Chinese worker leans over an imagined wall between China and Korea to slip a noose around the neck of an American composite figure armed with bombs. While the American prepares his sabotage, off scene North Koreans attack the invader with guns and bayonets from behind. (We might speculate that the hangman's noose, intended for the American imperialist, also alluded to the public executions of "enemies of the people" during the campaign against counter-revolutionaries that accompanied the war in Korea.[28]) With so much news being published in November 1950 about the highly sensitive spot of Andong on the Sino–North Korean border, such cartoons probably reflected and reinforced Premier Zhou Enlai's policy of "not sitting supinely by" as China's borders were threatened by a hostile foe.[29]

---

26 Ding, "Peaceful People."

27 Jie, "People's Shoreline."

28 On the contemporary, less violent "three-anti, five-anti" (*sanfan, wufan*) movements, see Mao, *Jianguo Yilai*, vols. 2 and 3; Tiewes, *Politics*.

29 Zhou Enlai's longstanding personal attachment to this idea is evidenced in a Memorandum of Conversation among President Nixon, Henry Kissinger, Zhou Enlai, Qiao

Figure 8 Ding Cong, "The Chinese and Korean People Unite to Resist America" *Xuanchuan huakan Ziliao*, No. 5, p. 15. (Hunter Collection)

In Figure 9, "Truman Tells Himself," a horned American president, recognizing the failures of Chiang Kai-shek and Syngman Rhee to roll back Communism in China and Korea, butts his head against a stout wall labeled "The Democratic Power of the Asian People."[30]

Figure 10 depicts a corpulent capitalist, apparently Harry Truman, plotting war against China.[31] The image plays upon an important dichotomy promoted in the new PRC: Socialist countries were inherently harmonious and consensual, while capitalist nations were predicated on raw coercive force. Figure 10, executed at the height of Chinese/North Korean military campaigns into southern Korea, depicts Truman attempting to cajole a group of imperialist leaders into signing a "Declaration to Invade China." Fearing to sign the declaration, the im-

Guanhua, et. al., in the Great Hall of the People, Beijing, February 22, 1972 (National Security Archive, Washington, DC), p. 22.

30   See Liu, "Meiguo qin Hua shi."

31   For Mao's contempt for overweight Westerners depicted in cartoons, see Chang and Halliday, *Mao*, p. 427.

Figure 9 Bing Hong, "Truman Tells Himself: Big or Small, None of Them Worked, So I Will Bang My Own Head!" (Yingzhe toupi, an qin zi peng!) *Manhua* No. 3, cover. (Hunter Collection)

Figure 10 Mi Gu, "How Dare You Put Down the Pen So Easily?" (Qi gan qing yi xia bi) (*Kangmei Yuanchao Manhua Xuan*, p. 22). (Hunter Collection)

perialists unanimously point out that "New China is too strong to oppose."

Such cartoons, depicting foreign reluctance to sign declarations, both contrasted and tallied with others celebrating the ostensible enthusiasm of young Chinese men to volunteer publicly for military duty in Korea. Within China, the Korean War had brought with it an intense campaign of mobilization including pledge drives of all types.[32] Students, women, farmers, and factory workers were encouraged and sometimes coerced to sign a host of banners declaring opposition to war, desire for peace, solidarity with the besieged North Korean people, material support for the Chinese People's Volunteers, and—most important—enrollment in the armies of defense. The cartoon may subtly allude to silent resistance to these campaigns among the Chinese populace by placing Truman in the position of an overbearing solicitor of signatures. At the same time, the cartoon was designed to

32 Gao, "War Culture."

encourage Chinese youth to sign up by noting that the imperialists were also trying to enlist support for their cause. The cartoon implies that, for both money-sodden imperialists and poor but patriotic Chinese, the act of signing a petition signaled but one overwhelming thought: China's substantial defensive capabilities.

This cartoon also places the image of Tiananmen in the collective imagination of the foreign powers, giving that symbol of China added significance. China's future strength, so different from its past weakness, will be enough, it seems, to keep the foreigners from invading. This idea so appealed to the editors of a major collection of "Resist America, Aid Korea" cartoons that they replicated the image inside the speech balloon of Figure 10 and printed it prominently on the collection's title page.

Two weeks after this cartoon appeared, another one used different images to reinforce the idea of China's changed status vis-à-vis its foreign adversaries. The CCP artist Mi Gu, who had thrown his barbs at Chiang Kai-shek from postwar Hong Kong, now focused on the United States' "reverse course" in Japan, dramatizing the American halt in war-crimes prosecutions and the U.S. sponsorship of the Japanese "self-defense force." In the first panel, MacArthur and a fascist Japanese soldier in the same bed "recall the past" when Japan had kicked down the flimsy door of the "Republic of China." This image reminds viewers of Chiang Kai-shek's past inability to protect China from Japanese aggression and the ostensibly unchecked continuation of Japanese militarists' dreams to restore Japanese influence on the continent. In the second panel, perhaps reflecting Chinese awareness of covert Japanese support for the American invasion of Korea, MacArthur sends the Japanese soldier off toward China, saying, "You're familiar with the gate and the road." In panel three, the Japanese soldier fails to smash the powerful new gate of the People's Republic of China, dramatizing the difference between the old and new China. Notably, MacArthur fears even to approach this new gate, having been bloodied by Chinese troops in the mountains and hills of Korea. Instead he ends up leading a retreat back into southern Korea, which Secretary of State Dean Acheson called the greatest U.S. defeat since Bull Run.

While Figure 11 dramatized the strength of the gate, the most exposed salient of the People's Republic's new wall of "socialist" wealth

Figure 11 Mi Gu, "The Gate Is Not the Same," *Kangmei Yuanchao Manhua Xuan* (Shanghai: Minzhong Chubanshe, 1950). (Hunter Collection)

and power, Chinese artists never supposed that China alone could defeat Japanese and American imperialism. In particular, one foreign country, the font of socialism, would help to deter Japanese militarism and offer fraternal support on the road to "modernization."

Walls as Icons of Solidarity with the Soviet Union

Artistic depictions of the Soviet Union, and of Sino-Soviet friendship, proliferated in the early years of the PRC and were particularly abundant in the months surrounding the Sino-Soviet alliance of February 1950. Because that alliance was defensive in nature, aimed against Japan and the unnamed state that might ally with it (i.e., the United States), perhaps the visual association of the Soviets with walls

Figure 12 Chen Yanqiao, "The Torch of Lenin Shines Over All Mankind," *Jiefang Manhua Xuan* (Shanghai, 1950), p. 67. (Hunter Collection)

redolent of national security should not be surprising. Though walls seemed incongruous, symbolically speaking, with Marx's praise of internationalism and belief in the universality of science, they also indicated the benefits of transnational cooperation in defense. One cartoon bridged the divide between the drag of anachronistic walls and the benefits of Soviet solidarity by depicting industry itself—in this case a dam—as a kind of "modern" bulwark (Figure 12).

China eagerly sought Soviet aid in building dams to produce hydroelectric power.[33] In the northeast, however, the CCP had to over-

33 Liu Shaoqi, "Telegraphs to Mao Zedong et al., Concerning the Request of Soviet Specialists to Repair Hydroelectric Plants in Manchuria," December 1949, in Liu Shaoqi, *Jianguo,* vol. 1, pp. 222–25. See also Mao Zedong, Telegraph to Liu Shaoqi, December 29, 1949, in Mao, *Jianguo,* vol. 1, p. 199; Liu Shaoqi, "Letter to Stalin and Soviet Communist

come deep anti-Soviet feelings resulting from the Soviet dismantling of Japanese industry at the end of World War II and its shipment to the war-devastated Soviet Union. The CCP strove to counteract people's suspicions of Soviet motives by associating the Soviet Union with defense against external enemies and downplaying its continued control over the major port of Lüshun.[34] The CCP argued that awareness of the economic benefits of dams should outweigh any rancor at past Soviet misbehavior and any shame in accepting foreign assistance.

The CCP's practice of printing overtly pro-Soviet and Soviet-style images in Shanghai in the late 1940s generated controversy. In response to those who criticized Soviet culture as imported and monotonous, the CCP trumpeted the strategic benefits of the Soviet alliance and invoked the values of nationalism and modernization. In one cartoon, Figure 13, the People's Political Consultative Conference, a kind of constituent assembly that drew up the first constitution of the People's Republic in 1949, was depicted as a thick wall around a Soviet-style building labeled "the Chinese People's Republic."

In this cartoon, a member of the People's Liberation Army, standing underneath the human-size characters for "people" (*renmin*), distributes handbills to workers and farmers. The soldier monitors a gap in the wall through which a path rises up toward the bright new compound, representing the People's Republic. Reflecting the general trend to dismantle city walls at the time, the wall's apertures are ungated, suggesting that the new government should be more accessible to the people. Assuming that the compound, like Tiananmen, faces south, the flags blow to the West and suggest thereby the prevalence of the east wind over the west wind (anticipating a later Maoist slogan).

Although depictions of new socialist architecture suggested a fresh start for the Chinese republic, Mao and the CCP ultimately decided to use a set of older symbols to represent the nation. In the "Propaganda

---

Party regarding the Need to Study Soviet Experience in Building a Republic," July 6, 1949, in Liu, *Jianguo,* vol. 1, p. 27.

34 For evidence of CCP sensitivity to the issue of Soviet technical assistance and the persistence of extraterritoriality for Soviet specialists, see Liu Shaoqi, "Comment on Letter Response from Zhang Zhongshi," November 6/7, 1949, Liu, *Jianguo,* vol. 1, p. 136. Interestingly, the U.S. military retained similar privileges by treaty with the Nationalist Government in 1945 that persisted in Taiwan after 1949.

Figure 13 Zhao Yan'nian, "Stepping Up," *Jiefang Manhua Xuan* (Shanghai, 1950), p. 28. (Hunter Collection)

Source Materials," the walls, gates and buildings of Beijing's Forbidden City and Moscow's Kremlin were presented as "bulwarks of liberation of the whole of humanity." Tiananmen (the principal entry to the Forbidden City), Qianmen (the city wall gate to the south) and the "Ten Thousand Li Long Wall" are juxtaposed with the crenellated towers of the Kremlin. These were the bastions of socialism—sometimes paired with human figures, but often standing alone, mute testimony to the strength of what was then widely regarded as "the Soviet bloc."[35]

If depictions of Moscow hinged on the Kremlin and Lenin's tomb, artistic representations of the United States dwelled on the capitol building.[36] The monthly pamphlet "Propaganda Source" depicted the capitol building in Washington, D.C., as fated to crumble under assault by the people of the world.[37] Although the capitol is mislabeled as the White House, the cartoon seems to suggest that the U.S. capitol was

---

35 *Xuanchuan huakan ziliao*, p. 1.
36 Chinese youth, who had been raised to revere Lenin, demonstrated against him at his tomb in Moscow during the Cultural Revolution. Ma, *Cultural Revolution*.
37 *Xuanchuan Ziliao*, p. 16.

Figure 14 Mengzi, "Sino-Soviet Cooperation Is Very Strong, and Will Not Allow the Japanese Pirates to Commit More Mischief," *Postcards to Prevent the American Revival of Japanese Militarism*, No. 20 (Hong Kong: 1950). (Hunter Collection)

destined to suffer the destruction similar to that which the United States was then visiting on the cities of North Korea.[38] Since the early 1950s, a similar image of a smashed heart of American power has been popularized by government artists in North Korea.

The violent destruction of the imperialists was contrasted with the peaceful construction of socialism. In a famous cartoon entitled "Sedan Chair Warriors of the Adventurists," the American general MacArthur is being transported across the sea from Taiwan and Korea toward Tiananmen and the Kremlin, symbols of the Sino-Soviet alliance shining with the beacon of peace.[39] China's shorelines are depicted as impregnable, high, uplifted, and unified. Doves or airplanes hover over the buildings, symbolizing both peace and defense. The imperialists, by contrast, are depicted as mired in antimodern violence.

38 For U.S. bombing of Korea during the Korean War, see Stratemeyer, *Three Wars*.
39 Zhang, "Sedan Chair Warriors of the Adventurists," *Renmin Ribao*, December 1, 1950.

The benefits of the Soviet alliance are seen in a different light in Figure 14. This postcard, interestingly, places Tiananmen on an even higher plane than the Kremlin, but the pairing of the two symbols shows the benefits of the defense alliance against Japan. If we were to put this in terms reminiscent of the Ming period, the PRC, having secured its northern frontiers with Russia, could turn its attention to the seaborne pirates of Japan. The wall as a symbol of Sino-Soviet solidarity emerges clearly in Figure 15. Here Mao and Stalin themselves, rather than stock depictions of the "working class," represent their respective states. Again Churchill and Truman approach the wall with crazed plans of invasion, again they are diminutive, and again Churchill's cigar smoke seems to react to the character "*tuan*" (militia, in *tuanjie*, unity) although this time rising toward it! The two socialist leaders, unlike the two comrades in Figure 14, do not stand arm in arm, and Stalin does not assume a protective pose. Instead, they are depicted as equals, their clothing and height indicating parity. Both men gaze beyond the petty imperialists below, but their visions extend in opposite directions. Mao's, perhaps not accidentally, is directed up to his left, perhaps toward the place where Marx had gone, as Mao would later say, to "see God." Mao is foregrounded and has both hands on the wall, suggesting perhaps his greater centrality and power.

Artists only infrequently paired Mao Zedong with the Sino-Soviet treaty in cartoons, perhaps because of his and his colleagues' doubts about the value of the agreement. Although cartoonists had Mao and Stalin share the spotlight in more than a few scenes, Mao's persona was already growing too grand to be limited by compromising undertakings with foreign mentors. Artists gradually depicted Mao, as much as Tiananmen itself, as the symbol of the new China. Because this notion would only grow, culminating in the huge rallies of the Cultural Revolution and the grim edifice of the chairman's mausoleum facing Tiananmen, Mao's association with Tiananmen in the early years of the PRC is worth closer examination.

Mao's Personal Association with Tiananmen

Mao's self-identification with Tiananmen was not coincidental, and it had consequences for the PRC. Tiananmen, the southern gate to the

Figure 15 Gu Bingxin, "Great Unity of 700 Million People," *Pierce the Paper Tiger*, p. 70. (Hunter Collection)

Forbidden City, afforded the chief passage through the massive walls around the Forbidden City dating from Ming times. Mao was at the apex, as if growing out of Tiananmen, where, of course, he had announced the founding of the People's Republic in 1949. The CCP obviously hoped that Tiannanmen, and by extension Beijing, would be a more durable symbol of a longer-lasting regime than the blue tile roofs of Nanjing, symbols of the Republic in the 1930s, had proved to be.

Out of Tiananmen would flow abundance, a result of the long pent-up productive potential of the Chinese people. Derk Bodde, a Fulbright scholar living in Beijing and studying classical poetry, filled the pages of his 1949 diary with images of the city being scoured by the Communists. Its lakes were dredged, its monuments restored, the earthen scars at the Temple of Heaven healed. The Chinese Communists thereby gave a nod to the "feudal past" represented by the gate even as they dedicated themselves to transcending that history.

The cartoonist Mengzi, celebrating China's having "stood up" in a series of postcards, refined the meaning of Mao's famous phrase by honing his caption into a more specific meaning: Japan can no longer spill Chinese blood. By using the phrase "China has stood up" in tandem with images of Tiananmen, Mengzi reminded viewers of Mao's electrifying declaration and implied that the establishment of the PRC would transform relations with Japan. In Figure 16, backed by an image of Tiananmen, a brawny Chinese man denounces a sword-wielding "Japanese devil," the worker's thoughts guided by the watercolor gaze of Chairman Mao, whose plump visage proudly surveys the proceedings, almost like a son of heaven. Rather than a Soviet worker-brother fending off the Japanese, as in Figure 14, here the evocation of Chairman Mao by a single outsized worker is sufficient to deter the bloodthirsty but diminutive Japanese.

It is not known what feelings stirred in the heart of the young Mao when he first beheld Tiananmen in 1918, but, like others who encountered the gate as fully conscious adults, he probably experienced the tug of history and the weight of "tradition." He must have become aware also of Tiananmen's potential as a symbol of tremendous strength. With the success of his revolution and the demise of the Republican regime in the southern capital of Nanjing, Mao's image would

14. 中國巨人站起來了，要向日寇討還血債。

Figure 16 Mengzi, "The Chinese People Have Stood Up, Preventing the Japanese Pirates from Spilling Blood Again," *Postcards to Prevent American Revival of Japanese Militarism*, no. 14. (Hunter Collection)

be changed as well. His previous association with the rough caves of Yan'an would be transformed into identification with the elegant gates of the Ming-Qing capital city. Like the "Great Within," which he first entered in 1949, Mao's thinking on the legacy of China's past rulers is not readily apparent. There is evidence, however, that he especially revered the commoner founders Han Gaozu and Ming Taizu.[40] Mao's marginalia in the dynastic histories and his own poetry make frequent mention of rural rebellions scattered through China's past.[41] Taking their cues from the Chairman, party propagandists would make repeated visual associations among Mao, China, and Tiananmen, fashioning the three into one indivisible symbol of the nation. Through Mao, the humiliations of the past would be transformed irrevocably into triumphs in the future.

In Figure 17, the masses combine uniformity with jubilance as they face south with Mao, whose image prior to 1949 had been banned by Chiang Kai-shek but now rises out of the gate at the back of the crowd. The red banners declare the "Chinese People's Republic," but these are abstractions compared with the dominant figure of Mao Zedong.

40   Andrew and Rapp, *Autocracy.*
41   Zhongguo Dang'an Chubanshe, *Mao Zedong.*

Figure 17   Mao and the Masses (*Manhua* No. 5, front cover). (Hunter Collection)

In Figure 18, published after the great ceremony atop Tiananmen on October 1, 1949, the artist surpasses the specific archetypes in the propaganda manuals by mixing together all manner of themes. This riotous visual shows that as long as glorification of the leader remained clear, artists were relatively free to elaborate on the state-approved models using their own imagination. As depicted on the back cover of *Manhua* magazine, the very important source of much of the graphic imagery in the new era, Mao's portrait on Tiananmen does not look squarely forward, but gazes upward and to his left as if to mimic the

Figure 18 Marching for Mao. (*Manhua* No. 5, back cover) (Hunter Collection)

living Mao's October First admiration of airplane formations flying overhead. If one opens the magazine to view both back and front covers simultaneously, it appears that Mao's immense head is rising out of the southern edge of the space that would become Tiananmen Square, remarkably near to the site of his sarcophagus today. Mao's personal association with the center of his new republic continues to have lasting consequences.

The teeming images in Figure 19, dating from 1950, helped develop the personality cult around Mao. No one could confuse him any more with Zhu De, the more plebian and modest commander, with whose

Figure 19 Ya Wen, "Greatly Celebrate New China's Helmsman" (*Manhua* No. 5, inside cover image). (Hunter Collection)

image Mao's had been regularly paired in street demonstrations in the late 1940s. Here Mao is identified instead with a gate resembling Tiananmen. From this site his personality infuses the new China. His is the guiding spirit of the revolution. Although natural science and technology (represented by the compass) are available to him as they were to his ancestors, Mao is able to steer forward intuitively by grasping the wheel of social science and ideology ("Marxism"). His sturdy clothing is that of a worker, his unbuttoned shirt suggesting a willingness to tackle any problem. The angle of the face, like that of the large portrait printed in the *People's Daily* (*Renmin Ribao*) on the day after the signing of the Sino-Soviet treaty, suggests visionary qualities.

This cartoon reverses the "traditional" *shan-shui* (lit., mountain/ water) order of painting in which background, foreground, and mid-

dle ground each unfold in succession. Now Mao, the "mountain" dominating the panel, is in the foreground. In the "water" element of the
picture, a trio (worker, soldier, and urban artist) pierce the illusion of
Guomindang and American strength in the Pacific. The worker takes
an immense sledgehammer to Chiang Kai-shek on Taiwan, an attack
buoyed by China's growing industrial wealth and potential naval
might. The boxes of supplies behind them, marked "Support the Front
Line," morph into a large gate symbolic of the nation. A small and
fedora-clad "bandit agent" is lifted from the ground by a righteous and
physically superior Communist official, indicative of the national pre-
occupation with counterrevolutionary activity in 1950 and 1951. This
protean depiction of Mao and of new China had only tangential connections to the propaganda manuals discussed earlier, indicating both
the fertility of the artist's mind and the limits on artistic expression in
1951. Mao was not yet entirely monopolizing depictions of Tiananmen.
But, it may be worth asking, who are the characters defending the critical "rear area" along the coast and at the foot of the gate? The answer is
not simply any old Chinese soldier or leader, but Mao himself. The row
of flags, a stock image of the time like the portrait of Lenin, forms a
wall of sorts, wherein political unity and a quasi-spiritual faith in socialism combine.

   To Mao's right, in the lower left corner of the frame, are piled bags
of grain and also what appear to be immense radishes, symbolizing the
agricultural bounty that would inevitably be achieved in the new order.
Farmers reap grain with new machinery, brandishing the "land reform
law," while merchants above them transact fair deals overseen by hon-
est cadre. Already adumbrating the grandiose agrifantasy of the Great
Leap Forward, the peasants are seen gladly pouring their yield into the
national granary, a longstanding Chinese symbol of responsible government.[42] Interestingly, the farmers literally have Mao's ear, and the
Chairman appears pleased by the sounds of grain pouring into the
state coffers.

   In Figure 19, however, nothing rises higher than Communist theory. In the upper left corner of the frame a large red banner identifies
the People's Congress, the prime locus of sovereignty in the People's
Republic according to its constitutions. Books are held high: one book
marked "Fascist Education" is destroyed, while a book of Marxism as

---

42   Will and Wong with Lee, *Nourish the People*; Leonard and Watt, *Achieve Security*.

large as a human is being lifted up like the Ten Commandments. Above it all, in the most striking of images, rise seven hands reading "Criticism, Self-Criticism," a Maoist version of a Buddhist mantra. Airplanes gild the sky, moving to the east. None of this utopian vision would be possible, the artist implies, without a strong defense. The artist, like Mao himself, chose carefully from the available repertoire in 1950, creating a potent amalgam of Chinese statecraft, proletarian internationalism, and national strength.

Images of walls continued to appear in the new China after 1949, enlisting ancient symbols in support of national strength. Renewal and destruction would coexist throughout Mao's reign, and the latter would arguably limit China's development. Mao's unshakeable belief in continuous revolution would ultimately take priority over the emphasis on strong defense characteristic of the political cartoons of the early 1950s. The promise of agrarian socialism, the fraternity with the communist bloc, and China's ability to hold at bay its external enemies would be put at risk by the anti-Rightist campaign, the Great Leap Forward, and the Cultural Revolution. By closing himself off in the great within of Zhongnanhai, part of the Forbidden City not open to the public, and by maintaining a wall of secrecy and superiority between himself and the people he led, Mao placed China at a great disadvantage at least in the immediate competition among the most powerful states. From 1949 to 1951, however, open speculations on such consequences of Mao's course were limited to a handful of Western observers in the Chinese peripheries of Hong Kong and Taiwan. Mao had thrust most foreigners to the very frontiers of China. The praise and portraits he received as a result helped to promote a national identity that was both new and deeply rooted in the past.

Works Cited

Andrew, Anita M., and John A. Rapp. *Autocracy and China's Rebel Founding Emperors: Comparing Chairman Mao and Ming Taizu.* Lanham, Md.: Rowman & Littlefield, 2000.

Bodde, Derek. *Peking Diary: A Year of Revolution.* New York: Henry Schumer, 1950.

Cathcart, Adam. "Chinese Nationalism in the Shadow of Japan, 1945–1950." Ph.D. dissertation, Ohio University, 2005.

————. "Cruel Resurrection: Chinese Comics in the Korean War," *International Journal of Comic Art* 1(2004), pp. 37–55.

Chang, Jung, and Jon Halliday, *Mao: The Unknown Story*. New York: Alfred A. Knopf, 2005.

Chang, Wen Ho. *Mass Media in China: The History and the Future*. Ames: Iowa State University Press, 1989.

Chu, Godwin C., and Yanan Tu. *The Great Wall in Ruins: Communication and Cultural Change in China*. Albany: SUNY Press, 1993.

Coble, Parks. *Facing Japan: Chinese Politics and Japanese Imperialism, 1931–1937*. Cambridge, Mass.: Council on East Asia Studies; distributed by Harvard University Press, 1991.

Cohen, Paul A. *History in Three Keys: The Boxer Rebellion as Event, Experience, and Myth*. New York: Columbia University Press, 1997.

Ding, Cong. "Peaceful People Must Be Vigilant at Every Moment against the Covert Sabotage of American Imperialism and Chiang Kai-shek," *Xuanchuan Ziliao* (Dec. 1950) No. 2, pp. 7–8.

Fitzgerald, C. P. *The Birth of Communist China*. Suffolk, England: Penguin, 1964.

Foreign Relations of the United States, 1946, The Far East: China. vol. X. Washington, DC: U.S. Government Printing Office, 1976.

Gao, James Z. *The Communist Takeover of Hangzhou: The Transformation of City and Cadre, 1949–1954*. Honolulu: University of Hawaii Press, 2004.

————. "War Culture, Nationalism, and Political Campaigns, 1950–1953." Pp. 179–203 in *Chinese Nationalism in Perspective: Historical and Recent Cases*, C. X. George Wei and Xiaoyuan Liu, eds. Westport, Conn.: Greenwood Press, 2001.

Hinton, William. *Fanshen: A Documentary of Revolution in a Chinese Village*. New York and London: Monthly Review Press, 1966.

Hung, Chang-Tai. "The Fuming Image: Cartoons and Public Opinion in Late Republican China, 1945–1949," *Comparative Studies in Society and History* 36(1, Jan. 1994), pp. 122–45.

Hunter, Edward W. Collection. Mass Education Materials Published in the Early Period of the People's Republic of China: Anti-Imperialism. China, 1949–1952. Center for Research Libraries, Chicago, Illinois.

————. *Brainwashing in Red China: The Calculated Destruction of Men's Minds*. New York; Vanguard Press, 1951.

Israel, John. *Lianda: A Chinese University in War and Revolution*. Stanford: Stanford University Press, 1998.

Jie, Kebao, "People's Shoreline" *Manhua* No. 5 (Shanghai, 1950), p. 26.

Johnson, Chalmers. *Peasant Nationalism and Communist Power: The Emer-*

gence of Revolutionary China, 1937–1945. Stanford, Stanford University Press, 1962.

Jordan, Donald. *Chinese Boycotts versus Japanese Bombs: The Failure of China's "Revolutionary Diplomacy," 1931–1932.* Ann Arbor: University of Michigan Press, 1991.

——. *The Northern Expedition.* Honolulu: University of Hawaii Press, 1976.

Leonard, Jane Kate, and John R. Watt, eds. *To Achieve Security and Wealth: The Qing Imperial State and the Economy, 1644–1911.* Ithaca: Cornell East Asia Series, 1992.

Li, Cunsong. "Pulling Up the Roots of Fascism," in Zhongguo quan guo, *Jiefang Shanghai*, p. 4.

Li, Hua. "Storming the Citadel," woodcut, *People's China* (Beijing: Foreign Language Press, January 1950).

Li, Zuopeng. "Under the Direction of Comrade Lin Biao: First Encounter on the Battlefield of the Northeast," originally printed in *Renmin Ribao*, Beijing, December 3, 1968, translated by American Consulate General in Hong Kong and published in *Current Background*, no. 896, Nov. 20, 1969, entitled *About Comrade Lin Piao*. Washington, DC: Center for Chinese Research Materials, Association of Research Libraries, 1970.

Lieberthal, Kenneth. *Revolution and Tradition in Tianjin, 1949–1952.* Stanford: Stanford University Press, 1980.

Liu, Danian, "Meiguo qin Hua shi" (A history of the American invasion of China"), wall poster (Beijing: Renmin Yishu Chubanshe, 1951), Library of Congress Prints and Photographs Division, call number POS-China. P44, no. 6 (B size).

Liu, Shaoqi. *Jianguo yilai Liu Shaoqi wengao* (Liu Shaoqi's manuscripts since the founding of the republic), 4 vols. Beijing: Zhongyang wenxian chubanshe, 2005.

Ma, Jisen. *The Cultural Revolution in the Foreign Ministry of China.* Hong Kong: Chinese University Press, 2004.

Mao, Zedong. *Jianguo yilai Mao Zedong wengao* (Mao Zedong's manuscripts since the founding of the People's Republic), 13 vols. Beijing: Zhongyang wenxian chubanshe, 1987.

Mitter, Rana. *The Manchurian Myth: Nationalism, Resistance, and Collaboration in Modern China.* Berkeley: University of California Press, 2000.

National Security Archive. Washington, DC: George Washington University, 2005. Available http://www.gwu.edu/-nsarchiv/nsa/publications/DOC_readers/kissinger/nixzhou/. Accessed November 11, 2008.

Peng, Zhen. "Zhangwo zhengquan, fadong qunzhong" (Seize political power and mobilize the masses), December 6, 1945, *Peng Zhen Wenxuan* (The writings of Peng Zhen). Beijing: Dangxiao chubanshe, 1995.

Potter, Pitman B. *From Leninist Discipline to Socialist Legalism: Peng Zhen on Law and Political Authority in the PRC*. Stanford: Stanford University Press, 2003.

Reilly, Bernard, Amy Wood, and Adam Cathcart. "Political Communications and Mass Education in the Early Years of the People's Republic," *Center for Research Libraries FOCUS* Vol. 22, No. 1 (2002): 9–11.

Schneewind, Sarah. *Long Live the Emperor! Uses of the Ming Founder across Six Centuries of East Asian History*. Minneapolis: Society for Ming Studies, 2008.

Shen, Kuiyi. "Lianhuanhua and Manhua—Picture Books and Comics in Old Shanghai," *Illustrating Asia: Comics, Humor Magazines, and Picture Books*, John Lent, ed. (Honolulu: University of Hawaii Press, 2001), pp. 100–20.

Shen, Zhihua. *Mao Zedong, Sidalin yu kang Mei yuan Chao*. (Mao Zedong, Stalin, and the Resist-America-Aid-Korea Movement). Guangzhou: Guandong renmin chubanshe, 2003.

Stratemeyer, George E. *The Three Wars of George E. Stratemeyer: His Korean War Diary*, William T. Y'Blood, ed. Washington, DC: U. S. Government Printing Service, 1999.

Su, Xiaokang. *Deathsong of the River: A Reader's Guide to the Chinese TV Series He Shang*, Richard W. Bodman and Pin P. Wan, trans. Ithaca: Cornell East Asia Series, 1991.

Tiewes, Frederick C. *Politics at Mao's Court: Gao Gang and Party Factionalism in the Early 1950s*. White Plains, NY: M. E. Sharpe, 1990.

Wang, Peiping. Dalian shi shi zhi bangongshi (Dalian history office), *Sulian Hongjun zai Lü Da*. (The Soviet Red Army in Lüshun and Dalian). Dalian: Dongbei caijing daxue yinshuachang, 1995.

Wasserstrom, Jeffery. *Student Protests in Twentieth-Century China: The View from Shanghai*. Stanford: Stanford University Press, 1991.

Weigelin-Schwiedrzik, Suzanne. "Party Historiography." Pp. 151–73 in *Using the Past to Serve the Present: Historiography and Politics in Contemporary China*, Jonathan Unger, ed. Armonk, NY: M. E. Sharpe, 1993.

Westad, Odd Arne. *Decisive Encounters: The Chinese Civil War, 1946–1950*. Stanford: Stanford University Press, 2003.

Will, Pierre-Étienne, and R. Bin Wong, with James Lee, eds. *Nourish the People: The State Civilian Granary System in China, 1650–1850*. Ann Arbor: University of Michigan Center for Chinese Studies, 1991.

Xuanchuan huakan ziliao (Visual propaganda materials), no. 4. Shanghai: Renmin meishu chubanshe, 1951.

Yang, Zhiguo. "U.S. Marines in Qingdao: Society, Culture, and China's Civil War 1945–1949." Pp. 181–206 in Xiaobing Li and Hongshan Li, eds., *China and the United States: A New Cold War History.* Lanham, Md.: University Press of America, 1998.

Yick, Joseph. *Making Urban Revolution in China: The CCP-GMD Struggle for Beiping-Tianjin, 1945–1949.* Armonk, NY: M. E. Sharpe, 1995.

Zhang, Ding. "Sedan Chair Warriors of the Adventurists," *Renmin Ribao* (People's Daily), December 1, 1950.

———. *Zhang Ding Manhua: 1936–1976* (Cartoons by Zhang Ding: 1936–1976). Shenyang: Liaoning meishu chubanshe, 1985.

Zhang Lianjun, Guan Daxin, and Wang Shuyan. *Dongbei Sansheng geming wenhuashi,* 1919.5.4–1949.10.1. (A cultural history of revolution in the Three Northeastern Provinces, May 4, 1919–October 1, 1949), Harbin: Heilongjiang renmin chubanshe, 2003.

Zhang Zhenglong. *Xue Bai, Xue Hong: Guo-Gong dongbei dajuezhan lishi zhenxiang* (White snow, red blood: A truthful history of the GMD-CCP decisive battle in the northeast). Hong Kong: Liwen Publishing House, 1999.

Zhongguo dang'an chubanshe (China archives press), eds., *Mao Zedong ping dian ershisi shi* (Mao Zedong's commentaries on the twenty-four histories), 3 vols. Beijing: Zhongguo dang'an chubanshe, 1997.

Zhou, Enlai. *Zhou Enlai xuanji* (Selected works of Zhou Enlai), 2 vols. Beijing: Renmin chubanshe, 1984.

CHAPTER SEVEN

Pathogen Traffic
Walls and Apertures

Richard V. Lee and Roger Des Forges

IN THE FALL OF 2002, a new, highly infectious disease broke out in China's southeastern province of Guangdong, taking the lives of patients and health care professionals who treated them. In February 2003, the illness that attacked the lungs but was impervious to antibiotics spread to Hong Kong, only recently brought under the authority of the People's Republic. From there it moved on to Taiwan, Singapore, Vietnam, and Canada. In March 2003, the pathogen was identified as a novel coronavirus (i.e., having a distinctive round shape) and was named Severe Acute Respiratory Syndrome (SARS). According to the available records, it took the lives of some 916 people worldwide before being brought under control by the following year. Meanwhile a highly pathogenic avian influenza (HPAI), Hemagglutin 5 Neuraminidase 1 (H5N1), which had infected eighteen people in Hong Kong in 1997, reappeared in south China and Southeast Asia. It took slightly more than two hundred lives worldwide over the next four years. It threatened to cause a pandemic equaling or surpassing that of 1918, which killed thirty to fifty million people.

The SARS epidemic now seems to have been contained and Avian flu H5N1 has yet to be easily or widely transmitted from humans to humans.[1] But fears of bioterrorism associated in some people's minds with the attacks in New York and Washington on September 11, 2001, and concerns about the emergence of new diseases in an age of global warming have combined to raise anxiety about the likelihood of a viral pandemic originating in China. The Acquired Immunodeficiency Syndrome (AIDS) pandemic has taken far more lives and is far more widespread, including in China, where there are some 1.5 million cases. But the unexpected and highly lethal SARS and H5N1 epidemics have raised questions about how they arose and spread so widely before they were brought under some kind of control.[2]

As the latest pathogens for which neither vaccines nor antiviral medicines have been developed, SARS and H5N1 continue to attract much attention, including academic conferences, journal supplements, conference volumes, and human-interest accounts.[3] In this chapter we draw on some of this literature to describe and analyze the complex roles that walls and apertures have played in the emergence, spread, and containment of these pathogens. We find that it was the breakdown in the wall between other animals' and humans' receptivity to the viruses and gaps in the wall between infected people and other people that allowed the SARS virus to become an epidemic. The H5N1 virus also jumped the wall between animals and humans but has so far been unable to migrate easily from one person to another. It has thus as of now failed to become the pandemic that was once feared and that, given its great lability (i.e., tendency to mutate) it is still likely to become.

Meanwhile, we note that it was the persistence of virtual barriers among Chinese bureaucratic units and between China's public health administration and international organizations combined with the diminution of material barriers to transport between China and the rest of the world that allowed the pathogens to travel so far and so fast. The absence of effective virtual walls of new vaccines and antiviral medicine led to heavy reliance on the more prosaic material "walls" of masks and isolation. On the other hand, it was the concomitant

---

1   In January 2008 three cases of Avian Flu among humans were reported in China.

2   Garrett, "Next Pandemic"; Karesh and Cook, "Human-Animal"; WHO Global Influenza Network, "Evolution."

3   Kleinman and Watson, SARS; Kleinman et al., "Avian"; Kleinman et al., "Asian"; McLean, SARS; Greenfeld, China Syndrome.

lowering of the barriers to domestic and international scientific communication that helped to limit the damage of the two epidemics. Close attention to the complex roles of various bulwarks and gaps in these two cases may be useful in ongoing efforts to prevent or at least minimize the impact of future outbreaks of these or similar diseases.

Emergence

Given that there are an estimated 1,400 human pathogens, it is not surprising that we humans have been contending with them on a regular basis ever since our appearance on earth many millennia ago. According to one theory, there have been three major periods in the development of diseases affecting humans. In the first, with the appearance of agriculture in the Neolithic era, humans became vulnerable to infectious diseases of many kinds. In the second, the industrial era, we developed the means of combating many infectious diseases through drugs but began to suffer more from chronic illnesses, such as heart disease and cancer. During the third period, beginning a few decades ago, we have been encountering the reemergence of endemic infectious diseases, such as tuberculosis; the emergence of new epidemic diseases, such as AIDS; and the development of new strains of old epidemic diseases, such as influenza, which are impervious—or at least highly resistant—to existing vaccines and medicines and therefore potentially productive of pandemics.[4]

In a slightly different but complementary view, infectious diseases have always been present around the world, including in North America, in recent centuries. They have included dysentery and fevers in the seventeenth century, smallpox and diphtheria in the early eighteenth century, yellow fever and cholera in the late eighteenth and nineteenth centuries, and polio and influenza in the twentieth century.[5] Although different in scope, these two periodizations agree in rejecting any simple linear development from human vulnerability to mastery and in positing a more complex and recurrent historical pattern of continuity and change.

---

4   Chuengsatiansup, "Ethnography," p. 53; Chen et al., "Angiostrongyliasis."
5   Rosenberg, "Siting," p. S4.

In light of the fact that 65 percent of all pathogens are zoonotic (capable of passing from other animals to humans and sometimes vice versa), and that various viruses, although only 5 percent of all pathogens, have been accomplishing this feat regularly since their appearance tens of thousands of years ago, it is also not surprising that there have been major epidemics on a fairly regular basis over the last four hundred years.[6] Even the sources of influenza pandemics have remained highly continuous if not constant. For example, the pandemics of 1918, 1958, and 1968 have all been traced to avian sources. From another perspective, endemic influenza viruses, when taken together, infect as many as 500 million people and cause 500,000 deaths worldwide every year. By comparison, the mortalities of the SARS and H5N1 epidemics of the last few years have been very modest indeed.[7]

The emergence of both SARS and H5N1 in Southern China had many precedents. In 1957 a novel strain of influenza originating in Hunan province in south-central China spread to the rest of the world under the name Asian flu. In 1968 another flu appeared in southern China, moved to Hong Kong, and became known to the world as Hong Kong flu. In 1997, a new strain of Influenza A appeared in the same region and killed much poultry before spreading to humans, proving fatal to six of the eighteen infected persons in Hong Kong, and causing financial losses estimated at one billion U.S. dollars. South China is a regular incubator of highly infectious disease largely because its people prefer to eat their meat as fresh as possible. That is reasonable enough given the warm climate of the region, but it means that birds and animals are slaughtered, dressed, cooked, and eaten in rapid succession. The people of Guangdong province and more precisely of its capital Guangzhou (widely known outside China as Canton) also are famous for having a taste for the flesh of all kinds of animals, including wild and exotic ones. This is perhaps partly because such viands are in short supply, making their consumption a status symbol, and partly because

6   Causey and Edwards, "Ecology," p. S29. Some observers have even posited the appearance of epidemics at regular intervals of from three to twenty-eight years or, even more precisely, every eleven years, but these schedules have sometimes led to mistaken policies for anticipating and combating outbreaks. Fineberg, "Preparing."

7   Chen et al., "Genetic," pp. S25–26.

they are regarded as therapeutic in their fresh, and sometimes nearly raw, form.

Unfortunately, such animals as civet cats are hosts of coronaviruses, some of which are also hosted by humans. It is still not clear whether the coronavirus that causes SARS is a totally new variant of the virus or simply new to human beings.[8] In any case, the virus apparently makes its jump to humans when animals are stored and sold in "wet markets" (so named because they are hosed down after hours), slaughtered at the market or in restaurants, and consumed in uncooked or under-cooked forms.[9]

The passage of H5N1 from animals to humans was also facilitated by conditions in south China. The virus was first isolated in 2003 from pigs raised in that region. Swine are generally thought to be natural mixing vessels of viruses and transmitters of them to poultry and hu-mans (see Figure 1). At any one time, China has a population of four-teen billion fowl of which it generally vaccinates only about 20 percent and of which some twenty-four million cross the border into Hong Kong each year.[10] About 70–80 percent of China's poultry are reared in "backyards" where they are allowed to roam at will and thus are ex-posed to interaction with wild and migratory birds.[11] It has been known since 1961 that some one hundred species of wild birds are asymptom-atic carriers of influenza viruses. It was discovered in November 2002, in Hong Kong, that wild water birds can be infected with the H5N1 virus.[12] Migratory swans and geese have been implicated in introduc-tions of avian H5N1 into flocks of domestic poultry and wild water-fowl. Waterfowl are particularly suspect as reservoirs and transmitters because they shed viruses that can last up to a month in cold water and even longer when embedded in ice. Although no migratory bird carry-ing an H5N1 subtype of human origin has yet been detected, the virus

8   Munster et al., "Mallards"; Xu et al., "Epidemiologic."
9   For a graphic description of conditions in a restaurant, see Greenfeld, *China Syndrome*, pp. 39–41.
10 Kaufman, "China's Health," pp. S9–S10; Thacker and Janke, "Swine Influenza," p. 19; Greenfeld, *China Syndrome*, p. 29.
11 The riverine form of this mode of agriculture was portrayed well in Flack and Wiese, *Story*, which was one of our favorite childhood books.
12 Kaufman, "China's Health," pp. S11–S12; Greenfeld, *China Syndrome*, p. 32.

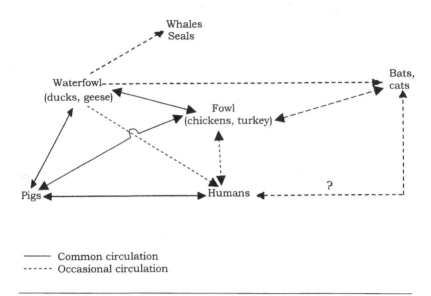

Figure 1 Influenza Viruses, Hosts, and Traffic.

is highly labile and can therefore pass from wild birds to poultry and pigs and then to humans (or even directly from wild birds to humans). Eventually, one fears, it will be able to move from infected humans to uninfected humans.[13]

Spread

The disease that came to be known as SARS was able to spread in part because it was caused by a new pathogen that resisted quick diagnosis. The first recorded case may have been a chef who was admitted to a hospital with members of his family in November 2002 in Foshan, a bustling industrial town an hour's drive south of Guangzhou. His symptoms and those of his close relatives were a cough, shortness of breath, and a fever. The first diagnoses were rickettsial pneumonia or tuberculosis, but the patients did not respond to broad-spectrum

---

13   Causey and Edwards, "Ecology," pp. S29–S33

antibiotics.[14] Suspecting that the disease might be viral, one doctor ordered a heavy dose of corticosteroids. That patient and his family were lucky and eventually recovered, but not before infecting four of their health-care attendants.

Then in December two patients were admitted to the hospital in Heyuan, two hundred miles north of Guangzhou. In this case the disease at first seemed to be different because not all family members and doctors exposed to the patients were infected.[15] This led to a tentative conclusion that the illness might not be highly infectious. In fact the new pathogen was not, we now know, as widely communicable as influenza, measles, or chicken pox. People contracting the disease do not become highly infectious until seven or eight days after the onset of symptoms, giving others warning to keep their distance. Because the disease remained unidentified and spread relatively slowly in Guangdong, apparently affecting only a tiny percentage of the population and killing only a few of the first three hundred infected, it was not considered serious enough by local health officials to be reported immediately to Beijing as an epidemic.[16]

The failure to make a quick diagnosis of the strange disease may have been partly a result as well of a general decline in China's public health system during the new era of reform and opening. During its first thirty years, the People's Republic had established a very robust public health system that eradicated smallpox and sexually transmitted acutely infectious diseases, contained tuberculosis and other chronic infectious diseases, and greatly reduced noninfectious diseases such as schistosomiasis. The result was a doubling of average life expectancy from thirty-five to nearly seventy by 1980. During the last twenty years, "relaxed government support and inadequate regulation" have resulted in the weakening of China's public health system.[17] With

14 Anthrax was ruled out although there was much concern about it in post-9/11 America.
15 Murray, "Epidemiology," pp. 17–19; Saich, "Is SARS," p. 74; Greenfeld, *China Syndrome*, pp. 62–70.
16 Murray, "Epidemiology," pp. 23–29. New viruses are often difficult to identify. The West Nile virus in New York City took a month to figure out. Saich, "Is SARS," pp. 73–76. Incidents of highly infectious diseases were to be reported to the Chinese central government.
17 Kaufman, "China's Health," pp. S7–S8.

the end of nearly free medical care and the introduction of fee for service, 21 percent of rural families remained below the poverty line because of medical expenses. In 2005 the State Council reported that 49 percent of the population could not afford to see a doctor and an estimated 30 percent were not hospitalized when necessary. As a result, tuberculosis and hepatitis B are now spreading unchecked, schistosomiasis has rebounded to affect one million people in an expanding area, and outbreaks of measles, meningitis, dengue fever, malaria, and encephalitis have become common in the Pearl River Delta.[18] Under these circumstances, some of the earliest victims of the new disease may never have come to the attention of the health system, allowing only more well-to-do patients to make their way to hospitals and public awareness. The growing gap between wealthy and poor in China, as in the world, has also permitted urban elites to purchase expensive, esoteric meat, the slaughter and consumption of which offer more opportunities for new pathogens to enter apertures in human defenses.

The spreading of the new disease was facilitated by gaps in the regulations designed to serve as walls against epidemics. It was at the same time abetted by walls erected among territorial and other units of the Chinese state and between China and the outside world. A law of 1989 required the reporting of many diseases by county officials to their provincial superiors and on up to Beijing, but reports on infectious diseases and epidemics were classified as state secrets that were not to be shared with the public. There were no requirements to report illnesses due to unknown causes.[19] The Ministry of Health in Beijing did not have the authority or ability to require reporting from the lower levels of government or even to supervise health infrastructure, financing, and pharmaceuticals. Those important domains were put in the hands of other ministries. Ever since the restructuring of 1978, the preponderance of authority and resources in China had been in the hands of provincial officials.

In January 2003 the authorities in Guangdong sent a team to investigate the "atypical pneumonia" in Heyuan. There was a flurry of reports in the Chinese press about the strange disease. Twenty-two foreign consulates in Canton warned their nationals about travel to the

---

18   Ibid.; Greenfeld, *China Syndrome*, pp. 36–37.
19   Kaufman, "China's Health," pp. S11–S12; Greenfeld, *China Syndrome*, p. 76.

region. The visit of the medical team to Heyuan spurred a panic in the town, however, and the provincial officials banned further newspaper reporting on the issue to avoid false "rumors."[20] This "wall of silence," motivated in part by the Sixteenth Party Congress being held in Beijing and the approach of the Chinese New Year, was soon extended to the foreign sphere. In early February the regional office of the World Health Organization (WHO) based in Manila became aware of earlier Chinese press reports and asked Beijing for permission to send a delegation to Guangdong to investigate. After a delay of ten days, the Ministry of Health refused the WHO request but allowed it to send a team to Beijing.[21] This confrontation is the principal reality behind charges that the Chinese government "stonewalled" foreign inquiries about the gathering crisis.

The spread of the new disease to Hong Kong reflected the crumbling of many walls that had once isolated the city from the China mainland. Hong Kong had returned to Chinese authority in 1998 after a century and a half of British rule. The burgeoning interaction with the mainland was evident in the development of a whole new city, Shenzhen, adjacent to Hong Kong. It also took the form of an increasing number of people—as well as chickens and civet cats!—crossing into Shenzhen and Hong Kong every day. One of the early victims of the new disease was a migrant worker, a butcher in a Shenzhen restaurant where a cook also came down with the disease. He was one of the 85 percent of the Chinese people without any health insurance; indeed he was one of the 150 million Chinese migrants who are too poor to obtain any serious health care whatsoever.[22] On February 21, a representative of a very different stratum of society, a physician from Guangdong already symptomatic with the infection for which he had been treating people at home, checked into a room on the ninth floor of the Metropole Hotel in Hong Kong. As a carrier of the disease that was at

---

20 Greenfeld, *China Syndrome*, p. 79. Suppression of "rumors," of course, can be a cover for concealing bad news, but the problem of mitigating fear in handling outbreaks of infectious diseases is a real one. For concern at the local level, see Pan and Zhang, "Surviving," p. 22. For the harmful effects of public panic in a case of bubonic plague in India in 1994, see Barrett and Brown, "Stigma," S34–S35.

21 Schnur, "Role," pp. 34–37.

22 Greenfeld, *China Syndrome*, pp. 34–42, 50–54.

its height of infectiousness, the visitor became the first of what came to be called "superspreaders," unwittingly passing the disease along to a dozen guests on the same floor.[23]

It was most appropriate that the physician had chosen to stay at the Metropole Hotel in Hong Kong, for its name captured the changing identity of China in the era of reform and opening. The hotel, in turn, was to be the site at which the new illness morphed into an epidemic and threatened to become a pandemic in full view of—and with great significance for—the entire world. Hong Kong has been a cosmopolitan city since its origins in the mid–nineteenth century, and it is estimated that 240 international flights leave the city's Chek Lap Kok airport every day. (Airline traffic has been growing worldwide at 6 percent a year for the last three decades.) In this context, a recent writer's warning is only slightly hyperbolic. Referring to a new and highly infectious pathogen of some kind that seems likely to appear in the near future, he wrote: "The virus will reach your hometown just twenty-four hours after it reaches Hong Kong."[24] In the case of SARS, among the twelve people infected by the superspreader at the Metropole, one was a businessman who went to Hanoi and infected people there, another was a woman who went home to Singapore and was the source of one hundred cases there, and a third was a woman who initiated a cluster of 132 patients in her native city of Toronto, of whom twelve died. By mid-March 2003 the disease had spread to seven countries and territories, including Taiwan. By late March over 1,320 cases were reported worldwide, among which there were already fifty fatalities.[25]

Control

On March 15, 2003, the WHO issued the first global health alert in its history. Two days later it set up secure websites for laboratory, epidemiological, and clinical aspects of the disease, initiating "unprecedented collaboration" worldwide to identify the causes of the

---

23 Murray, "Epidemiology," pp. 18–19.
24 Greenfeld, *China Syndrome*, p. 29. See also Mangili et al., "Transmission."
25 Murray, "Epidemiology," pp. 18–19.

disease.[26] By the third week in March, research groups in various countries had identified a novel coronavirus from the secretions of patients and named it the Severe Acute Respiratory Syndrome (SARS-CoV). On April 2, the organization issued, for the first time in its history, a travel advisory for Hong Kong and Guangdong, recommending postponement of all but essential travel. After erecting this virtual wall against unnecessary exposure to the disease, a WHO team promptly went through an aperture in the wall to visit Guangdong on April 3. After five days it reported to the Ministry of Health in Beijing that the province was "responding well to the outbreak," but it warned that similar success would be difficult to replicate if the disease should spread to the rest of the country. The WHO criticized the Ministry for claiming that there were only thirty-seven cases of the disease in the capital, whereas it estimated there were at least one to two hundred probable—and over one thousand suspected—cases.[27]

If the Ministry of Health's "stonewalling" of the WHO request on February 20 to visit Guangdong can hardly be blamed for the transmission of the disease to Hong Kong on the very next day,[28] its delays in publicizing the disease during the National People's Congress held in Beijing in the first two weeks of March compromised efforts to keep it from spreading to the capital.[29] Even after the Congress was over, it was only pressure from the WHO and the cancellation of two international events in Beijing that forced the ministry to acknowledge a problem with the disease in the capital. On April 20, faced with the refusal of the minister of health and the mayor of Beijing to acknowledge publicly the actual number of SARS cases in hospitals of the city, and embarrassed by the public charges of a prominent Chinese doctor that there were over 120 cases in a single military hospital, the newly established leadership of General Secretary Hu Jintao and Premier Wen Jiabao replaced the minister and the mayor with new

26 Some of this was a product of post-9/11 investments in global health-information systems, surveillance, and rapid response planning. Kaufman, "China's Health," p. S7.

27 Murray, "Epidemiology," pp. 21–22; Schnur, "Role," pp. 37–41. The ministry's misrepresentation of the situation in military hospitals was at least in part a product of its lack of authority, mentioned above. Kaufman, "China's Health," p. S8.

28 Pace Kaufman, "SARS," p. 55.

29 Saich, "Is SARS," p. 78.

and more energetic personnels.[30] Soon thereafter the epidemic peaked with perhaps two thousand acknowledged cases in the capital and with one hundred new ones being reported each day.

Laboratory research facilitated by electronic communication soon revealed that SARS was a novel coronavirus, or at least one that was new to human beings, and that it could cause severe respiratory disease or even death. Scientists looking in the live animal markets of Guangdong found a closely related virus in masked palm civet cats and raccoon dogs. Those animals may not have been the sources of the pathogen; in fact they may have been infected by humans. But the research showed that, at the least, the species barrier had been breached. This finding was "supported by the ease with which SARS-CoV infected a range of cell lines from different species in vitro."[31] Unfortunately, no similar scientific breakthroughs occurred in developing vaccines, therapies, and curative medicines for the new disease.[32]

Under these circumstances, the Chinese continued the usual range of methods for dealing with epidemic disease. In other words, they established walls of various sorts to contain the epidemic. They isolated those known or suspected to be infected and sometimes even those who had simply been exposed to the infected persons, including family members and health-care personnel. They required health-care workers to wear face masks and encouraged others in or near infected areas to do the same, something that was easy to do given the common practice of wearing such masks to prevent the transmission of illness in East Asia. They also mobilized people to conduct temperature checks at borders and gates, closed down schools and businesses, and disinfected public places (especially live markets). They turned any hospital with a SARS patient into a quarantine institution and/or moved infected patients from public hospitals to special facilities.

Aware that the previous leadership had been reluctant to publicize the crisis so as not to jeopardize business during the bustling Chinese New Year festival, General Secretary Hu Jintao adopted a different

---

30 Schnur, "Role," p. 41; for the politics of this shift, see Saich, "Is SARS," pp. 79–82. More than one thousand cadres lost their jobs or were severely punished because of SARS-related dereliction of duty. Lam, *Chinese Politics*, pp. 27, 111, 140.

31 Murray, "Epidemiology," pp. 22–23.

32 Schnur, "Role," p. 43.

policy. He shortened the May Day vacation from seven days to one and used May 1 to proclaim a "people's war against SARS."[33] The new head of the Ministry of Health made daily public reports on the crisis and required all provinces to do the same. The new mayor of Beijing arranged to have built, in less than a week, a special one-thousand-bed SARS facility at Xiaotangshan on the outskirts of the capital.[34] The central government appropriated two billion yuan to fund the campaign against SARS. As part of its repeatedly stated concern for segments of the population left behind by the reforms, the new leadership set aside ninety million yuan to provide free care for SARS victims in nine of the poorer provinces of central and western China.[35]

The rapid countywide deployment of surveillance and quarantine teams during 2003 was described by English travel writer Colin Thubron in his book, *Shadow of the Silk Road*, first published in 2006.

When I returned to my hotel, a phalanx of masked, white-coated men fanned out to meet me. The SARS virus had leapfrogged west to Lanzhou, bringing panic and bureaucracy. In the foyer, while passers-by crowded in to watch, I was inquisitioned about my itinerary, a thermometer stuck under my armpit and blood extracted from my earlobe by a nurse with a surreptitious needle. I might be quarantined, they said, if my temperature was up. After a while I was handed my haematology report, which I could not decipher, and a histogram whose graph featured a low, solitary hump, like the tomb of the Yellow Emperor. Then they all smiled, apologized, filled in their forms and departed. But I feared for my journey.[36]

Three weeks later Thubron reached Cherchen, one of the oasis towns on the southern route around the Taklamakan Desert, where he was not so lucky.

But in the centre our bus was flagged down and a team of SARS officials boarded: a faceless policeman, a lanky municipal worker and

33   Saich, "Is SARS," pp. 82–86.
34   Ibid., p. 83; Schnur, "Role," p. 41; Kleinman and Watson, *SARS*, p. 4.
35   Kaufman, "SARS," p. 67; Saich, "Is SARS," p. 98.
36   Thubron, "Shadow," p. 73.

an official in a peasant cap and dark glasses. An edict had gone out from Beijing, the official said, that any travelers who couldn't prove their movements must be quarantined for two weeks, the length of time the virus took to develop.

I fixed my mask uselessly over my mouth. But my luck had run out. SARS had broken out in Jiayuguan, the official said (it seemed to be following me). He was very sorry. I answered, with deepening hopelessness, that Jiayuguan was already a thousand miles behind us, but five minutes later a truck was taking me to a quarantine compound. I felt the irrational guilt of someone already ill. The driver averted his face from me.

It was an empty municipal building, stranded in fields. The official released the chain across its entrance, and stayed on the other side. "You can't leave here." In the weak moonlight his dark glasses gaped like eye-sockets. Perhaps some second-hand memory of camps or sanatoria tinted this harmless scene with horror, because I began instinctively to look for an escape.

A grizzled doctor came to the gate to meet us, but did not dare shake my hand. A bevy of nurses flittered behind him. Above their masks their eyes were wide with alarm and curiosity. One of them led me inside to a big room. Under a birth-control poster in Uighur, a white bed stood on a white-tiled floor, with a rickety table. The doctor pointed out a makeshift lavatory built in the grounds a few days earlier. It already stank.

"In two weeks you will be dead," he said, "if you have it." But he spoke gently, as though apologizing to me.[37]

Thubron suffered, of course, not only from the general fear of contagion that spread across China at the time but also from the crudely expressed worst-case prognosis, a common problem for English-speaking foreigners without Chinese-language capability dealing with Chinese medical personnel with only limited English. Fortunately, with no evidence of fever or coughs, Thubron was released a few days later and continued on his journey to the West without further delays.

---

37 Ibid., p. 104.

During the campaign, the Chinese state and people deployed the image and the substance of walls in efforts to resist the disease. On May 15, the *People's Daily* published a front-page story under the headline: "Build Our New Long Walls—On the Great Spirit of the Fight against SARS." Some residents of Beijing were reported to have established barricades outside the city to monitor, presumably through temperature checks, those coming from SARS-infested areas. Some villages joined in erecting walls to regulate the comings and goings of outsiders. Perhaps only half jokingly, someone modified the national anthem with its theme of the Great Wall as follows:

Arise, Ye who refuse to be infected,
With our money,
Let us build our long walls against SARS!
The peoples of China are in a most critical time,
Everybody must roar his defiance.[38]

Whether or not they were inspired by such versifying (which certainly lost much in this translation!), many health care workers, medical students, and other citizens put their lives on the line to care for SARS victims and thus helped to bring the threatened epidemic to an end. In line with established party policy that Mao Zedong had been 70 percent correct, they replicated some of the style and achievements of the campaign that had wiped out smallpox in the first decade of the People's Republic.[39]

To be sure, after a period of costly delay, the Chinese, like others, sometimes went to extremes that were, in retrospect, unnecessary and, in some cases, harmful. Since people infected with the disease do not immediately show signs and are not highly infectious even for some days after having symptoms, not all who had been exposed to infected persons (as opposed to infectious persons) had needed to be quarantined. Thus it has been noted after the fact that many of the thirty thousand people who were held in isolation in Beijing and some of those many people similarly quarantined in Hong Kong, Singapore,

38 Eckholm, "SARS," pp. 127, 130; Kleinman and Lee, "SARS," p. 179; Zhang, "Making," p. 156.
39 Kleinman and Watson, *SARS*, p. 9.

and Taiwan had not needed to be isolated so completely. A strategy focused more sharply on identifying and isolating those persons known to be already infected would have been more efficient and less disruptive.

The strategy, considered after a threatened revival of the disease in summer 2003, of slaughtering large numbers of animals under suspicion of harboring the disease might have needlessly risked the infection of the workers doing the killing. Outlawing the sale of certain exotic animals, another measure under consideration, might simply have driven the trade underground, where it would have been more difficult to regulate.[40] The forceful quarantine of large numbers of suspected persons in Beijing led to panic among some people, who fled the city to avoid being virtually incarcerated.[41] Some victims of the disease and members of their families were needlessly ostracized. In some cases the anti-SARS campaign was even used as a cover for repressive political and social policies such as arresting members of the religious sect Falungong on the grounds they opposed medical treatment and placing in quarantine people who protested their displacement by the Three Gorges Dam project.[42]

Some observers criticize such policies adopted in China and Singapore as "authoritarian" and unacceptable in "democracies."[43] General Secretary Hu Jintao did state during the crisis that people should "unite their thoughts and action based on the planning of the central authorities." He added, however, "We must uphold the principles of relying on the masses, relying on science, and working hard with one heart and mind." Even Hu thus adopted a somewhat populist, rational, and inclusive—if not democratic—approach.[44] Others point out the "beneficial aspects of authoritarian government" that more "individualistic" polities might take note of.[45] In fact, during

40 Murray, "Epidemiology," pp. 28, 30.
41 Kaufman, "SARS," p. 56. Fortunately, unlike in India in 1994, the exodus did not include physicians and health care workers.
42 Saich, "Is SARS," p. 89. For the negative effects of stigma in the course of epidemics, see Barrett and Brown, "Stigma," pp. S34–S37.
43 Rawski, "SARS," p. 120.
44 Lam, *Chinese Politics*, p. 42.
45 Kleinman and Watson, *SARS*, p. 3. See also Wang and Zheng, *SARS Epidemic*, for a balanced approach.

the height of the crisis, the United States for all its vaunted individualism imposed a very harsh ban on travel to hot spots. President George W. Bush issued an executive order that authorized the forcible quarantining of suspects, none of whom turned out to be infected with SARS-CoV.[46] It is not only in China that national crises lead to enhanced efforts at central authority.

Despite delays, mistakes, and excesses, the Chinese campaign against SARS resulted in containment of the disease. By May 29, 2003, there were no new cases reported in Beijing and very few throughout China. No cases were reported after early June. On July 5, the WHO announced that the disease was under control worldwide.[47] China, of course, had been the origin of the epidemic and it also suffered the most from it. On August 7, it was announced that of 8,422 cases of infection in thirty countries, 5,327 of them had occurred in China, and of a total of 916 deaths worldwide, 349 were in China.[48] China thus had some 63 percent of the total number of cases but only 38 percent of the fatalities. Assuming that the statistics are accurate, they would seem to suggest that the Chinese managed fairly well in keeping the mortality relatively low.

While recognizing the need for closer international cooperation and changes in China's system of reporting in the future, the WHO representative in China at the time concluded, "In the end, it was what China did that mattered most in controlling the outbreak."[49] Some would attribute whatever success was achieved to the appearance—or at least an occasion for the appearance—of "modern leaders concerned for the welfare of their people."[50] But most observers also acknowledge that the People's Republic suppressed the SARS epidemic mainly by

---

46 Kleinman and Lee, "SARS," p. 18; Watson, "SARS," p. 200.
47 Schnur, "Role," p. 42. Given the problems in China's public health system noted above, it is difficult to be sure that all cases of this highly infectious disease, especially those occurring among the poor, are being reported to the authorities. But reforms in the system centralizing authority over public health and linking all counties directly to Beijing by Internet may be reassuring. Kaufman, "China's Health," pp. S11–S12.
48 Kaufman, "SARS," p. 57.
49 Schnur, "Role," p. 50. "What China did," of course, could include its understating of the number of infected persons in Beijing.
50 Saich, "Is SARS," pp. 71, 83.

using methods of "mobilization" that were "archaic" and/or "Maoist."[51] Certainly it was concern with economic interests, including those of urban businessmen opposed to harmful "rumors" and rural entre- preneurs profiting from side-line production, that motivated some officials to keep the SARS issue quiet and to oppose restrictions on wet markets. Somewhat ironically, some foreign observers have called for China to pay more attention to "public goods" and to social equity in health care to help prevent future epidemics from turning into national disasters and global pandemics.[52]

The recent outbreak and present control of SARS should be kept in perspective. Although a crisis of sorts, the epidemic took the lives of fewer than one thousand people worldwide before dying out (we now think) in summer 2003. In contrast, AIDS killed an estimated three million people in that year alone and is still going strong.[53] SARS became a crisis, in part, because it spread to big cities and foreign countries, potentially threatening the lives of urban elites around the world. Other diseases, such as malaria and tuberculosis, which regularly kill millions of people in the poorer parts of the world, create no comparable sense of crisis.[54] Of course, "As the first global health crisis of the twenty-first century, the SARS epidemic demonstrated the continuing threat posed by communicable diseases to public health and the risk of new and reemerging diseases quickly affecting all countries in the age of globalization."[55] "In retrospect, SARS is probably best seen as a harbinger of future events that might be catastrophic for the global system as we know it today."[56] Certainly, we agree on the need for a new approach of "transdisciplinary research" to deal with such crises, although we also recognize that the "isolationist (and

---

51   Kleinman and Watson, *SARS*, p. 3; Schnur, "Role," p. 51; Eckholm, "SARS," p. 127; Shaw, "SARS Scare," pp. 48–57.

52   Schnur, "Role," p. 49; Kaufman, "SARS," pp. 57–59.

53   Kleinman and Watson, *SARS*, p. 1. This is a clear instance of stigma inhibiting effective treatment, again a phenomenon not restricted to China. Barrett and Brown, "Stigma," p. S34; Pan and Zhang, "Surviving," p. 29.

54   Kleinman and Lee, "SARS," p. 186.

55   Schnur, "Role," p. 48.

56   Kleinman and Watson, *SARS*, p. 1.

elitist) conventions of traditional academic disciplines make it difficult for younger scholars to engage in this type of team research."[57]

Avian Influenza A-H5N1

Control over SARS was hardly accomplished when, in November 2005, the "highly pathogenic avian influenza" (HPAI) strain H5N1, which had infected a few residents of Hong Kong in 1997, reappeared. Although, as we have noted, this pathogen has yet to achieve easy transmission from person to person, it is in some other ways more worrisome than SARS.[58] Unlike SARS, which takes some time to develop and to become infectious, HPAI/H5N1 has a short incubation period, multiplies quickly, becomes infectious even before symptoms appear, and, being a single-stranded RNA, can mutate easily and rapidly. The success of influenza viruses as multiple-species pathogens has to do with their genetic lability, the seeming ease with which they change their genetic instructions. When two variants of influenza virus infect the same host they may recombine their nucleic acids in the course of their multiplication so that infectivity and virulence traits can be traded. That results in some of the recombinant viruses possessing capacity to be easily transmitted and to be highly virulent in a new host species.[59] Once adapted to humans it might easily mutate to be able to be transmitted from one human to another. Influenza viruses adapted to human hosts are easily transmitted by small airborne droplets from coughs and sneezes that are inhaled or ingested from contaminated surfaces, e.g., hands and glassware. They are already widespread among pigs and poultry in many parts of the world, including the United States, and their continuing and accelerating spread means that they still offer a real threat of becoming pandemic.[60]

---

57   Ibid., p. 14.
58   That there are so far so few documented cases of transmission from human to human suggests how difficult such transmission is but also how important it is to prevent future cases. For one case in Thailand, see Chuengsatiansup, "Ethnography," p. 54; Auewarakul et al., "Institutional," p. 62.
59   WHO Global Influenza Network, "Evolution," pp. 1515–21.
60   For the situation in the United States, see Thacker and Janke, "Swine Influenza," pp. S19–S24. For China, see Kaufman, "China's Health," pp. 10–11.

China, to be sure, learned something from the SARS crisis, but some lessons appear to be either short-lived or insufficient to deal with the new contagion. Between October 2005 and February 2006, the Ministry of Agriculture, Ministry of Finance, and the State Council published fifteen regulations, guidelines, and policies related to avian influenza, including prevention, control, reimbursement, and assistance to poultry farmers. A strengthened Ministry of Health with its new Centers of Disease Control has established direct Internet connections with 93 percent of hospitals down to the county level and with 43 percent of hospitals at the township level. Many live markets were shut down, but some have reopened and have been allowed to operate on the grounds that banning them would only drive them underground and make them more difficult to regulate. To provide a wall between poultry and wild birds known to carry the new virus, officials in Anhui responded to the infection of one person by requiring farmers in that province to keep all backyard poultry in cages. That proved to be a local ordinance that was difficult to enforce in Anhui, however, let alone extend to the rest of the country. As noted, the Chinese have vaccinated some 20 percent of their chickens but the vaccines may be only mildly successful and may lead to the selection of even more virulent viruses. Although the People's Republic supplied the WHO with some twenty samples of the virus for research in 2004–2005, it remains reluctant to share such samples with the United States and the United Kingdom, arguing that they have misused such samples in the past. As a result, even an observer sympathetic to China concludes, "If an avian influenza pandemic among humans were to emerge, its likely source would be China."[61]

Worldwide efforts to prevent or at least control a future avian influenza epidemic confront several major problems. Existing vaccines, most commonly with killed or cold-adapted viruses, prevent illness from infection in only 70–90 percent of healthy adult humans and in

---

61 Kaufman, "China's Health," pp. S12–S13. For local task forces that monitor health conditions in a town in Zhejiang, near Shanghai, see Pan and Zhang, "Surviving," p. 23. For successful efforts to keep backyard poultry separate from wild birds in a village in the New Territories, adjacent to Hong Kong, see Liu, "Custom," p. 11. For Indonesians' concerns about lack of access to vaccines based on samples of H5N1 they sent to WHO, see Chuengsatiansup, "Ethnography," p. 57.

only 30–40 percent of infants, the elderly, the immuno-compromised, and the chronically ill. Existing vaccines, of course, also have adverse effects and will not work against new and unexpected viruses. It normally takes four to six months to formulate and ramp up new vaccines and take them across regulatory hurdles. There are four existing antiviral drugs for prophylaxis and treatment that are used as adjuncts in controlling outbreaks, but they must be administered within the first twenty-four to forty-eight hours after the development of symptoms. They also have unwanted side effects, require careful monitoring, are in limited supply, and are quite expensive. They can also produce drug-resistant strains and some have been discontinued by the U.S. Center for Disease Control for that reason.

Under these circumstances, one Chinese researcher working in the United States has proposed a proactive and complementary strategy of using RNA-interference technology to produce transgenic, or influenza-resistant, poultry. This method, he claims, has been effective with polio, hepatitis B, dengue, HIV, and SARS in cell cultures and, in a few cases, in animals. He readily acknowledges that there are problems with this strategy as well. So far it has not been demonstrated experimentally, it would need the consent of corporations and states, it would have to be field tested and monitored, it would take years of very stable transmission to become effective, and it would result in a genetically modified organism (GMO) that would face resistance in some industrialized countries. Opposition might be less in Asia, however, where new viruses seem most likely to arise. Such poultry have the potential to reduce the incidence of H5N1 influenza among poultry and therefore humans. For these reasons, he concludes, a research effort in that direction should be funded.[62]

Meanwhile, the spread of the H5N1 pathogen through the world continues to accelerate. In April 2005, there was a massive dying off of migratory birds in the Qinghai Lake nature reserve in northwest China. By the end of 2006, some fifty-five countries reported outbreaks of H5N1 in wild birds and/or poultry.[63] The transmission of the virus from animals to humans has been most common in Asia. As of July 2007, Indonesia reported the world's largest number of confirmed cases of

62 Chen et al., "Genetic Strategy," pp. S24–S28.
63 Kaufman, "China's Health," pp. S12–S13.

avian flu in humans, 102, as well as the highest fatality rate, 81. Vietnam had 95 cases, of which 42 were fatal; Thailand had 25 people infected, of whom 17 died. In these Southeast Asian countries, as in China, poultry are generally raised in backyard open ranges where they have contacts with wild birds, and they are sold in wet markets where they have close contacts with humans. Studies show that the many small farmers in these countries generally wish to maintain their present way of life, which, they believe, provides them with fresh and healthful food. Some doubt that flu among poultry can infect humans. Some suspect that the "crisis" is manufactured by the press to sell newspapers. Some believe that large commercial farms use the "crisis" and manipulate public policy (e.g., to require massive culling and/or vaccination) to restructure the market to their advantage and the disadvantage of small farmers. Some surmise that corrupt officials and central governments use the issue to increase their wealth and power at the expense of the people, including themselves. Instead of imposing massive culling of sick poultry that is often economically ruinous and instead of requiring widespread vaccinations that are expensive and only partially effective, some Asian farmers feel that wealthy and powerful countries should devote more resources to developing cheaper and more effective vaccines to assist poor and weak countries in building an "epidemic firewall against the global spread of infection."[64]

As long as H5N1 remains unable to pass easily from person to person, the main conveyors of this pathogen will probably continue to be migratory birds. The rapid spread of avian influenza viruses among wild waterfowl and the household flocks close to wetlands on water-fowl migration routes has been documented in Europe.[65] Perhaps more destructive but slower, multistage transmission of avian influenza follows the commercial trade in domestic poultry: chickens and chicken products, fighting cocks, and exotic birds. The entrance of HPAI H5N1 into Africa has been the result of importing infected chickens and chicken products into Egypt and Nigeria. To

---

64 Padmawati and Nichter, "Community," pp. 31–51; Chuengsatiansup, "Ethnography," pp. 53–59; Auewarakul et al., "Institutional," pp. 61–67; Olsen et al., "Poultry-Handling." For evidence that poultry industries in industrial countries have benefited from—if not abetted—distress in the poultry industries of poor countries, see Davis, *Monster*, p. 166.

65 Karesh and Cook, "Human-Animal," pp. 38–50.

date the pathogen has not been detected among birds along the African or the Western hemisphere flyways, but that may change.

Once established in a region with widespread domestic poultry, avian influenza has been rapidly disseminated among fighting roosters and exotic birds. The source of the sudden northern and western spread of the H5N1 virus has been migratory waterfowl, especially the bar-headed goose. In 2005, the northern hemisphere autumnal migration of waterfowl began in August and the virus appeared in distant foci in Tibet, Mongolia, Russian Siberia, Kazakhstan, Turkey, Romania, and Bulgaria. Culling and quarantine of domestic birds did not close the aperture of migratory wild birds.

Conclusions

The pathogens we call viruses are nothing but tiny bits of nucleic acid that can hardly be said to be alive, but they are remarkably persistent and adaptable in reproducing themselves and seem destined to evolve along with their various hosts. They survive by penetrating the walls of animal cells and spread by jumping the walls (not very formidable as it happens) between animals in general and the specific species called human, and, in some cases, the walls (e.g., outer skins) between one human being and another. New forms of virus, such as SARS and H5N1, are constantly appearing, and humans have only limited means to control their spread. We can separate more domesticated and sedentary animal hosts, such as pigs and chickens, from wild and migratory carriers, such as ducks and geese, and we can develop vaccines to prevent and antiviral medicines to treat clinical disease resulting from infection. But the history and the medicine of pathogens conjoin to deny that there can ever be a "total victory" of humans over germs or even a foolproof method of predicting and preventing epidemics and pandemics in which large numbers of people succumb to their adversaries.[66]

What should be more possible is to understand the conditions under which pathogens such as viruses produce diseases that become

---

66 For the U.S. surgeon general's false, or at least premature, declaration of victory over infectious diseases, see *Lancet* 372(2008), p. 110. For the strength and persistence of germs and even plagues, see Mc Neill, *Plagues*; Diamond, *Guns*.

epidemic and pandemic and the roles of various kinds of walls in inhibiting or at least mitigating these threats to human life and well-being. In the cases of SARS and H5N1 it was a combination of local practices such as backyard poultry farming and the consumption of fresh and exotic meats together with a decline in the public health system, the persistence of bureaucratic barriers, and the increase in ground and air traffic that led to the SARS epidemic and that perpetuates the risk that some novel form of H5N1 will become the next pandemic. At the same time, closer regulation of farming and culinary practices, greater attention to public health and social justice, and improved communication within China and between China and the outside world promise to allow for more precision in anticipating a possible outbreak and more effectiveness in containing any pandemic.

At the very least, this record of the SARS and H5N1 crises should help to disabuse us of some of the more simplistic and damaging mythology surrounding such events. The continuing centrality of China in the history of viral epidemics can be seen not as evidence of some kind of persistent or recurrent "yellow peril," but as a reminder of that polity's enormous size, high density, and, perhaps, continuing quest for fresh meat and culinary pleasure, surely excusable passions.[67] Any move to blame China for being a perennial source of viral epidemics will be no more productive—in fact it will be just as destructive—as north Chinese criticism of Cantonese as omnivorous, urban Chinese castigation of rural migrants as unclean, Indian Hindu association of Muslims with bubonic plague, or Indonesian Muslims' suspicions of American-Christian-Israeli bioterrorism.[68] Even the widespread assumption, which lies behind our analysis, that backyard farms are more vulnerable than large commercial farms to infection from wild birds and the common idea, which even many Asians continue to hold, that massive vaccination can protect animals, including humans, from sources of infection, are being called into

---

67 For the danger of new forms of "yellow peril" ideology and "xenophobia about non-Western societies," see Lam, *Chinese Politics*, p. 168; Rosenberg, "Siting," p. S6.

68 Northern Chinese express their prejudices humorously in the saying: "The people of Harbin will wear anything, the people of Henan will say anything, and the people of Guangdong will eat anything." For the case of India, see Barrett and Brown, "Stigma," p. S35; for Indonesia, see Padmawati and Nichter, "Community," pp. 36, 43.

question by recent research into the biosocial dimensions of epidemic disease.[69]

More positively, there is a growing consensus, in China and abroad, on the need for more emphasis on broad public health programs and more social justice if we are to effectively mitigate the effects of future epidemics that appear to be unavoidable. In the words of Guangdong epidemiologist, Dr. Zhong Nanshan, a veteran of the SARS crisis, "The degree of a country's modernization shouldn't be reflected just by GDP [Gross Domestic Product] growth. . . . Social development is just as important." The Chinese Premier Wen Jiabao agreed with that emphasis when he said: "China has always paid a lot of attention to economic development. . . . Yet social development is just as important."[70] Similarly, Komatra Chuengsatiansup, of the Ministry of Health in Thailand, has called for "health education and prevention efforts that rely on community co-operation and individual behaviour change for their implementation." Arthur Kleinman, professor of anthropology and social medicine at Harvard University, has concurred in his recent introduction to a set of papers, writing: "The need to build public trust and public health infrastructure is one of the primary messages of this collection."[71] Just as the health of the Chinese body politic depended historically not only on the maintenance of long walls across its northern frontier but on the general well-being of the entire polity, so the health of the Chinese people today depends not just on walls against epidemic disease but on the general day-to-day prosperity of the entire population. The same, we would suggest, can be said of the world at large.

Works Cited

Auewarakul, Prasert, Wanna Hachaoworakul, and Kumnuan Ungchusak. "Institutional Responses to Avian Influenza in Thailand: Control of Outbreaks in Poultry and Preparedness in the Case of Human-to-Human Transmission," in Kleinman et al, "Asian," pp. 61–67.

---

69 Kleinman et al., "Avian," p. S3.
70 Lam, *Chinese Politics*, p. 72.
71 Kleinman et al., "Avian," p. S1.

Barrett, Ron, and Peter J. Brown. "Stigma in the Time of Influenza: Social and Institutional Responses to Pandemic Emergencies." Pp. S34–S37 in Kleinman et al., "Avian."

Causey, Douglas, and Scott V. Edwards. "Ecology of Avian Influenza Virus in Birds." Pp. S29–S33 in Kleinman et al., "Avian."

Chen, Jianzhu, Steve C. Y. Chen, Patrick Stern, Benjamin B. Scott, and Carlos Lois. "Genetic Strategy to Prevent Influenza Virus Infections in Animals." Pp. S25–S28 in Kleinman et al., "Avian."

Chen X.-G., Li H., and Lun Z.-R. "Angiostrongyliasis, Mainland China," *Emerging Infectious Diseases* 11(2005), pp. 1645–1647.

Chuengsatiansup, Komatra. "Ethnography of Epidemiological Transition: Avian Flu, Global Health Politics and Agro-Industrial Capitalism in Thailand." Pp. 53–59 in Kleinman et al., "Asian."

Davis, M. *The Monster at Our Door: The Global Threat of Avian Flu*. New York and London: New Press, 2005.

Diamond, Jared. *Guns, Germs, and Steel*. New York: W. W. Norton, 1997.

Eckholm, Erik. "SARS in Beijing: The Unraveling of a Cover-Up." Pp. 122–32 in Kleinman and Watson, *SARS*.

Fineberg, Harvey. "Preparing for Avian Influenza: Lessons from the 'Swine Flu Affair.'" Pp. S14–S18 in Kleinman et al., "Avian."

Flack, M., and K. Wiese. *The Story About Ping*. New York: Viking, 1933.

Garrett, L. "The Next Pandemic," *Foreign Affairs* 84(2005), pp. 3–23.

Greenfeld, Karl Taro. *China Syndrome: The True Story of the 21st Century's First Great Epidemic*. New York: Harper Collins, 2006.

Karesh, W. B., and R. A. Cook. "The Human-Animal Link," *Foreign Affairs* 84(2005), pp. 38–50.

Kaufman, Joan A. "SARS and China's Health-Care Response: Better to Be Both Red and Expert!" Pp. 53–70 in Kleinman and Watson, *SARS*.

———. "China's Health Care System and Avian Influenza Preparedness." Pp. S7–S13 in Kleinman et al., "Avian."

Kleinman, Arthur M., Barry R. Bloom, Anthony Saich, Katherine A. Mason, and Felicity Aulino. "Introduction: Asian Flus in Ethnographic and Political Context: A Biosocial Approach," *Anthropology and Medicine*, 15.1(April 2008), pp. 1–5.

———. "Introduction: Avian and Pandemic Influenza: A Biosocial Approach," *Journal of Infectious Diseases*, 197(February 15, 2008), pp. S1–S3.

Kleinman, Arthur M., and Sing Lee. "SARS and the Problem of Social Stigma." Pp. 173–95 in Kleinman and Watson, *SARS*.

Kleinman, Arthur, and James L. Watson. *SARS in China: Prelude to Pandemic?* Stanford: Stanford University Press, 2006.

Lam, Willy Wo-Lap. *Chinese Politics in the Hu Jintao Era: New Leaders, New Challenges*. Armonk, New York: M. E. Sharpe, 2006.

Liu, Tik-Sang. "Custom, Taste and Science: Raising Chickens in the Pearl River Delta Region, South China." Pp. 7–18 in Kleinman et al., "Asian."

Mangili A., and M. A. Gendreau. "Transmission of Infectious Diseases during Commercial Air Travel," *Lancet* 365(2005), pp. 989–96.

McLean, Angela, ed. *SARS: A Case Study in Emerging Infections.* Oxford: Oxford University Press, 2005.

McNeill, W. *Plagues and Peoples.* Garden City, New York: Anchor Press/ Doubleday, 1976.

Munster, V. J., A. Wazzenstein, C. Bass, et al. "Mallards and Highly Pathogenic Avian Influenza Ancestral Viruses, Northern Europe," *Emerging Infectious Diseases* 11(2005), pp. 1545–51.

Murray, Megan. "The Epidemiology of SARS." Pp. 17–30 in Kleinman and Watson, *SARS.*

Olsen, S. J., Y. Laosiritaworn, S. Pattanasin, et al. "Poultry-Handling Practices during Avian Influenza Outbreak, Thailand," *Emerging Infectious Diseases* 11(2005), pp. 1601–3.

Padmawati, Siwi, and Mark Nichter. "Community Response to Avian Flu in Central Java, Indonesia." Pp. 31–51 in Kleinman et al., "Asian."

Pan, Tianshu, and Zhang Letian. "Surviving the Crisis: Adaptive Wisdom, Coping Mechanisms and Local Responses to Avian Influenza Threats in Haining, China." Pp. 19–30 in Kleinman et al., "Asian."

Rawski, Thomas G. "SARS and China's Economy." Pp. 105–21 in Kleinman and Watson, *SARS.*

Rosenberg, Charles E. "Siting Epidemic Disease: 3 Centuries of American History." Pp. S4–S6 in Kleinman et al., "Avian."

Saich, Tony. "Is SARS China's Chernobyl or Much Ado About Nothing?" Pp. 71–104 in Kleinman and Watson, *SARS.*

Schnur, Alan. "The Role of the World Health Organization in Combating SARS, Focusing on the Efforts in China." Pp. 31–52 in Kleinman and Watson, *SARS.*

Shaw, Jonathan. "The SARS Scare," *Harvard Magazine*, 109.4(March–April 2007), pp. 48–57.

Thacker, Eileen, and Bruce Janke. "Swine Influenza Virus: Zoonotic Potential and Vaccination Strategies for the Control of Avian and Swine Influenzas." Pp. S19–S24 in Kleinman et al., "Avian."

Thubron, Colin. *Shadow of the Silk Road.* New York City, HarperCollins, 2008.

Wang, John, and Zheng Yongnian, eds. *The SARS Epidemic: Challenges to China's Crisis Management.* New Jersey: World Scientific, 2004.

Watson, James L. "SARS and the Consequences for Globalization." Pp. 196–202 in Kleinman and Watson, *SARS*.

WHO Global Influenza Network. "Evolution of H_5N_1 Avian Influenza Viruses in Asia." *Emerging Infectious Diseases,* 11(2005), pp. 1515–21.

Xu, R.-H., J. E. He, M. R. Evans, et al. "Epidemiologic Cues to SARS Origin in China," *Emerging Infectious Diseases* 10(2004), pp. 1030–37.

Zhang, Hong. "Making Light of the Dark Side: SARS Jokes and Humor in China." Pp. 148–72 in Kleinman and Watson, *SARS*.

CHAPTER EIGHT

Realizing the Four Modernizations with a New "Long Wall"

China's Effort to Use a "Big Fire Wall" to Control the Internet

Junhao Hong

DURING THE LAST DECADE OR SO, the People's Republic of China has developed the Internet in pursuit of two concrete but competing goals. Economically and technologically, the government has deployed the Internet to accelerate the country's march toward the "Four Modernizations": in agriculture, industry, science and technology, and the military. Politically and ideologically, it has established a "great firewall" (*da huo qiang*) to monitor and control Internet communications to insure the continuing authority of the Communist Party.[1] Some people think that China's effort to control the Internet is quixotic. United States President Bill Clinton in 2000 stated that the Chinese effort to crack down on unacceptable use of the Internet would be like "trying to nail Jell-O to the wall."[2] Soon after in 2005, however, John Palfrey, an

---

1   Hong and Huang, "Split;" Lagerkvist, *Internet*; Zhou, *Historicizing*.
2   Kurtlantzick, "Dictatorship," cited in Lovell, *Great Wall*, p. 340. George W. Bush concurred that, with the Internet, "freedom's genie will be out of the bottle." Ibid.

American expert on the Chinese Internet, argued that "China has been more successful than any other country in the world to manage [*sic*] to filter the Internet despite the fast changes in technology."[3] While some Chinese, including the present writer, believe that the Internet will ultimately make China a more liberal polity, others argue that, at least so far, China has invented the most effective electronic firewall in the world.[4] Interestingly, the Chinese call this digital barrier a new "Long Wall" (*changcheng*), alluding to the frontier fortifications that attained their height in the Ming dynasty.

In this chapter I trace the development of the Internet and efforts to control it over the last decade and a half. My principal thesis is that the "new long wall" may help China maintain economic growth and political stability for some time, but it will eventually have a strongly negative effect on China's "informatization" and "democratization," two essential components, in my view, of any genuine "modernity." At the same time, I am aware that some scholars question the so-called Whig interpretation of history, that wealth and power automatically produce liberalism and democracy and that all good things can be achieved together over time. Indeed one interpretation, associated with postmodern theory, holds that the "modern era" is actually characterized by increasingly powerful states that exert ever closer control over the activities of people. Instead of enjoying more freedom, people may actually lose much of the autonomy and agency once associated with "citizenship."[5]

In this chapter, therefore, I shall attempt to delineate conditions that help to determine how the Internet actually functions, whether to give voice to its users—or "netizens"—or to enhance the control of the state. In some cases these two uses may be complementary, even

---

3   "Chinese Control," cited in Lam, *Chinese Politics*, p. 232. Lovell agrees that "the rulers of Communist China have proved themselves just as good as—if not better than—any of their imperial predecessors at building, maintaining, restoring and guarding walls." Lovell, *Great Wall*, p. 346.

4   Du interview. Operating from a different perspective on "freedom," one comparative study concludes that the People's Republic has evinced greater confidence that it can keep the Internet free from foreign control than the Qing dynasty showed vis-à-vis the telegraph. See Zhou, *Historicizing*, pp. 137, 232.

5   See, for example, the work of Michel Foucault, including his *Discipline and Punish*, and the work of Habermas, including *The Structural Transformation of the Public Sphere*.

identical; in others they will be at odds with one another. In the end, perhaps, there will be no clear victory of one over the other or any clear linear process in one direction or another. Instead, there will more likely be a constant or, more precisely, periodic exchange of power in which people and state, China and the world play significant roles. This, at least, seems consistent with what we know about the functioning of long walls in earlier periods of Chinese history.[6]

The Importance of the Internet in China Today

I begin this discussion as a specialist in communication impressed with the significant place the Internet has assumed in China at the outset of the twenty-first century. Some basic statistics will help to set the scene. In 2007 there were around 180 licensed web media services in operation, along with an uncountable (because unlicensed) number of news websites. More than 80 percent of Chinese netizens were frequent web media users.[7]

Most of this growth has occurred in the last decade. According to the China Internet Information Center, the number of Internet users rose from 62 million in 1997 to 79.5 million at the end of 2003, with 55,900 new netizens entering the net-space each day.[8] By 2005 there were over 100 million, and since then on average 20 million more have joined in each year. The majority of Internet users are young and relatively well educated, suggesting that the technology still serves mainly a small but strategic elite. Most netizens have a high school education or above, with 31.3 percent having a high school degree, 23.3 percent having a three-year college degree, and 25.8 percent having a four-year BA or BS degree.[9]

The influence of web media on the Chinese people and society has become not only extensive but intensive. The average time spent by users on the web in 2007 was 16.9 hours per week, or more than 2.4 hours a day. Such massive exposure naturally raises concerns in vari-

---

6   Lovell, *Great Wall*, pp. 348–49; Lam, *Chinese Politics*, p. 232.

7   *China Internet Network Information Center 2007 Report*; *China Internet Network Information Center 2008 Report*.

8   Zhao, "The Current Situation;" "China's Web Business."

9   *China Internet Network Information Center 2007 Report*.

ous quarters about the influence of the Internet, particularly that of web media. While the state worries about breaches of security, others may be concerned about the glorification of violence. In fact, most people access the Internet innocuously enough, primarily to obtain information, especially the latest news. According to a national survey, the largest group of Internet users, 46.2 percent of the surveyed, go online for such information. The second largest group, 32.2 percent, go online for entertainment. According to the same survey, among the 46.2 percent of Internet users looking for information, 59.2 percent use the Internet mainly for reading news and 18.8 percent mainly for accessing net forums, such as Bulletin Board Services (BBSs). In only ten years the Internet has become the main tool for many Chinese people to obtain information. In fact, 99.8 percent of the users say they will use the Internet first when they want to search for information, and 70.9 percent of them say their most sought after information is news. Websites in China have also grown rapidly. By 2007 domain names registered under .cn reached 1,800,000 and the number of www websites, including .cn, .com, .net, and .org, reached 843,000. The majority of web users still prefer Chinese websites. Among the online information searchers, 81.6 percent visit domestic Chinese websites; 24 percent of adult users and 40 percent of young users sometimes also visit overseas websites.[10]

The Origins and Growth of the Internet in China

The Internet originated with the United States military in the 1960s and became popular throughout the world with the development of the world wide web in the 1990s.[11] This coincided with the People's Republic's emphasis on state stability and economic development in the wake of the widespread urban demonstrations of 1989. In line with Deng Xiaoping's calls for reform and opening reiterated in his "southern tour" from January 18 to February 21, 1992, his successor Jiang Zemin, an engineer by training, moved quickly to place China in the forefront

---

10   Bai, *Analysis*; *China's Online News*; *China Internet Network Information Center 2007 Report*.

11   Zhou, *Historicizing*, p. 135. The United States laid down strict conditions for the linking of China to the Internet in the early 1990s. Ibid., p. 138.

of the new technology. Web media in China did not emerge as completely new and independent but arose from existing newspapers, magazines, and radio and television stations. The first web media service was the online version of the magazine *Chinese Scholars Abroad* (*Haiwai xueren*), launched on January 12, 1995. This web magazine was (and is) a weekly digest that provides news and information gathered from dozens of leading newspapers and magazines mainly to serve the hundreds of thousands of Chinese students studying abroad. The first web newspaper was the online version of *China Trade* (*Zhongguo maoyi*), which was launched on October 20, 1995. It provides trade information to foreign companies around the world. In the following year, the first web radio was launched by Guangdong Radio Broadcasting Station, and several months later China Central Television (CCTV) opened its online service. By the end of 1995 there were about ten online news services, all of them electronic versions of the established media. Meanwhile, numerous nonofficial—either commercial or individual—websites also provided news.[12]

The ten-year development of web media can be analyzed in three stages. During the first, from 1995 to 1997, web media grew rapidly but remained limited. By the end of 1997, around sixty leading news organizations had launched their web versions, including *People's Daily*, *Market Daily*, *Economy Daily*, *Finance Daily*, *China Consumers*, *International Business*, *Farmers' Daily*, *Popular Movies*, *Tourism*, *Stock Market*, *China Youth*, and *Beijing Review*. In addition, China's two wire news services—Xinhua News Agency and China News Service—opened online versions. Moreover, China Web, the first government website designed to produce external propaganda—or "foreign publicity" in the new locution of the Chinese government—was launched by the State Council Information Office.[13] Still, of a total of more than 2,000 newspapers and nearly 8,000 magazines available at that time, less than 1 percent had launched online services by 1997.

Web media services encountered several problems at this stage. They were almost all electronic versions of the existing media. They lacked financial resources, reliable technology, and well-trained web media professionals. Among the mainstream influential web media

---

12   *Chronicle.*
13   Wang, "Build the Web."

services, none was commercially or privately owned. All had limited resources and potential for expansion in the new economic environment of the time. Moreover, many of the web media sites were of low quality and did not provide much information. Some of them were not updated for long periods or were frequently out of service. Not surprisingly, therefore, the number of web media users was small and the impact of web media was still insignificant.[14]

During the second stage of development, from 1998 to 2002, leading news organizations, such as *Guangming Daily* and China Radio International, developed web versions and several large commercial websites, such as Sina, Sohu, and NetEase, were allowed to provide news services. Sina, launched by a private commercial company in Beijing on December 1, 1998, soon became the largest commercial Chinese language website in the world. A total of 400,000 people visited Sina the day it opened, immediately surpassing the number of users of Yahoo's Chinese website.[15] In the wake of Sina's opening, Sohu and NetEase were also launched and licensed. These nonofficial websites did not enjoy the right of "independent news coverage," but they immediately attracted a large clientele.[16] Their strategies included providing abundant, up-to-date, real-time, continuous news, as well as all-around news background information. In addition, they used "discussion forums," user-friendly news selection, and sensational column layout to compete with the official web news services for web media users.[17] Soon their broader news coverage, more current information, more human-interest stories, and more relaxed news formats knocked out all of the official web media services. More independent of the state, these commercial services enjoyed a kind of "freedom" that gave them advantages over the official print, radio, and television media.[18]

---

14   He, "Current Status."
15   Bai, *On the Web.*
16   Such a system of state licensing and private management might be compared with the officially managed and merchant-operated firms of the late Qing period. See Zhou, *Historicizing*, p. 172.
17   Chen, *Immature.*
18   "Freedom," of course, is a highly loaded word with much ideological content and social significance. Zhou, *Historicizing*, p. 238; see also Jean Oi's essay in Kirby, *Realms*, pp. 264–84.

During this stage, thousands of local media organizations—at the provincial, regional, municipal, and even down to the county level—launched their online services. By the end of 2002, the total official web services of both print and broadcast media had reached several thousands. It is estimated that by that time about one-third of China's 2,100 newspapers, 9,000 magazines, and 700 radio and television stations had launched online services.[19] An even more meaningful change was that many of the web media services were no longer just the electronic versions of the existing media, but had departed from their "parents." Instead of mainly posting news copied from newspapers, radio, and television on the web, some web media services started providing their own news coverage and commentaries. Some also offered other kinds of consumer-oriented services, such as weather, stock, and tourism information. Another important change in 1999 was web media use of Bulletin Board Services (BBS). The *People's Daily*'s web service launched China's first news BBS, "Strengthen the Nation Forum" (*qiangguo luntan*) on June 19, 1999, right after the United States' bombing of the Chinese embassy in Yugoslavia.[20] Although the initial purpose of opening this forum was to give the public a venue to criticize the United States and to express their patriotic emotions, the forum also gave the public an opportunity to interact with news providers much more easily, quickly, and directly. Very soon, the public began to use the BBSs to post their own news and comments, including criticisms of the party and government.[21] It would not be the first, or last, time state-approved institutions in China were used by the populace to advance their own agendas.

During the third stage of development, since 2003, web media spread to most of the rest of Chinese territory, including distant and relatively poor frontier areas such as Xinjiang and Tibet. In the last few

---

19 Zhao, "Brief History."

20 *Chronicle of Web Development*. For a website focused on the "Great Wall" launched at the same time, see Chapter 1 in this volume.

21 In this sense, BBSs could be likened to the walls on which large-character posters were mounted during the Cultural Revolution and to the Xidan Democracy Wall that had appeared during Deng Xiaoping's return to authority in 1978–1979. These forms of public expression had been outlawed as destabilizing forms of "Big Democracy" (*da minzhu*) in the early 1980s. See Zhou, *Historicizing*, p. 178.

years, the development of web media has also become more "rational" in the sense of being better organized.[22] In addition to seeking quantitative expansion, the web media services have emphasized quality. Small, local web media services have merged to form a few larger, more competitive regional or national web media that have more financial resources, better trained professionals, and better information technologies. For example, nine leading local web media services in Beijing merged to form Qianlong Net, significantly named after the reign during which the Qing dynasty reached its full efflorescence in the eighteenth century.[23] Similarly, eleven leading web media services in Shanghai merged to form East Net, an allusion, perhaps, to China's "peaceful rise" (in the Maoist lingo the East was "red") as well as to the location of Shanghai on the coast.[24] Both websites provide a variety of services but focus on news. They are now among a handful of the most popular and influential web media in China.

In the current stage, web media have developed along two dimensions. They have become more like corporations than party agencies, and thus somewhat more independent of the state; but, at the same time, they have become more subject to regulation than previous private and commercial web media had been.[25] Although the majority of the web media were derived from the existing media and many of them are institutionally still part of that media, they have been successful to various degrees in departing from such media in areas ranging from fundamental concepts to daily operations. Web media have been exploring a model suitable for survival in the Chinese context, especially in the existing political and cultural environment. After mergers and consolidations, thousands of official web media services have been reduced to a couple of hundred larger ones. Nevertheless, in spite of the mergers and consolidations, the most popular, most influential,

---

22 Ming interview.

23 For the concept of efflorescence, see Goldstone, "Neither Late."

24 Williams, "Brief History."

25 Xie and Zhou, *Theories.* For the roots and contemporary manifestations of this characteristically Chinese mix of public and private identities, see Brook and Frolic, *Civil Society*, esp. chs. 1–2, 5.

and perhaps most powerful websites are still the three commercial ones—Sina, Sohu, and NetEase.[26]

An interesting phenomenon is that, while the three commercial web services have been trying to become more news-oriented in order to make themselves more authoritative, the official web media have been trying to become more commercialized in an attempt to make themselves more popular. The two opposite approaches are for the same purpose, i.e., to obtain more users and larger market shares. In this competition so far, the commercial services are well ahead of the official ones. Importantly, Sohu has publicly proclaimed its criteria for covering the news: humanistic value, social responsibility, and factual credibility. These claims suggest that a somewhat new type of media philosophy has emerged in China, which emphasizes "serving people and society" rather than "serving party and government." The claims would appear to combine the Maoist-era slogan of serving the people (*wei renmin fuwu*) with the more contemporary idea of serving the "public," defined, perhaps, as the putatively emerging urban and educated middle-class or elite.

By 2006, a multilevel and multisystem web media infrastructure was established. Among the 170 or so licensed websites that were involved in news services, the great majority were official, state-owned, and noncommercial. However, the minority, consisting of commercial web media services, get the most users, followed by the middle-level government services, and then the central-level government services. Web media have not just entered the consciousness of many Internet users, but have also entered the awareness of a much larger number of people—hundreds of millions of mobile phone users.[27] For example, by the end of 2003, China's mobile phone users had reached 250 million, and many of them were subscribers to web news services able to check the news through their mobile phones.[28] Therefore, altogether web media services are accessible to a great number of people although still a fairly modest minority of the entire population.

---

26   *Top Ten*; *Top 100*.

27   As early as 2004, mobile phone users were estimated to number 350 million and to have sent 220 billion text messages, more than the rest of the world combined. Lam, *Chinese Politics*, pp. 229–30.

28   Liu, "Obstacles."

In addition to proliferating, in this stage China's web media have also become increasingly influential, especially among young people. The Internet has been providing a variety of ways for the public to obtain news, and many users have been getting news through many different online channels. For instance, in 2004 while 89.0 percent of web users went to web media sites for news, 43.8 percent of them also got news through BBS, 17.8 percent from e-mails, 12.3 percent from news groups, 9.6 percent from chat rooms, 2.7 percent from mobile phone short messages (SMS), and 1.4 percent from blogs.[29] In 2003, the five most popular web media sites were Sina, Sohu, People Net, Xinhua Net, and CCTV Net, with the first two commercial websites being used by 70 percent of the total web media users. Most users have gone online mainly for international and domestic political news.[30] This is not strange because the official media censor international and domestic news or present it in a politically biased fashion.[31] Therefore, web media, mainly the nonofficial commercial web media, provide an irreplaceable alternative source for the public to access otherwise unreported international and domestic political news. A related phenomenon is that nowadays all kinds of international and domestic entertainment and sports news, even if they are very vulgar, are rarely censored and are available on all media outlets. This gives web media a greater opportunity than before for growth and impact in nonpolitical domains.

The Strategy of Using and Controlling Web Media

The Chinese government was enthusiastic about the web not only because it was a cutting-edge technology that could encourage business and investment but also because it could be used to advance political and social agendas. The resulting state regulations, policies, and laws on web media have also experienced three phases of development, only slightly different from the stages of web media growth discussed above. During the first phase, 1995–1997, there were no regulations that were specifically designed for web media. As a result, across the nation many

---

29   "Online Battle."
30   Chao, "Four Web CEOs."
31   Media "bias," of course can be alleged—and often found—in any society.

websites were already involved in providing unregulated news, and the majority of them were operated by small, commercial individuals or companies.

To be sure, electronic communication had started in China as early as September 1987, when a Chinese professor of computing had sent an e-mail containing the slogan: "Go beyond the Great Wall, March toward the World."[32] The Chinese established their first network in 1994 and their first public Internet service the following year. In February 1996 the government established the first regulations on the Internet, requiring users to file reports with the Public Security Bureau and to sign a pledge not to read or transmit material that "endangers the state, obstructs public safety, or is obscene or pornographic." In late 1996 and early 1997, the Public Security Bureau created a new department that began the construction of the "great firewall." The firewall has been characterized as a "sprinkling of servers guarding the five gateways at which the Chinese Internet met that of the outside World."[33] It was programmed to block sensitive sites from abroad, including some foreign newspapers, pro-Tibetan or Taiwanese independence organizations, religious cults, human rights groups, and pornography, all from a list updated every two weeks. Within five years, the system was armed with "packet sniffers," software able to detect problematic words such as Falun Gong, Jiang Zemin, freedom, and sex that would trigger a freezing of the relevant terminal.[34]

This general effort to control the Internet naturally had some impact on web media. In March 1997 the State Council Information Office issued the first regulations on web media, initiating the second stage in state relations with that media.[35] During this period, 1997–1999, however, most government regulations were either too general, and thus ineffective, or quickly outmoded, and thus meaningless. For instance, the government issued regulations that forbade commercial and individual websites from operating news services, but many such websites still found various ways to provide such news. Due to the lack of specific regulations or effective enforcement, the web media envi-

---

32   Lovell, *Great Wall*, p. 339.
33   Ibid., p. 340.
34   Ibid., pp. 340–41; Ming, "Where Does."
35   Ming, "Where Does."

ronment remained rather chaotic. Fake news and copyright violations were very common. Thus this period was not much different in fact from the first period, which had no regulations.

During the third phase, 2000–present, several specific regulations, policies, and laws have been established and effectively implemented. In the year 2000 alone, the state issued nine regulations on web media. On November 7, 2000, the State Council Information Office and the Ministry of Information Industry jointly issued the "Temporary Act on Websites Involving News Operation," which is the country's first specific lawlike policy on web media. On July 15, 2002, the State Council Information and Publishing Office and the Ministry of Information Industry jointly issued another regulation, the "Temporary Act on Websites Involving Publishing."[36] By 2003 the government had established and implemented a relatively complete set of policies and regulations on web media. Because of this, the web media have become better ordered but of course they have also become more controlled.

The most important and distinctive characteristic of China's web media policy is its two contradictory or opposite dimensions. In principle, the Communist party and PRC government strongly encourage and promote the development of web media. In 1999, Jiang Zemin, then party general secretary, called on all the existing media to take advantage of the Internet to launch online versions in order to maximize the scale, speed, and effects of their news services. The Propaganda Department of the Party's Central Committee and the External Propaganda Department of the State Council ordered all leading central media organizations to open their online versions as soon as possible. Meanwhile, they also ordered each province and big city to set up an influential web media service to make the news services more attractive, timely, and effective. In 2000, Jiang Zemin again called on party committees and government agencies at all levels to fully recognize the importance of the Internet and web media. This time, however, he shifted the emphasis from the development of the Internet to the "safe administration" of the Internet, a euphemism for exerting more state control.[37] The relevant party committees and government agencies later issued several directives to warn their members about

36   "Regulations."
37   "Speech of Jiang Zemin."

the negative impact of the Internet and web media. In 2001, the party leaders put forth a new initiative for developing the information industry as part of the country's Tenth Five-Year Plan. The initiative once again emphasized the importance of the Internet and web media but it also called for "healthy development." It particularly stressed the necessity of regulating the Internet and web media and implementing the existing regulations and policies.[38]

As a result of these contradictory and shifting guidelines, many of the specific regulations and policies tend to be more restrictive than supportive. The constraints are mainly directed at the web media's political and ideological content, not its pornographic or violent content. The regulations require all websites to obtain a license from the State Council for operating news services. In order to obtain such a license, a website must meet the political criteria set by the party and government: no content should "be against the party's 'Four Cardinal Principles'" (adherence to socialism, proletarian dictatorship, Communist party leadership, and Marxism-Leninism), "endanger state security," or contain elements of "national or ethnic discrimination." Websites that want to be licensed must also meet other professional standards, such as having "the necessary news editing organization, sufficient financial resources, and up-to-date IT equipment and offices." Moreover, the website must also have a group of "experienced senior news professionals."[39]

Obviously, under these strict and sometimes unreasonable requirements, only the official media services or government/party agencies, along with a few large commercial web services, will qualify to obtain such a license. It is not clear whether this is what the party and government intended, but it is what has been happening. These regulations have greatly altered China's web media landscape. Now, only a handful of nonofficial commercial websites have obtained news service licenses, and all other commercial or individual websites are illegal (and therefore uncountable). When discovered, the unlicensed websites may be prosecuted and punished at any time if they are considered to have crossed the party's political line or otherwise exceeded the permissible limits. The regulations further prohibit the licensed commer-

---

38   Sun et al., *Security Law.*
39   *Temporary Regulations.*

cial websites from producing news on their own, with the exceptions of covering big news events and getting special permission on a case-by-case basis. As a result, in general these licensed commercial web media services are restricted in selecting news from the existing media services or other domestic web media services and posting it on their sites. They cannot obtain news from websites outside China without special permission from the State Council Information Office on a case-by-case basis.[40]

Therefore, although China now has the largest number of Internet users in the world (followed by the United States), the Communist party's willingness to develop and to use the Internet and web media has done nothing to dispel its ambivalence toward them.[41] In other words, the leaders' attitude toward the Internet and web media is split between a recognition that the Internet and web media are critical tools for China's modernization and a desire to control online information available to the public. When the Internet had just emerged in China, the party was already warned by its senior consultants that opening to the Internet would unleash an uncontrollable flood of information that might eventually lead to the collapse of the Communist ideology. In the last decade the party has demonstrated that it can both censor and, to some degree, tolerate the flow of information over the Internet and web media. Thus, the leaders see that the Internet can be a powerful and popular channel for both the authorities and the public to hear and to be heard. They want to use it as a new tool to realize their political and economic goals even at the price of incurring a certain number of complaints and criticisms.[42]

The government uses several different methods to control the web media. First, it forbids commercial websites to gather and release news—particularly political news—independently. They may post only the news stories provided by the official, existing media or other approved web media services. Second, tens of thousands of specially established and reportedly well-paid government agents, known as the "web police," have been installed in the security bureaus at all levels to

---

40   Yan, "Analysis."
41   "China's 'Netizens.'"
42   Li, "Internet's."

monitor websites.[43] When a news message crosses the line or exceeds the limits—particularly the political line and the ideological limits—the web police will not only censor or delete the news, they will also pursue the poster and punish him or her with up to a life sentence.[44] The government filters public access to thousands of international and domestic websites run by dissidents, human-rights groups, and some Western "rightist" news organizations. Third, using the firewall technology and other advanced filtering IT devices, the government also puts great effort into suppressing information and messages related to sensitive topics on the Internet. More recently, the government has been closely monitoring chat rooms, BBSs, and other online venues where web users increasingly vent frustrations and air criticisms.[45] Nonofficial and commercial websites select, repackage, and lay out news from the available pool that is much less propaganda-oriented and much more human-interest-oriented than that on other web sites. Moreover, with the interactive function of e-mail, ICQ (shorthand for the phrase "I seek you," an instant messaging computer program), and discussion forums, millions of users actively exchange, forward, publish, and verify news information among themselves. These activities often reach a peak when official media lose their voice or credibility in a social crisis such as SARS or during a politically sensitive social event.

Since 2003, fearing the appearance of overt "dissent," the government has become increasingly concerned with the operation of the Internet and web media. It has been tightening control on web media, especially during politically sensitive periods, such as the anniversaries of the June 4 Tiananmen Square prodemocracy movement in 1989.[46] In 2003, a Reporters Without Borders investigation of content filtering by Chinese websites showed that only 60 percent of messages posted to

---

43 "China Establishes." Estimates of the numbers of these web police vary from 30,000 (Lovell, *Great Wall*, p. 344) to more than 50,000 (Lam, *Chinese Politics*, p. 230). The numbers, of course, are neither widely publicized nor officially confirmed.

44 By 2004 an estimated sixty-one activists on the net, called "netivists," had been imprisoned, some without charges for up to a year. Lovell, *Great Wall*, p. 341.

45 Chiu, "Chinese Net;" Yu, "On Freedom." Blogs, on the other hand, are more private and less subject to surveillance. Lovell, *Great Wall*, p. 342.

46 Wang, *Mixing Three*.

discussion forums over a period of one month appeared online. That
number fell to 55 percent for messages with content deemed controversial by the censors. Of that 55 percent, more than half were subsequently removed by webmasters tasked with overseeing the online forums. Although the level of filtering varied from site to site, discussion
forums run by commercial sites were generally more open than official
websites. The report noted that no messages criticizing the party or
government were posted to the discussion forums of China's official
online news services, such as the Xinhua News Agency and *People's
Daily*. By comparison, 50 percent of the messages that appeared on the
discussion forum run by Sina criticized the party or government.[47]

The rationale for the party's split and fluctuating policy is that it
permits the public to blow off "steam" so that discontent does not ac-
cumulate and result in an explosion. Thus, even the official website of
People's Daily operates the Strengthen the Nation Forum, where the
public may vent its frustration and "light" criticism so long as it does
not challenge the legitimacy of the party. Not surprisingly, many people are still unhappy about the party's control-oriented regulations and
policies.

The Problems of China's Web Media

There are several obvious—or not so obvious—problems associated
with China's web media. First, web media in China have been growing
rapidly. By 2007 there were around 180 major licensed web media
services that contained thousands of media websites. But very few of
them are independent from the political system. In fact, the majority of
media websites are the online or electronic propaganda apparatus
of the party and government. Web media as a whole are under the close
supervision of the party. The party and government pay a lot of attention
to the development of web media, but the fundamental purpose is to
insure effective service to the party and government. In the view of the
party, web media, like all other kinds of media, are just part of the
overall political machine. In fact, in my judgment, most of the web
media services do not provide the public with the news they really

---

47   Shen, "Law-Related."

want. Mainly, they are just posting the news gathered from the regular media with some modifications. We may therefore consider China's web media to be far from "free and independent" by Western ideal standards.[48]

However, technologically, the government is unable to prevent individuals from posting news information on discussion forums. They can only delete it after the news is posted. Thus, the net forums give the public a kind of evanescent free speech that may never reach a large audience because it may be deleted as soon as the web police notice the red flags.[49] Nonetheless, a national survey in 2004 showed that 2.4 million people frequently post new information on BBSs.[50] Thus, a popular, quasi-news service has emerged. In China, all major portal sites and websites host multiple net forums treating politics, finance, military, sports, health, and lifestyles. A typical net forum features a threaded discussion format that is similar to online newsgroups, but email addresses of those who post are concealed from the public. The posters are known only by their net names, which gives them some degree of protection against government reprisals.

Second, despite the fact that by June 2008 the Chinese comprised one of every nine netizens in the world and the total number of Chinese netizens reached 162 million, the nation's Internet development can still be said by other measures to be in its primary stage.[51] For example, in 2004, only 7.9 percent of China's total population used the Internet—nearly 50 percent less than the average per capita global percentage. In early 2008, the Internet penetration rate in China reached 19 percent, but it was still lower then the world's average Internet penetration rate of 22 percent. Predictably, the proportion of people exposed to the Internet in smaller cities and the countryside has been

---

48 Of course, those standards are often honored in the breach even in so-called democratic countries. Goody, *Theft*, ch. 9. Indeed, the supposedly "liberal" washingtonpost. com "has control mechanisms very similar to those of People's Daily Online." Zhou, *Historicizing*, p. 153. The U.S. media have engaged in egregious self-censorship in not printing photographs of U.S. casualties during the U.S. war in Iraq.

49 Cheng and Shen, "Impact."

50 *Thirteenth Statistical.*

51 "Global Web Users."

even lower. Most middle-aged and older people have been non-users, and Chinese netizens have been mainly male.[52]

Third, participating in net discussions is still a potentially dangerous activity and periodically leads to prosecution by the government if the content of the message crosses the party's line. To be safe, the majority of contributors use pseudonyms, especially when posting politically sensitive messages.[53] Although the issue of Internet censorship, including the government's attempts to block access to some websites and to censor discussion groups, is routinely met with harsh criticisms from human rights groups in Western countries, the Internet censorship and restricted access to information in China are still controversial issues among the Chinese public and there is no solid consensus on them. Concerns for "order" often trump quests for "freedom" in Hu Jintao's China. A 2002 study conducted by Harvard University on Internet and society found that 18,931 out of a total of about 200,000 websites (including both domestic and foreign) were inaccessible from two different proxy servers in China on two different days. Thus nearly 10 percent of websites in China were inaccessible to web users. While some of the sites that were blocked were sexually explicit, others simply offered news, health information, education, and entertainment.[54]

However, I believe the most important thing is that the party's heavy censorship cannot completely block the public's access to online information. In fact, some web users are often able to access politically sensitive information despite the best efforts of the censors. Resourceful netizens can find their way around the "net wall" (*wangqiang*) by various means. For example, in 2004 Chinese users of Google accessed the search engine's results by using ElgooG, a mirror-image version of the original site that originated as a computer-nerd joke.[55] Users often gain awareness of information contained on websites blocked by censors, thus reducing the significance of the party's censorship efforts. Also, web users who post content online or participate in discussion groups are generally savvy enough to avoid topics that transgress the government's red lines. Accordingly, they subconsciously

52   "China's Internet."
53   Rodriquez, "Burning"; Yu, "Freedom."
54   Liu, "Obstacles."
55   Lovell, *Great Wall*, p. 342.

temper their remarks through self-censorship. Consequently, most web users do not pose a direct challenge to the party's ideology or to the government's policies and thus avoid government harassment and prosecution.

Implications of the Battle over Web Media

Web media in China have already formed a comprehensive system and an advanced infrastructure. As in the case of newspapers, magazines, radio, and television stations in an earlier era, web media have been having various kinds of overt and covert impacts in the time of reform and opening. The web media are competing with the existing media, facilitating public surveillance of the ruling political party, and encouraging China's transition toward more political civility and democratization. In theory, web media should eliminate the last obstruction to the free flow of information, and, in practice, they greatly multiply the potential sources of information.[56] Under certain conditions, the Internet can come close to realizing its full potential. During the SARS crisis in 2003, for example, the state-run media lost their credibility when they failed to publicize the full extent of the problem even after they became aware of it (see Chapter 7 in this volume). In that situation, the Internet and web media quickly became the general public's most important sources of information about the epidemic. According to a survey in 2004, while a total of 38.8 percent of the people surveyed used print media for news about SARS—9.9 percent from newspapers and magazines and 28.9 percent from radio and television—57.8 percent of the surveyed used websites for news about the disease. Given that in 2003 more than 90 percent of the Chinese households had access to newspaper, radio, and television, and less than 5 percent had access to the Internet, the above figures are very meaningful, though subject to different interpretations. On the one hand, they show that people with access to the Internet can easily rely on it to the exclusion of other, slower, and less reliable media. On the other hand, these statistics remind us that the vast majority of the Chinese people still do not have that option.[57] In any case, according to

---

56 Hachigian, "Internet"; Li, "Real Challenges."
57 Cheng and Shen, "Impact."

another study in 2004, 50 percent of urban web users increased their use of the Internet and web media in the wake of the SARS scare.[58] Similarly, net forums and chat rooms have been providing an alternative source of news to the more fully controlled media.[59]

Second, the Internet and web media not only provide an alternative venue for information flow, but also function as a public forum in which netizens can discuss politics and many other sensitive topics. The Internet and web media have opened paths for two-way communication, reminiscent of various historical forms of the "word road" (*yanlu*) and the more recent Maoist ideal of "from the people, to the people," which are all in contrast to China's other longstanding and better known, top-down-indoctrination-oriented, media systems.[60] These media have also become public forums for people to exchange ideas and viewpoints among themselves.[61] Given the limits of China's political environment, these public spaces may be seen as already containing some key elements of the "public sphere."[62] According to Jurgen Habermas, the public sphere is the social space generated in communicative action, especially in times of transition from one kind of social system to another. Free information flow and public political communication are two of the essential elements in the formation of a "civil society."[63] Thus the formation of public forums in China's web media may be an important step in the country's transformation and political democratization. The development of the Internet and web media has brought much more access to information and more diversity to discussion than in the past. This venue of public political communication, although still in its infancy, makes it possible for people to form a "public community" that is able to criticize the legitimacy, scru-

---

58 Zheng and Jiang, "Web Media."

59 "Zhang Chaoyang."

60 Popular complaints posted on the net against official corruption can sometimes have an influence on the state's personnel policy. See Lovell, *Great Wall*, pp. 342–53; Lam, *Chinese Politics*, p. 229.

61 The Falun Gong sect used electronic communication to organize their demonstration against the government in April 1999, and Chinese human rights organizations use the technology to keep in touch with foreign sympathizers and supporters. Lovell, *Great Wall*, p. 342; Lam, *Chinese Politics*, p. 228.

62 Ming interview; Zhang, "Window"; Qu, "Will the Internet."

63 Habermas, *Between Facts*.

tinize the validity, and evaluate the objectivity of the official media's representations of news events.[64]

In theory, web users are free to provide their chosen information anonymously and to discuss topics freely. In fact, the censors are incapable of keeping pace with the information posted on web media, and many people's attitudes are being shaped more by the information on the nonofficial web media, net forums, and chat rooms than by the official media.[65] It was estimated in 2004 that there were some 300,000 web columns and blogs in China.[66] There has never been an accurate official number of bloggers in China; all the numbers are estimates, because there is no way to calculate the ever-changing number of bloggers. According to China Internet Network Information Center, however, in 2008 the number of bloggers in China was estimated to be 47 million. Only a tiny percentage of them were politics- or sex-oriented and thus subject to close state scrutiny. These websites and blogs cover various subjects, from politics to pop music, but most carry simply the personal musings of some of the country's millions of Internet users.[67]

In a country where freedom of political expression was very limited for half a century or more, the impact of such changes should not be underestimated.[68] According to Li Xiguang, web media have a special political importance in China because they can carry information unavailable in the governmental media.[69] Moreover, in China, the web media give individuals more opportunities to express their views, to communicate with the public, and to search for reliable information. Of course, to some extent, this is true of the Internet in all societies because mainstream media are everywhere constrained by pressures, economic as well as political, to carry All the News That's Fit to Print,

---

64 Cheng and Shen, "Impact."

65 Li, "Real Challenges."

66 Bosco, "Weblogs."

67 Yu, "China's Netizens."

68 For limitations on freedom of expression in the Republic, now somewhat idealized by Chinese young people critical of the People's Republic, see Kirby, *Realms*, esp. chs. 4, 5, and 7.

69 Li, "Internet's Impact."

as the *New York Times* puts it.[70] But in the People's Republic before the
Internet and web media, Chinese citizens had only "new democracy"
and "democratic centralism" defined by the party and government, liberal democracy of the fleeting "hundred flowers" variety, and/or "mass
democracy" of the Cultural Revolution type. Now, under the policies
of reform and opening, China's netizens have arguably started to experience a new type of liberalism made available by the public forums on
the Internet and web media.

Third, equally if not more importantly, the online public communication and discussion have begun influencing the decision-making
procedure of the party and government, especially in regard to public
policies.[71] In some cases, they have even helped to change several important public policies or laws. One example was the case of the Acquired Immunodeficiency Syndrome (AIDS) crisis that resulted in
part from the unsupervised sale of blood in Henan province in the late
1980s and early 1990s. That public health disaster was finally brought
to public attention in part through the web media and efforts to deal
with it became more serious following the SARS crisis.[72] Although it
would be too optimistic to think that this change in procedure will be
adopted in all decision-making processes in the future and will be extended to all other fields in the society, given that the online "public
sphere" in China is growing so vigorously and that the country will
either choose or will be forced to become more "open," the potential of
the influence of public pressures on the party's decision-making will
only become bigger and, I think, irreversible.[73] For instance, 2003 was
hailed as the "year of protecting civil rights on the Internet" by web
users in China. The hottest issues in 2003 and afterward included "the
death of detainee Sun Zhigang," a case of exposing severe human rights
abuses; "the BMW car accident," a case revealing elite brutality toward

---

70 It might be argued that there is more diversity of opinion in the People's Republic than
    in the United States over basic issues such as whether to take the "socialist" or "capital-
    ist" road, but I still think that there is more open discussion of political issues such as
    the quality of current leaders and their policies in the United States and other self-
    proclaimed liberal democracies than in the People's Republic.
71 "China's 'Netizens.'"
72 Lovell, *Great Wall*, p. 342; Lam, *Politics*, pp. 98–99.
73 Yu, "Freedom"; Lemon, "Chinese Internet."

the common people; and the "resentencing of Shenyang mafia Godfather Liu Yong," a case of justice versus corruption in the judicial system. All of these issues were considered "negative news" by the other forms of media and got very limited coverage. The web media's coverage, however, turned these news events into household items among those with access to computers. The results were, first, a strong public opinion wave, then a push for the regular media to follow the trend, and finally the formal involvement of the party and government in changing some relevant policies and laws.[74] Because of the widespread exposure of these news events on the web, they became concerns of the public and the foci of the society. Public opinion (*yulun*) has played an important role at many moments over the course of Chinese history, but this was one of the first times the Internet was used by netizens to press the party and government into revising its policies and laws.[75]

The public's criticisms of the party and government on the web have become a significant new societal force. Some government ministers and high-ranking party officials have communicated online with the public, answering their concerns or providing explanations about some issues. China's top leaders, including President Hu Jintao and Prime Minister Wen Jiabao, have publicly acknowledged that they routinely log onto the web to stay informed about "public opinion."[76] Besides People Net, other major news websites such as Xinhua Net and CCTV Net have all devoted sections in their homepages to "Netters' Posts." There is no doubt that these interactions between the leaders and the public are helpful to China's transition toward what the party calls "political civilization" and "democratization." To a certain degree, this kind of interaction itself may be viewed as a sign of democracy, at least in the case of China. Realistically speaking, this type of democracy, elitist and limited though it may be, is probably the only kind or degree the Chinese people can enjoy at this moment.[77] In the long

---

74 Kloet, "Weblogs."

75 Lemon and Williams, "Finding Freedom." For ruminations on various forms and concepts of democracy and civil society in Chinese history and culture, see Des Forges, "Democracy" and "States."

76 Yu, "On Freedom."

77 For reflections on contemporary Chinese forms of democracy, see Shih, *Collective Democracy*; Lam, *Chinese Politics*.

term, the power of online public opinion seems likely to exert a profound impact on China's longstanding and recurrently authoritarian
political system.

Conclusion

The Chinese Communist party has attempted to control the media ever
since it began to gain authority over parts of China more than eighty
years ago. Today, however, in addition to thousands of party-run
newspapers, magazines, and radio and television stations, there are
also almost 600,000 official or nonofficial websites.[78] Hundreds of
millions of Chinese people can now obtain, either directly or indirectly,
news and other information from websites as well as from the usual
official media. Web media have opened the door a little for many people
to have more freedom of information. Technologically and potentially,
the BBSs and chat rooms have provided the public with an unlimited
space for exchanging information and ideas freely and anonymously,
although politically and practically the state continues to try to limit
this space.

From an optimistic perspective, the Internet and web media have
become a source of political democratization, offering a virtual public
space for civic discourse and manifesting some characteristics of a
public sphere.[79] From a pessimistic point of view, the party and government have institutionalized the Internet and web media into a
control apparatus by successfully implementing various legal—or not-
so-legal—regulations and policies and by effectively configuring the
systems to filter a large number of overseas websites.[80] Regardless of
one's perspective, the Internet and web media in China are increasingly gaining a silent but salient influence and exerting a quiet but significant impact. They are playing an important role as an alternative
source of information and as a venue for the public to express opinions. They are providing the public with different voices and are creating a public community capable of interpreting and verifying "reality"
on its own. With the number of Internet users expanding by millions

---

78   *Thirteenth Statistical*; Liu, "China Has."
79   Meng, "Development."
80   Rodriquez, "Burning."

each month, the Chinese people as a whole have obtained unprecedented opportunities to receive uncensored information, to express views, and to have their voices heard by millions of fellow citizens.[81]

The party's concern over the Internet and web media is not baseless. Political discussion seldom ends without attempting to effect social change; very often, informal discussion groups become bases for organized political actions. Suggestions, petitions, and signature collections for certain activities have already been regularly seen on many net forums, and these net forums can easily become venues for political movements.[82] Controlling the Internet and web media effectively has become increasingly difficult, if not impossible. As Li comments, in today's China the only effective way to staunch information flow would be to assign a policeman to every computer in the country—and of course it would also have to be arranged that the policemen were not corruptible. There is another reason as well for the party's control over the Internet and web media to become more and more difficult: the Internet and web media will increasingly belong to the information technology industry.[83] Once international businesses begin to invest in China's information technology industry—including the Internet and web media—under the rules of the World Trade Organization (WTO), it will become more difficult for the propaganda (or publicity) authorities to control the online information flow based on political or ideological criteria.[84]

Probably because of these difficulties, the party and government have recently tried to adjust the control mechanisms and have adopted a "new" approach. Under the guidance of the State Council Information Office, more than thirty leading web media services have formed

---

81 Chiu, "Chinese Net."

82 See, for example, the organization of demonstrations against Japan and against state policies toward military veterans in 2005. Zhou, *Historicizing*, p. 237; Lovell, *Great Wall*, pp. 345–47; Lam, *Chinese Politics*, p. 230.

83 Of course, the global information technology industry is also capable of cooperating with—and even assisting—the Chinese government in supervising the net as the recent cases of Google and Yahoo and other multinational corporations have shown. Lovell, *Great Wall*, p. 341; Lam, *Chinese Politics*, p. 231; Shao and Wang, *Media*.

84 The WTO, of course, has its own ideology and does not always enforce its regulations equitably or even at all. See the report by its former head, Moore, *World without Walls*.

the China Web Media and Information Service Association.[85] Although this organization has an official background, it is not a party or
government unit.[86] It will assume responsibility for drafting and implementing "self-regulating" policies and bylaws to ensure that all web
media services will fully obey the government regulations, policies,
and laws, and to accept supervision by the public, i.e., the state. The
association calls on all web media services to refrain from posting
"dirty and poisonous" materials and information and to make sure all
content will meet the requirements of the party, government, and public.[87] This new approach may show some kind of policy shift and
change in the control paradigm, i.e., a change from the party's and government's direct control to indirect control and self-regulation, as a
result of realizing the increasing ineffectiveness and difficulties of direct control and hoping to find an updated, more efficient control
mechanism.[88]

China's web media have already had effects that have been felt by
more and more people. In the last several years, the close and complex
relationships among web media, people, society, and politics have become clearer. Despite the fact that there are still many constraints and
restrictions, despite the fact that the web media are still far from being
considered as an independent social institution, and despite the fact
that in China the public sphere or virtual democracy may never become a reality as long as the present political system remains intact, the
Internet and web media have been not only greatly changing organizations' and individuals' ways of conducting economic activities, but also
silently yet saliently altering the way people think, particularly about
public surveillance and democracy. The impact may not be revolutionary and overt; instead, it may be evolutionary and covert. But the Internet and web media have begun serving as a starter and accelerator for

---

85 Ming interview.
86 For the role of such associations in establishing a form of civil society, see Frolic, "State-
    Led Civil Society."
87 Liang, "Four Net CEOs."
88 For articulation of the rationale for this policy by one of the founders of the firewall as
    early as 1997, see Lovell, *Great Wall*, p. 343. This form of political organization also has
    a long history in China. See Brook, "Auto-Organization."

the country's historical transformation.[89] It is true that in China as elsewhere the future is unpredictable, but one thing about the Internet seems to me to be sure: it will get freer and freer. As both Lemon and Lagerkvist suggest, the Internet in China will be freed up not because the authorities desire democracy but because it makes business sense.[90] Or, in a different scenario, the Internet will be liberalized to the extent that sensitive issues, such as political corruption, social inequality, environmental pollution, and the status of Tibet and Taiwan are addressed and resolved. On these questions, as on many others, China cannot act alone.

Works Cited

Bai, Wenbo. *Analysis of the Netizens*. Beijing, China: Beijing University Press, 2003.

———. *On the Web Media*. Beijing, China: Qinghua University Press, 2003.

Bosco, J. "Weblogs in China," *Chinese Internet Research* (online publication), May 13, 2004.

Brook, Timothy. "Auto-Organization in Chinese Society." Pp. 19–45 in Brook and Frolic, *Civil Society*.

Brook, Timothy, and B. Michael Frolic, eds. *Civil Society in China*. Armonk, New York: M. E. Sharpe, 1997.

Chao, Zhulin. "Four Web CEOs On Characteristics of Web Media," *China Journalism Technology Net* (online publication), December 21, 2003.

Chen, Lidan. *The Immature Web Media Communication*. Beijing: Center for China Journalism Research, 2003.

Cheng, Y., and L. Shen, "The Impact of the Internet on Chinese Television News: A Case Study of CCTV during the SARS Outbreak." Paper presented at International Communication Association 2004 Annual Convention, May 27–31, 2004, in New Orleans. (Cited with the author's permission.)

"China Establishes Web Police," *United Morning*, July 25, 2002, p. B3.

---

89 Lemon and Lawson, "Networking."

90 Ibid.; Lagerkvist, *Internet*. This, of course, is what Marxists would call "bourgeois liberalism," or the theory that private property is the only possible basis for individual liberty and is a certain one to boot. For a less optimistic view, warning against the dangers of Western liberalism and technological determinism, see Zhou, *Historicizing*, pp. 238–40. For the repressive aspects of "neoliberalism" in China and around the world, see Wang, *China's New Order*.

China Internet Network Information Center 2007 Report. Beijing: China Internet Network Information Center, 2007.

China Internet Network Information Center 2008 Report. Beijing: China Internet Network Information Center, 2008.

"China's Internet: Behind the Attractive Statistics," *Xinhua News Agency*, January 17, 2004.

"China's 'Netizens' Log On To Parliament," Taipei Times, May 14, 2004, p. B1.

China's Online News Readership. Beijing, China: China Internet Network Information Center, 2003.

"China's Web Business Has a Promising Future," *China Press*, March 11, 2004, p. A2.

Chiu, Cengceng. "Chinese Net Protestors Face Continued Government Censorship," *Chinese Internet Research* (online publication), May 17, 2004.

Chronicle of Web Development in China. Beijing: China Internet Network Information Center, 2003.

Des Forges, Roger. "Democracy in Chinese History." Pp. 21–52 in Roger Des Forges, Luo Ning, and Wu Yen-bo, eds., *Chinese Democracy and the Crisis of 1989: Chinese and American Reflections*. Albany: SUNY Press, 1993.

——. "States, Societies, and Civil Societies in Chinese History." Pp. 68–95 in Brook and Frolic, *Civil Society*.

Du, Junfei. Director of the Institute of Internet Research, Nanjing University, China. Interview by author, March 2004, Nanjing.

Foucault, Michel. *Discipline and Punish: The Birth of The Prison*. Alan Sheridan, trans. New York: Random House, Vintage, 1979.

Frolic, B. Michael. "State-Led Civil Society." Pp. 46–67 in Brook and Frolic, *Civil Society*.

"Global Web Users Will Reach 655 Million." *Agence France-Presse*, November 20, 2002.

Goldstone, Jack. "Neither Late Imperial nor Early Modern: Efflorescences and the Qing Formation in World History." Pp. 242–302 in Lynn Struve, ed., *The Qing Formation in World-Historical Time*. Cambridge: Harvard University Asia Center, Harvard University Press, 2004.

Goody, Jack. *The Theft of History*. Cambridge: Cambridge University Press, 2006.

Habermas, Jurgen. *Between Facts and Norms: Contributions to a Discourse Theory of Law and Democracy*. Cambridge, Mass.: MIT Press, 1996,

——. *The Structural Transformation of the Public Sphere: An Inquiry into a Category of Bourgeois Society*. Thomas Burger and Frederick Lawrence, trans. Cambridge, Mass.: MIT Press, 1991.

Hachigian, Nina. "The Internet and Power in One-Party East Asian States," *Washington Quarterly*, 25.3(2002), pp. 41–58.

He, Jiazheng. "The Current Status and Future Development of News Websites in China," *Journalism Frontier*, 9(2001), pp. 28–36.

Hong, Junhao, and Li Huang. "A Split and Swaying Approach to Building Information Society: The Case of Internet Cafés in China," *Telematics and Informatics*, 22(2005), pp. 377–93.

Kirby, William C., ed. *Realms of Freedom in Modern China*. Stanford: Stanford University Press, 2004.

Kloet, J. "Weblogs in China," *Chinese Internet Research* (online publication), May 13, 2004.

Kurtlantzick, Joshua. "Dictatorship.com: The Web Won't Topple Tyranny," *New Republic*, 230.12(4 May 2004).

Lagerkvist, Johan. *The Internet in China: Unlocking and Containing the Public Sphere*. Lund, Sweden: Lund University Press, 2006.

Lam, Willy Wo-Lap. *Chinese Politics in the Hu Jintao Era: New Leaders, New Challenges*. Armonk, New York: M. E. Sharpe, 2006.

Lemon, Sumner. "Chinese Internet Users Work to Make Knowledge Free," *International Data Group News Service* (online publication), May 17, 2004.

Lemon, Sumner, and Stephen Lawson. "Networking A Place in Chinese History," *International Data Group News Service* (online publication), May 17, 2004.

Lemon, Sumner, and Martyn Williams. "Finding Freedom Behind China's Great Firewall," *International Data Group News Service* (online publication), May 17, 2004.

Li, Xiguang. "The Real Challenges from the Virtual Cyberspace," *People Net* (online publication), December 18, 2001.

———. "The Internet's Impact on China's Press," paper presented at Asian-Pacific Journalists Meeting, Beijing, October 26–28, 2001. (Cited with the author's permission.)

Liang, Ping. "Four Net CEOs on Web's Responsibility," *China Journalism Technology Net* (online publication), December 21, 2003.

Liu, Cun. "On Obstacles to China's Web Development," *China Culture and Information Net* (online publication), August, 12, 2003.

Liu, Juhua. "China Has Nearly 600,000 Websites," *People's Daily*, April 2, 2004, p. 4.

Lovell, Julia. *The Great Wall: China Against the World, 1000 BC–AD 2000*. New York: Grove, 2006.

Meng, Can. "The Development Tends of China's Web Media Forums," *People Net* (online publication), December 13, 2001.

Ming, Dahong, Research Fellow in the Institute of Journalism and Communication, Chinese Academy of Social Sciences. Interview by author, March 2004, Beijing.

_____. "Where Does the Influence of Web News Sites Come from?" *People Net* (online publication), December 18, 2001.

Moore, Mike. *A World Without Walls: Freedom, Development, Free Trade and Global Governance.* Cambridge: Cambridge University Press, 2003.

Oi, Jean C. "Realms of Freedom in Post-Mao China." Pp. 264–84 in Kirby, *Realms.*

"The Online Battle of Chinese Websites," *China Net* (online publication), May 10, 2004.

Qu, Beiying. "Will the Internet Be A Public Sphere?" *MediaChina Net* (online publication), February 17, 2004.

"Regulations on Web News Service Established," *China Journalism Technology Net* (online publication), December 21, 2003.

Rodriquez, Felipe. "Burning the Village to Roast the Pig—Censorship of Online Media." Paper presented at the Freedom of the Media and the Internet Workshop, New York, November 29, 2002. (Cited with author's permission.)

Shao, Le, and Yang Wang. *Media in the Information Age.* Chengdu: Sichuan People's Press, 2000.

Shen, Wei. "The Law-Related Issues of China's Web Media Development," *Journal of Chinese Academy of Social Sciences*, 2(2006), pp. 36–44.

Shih, Chih-yu. *Collective Democracy: Political and Legal Reform in China.* Hong Kong: Chinese University Press, 1999.

"Speech of Jiang Zemin at the Law Seminar of the Central Committee of CCP," *People's Daily*, June 12, 2001, p. 1.

Sun, Changjun, Yuanmin Zheng, and Zhibin Yi. *Security Law for the Web.* Changsha: Hunan University Press, 2002.

The Temporary Regulations on Web Media Services. The State Council of China. Beijing: Center for China Journalism Research, 2002.

The Thirteenth Statistical Survey on the Internet Development in China. The State Council of China. Beijing: China Internet Network Information Center, 2004.

"The Top 100 Most Popular Websites in China". China Internet Network Information Center. *Feifan Net* (online publication), March 9, 2004.

The Top Ten Most Popular Websites in China. China Internet Network Information Center. Beijing: China Internet Network Information Center, 2000.

Wang, Hui. *China's New Order: Society, Politics, and Economy in Transition,* Theodore Huters, ed. Cambridge, Mass.: Harvard University Press, 2003.

Wang, Yi. *Mixing Three Kinds of Freedoms: Criticism of the Temporary*

Regulations on Web Media Services, Beijing: Center for China Journalism Research, 2004.

Wang, Zhi. "Build the Web with Chinese Characteristics," *Computer World*, January 15, 2001, pp. 18–20.

Williams, Martyn. "A Brief History of the Internet in China," *International Data Group News Service* (online publication), May 17, 2004.

"WTO and the Development of China's Digital Media," *STUDA Net* (online publication), February 19, 2004.

Xie, Xinzhou, and Xisheng Zhou. *Theories and Practices of Online Communication*. Beijing: Beijing University Press, 2004.

Yan, Wei. "Analysis of the Current Laws on China's Web." *MediaChina Net* (online publication), December 15, 2003.

Yu, Jie. "On Freedom of Speech and the Internet in China." Speech at the University of Chicago, April 30, 2004. (Cited with author's permission.)

Yu, Zeyuan. "China's Netizens Reach 68 Million," *United Morning*, July 22, 2003, p. B3.

Zhang, Cui. "The Window of Public Opinion," *United Morning*, January 19, 2004, p. B3.

"Zhang Chaoyang On Web's Responsibility," *Economic Observation*, January 5, 2003, p. 2.

Zhao, Qing. "The Current Situation and Future Trends of China's Web News Development," *Journalism Frontier*, 2(2003), pp. 1–5.

Zhao, Yongfang. "A Brief History of China's Web Development," *China Culture and Information Net* (online publication), May 18, 2003.

Zheng, Yanan, and Defeng Jiang. "Web Media and Their Impact on China's Political Democratization," *MediaChina Net* (online publication), January 30, 2004.

Zhou, Yongming. *Historicizing Online Politics: Telegraphy, the Internet and Political Participation in China*. Stanford: Stanford University Press, 2006.

PART FOUR

China in the World

AS A GEOGRAPHICAL ENTITY, "CHINA" has been "in the world" since it began; as a human population, it has presumably existed since homo sapiens left East Africa several tens of thousands of years ago; and, as a distinctive civilization, it has flourished since the development of agriculture and pastoralism circa 10,000 BCE. More recently as a constructed polity, the central state(s) has (have) been much more involved in the world (and the world in it/them) than is often thought, although, to be sure, that involvement has varied frequently and widely over the course of the last four millennia. Having already addressed some of those twists and turns in earlier parts of this book, we move on in this part to "greater China's" (including Taiwan and the Chinese diaspora) considerably intensified interaction with the rest of the world since the "new era" of "reform and opening" beginning in the late 1970s.

Once again our approach is interdisciplinary. We first take up the field of literature and, more specifically, poetry, and explore to what extent Chinese verse, imbued with the Daoist emphasis on naturalness (*ziran*) and nonpurposive action (*wuwei*), is able to represent the material world more directly and successfully than other poetics. We also examine to what degree translations of that poetry into Western languages, such as English, can embody and transmit those special insights. We then turn to the field of aesthetics and, more especially, to performance or behavioral art, and look at the work of four "ethnic" Chinese hailing from China's Central Plain, the heartland of Chinese civilization, from the near periphery of Hong Kong and Taiwan, and from the far periphery of North America. These artists who all use their bodies to express their ideas and become sojourners in the United States cannot avoid the issue of ethnic identity, but they draw on their own personal experiences to grapple with the arguably more important matter of cultural authenticity. Finally we examine Chinese historians in the People's Republic who have recently attempted to transcend the walls of the Marxian five-stage theory of social history and the barriers between the subdisciplines of Chinese and world history in efforts to rewrite world history so as to take better account of the vast majority of the world's people who have lived—and continue to live—outside Europe and North America.

In analyzing these three facets of China's increasing immersion in global culture and history, we are struck by both the considerable achievements and the persisting limitations of the Chinese actors. The Chinese language and script, it seems, is not conclusively more effective than others in breaking down the wall between the world and human representations of it. Similarly, Chinese poet-translators can go only so far in capturing the essence of the original Chinese texts in their English translations. Chinese behavioral artists for their part have sometimes succeeded in incorporating their Chinese bodies, experiences, and outlooks into aesthetic hybrids of universal import, but they continue to suffer from cultural discrimination and the problematic of authenticity in an increasingly malleable, rapidly changing, and artificially constructed global civilization. Chinese historians have taken several steps toward revising world history to give a larger place to non-Western (or non-Euro-American) peoples, but they continue to be constrained by the nineteenth-century Marxian and twentieth-century Weberian quests for scientific history that privilege "capitalism/socialism" and "modernity/postmodernity." In the process, we believe, they continue to underestimate the potential importance of earlier ages and non-Western cultures in the construction of the more integrated—but also possibly more explosive—global civilization of the twenty-first century.

CHAPTER NINE

Breaking Down the Wall between East and West in the "Daoist Poetics" of Wai-lim Yip

Jonathan Stalling

AN EFFORT TO COME TO terms with the different ways in which "China," or the central state(s), has/have been "in the world" might begin with a recognition that this could involve two different, if related dimensions. The first is the way in which the people we call Chinese have perceived "the world" as the material environment in which they, along with all other humans, have long lived and died. The second is the way in which those same people think about and interact with other peoples on the globe who are not Chinese in ethnic or cultural identity. Spoken and written languages are both potential keys to understanding both dimensions, but, given the early appearance and cultural significance of writing in Chinese civilization and the presumed close relationship between Chinese script (Hanzi, or Zhongwen) and the material world it attempts to capture, we shall focus in this chapter on a particular form of writing or literature, namely, poetry or poetics, and what it can tell us about how Classical Chinese poetics and philosophy have been remobilized in our current period to articulate the differences between "Chinese" and "non-Chinese" ways of conceiving of the interface between language and the "life-world."

In this chapter we will explore the thesis, as put forth by the trans-Pacific poet-critic Yip Wai-lim (葉維廉), that Chinese poetry infused with Daoist philosophical discourses has developed various methods of "disclosing" the natural world with a minimum of human interference, and that by extension these Daoist concepts can be mobilized in our current era to break down the wall between Eastern and Western ways of seeing more generally.

Since the mid-1970s, Wai-lim Yip has offered Anglophone readers a description of Classical Chinese poetry as an immanent vision of the "real-life world" unmediated by egoistic, temporal, spatial, or logical frames. He gives us a vision of a poetics of emptiness, whereby poets and even poetry itself step out of the way to let things present themselves "as they are." Yip refers to Chinese poetry and poetics as a kind of *wuyan* 無言 ("empty language")[1] capable of putting into practice a Daoist conception of stepping aside to let the world arise as if untouched by language. To illustrate what he sees as the difficulty of his critical Daoist project, Yip cites an imaginary dialogue with a Japanese intellectual penned by Martin Heidegger. Heidegger "records" the dialogue this way:

> [Heidegger]: The danger of our dialogue was hidden in language itself, not in what we discussed, not in the way in which we tried to do so.
>
> Japanese [visitor]: But Count Kuki[2] had uncommonly good command of German, and of French and English, did he not?
>
> H: Of course, he could say in European languages whatever was under discussion. But we were discussing *Iki*[3] and here it was I to whom the spirit of the Japanese language remained closed— as it is to this day.

---

1   I shall discuss this term later in the chapter. Yip discusses the term in *Diffusion*, pp. 66, 98, and throughout his essay "Taoist Aesthetic." Also see an expanded discussion of this term and Yip's work in my monograph *Poetics of Emptiness*.

2   Count Kuki Shūzō was a student of Heidegger and was a friend of Sartre. See Kuki, *Philosopher's*. The first book-length study of Heidegger was Kuki, *Philosophy of Heidegger*, published in Japan in 1933.

3   An allusion to Kuki's work *Iki no kōzō*. It has been translated by John Clark as *Reflections on Japanese Taste* and by Hiroshi Nara as *The Structure of Detachment*. The Japanese aesthetic term *iki* いき is often represented as 粋.

J: The languages of the dialogue shifted everything into European.

H: Yet the dialogue tried to say the essential nature of Eastasian art and poetry.

J: Now I am beginning to understand better where you smell the danger. The language of dialogue constantly destroyed the possibility of saying what the dialogue is about.

H: Sometime ago I called language, clumsily enough, the house of Being. If man by virtue of his language dwells within the claim and call of Being, then we Europeans presumably dwell in an entirely different house than Eastasian man.

J: Assuming that the languages of the two are not merely different but are other in nature, and radically so.

H: And so, a dialogue from house to house remains nearly impossible.[4]

A house, to be a house—even the house of being—needs walls, and here it is clear that Yip is offering a paradox. He endorses Heidegger's notion of insurmountable cultural walls, but in a second move he argues that Daoism, by virtue of its ability to dissolve the dualism of subject and object, may hold the key to dissolving the walls between the East and West. He contends that the concept of *ziran* 自然 (conventionally translated as "naturalness"),[5] a category of unmolested alterity (absolute otherness), and *wuwei* 無為 ("nonaction"),[6] the principal stance whereby one integrates the self's *ziran* with the *ziran* of other (-ness) without appropriation or distortions, can together provide a metaphysical foundation for an ethical, heterocultural dynamic heretofore unavailable within Western philosophy.[7] Yip writes (using an

---

4   Heidegger, *On the Way*, pp. 4–5; Yip, *Diffusion*, p. 15. Lydia Liu quotes a different section of this text and, like Yip, appears to share much of Heidegger's skepticism toward cross-cultural communication. See *Translingual Practice*, pp. 4–6. See both Nishida Kitarō's "Problem," p. 859, and "Towards a Philosophy." Also see Sharf, "Zen." For a Buddhist critique of Japanese nationalist Buddhism, see Hubbard and Swanson, *Pruning*.

5   Yip, *Diffusion*, pp. 78, 114.

6   Ibid., pp. 72, 104, 140.

7   The term *ziran* appears in the *Daodejing* verse 25, "*Dao* follows the law of *ziran*." And the term *wuwei* appears in ch. 63 of the *Daodejing* in the phrase *weiwuwei* 為無為. The actual phrase *wuwei* shows up only three times in the inner chapters of the *Zhuangzi*,

old Romanization system): "The Taoist worldview rejects the premise that the structure of phenomenon (Nature), changing and ongoing, is the same as we conceive it to be. All conscious efforts to generalize, formulate, classify and order it will necessarily result in some form of restriction, reduction or even distortion." He continues: "We impose these conceptions, which, by definition, must be partial and incomplete, upon phenomena at the peril of losing touch with the concrete, original appeal of the totality of things."[8] Yip is drawing upon a notion of *ziran* that is as negative as it is positive. Qingjie Wang argues that we should, like Yip, read *ziran* as not only "self-generating," but also as "other-ing" since implied in Lao Zi's usage of the term is a focus on the need to allow "otherness" to become "itself" without being intervened upon, hence the need for the corollary term, *wuwei*.[9]

Upon closer examination, this "Taoist worldview," insofar as Yip is describing it here, is not entirely distinct from views familiar to "Western" philosophy. Whether one is concerned with Platonic idealism, Christian metaphysics, or the Kantian distinction between noumena and phenomena (among many more such concepts), Western philosophy has long taken nature to be something distinct from how we conceive it to be. The difference with which Yip's Daoism is concerned, however, is that the primary obstacle or "wall" standing between nature and its perception is the language we use (or do not use) to describe it. Of course, this idea can also be found throughout Western philosophy (apophatic Christianity, which claims that the nature of God cannot be captured in language, comes to mind). Yet both the *Daodejing* (or *Laozi*) and *Zhuangzi* (or, taken together, *Lao-Zhuang*) take the linguistic barrier as the central concern and springboard for their philosophical agendas, in ways that, assuming some commonly accepted standard, would appear to exceed those of Western philosophy and theology.

---

but becomes a term of major philosophical and aesthetic import in and after neo-Daoism.

8   Yip, "Taoist Aesthetic," p. 18.
9   See Wang, " 'It-self-so-ing.' "

For Yip (who echoes the positions of many earlier Chinese poet/
critics such as Lu Ji 陸機, Sikong Tu 司空圖, Su Dongpo 蘇東坡,
and Yan Yu 嚴羽)[10] Classical Chinese poetry prolongs *Lao-Zhuang*
thought's critique of language by developing poetic forms that attempt
to avoid cognitive reductions and what Yip calls "epistemological elaborations." "The main aim [of Chinese poetry]," Yip writes, "is to receive, perceive, and disclose nature the way nature comes or discloses
itself to us, undistorted."[11] By following nonpurposive action (*wuwei*)
to behold the natural (*ziran*), poets can avoid "disfiguring things in
their immanent presences by allowing them to disclose the dimension
of their immediate thereness."[12] If translators did the same, they, too,
according to this logic, could avoid "disfiguring" the original's ability to
"allow things to disclose themselves." But at this point the shadow of a
"European language" falls across the Chinese poem.

Yip claims to have found in Daoism a way to both acknowledge and
challenge universal claims made by Western structures of knowledge.
He applied these critiques to translation practices years before Edward
Said's critique of "Orientalism," which according to Said involved a
similar misreading of other cultures, and decades before the postcolonial translation theories of Tejaswini Niranjani and Lawrence Venuti,
which emphasize the link between imperialism and translation and
attempt to find ways of preserving the alterity of the foreign texts' original cultural particularities, which might otherwise be assimilated and
domesticated into the imperial tongues.[13] Yip situates his ideas within

---

10 Yip quotes a series of Chinese literary figures to support his ideas throughout his work,
including Lu Ji (pp. 261–303): "The mind is cleared to crystallize contemplation" 罄澄
心以凝思; Sikong Tu: "Live plainly: wait in silence/It is here the Scheme is seen" 素處
以默/ 妙機其微; Yan Yu: "The last attainment of poetry is entering into *shen* (spirit)"
詩之極致有一 曰入神; and Su Dongpo: "In the state of emptiness, one takes in all the
aspects" 空故納萬境. Yip cites all of these passages in "Language," a chapter in his *Diffusion*, pp. 75–76, and in his essay "Taoist Aesthetics."

11 Yip, *Diffusion*, p. 50.

12 Ibid., p. 65.

13 Yip's work in the late sixties through the seventies predates Edward Said's *Orientalism*
(1978) by nearly a decade and the birth of translation theory by decades. Tejaswini Niranjani influential book *Siting Translation* did not come out until 1992 and Lawrence

the broader context of what Robert Duncan, the great American modernist poet, called a "symposium of the whole, . . . a totality [in which] all the old excluded orders must be included. The female, the proletariat, the foreign, the animal and the vegetative; the unconscious and the unknown."[14] Such a "symposium" gives non-Western philosophical concepts, and other "minority" Western ones renewed critical import by questioning the discriminatory hegemony of Eurocentric claims to universal objectivity.

For Yip, East/West studies and poetics will have an invaluable part to play in the "symposium of the whole." Yip asks "whether the indigenous aesthetic horizon is allowed to represent itself *as it is (ziran)* and *not as it is framed* [i.e., acted upon, the opposite of *wuwei*] within the hermeneutical habits and the poetic economy of the West."[15] For if the inclusion of "all the old excluded orders" takes place through deforming domestications and distorting appropriations, we will still be far from realizing Duncan's vision. Since the publication of Said's *Orientalism* in 1978, most discussions of cultural appropriations and distortions have taken as their starting point the colonial, postcolonial, and neocolonial contexts of cultural exchange. Distortions take place because Western representations of the other serve to reify cultural differences as a means of legitimating political and cultural hierarchies, or in Said's words, "dominating, restructuring, and having authority over the Orient."[16]

While Yip's work may be sympathetic to the last point, he would have to disagree with Said's assertion that Orientalism (in its most pernicious sense) is a "style of thought based upon an ontological and epistemological distinction made between 'the Orient' and (most of the time) the 'Occident.' "[17] On the contrary, Yip's work presupposes that the primary obstacle to more effective cross-cultural interpretation *is* the a priori existence of radically different cultural paradigms. In Yip, as in Benjamin Whorf long before him, tacit linguistic and

---

Venuti's works on translation theory *(Translator's Invisibility; Scandals of Translation)* did not appear until the mid-1990s.

14   Yip, *Diffusion*, p. 1.
15   Ibid., p. 2.
16   Said, *Orientalism*, p. 3.
17   Yip, *Diffusion*, p. 2.

metaphysical presuppositions impede communication before and apart from power relations.[18]

Yip is particularly interested in phrases that embody the constitutive negation at the heart of his wider cultural project: 無我 (wuwo, empty/non-self), 無知 (wuzhi, empty/non-knowledge) and 無言 (wuyan, empty/non-language). In each case the first term of the binome 無 (wu), which is itself a complex philosophical term that can be translated in a variety of ways in different contexts ("the unseen," "the undifferentiated void," "nothingness," "nonbeing," etc.) but works similarly to the English prefix "non-," in this case transforming the function of the second term without destroying its existence in space. There is a self, but it is empty of ego. There is knowledge, but it is empty of cognizable information. And, finally, one acknowledges a language, but it is empty of grammar and syntax. These terms all share the notion of a *housed emptiness*. While Yip often translates the term *wuyan* as the "nonverbal world," this is the world he sees "housed" in the transparent body of Classical Chinese poetry, which is why I feel the phrase *wuyan* is perhaps the best term for describing the language Yip claims can "get out of the way."

To ground the otherwise abstract theoretical notion of an empty or transparent language of Classical Chinese poetry (*wuyan*), Yip returns to the rhetorical and methodological trope of translation. For example, Yip gives his translations of the first two lines of Li Bai's poem "Song youren," 送友人 ("Seeing Off a Friend"):

清　　山　　横　　北　　郭
green / mountain(s) / lie across / north / wall
白　　水　　遶　　東　　城
white / water / winds around / east / city[19]

Throughout both his critical prose and his anthologies of Chinese poetry, Yip gives readers word-for-word translations of the poetic lines so that they can try to *see* their meanings without significant alteration.

---

18 Carroll, *Language*.

19 Ibid., p. 40.

He wants the reader to notice the absence of authorial presence, the bare, nearly paratactic or juxtaposed quality of the lines whereby *things* are allowed to exist side-by-side, as they might in a painting, which is to say without what he calls "epistemological elaborations."

Yip then compares his literal translations to two canonical English translations:

> *Where* blue hills cross the northern sky,
> *Beyond* the moat which girds the town,
> 'Twas here. . . . Giles, 1898 [Yip's emphasis]

> *With* a blue line of mountains north of the wall,
> And east of the city a white curve of water,
> Here you must. . . . Bynner, 1920 [Yip's emphasis]

Yip then writes, "Whereas in the original we see things working upon us, in the versions of Giles and Bynner we are *led* to these things by way of intellectual, directive devices ('where,' 'with,' etc.)."

Clearly, what has happened here is that a different sort of hermeneutical habit of perceiving and reading has intruded upon "a rather clear-cut condition or state of being."[20] Yip is not describing a merely inaccurate or excessive translation. He makes the more powerful metaphysical claim that the reason the English fails to capture the original is that Classical Chinese poetry is, in its essence, a *transparent* language. For Yip most Western translators cannot stay "out of the poem," nor can they "think with the things," and therefore they cannot transmit the original's noninterventionist language.

This claim is not an easy one to demonstrate. By arguing that Chinese poetry can be used as a transparent language (or perhaps a *wuyan*—a non- or "empty" language) capable of "getting out of the way of 'things themselves,'" Yip perhaps inadvertently replaces transcendent signifieds with translative origins, or in other words, he replaces the idea that there are universal ideas that language points to with the Chinese poem itself. Often we come to language assuming that words point to meanings that are out in space somewhere, and

---

20 Ibid.

that different languages all point to these same "objective" and "transcendent" ideas. Yet structuralism and poststructuralism have problematized this metaphysical understanding of language by demonstrating that meanings are not "present" as "things" in themselves and languages are not conduits transmitting these "things," but are instead highly complex differential oppositions of phonemes that make up vast webs of potential significations taking place through myriad layers of contextualization. So when Yip moves to replace "transcendent" meanings "behind" language with the Chinese characters "behind" the English translations, a little caution might be warranted. For if this were the extent of Yip's attempted "Daoist" disruption of Western metaphysics and poetics it would likely fail to address today's cross-cultural concerns, which are centered on unequal power differentials. So too might we want to be cautious about the ocular-centric (i.e., privileging seeing) and positivist claims now criticized as the very foundation of Orientalist reification of cultural differences.[21]

That is to say, in the context of translation, his terms situate Chinese poetry *as* the "real-life world"; this real-life poetry is then dislocated from its pre-predicative (i.e., autonomous) state when translated into "obfuscating language" (namely, discursive English). Language, therefore, splits into two kinds: *wuyan* as embodied in the so-called nonobfuscating forms of nouns and verbs common to Classical Chinese poetry, which Yip claims throws "a spotlight that brightens objects emerging from the real world," and the obfuscating, predicative (hence dependent) particles common to English, which force "the world" into closed "epistemological elaborations" removed from the

---

21 In recent years Western literary criticism and philosophy have directly challenged truth-claims based upon vision and visual language. Michel Foucault's work provides one of the most sustained analyses of visual knowledge claims, arguing that vision has dominated such claims throughout Western history, and that the hegemony of vision has "real-life" implications for us all. He analyzes the "cold medical gaze" of the rationalistic scientist directed toward a corpse on a table, as well as the totalitarian gaze of the "panopticon," symbolizing the all-seeing gaze of social domination and control. (See Foucault, *Birth* and *Discipline*.) These writings have contributed to a general tendency in Western theory to criticize vision as a limited way to perceive. This tendency informs Edward Said's *Orientalism*, and Johannes Fabian's *Time*.

perceptual act itself.[22] The bifurcation of language into these two distinct *kinds* not only overdetermines the transparency of Chinese, but also overconcretizes English (written in a discursive fashion) into a rigid system incapable of interpretive flexibility, a truly questionable claim.

By using translation to replace the golden thread between signifier and transcendental signified with a new thread between English signifiers and Chinese signifieds (which serve as both sign and referent), Yip's ethnographic mediation grants him a unique, almost oracular proximity to the "Real." I say "oracular" because Yip's translations work as an oracle through which he believes he can *see* the "real-life world" without linguistic mediation. The transparency of a poetry of *wuyan* or nonlanguage allows for a direct *vision,* whereby the Chinese reader (in this instance Yip) can *see* the nature of nature, while non-Chinese readers must make do with translations. If this had been the full extent of Yip's argument, we could only follow behind him in the hope that he would turn around and share his vision (and that of the Chinese poet) of the real with us.

In a later essay, "Syntax and [the] Horizon of Representation," however, Yip argued that the Ezra Poundian strain of Modernism, drawing upon Chinese poetry, found a means of accommodating the Daoist worldview in English. Yip writes, "In 1911, before he came into contact with Chinese poetry, Pound argued, 'The artist seeks out the luminous detail and presents it. He does not comment.' After his contact with Chinese poetry, he [Pound] wrote, 'It is because certain Chinese poets have been content to set forth their matter without moralizing and without comment that one labors to make a translation.' "[23] Later Yip quotes William Carlos Williams's famous dictum "no ideas but in things" and argues that "Williams wanted to see 'the thing itself' with-

---

22 Yip's bifurcation of language into these two types is itself present within the classical Chinese definition of particles as "empty words" (*xu zi*), yet interestingly, Yip points to the near absence of these words as his proof of his "*wuyan*" thesis. François Cheng, meanwhile, points to the existence of these so-called empty words as his principal claim that "emptiness" undergirds classical Chinese poetry more generally. See Cheng, *Chinese Poetic Writing.*

23 Yip, *Diffusion, p.* 50.

out forethought or afterthought but with great intensity of perception."[24] Finally, to complete his identification with the Pound/Williams/New American Poetry lineage, he quotes Charles Olson and Robert Creeley, who, "in step with Pound and Williams, postulated that 'The objects which occur at any given moment of composition . . . are, can be, must be treated exactly as they do occur therein and not by any idea or pre-occupations from outside the poem . . . [they] must be handled as a series of objects in field . . . a series of tensions . . . space-tensions of a poem . . . the acting-on-you of the poem.'"[25] Yip's identification with this strain of American Modernism holds only so far as it tends to sub-scribe to the "peculiar mode of representation constituted by Chinese syntax," as distinct from a more conventional English syntax, in which connectives direct discursive thought from point to point.

If we return to Yip's initial allusion to Duncan's "Symposium of the Whole," we can see that for Yip, the Pound/Williams lineage of American Modernism succeeded in widening the "Western aesthetic horizon" to accommodate the "Chinese mode of perception."[26] By attempting to recover "the original ground, where we find the given as given," American Modernists like the Classical Chinese poets "liberate themselves from the accustomed house of thought so that language acts try not to disfigure things in their immanent presences but to make them disclose the dimension of their immediate thereness."[27] For Yip, therefore, one can deploy modernist aesthetic conventions to translate Clas-

---

24 Ibid.

25 Ibid.

26 Ibid., p. 48.

27 Ibid., p. 65. The bulk of Yip's criticism gestated in the late 1960s to mid-1970s and his own poetic production can be included in the "tradition" of Donald Allen's *New American Poetry*, which set itself against the then still entrenched New Critics and T. S. Eliot. In this context, Yip tends to privilege what Lazlo Géfin calls the *ideogrammic stream* (imagist-objectivist-Black Mountain) as a break from so-called traditional Western poetics. I am using this term "traditional" since Yip himself does in pointing to the work of the New Critics, which focused on earlier forms of scansion and thematic analysis, as opposed to the poetry and criticism gathered together under the heading of New American Poetry. Therefore, we might extend the similarities between New American Poetry and Daoist poetics beyond their metaphysical claims, to the fact of their mutual "otherness"—to what Yip considers "traditional Western poetics." See Géfin, *Ideogram*.

sical Chinese poems while preserving what Yip sees as the Daoist *wuyan*, the "transparent language" of the originals.

Take for instance the following translation of Meng Haoran's "Su Jiande jiang" (宿建德江 "Staying Over at Jiande River"):

yí	zhōu	jì	yān	zhù
移	舟	泊	煙	渚
move	boat	moor	smoke	shore
rì	mù	kè	chóu	xīn
日	暮	客	愁	新
sun	dusk	traveler	grief	new
yě	kuàng	tiān	dī	shù
野	曠	天	低	樹
wilds	far-reaching		sky	low/er tree
jiāng	qīng	yuè	jìn	rén
江	清	月	近	人
river	clear	moon	near/s	man

Yip translates this poem as,

A boat slows,
Moors by
Beach-run in smoke.
Sun fades:
a traveler's sorrow
freshens.
Open wilderness.
Wide Sky.
A stretch of low trees.
Limpid river:
clear moon
close to
man.[28]

---

28 Yip, *Chinese Poetry*, p. 231.

Compare the presentation of this poem to William Carlos Williams or to any number of Modernist American poets who employ the left-aligned, short-lined, vertical form of free verse. The utilization of short line breaks distributes the weight of a/the poem away from syntax's linear grammar toward an archipelago of visual data suspended paratactically. The effect in English is not so dissimilar from the "horizon of syntax" Yip attributes to Daoism-infused Classical Chinese poetry insofar as the poet recedes into the background, and the differentiae of what Yip calls the "real-life world" are presented without "epistemological elaborations."

Yip's argument is most poignantly illustrated by his continual references to the work of Gary Snyder and particularly by a series of modernist montage poems by Robert Duncan that appear in Yip's essay, "Syntax and Horizon of Representation."

The Fire					Passages 13
jump	stone	hand	leaf	shadow	sun
day	splash	coin	light	downstream	fish
first	loosen	under	boat	harbor	circle
old	earth	bronze	dark	wall	waver
new	smell	purl	close	wet	green
now	rise	foot	warm	hold	cool[29]

The above example reveals for Yip how Modernist montage, like Classical Chinese poetry, allows words to stretch out into a horizon that "radiates more connections than conventional syntactical structures can handle."[30]

Thus Modernist poetry, by which I want to signal the tradition of American poetry that begins with Ezra Pound's publication of *Cathay* in 1915 through the post–World War II movements collectively known as New American Poetry (which includes the writing of the San Francisco Renaissance, Black Mountain, the New York School, and the

---

29 Yip, *Diffusion*, p. 62.
30 Ibid.

so-called Beats[31]) vindicates the Chinese example and makes possible by legitimating example, a faithful translation from the original words or things. While Yip does not go as far as Chen Xiaomei in tracing the reciprocal influence of American Modernism (inspired by Classical Chinese poetry) upon contemporary Chinese poetry,[32] both Yip's verse and his prose point to this trans-Pacific mutual influence. In an interesting follow-up, the ability of Modernist montage to break through the limitations of Western discursive language becomes Yip's model for contemporary Chinese poetry, which he feels is in danger of losing its Daoist worldview to Western linguistic and epistemic encroachments. In *Modern Chinese Poetry* (1970), Yip discussed the Westernization of *baihua* (modern, colloquial Chinese) as a danger to contemporary Chinese (in this case Taiwanese) poetry, and introduced his Modernist/Daoist poetics as a possible model of resistance. In this work, Yip departed somewhat from his role as literary critic and spoke as a "Daoist" Modernist poet describing a state of mind he reached during a transpacific flight:

> One passenger, who is not sleeping, unconsciously becomes silence itself . . . Limits of space and limits of time do not exist in the consciousness of this passenger. He has *another hearing, another vision.* He hears voices we normally do not hear. He sees activities across a space not to be seen by the physical eye. Nor is the passenger conscious of any linear, causal developments between or among these things . . . and prose is a linear structure defined by limits of space and time, so this passenger writes a poem.[33]

The "passenger" in Yip's poetics statement is himself, but we could extend the label to cover any Chinese poet today who shares his Daoist/Modernist poetics. As a poet, Yip chooses to include far more Classical Chinese words in his poetry than his contemporaries do. He knows that he cannot go back to writing regulated verse forms (for Yip is a Modernist), but he admonishes his fellow poets to adopt the Daoist metaphysics that underlie *wenyan*, Classical Chinese. For he argues

---

31   See Allen, *New American Poetry.*
32   See Chen, *Occidentalism.*
33   Yip, *Modern Chinese Poetry*, p. 77.

that *wenyan*, as opposed to *baihua*, is "conducive to this cinematic presentation which emphasizes phases of perception through spotlighting activities rather than through analysis."[34] Yip, following Ernest Fenollosa, scorns the "analytical" abstraction of discursive English. Yip explains that the discursive quality of *baihua* results from its origin in Classical narrative prose, which relies on linear plot developments, explanation, and causal relationships.

Yet Yip argues that, if the problem started in the evolution of Chinese language,

> The situation is worsened by the intrusion of Western sciences, systems of logic, and forms of poetry. The *baihua* is being Europeanized (as the Chinese called it) in the process of translation (both journalistic and literary) . . . introduction of Occidental syntax, adoption of foreign grammatical frameworks as bases for the Chinese sentence, and application of punctuation to regulate and clarify Chinese linguistic structures. All of these were intended, no doubt, to tell the world that we have just as much logic and are just as scientific as the West, as if poetic ambiguity and richness were a shame![35]

Yet Yip holds out hope for *baihua* poetry since even contemporary Chinese poets (who rely heavily on *baihua*) can eliminate connectives and other discursive particles, merge with objects, and use "antilinear structures," etc. When addressing contemporary Chinese poets (and readers), Yip tends to emphasize not only the negative trans-Pacific influences upon Chinese poetry (e.g., the imposition of discursive logic), but also the positive influence of paratactic, montage, or elliptical compositional modes in Modernist poetry as well.

While Yip may suggest that American Modernism offers contemporary poets (both American and Chinese) techniques capable of breaking down the wall he and Heidegger see separating classical Daoist and Western worldviews, Yip's aesthetic choices and the poetics that undergird them come at a price. The similarities pointed to by Yip between Classical Chinese and American Modernist poetry—sparing use of words, maximum imagistic appeal, and limited use of nonimag-

---

34   Ibid., p. xv.
35   Ibid., p. xvii.

istic language (often creating asyntactic assemblages)—are arrived at
ahistorically and transculturally and are decontextualized from the
traditions within which they are situated.

Anthologies and canons always decontextualize. Yip's canon is no
exception. Yip's understanding of Chinese poetics (like that of many
poet-critics working out of American Modernism) is drawn from a
relatively homogeneous selection of Classical Chinese poems. Relying
on highly imagistic, syntactically ambiguous Chinese poems like Wang
Wei's "Deer Fence," Ma Zhiyuan's "Sky Pure Sand," and palindromic
verse (which can be read backward as well as forward), he tends to reduce the tradition's great stylistic diversity to a single description. Similarly, he tends to reduce "Daoism" and/or Daoist poetics to "*Lao-
Zhuang* thought" (or the Daoism of its two most canonical texts: the
Daodejing—or *Laozi*—and the *Zhuangzi*) in ways that need to be
addressed.

That American poets (a group to which Yip belongs, along with
other groups) have been interested in models of poetic emptiness derived from *Lao-Zhuang* thought should come as no surprise, since
what awareness most Americans have of Daoism comes from the ubiquitous translations of the *Daodejing* and the *Zhuangzi*. The popularity
of these texts is no coincidence, but results from the historical privileging by both Confucian and Western scholars of "philosophical Daoism," a school of thought and body of texts that they described as
something wholly separate and distinct from "religious Daoism." Although Daoism certainly evolved and changed over time, this now dis-
credited bifurcation of Daoism into *Daojia* (Daoist philosophy) and
Daojiao (Daoist religion) can be traced to sinologists like Henri Maspero, Fung Yu-lan and H. G. Creel.[36] Furthermore, their predecessors,
nineteenth-century sinologists like Giles and Legge, relied on late Qing
Confucian scholars who, for various reasons, chose to focus on only
two early Daoist texts: the *Daodejing* and the *Zhuangzi*. While a few
nineteenth-century scholars like Abel Rémusat (1788–1832) and Père
Léon Wieger (1856–1933) also translated more "religious" texts like the
Liezi and *Ganying pian*,[37] most Western readers would come to identify

---

36   See Fung, *Short History*; p. 3; Maspero, *Taoïsme*; and Creel, *Chinese Thought*.
37   Thanks to Haun Saussy for pointing these out to me.

"philosophical" Daoism as the more important tradition while "religious" Daoism became a label for derivative folk or cultural practices.

In a manner not unlike the textualist and doctrinal approach taken by early Western Buddhology, Daoism, when reduced to two texts, gave Westerners a means to claim a superior understanding of "pure Daoism" unclouded by over two thousand years of "superstitious cultural accretions."[38] In this way, any Daoist practitioner working as an "informant" could only provide interesting examples of "derivations" from the pure philosophical texts, rather than new exegetical insights. Daoist scholarship has improved steadily since the 1970s and currently offers English readers far more complex accounts of Daoism, translations of many of the tradition's most important texts, and a growing body of work historicizing the study of Daoism itself.[39] Yet these works rarely make it into the hands of nonspecialists. Instead, contemporary American bookstores are flooded with texts entitled "The Tao of . . . ," which strip Daoism of its cultural and historical particularities.[40]

While Yip supports his theories of Chinese poetry based largely upon references to Lao-Zhuang thought, to his credit most of his theories are textually grounded within language cited from Guo Xiang, a Western Jin commentator on the Zhuang Zi. Guo Xiang (郭象 d. 312 CE) is known as one of the two founders of what has been called "neo-Daoism" (known as 玄學 xuanxue, lit., dark/obscure learning); he is also credited with assembling the present form of the Zhuang Zi.[41] Toward the end of his essay "Language and the Real-Life World," Yip addresses the ways in which Guo Xiang's commentaries on the Zhuang Zi challenge and revise potential ontotheological readings of Lao-Zhuang

---

38 To be sure, there continue to be excellent new translations of the Daodejing, reputed to be the most frequently translated Chinese "classic," and the Zhuangzi, that do not make these claims. See e.g., Roberts for the former, Graham for the latter.

39 One will want to explore the work of Seidel, Kaltenmark, Girardot, Robinet, Kohn, Strickmann, etc., as well as Zheng Liangshu, Ge Zhaoguang, Zhang Longxi, etc.

40 For a good introduction to the Western reception of Daoism see Clark, Tao.

41 Neo-Daoism is a term indicating the second flowering of Daoist thought by a small but influential group of thinkers like Guo Xiang and Wang Bi. The movement is associated with the debate activity of "pure talk" (qingtan) 清談 and is further linked to the so-called Seven Worthies of the Bamboo Grove 竹林七賢 often depicted in paintings about the period. See Johnston, "Neo-Taoism." For a more comprehensive study of neo-Daoism, see Ziporyn, Penumbra.

thought. "Guo Xiang helped to clear away the possible mystical as well as metaphysical meanings unduly attributed to the word Dao. . . . He [Guo] unequivocally said in his preface 'Above, there is no Creator, below, things create themselves.' "[42] Mystical meanings have long been attributed to Daoist texts. The famous first lines of the *Daodejing* read:

道可道 非常道
名可名 非常名

The Dao that can be spoken of is not the eternal Dao
The name that can be named is not the eternal name.[43]

Note that the skepticism toward language as a medium for ultimate knowledge actually seems to propose the existence of an extralinguistic (non-)being or at least unseen being, an a priori, eternal Dao. But Guo Xiang undermines this idea of a preexistent nonbeing, which suggests a generative monism, by introducing new terminology less invested in monistic thought. Again Yip cites Guo Xiang: "All things are what they are without knowing why and how they are . . . although things are different [in many ways] they are the same in that they exist spontaneously as they are.' "[44] Here Guo Xiang shifts the emphasis away from the monistic Dao toward his central concept of *ziran*, which, as we have already seen, becomes central to Yip's poetics. What Guo Xiang's notion of *ziran* does is to replace the "unknowability of the Eternal Dao" with the unknowability of all existing things, individually. While I believe that the fact Yip goes to Guo Xiang's commentaries as inspiration for his poetics shows a resourcefulness and comfort with more nuanced aspects of *Lao-Zhuang* thought, his application of Guo's *ziran* as a linguistic/translative practice whereby one "is to receive, perceive, and disclose nature the way nature comes or discloses itself to us, undistorted"[45] gives me pause. Yip's emphasis on unmediated disclosure is where his reading of Guo Xiang departs from my own. Yip is interested in using Guo's theories to support his description of poetry

42   Yip, *Diffusion*, 96.
43   My translation.
44   Yip, *Diffusion*, p. 71.
45   Ibid.

as something capable of offering "direct" or "bare" perception or apprehension (understood as a "vision") of the real, whereas I believe Guo Xiang is arguing for a very different relationship to *ziran*.

At the same time as Yip makes Guo Xiang the foundation of his theories, he has had to ignore prominent elements of Guo Xiang's neo-Daoism, which, had he included them, would have directed his poetics away from the ocular-centric essentialism that informs it. Guo Xiang seeks to reveal the violence of vision as a form of cognition by offering an alternative to *mingbai* (明白, which implies visual clarity and is privileged by Yip): he argues that the way to *ziran* lies in the *ming* (冥 dark or obscure). Guo uses *ming* (冥—obscure—not *ming* 明—bright) not in its normative adjectival or nominal sense but as an action verb "one *mings* with things, with transformations, with what one encounters . . . as a way of relating to them without the mediation of traces, and hence it is precisely the opposite of *ming*, brightness."[46] Brook Ziporyn defines this "dark" *ming* as "vanishing into," which "implies a 'dimming' and 'darkening' of the perceived object, and a 'dimming' or 'darkening' of oneself *into* that thing."[47] Following this reverse heliotropism, Guo argues one can move beyond the cognitive consciousness delivered through the clarity of vision and language (conceptually framed by vision) by leaving the self and others (things) in their uncognized solitude, "free of the reflections and comparisons to other things that they would have if made objects of relative knowledge."[48] Clearly, the "disclosure" of "things in themselves" is very different from *wuwei* and *wuyan* according to Guo Xiang and his exegetes who, I believe, would find this "clarity" an undesirable imposition on the mysterious becoming of the obscure (*ziran*) of otherness. Yet one can see why Yip might not agree with my reading of Guo since it might be hard to see how a poet, as opposed to, say, a hermit, could adopt this scale of values.

Beyond the question regarding the privileging of vision in Yip's "Lao-Zhuang" poetics, it is important to note what this limited definition of Daoism leaves unconsidered in Classical Chinese poetic form. Yip cites the Six Dynasties genre of "mountain and water" or "land-

---

46 Ziporyn, p. 66.
47 Ibid.
48 Ibid., p. 68.

scape poetry" (*shanshui shi*) as the origin of his *wuyan* poetics, but he
can do this only by ignoring its formal integration of correlative cosmology in the form of parallelism in that verse. Yip argues that *shanshui* poetry "calls for the poet to release the objects of Phenomenon
from their seeming irrelevance and bring forth their original freshness
and thingness—return to their first innocence, so to speak—thus,
making them relevant as 'self-so-complete' [*ziran*] objects in their co-
extensive existence." He continues, "The poet's job is to approximate
the cuts and turns of our immediate perceiving contact with the objects in their original condition."[49] Such an argument rests upon the
omission of any discussion of parallelism, formal prosody, in short,
style.

For *shanshui* poets like Xie Lingyun, parallelism creates the meaning of the scenes described.[50] But parallelism contradicts the so-called
transparent "presentation" (as opposed to representation) of a scene
"unmodified by the poet's mediation." Here the function of parallelism
signals one of two things: It reveals either that one grasps the spiritual/
cosmological reality underlying a scene's beauty by presenting its balance and harmony, or that the parallelism is more a function of poetic
agency, an "ordering" or "harmonizing" of the natural world itself, as a
"traditional" Chinese doctor may try to promote correlative harmony
in an ailing human body. The importance of correlative thought in the
Six Dynasties poetics is clear throughout Liu Xie's great work of literary theory, *The Literary Mind and the Carving of Dragons (Wenxin
Diaolong)*, which elevates human writing, *wen*, to a new cosmological
significance implying a role for poets as not only seers but agents
of cosmic harmonization. In the chapter "Li Ci" (Paired Expressions)
of this work, Liu Xie points to the cosmological foundation of
parallelism:

> Nature, creating living beings, endows them always with limbs in
> pairs. The divine reason operates in such a way that nothing stands
> alone. The mind creates literary expressions, and organizes and

---

49 Yip, *Chinese Poetry*, p. 130.
50 For a lengthy exploration of parallelism in shanshui verse see Chang, *Six Dynasties
    Poetry*.

shapes one hundred different thoughts, making what is high supplement what is low, and spontaneously producing parallelism.

造化賦形，　支體必雙，　神理為用　事不孤立。
夫心生文辭，運裁百慮，　高下相須　自然成對。[51]

Yip's *Lao-Zhuang* poetics would have to disavow such an idea as un-Daoist (after all such a notion of poetic agency directly conflicts with his understanding of *wuwei*). But such a form of agency dominates in many forms of Daoism: one has only to consider classic works like the 內業 (*Nei Ye*) and 淮南子 (*Huainanzi*), not to mention the huge corpus of "self-cultivation texts," which all discuss human agency in cosmological terms.[52]

What then should we make of Wai-lim Yip's Daoist poetics? Is it "Daoist"? Is it a "romantic Western invention"? Or is it something else entirely? I would opt for a combination of these. I believe Yip's poetics may not break down the wall he sees between East and West through a recourse to a "pre-predicative *wuyan*." Nevertheless, his work does still break down these walls by the sheer fact of his work's incredible hybridity. Thus I would argue that we can read his literary and scholarly works as important instances of heterocultural production more in line with his Daoist poetics than one may think. To help support this thesis, let me turn to a diagram Yip offers to clarify his idea of a "cross-cultural poetics."[53]

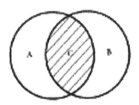

51　From ibid., p. 65 (with modifications made by Chang).

52　For an excellent annotated bibliography of "self-cultivation" texts see Komjathy, "Daoist Texts in Translation."

53　Yip, *Chinese Poetry*, p. 18.

Yip argues that circle A and circle B represent two distinct cultural models, and the shaded area of C, where the two overlap, "represents resemblances between the two models" and can serve as "the basis for establishing a fundamental model."[54] To produce such a model Yip argues that the poetics of culture A must not be subjected to the terms of the poetics of nature B or vice versa. In his Daoist language, circle A's and circle B's *ziran* must not be distorted by the other, and one achieves that by adopting *wuwei* as one's comparative methodology. Yet Yip's desire to find a universal or "fundamental model" for both East and West poetics does not seem to follow from his concept of *wuwei* since such an imposition of (or quest for) a "fundamental model" would, by its very nature, intrude upon the different patterns of *ziran* mysteriously unfolding within each circle. Yip's ocular-centrism may prevent him from "seeing" that *ziran* is not a perceptual category in the first place. I would argue that one cannot perform linguistic *wuwei* in order to better perceive something in its unaltered state since perception is only ever accomplished by way of alteration, as knowing alters the "known." Following Guo Xiang's dark "*ming*" as a form of nondistorting attention, however, perhaps we can think of Yip's work as a "darkening" or a "sinking into" multiple cultural discourses at the same time. By "darkening/sinking," I hope to suggest the loss of conceptual clarity offered by the distinctly pure cultural autonomies suggested by the comparative hubris of the above diagram. Yip's work loses this clarity—in a salutary way—when he integrates American Modernist and classical Daoist poetic methodologies and aesthetics. The result is neither purely Western nor Eastern but heterocultural.

As visual aids, diagrams like Yip's can be helpful, but also harmful. What would a diagram presenting Yip's own heterocultural scholarship and poetry look like? Would the multiple circles drawn circumscribe cultural phenomena associated with individual nation-states, ethnicities, cultures, and/or races? Such circles, like Heidegger's separate "houses of being," are too essentializing. Take China, for example (but you could take America, Europe, or Russia as easily). China con-

54   Ibid.

ceived of as a nation-state, a unified culture, or a "race" is an illusion, or to be more specific, an ideological formation (something discussed in many chapters of this volume). These terms are and have been deployed to consolidate power over a heterogeneous population, and drawing a circle around China reinforces this hegemonic ideology. The ideological power of visually represented boundaries common to Yip's diagram, map-making, or even the Chinese character for nation–state 國, traffic in the language of siege warfare, and I believe they cannot be relied upon to explore the intricacies of heterocultural literary productions. Yip may not have been successful in offering a way of escaping languages' representing mediation as he hoped, but this is not as important as the ways in which he has successfully mobilized different cultural discourses to make a compelling trans-Pacific vision of poetry, which shows how cultural purities (or conceptual claims to purity) give way to new heterocultural formations that emerge in ways circles, houses, and walls cannot hope to map or prevent.[55]

Works Cited

Allen, Donald. *New American Poetry 1945–1960*. New York: Grove, 1960.

Carroll, John B., ed. *Language, Thought, and Reality: Selected Writings of Benjamin Lee Whorf*. Cambridge, Mass.: MIT Press, 1956, 1997.

Chang, Kang-i Sun. *Six Dynasties Poetry*. New Haven, Conn.: Yale University Press, 1983.

Chen Xiaomei. *Occidentalism: A Theory of Counter-Discourse in Post-Mao China*. Lanham, Md.: Rowman & Littlefield, 2002.

Cheng, François. *Chinese Poetic Writing*. Donald A. Riggs and Jerome P. Seaton, trans. Bloomington: Indiana University Press, 1982.

Clark, J. J. *The Tao of the West: Western Transformations of Taoist Thought*. London, New York: Routledge, 2000.

---

55 I use the term "heterocultural" in a way similar to that of Lydia Liu in her work *The Clash of Empires*. In Chapter 2, Liu focuses on the heterocultural conditions of terms like 夷 ("*yi*," as an example of a "supersign," which Liu describes as "a linguistic monstrosity that thrives on the excess of its presumed meanings by virtue of being exposed to, or thrown together with, foreign etymologies and foreign languages" (p. 13). While the reduction of *yi* to "barbarian" was indeed monstrous, not all supersigns need be so. Mixed up, excessive, stained by multiple cultural idioms, languages, and historical desires, Yip's poetics is not monstrous, but simply unstable, plural, and deeply hopeful.

Graham, Angus C. *Chuang-Tzu: The Inner Chapters*. London: George Allen & Unwin, 1981.

———. *Chuang-tzu: Textual Notes to a Partial Translation*. London: School of Oriental and African Studies, 1982.

Creel, Herrlee G. *Chinese Thought from Confucius to Mao Tse-tung*. Chicago: University of Chicago Press, 1953.

Fabian, Johannes. *Time and the Other: How Anthropology Makes Its Object*. New York: Columbia University Press, 1983.

Foucault, Michel. *The Birth of the Clinic: An Archaeology of Medical Perception*, Alan Sheridan, trans. New York: Vintage, 1973.

———. *Discipline and Punish: The Birth of the Prison*, Alan Sheridan, trans. New York: Vintage, 1979.

Fung Yu-lan. *A Short History of Chinese Philosophy*, Derk Bodde, ed. New York: Free Press, [1948] 1966.

Géfin, Laszlo. *Ideogram: History of a Poetic Method*. Austin: University of Texas Press, 1982.

Heidegger, Martin. *On the Way to Language*, Peter D. Hertz, trans. New York: Harper and Row, 1971.

Hubbard, Jamie, and Paul Swanson, eds. *Pruning the Bodhi Tree*. Honolulu: University of Hawaii Press, 1997.

Irigaray, Luce. *Speculum of the Other Woman*. Trans. Gillian G. Gill. Ithaca: Cornell University Press, 1985.

Johnston, Ellen. "Neo-Taoism and the 'Seven Sages of the Bamboo Grove' in Chinese Painting." *Artibus Asiae*, 36(1/2, 1974), pp. 5–54.

Komjathy, Louis, and Kang Siqi, "Daoist Texts in Translation." Center for Daoist Studies. http://www.daoistcenter.org/texts.pdf.

Kuki Shūzō. *A Philosopher's Poetry and Poetics*. Michael Marra, ed. Honolulu: University of Hawaiì Press, 2004.

———. *Reflections on Japanese Taste*, John Clark, trans. Sydney: Power Publications, 1997.

Liu, Lydia. *Translingual Practice*. Stanford: Stanford University Press, 1995.

———. *The Clash of Empires: The Invention of China in Modern World Making*. Cambridge, Massachusetts: Harvard University Press, 2004.

Liu, Xie. *The Literary Mind and the Carving of Dragons*. Vincent Yu-chung Shih, trans. Hong Kong: Chinese University Press, 1983.

Maspero, Henri. *Le Taoïsme et les religions chinoises*. Paris: Gallimard, 1971.

Nara, Hiroshi. *The Structure of Detachment: The Aesthetic Vision of Kuki Shūzō*, Honolulu: University of Hawai'i Press, 2004.

Niranjani, Tejaswini. *Siting Translation: History, Post-structuralism and the Colonial Context*. Berkeley: University of California Press, 1992.

Nishida, Kitarō. "The Problem of Japanese Culture," Masao Abe and Richard DeMartion, trans. In *Sources of Japanese Tradition*, Ryusaku Tsunoda, William Theodore de Bary, and Donald Keene, eds. New York: Columbia University Press, 1958.

———. "Towards a Philosophy of Religion with the Concept of Pre-Established Harmony as Guide," David A. Dilworth, trans. *Eastern Buddhist*, n.s., 3(1,1970), pp. 19–46.

Roberts, Moss, trans. *Daodejing: The Book of the Way*. By Laozi. Berkeley: University of California Press, 2001.

Said, Edward. *Orientalism*. New York: Random House, 1978.

Sharf, Robert H. "The Zen of Japanese Nationalism." *Curators of the Buddha: The Study of Buddhism Under Colonialism*. Donald S. Lopez, ed. Chicago: University of Chicago Press, 1995.

Venuti, Lawrence. *The Translator's Invisibility: A History of Translation*. London: Routledge, 1995.

———. *The Scandals of Translation: Towards an Ethics of Difference*. London and New York: Routledge, 1998.

Wang, Qingjie (James). "'It-self-so-ing' and 'Other-ing' in Lao Zi's Concept of Zi Ran." Pp. 225–24 in *Comparative Approaches to Chinese Philosophy*. Bo Mou, ed. Burlington, Vermont: Ashgate, 2003.

Yip, Wai-lim. *Modern Chinese Poetry*. Iowa City: University of Iowa Press, 1970.

———. "The Taoist Aesthetic." Pp. 17–32 in *China and the West: Comparative Literature Studies*, William Tay, Ying-hsiung Chou, and Heh-hsiang Yuan, eds. Hong Kong: Chinese University Press, 1980.

———. *Diffusion of Distance*. Berkeley: University of California Press, 1993.

———. *Chinese Poetry*. Durham: Duke University Press, 1997.

Ziporyn, Brook, *The Penumbra Unbound: The Neo-Taoist Philosophy of Guo Xiang*. Albany: State University of New York Press, 2003.

CHAPTER TEN

Near Far

The Dispersion, Relocation, and Mobility of Contemporary Chinese Artists

Millie Chen

IN THE 1960S A CENTURY of discriminatory legislation restricting the immigration of Chinese to the United States and Canada finally came to an end. In the 1970s the People's Republic of China began to allow its citizens to travel and work abroad. In the 1980s many Chinese took advantage of these new opportunities. The numbers increased considerably in the 1990s after the forceful suppression of the 1989 urban prodemocracy demonstrations, including those in Beijing's Tiananmen Square. It was at that time that the centuries-old walls between Chinese artists in China and Chinese artists in the rest of the world were being dismantled. The increased interactions among indigenous and diasporic Chinese artists strengthened and enriched both communities. At the same time, the resulting expansion of cultural exchanges with the West, the escalation of global economies and transnational mobility, and the deepening assimilation of diasporic populations called into question the very nature of Chinese identity in an ever more integrated and globalized world. In this world, the questions arise: Which artists and what art should be regarded as more "authentically" Chinese? Is the time coming when the category "contemporary Chinese artists" should be expanded beyond those living in territorial China to include artists in the diaspora? Or should the categorization give way altogether to the ethnically and culturally nonspecific term "contemporary artists"?

These questions are particularly challenging, perhaps, for ethnic Chinese who incorporate performance art or performativity into their work. Since the ethnically distinguishable bodies of this subgroup are central to their work, they can claim Chinese identity and expect other ethnic groups to recognize it even if their art might not be automatically accepted as "authentically" Chinese. Their ethnic identity is particularly secure in the West, where ethnicity is often confused with the highly problematic and often treacherous category of race. But even these artists face the problem of appearing to lose their "authenticity" when they adopt so-called modern artistic practices that are usually presumed to have originated in the West. Compounding this situation is the fact that many diasporic artists choose to downplay their ethnicity in an effort to avoid the authenticity debate, which they believe might obscure other more pressing and more universal issues in their work.

In this chapter I select from among the many diasporic artists living and working on several continents in recent decades four contemporary figures, three of whom traveled to North America from different parts of China at different times and are currently well known and studied. The fourth artist under review here was born in the United States and has recently begun to gain international recognition. In each case I analyze the different ways in which their art reflects their times and places of origin, their varying relationships to North America, and their ultimate locations near or far from China and Chinese culture. What these artists share is not the broadcasting of a unified, authentic voice but the breaking down of ethnic authenticity altogether.

In cultural circles, the term "contemporary Chinese artists" usually refers to residents of or recent emigrants from mainland China and Taiwan, yet we may expand this term to include artists of Chinese descent, like me, who have lived most or the whole of their lives in the diaspora and whose ties to Chinese territory are mainly ancestral and, at least until very recently, quite remote. As a fascinated (if anxious) outside world increasingly scrutinizes China's every cultural/political/economic/social movement, there has been an undeniable pull of the

"Middle Kingdom" [or Central State(s)] on the psyches of those whose ancestors originated there as well as on those who have traveled abroad from there.[1] In this inquiry I seek to understand how this pull affects cultural production within the increasingly linked artistic communities inside and outside China. To the revived "culture of China," the sway of the global marketplace exerts a countervailing force. Some would see that marketplace, or capitalism, as Western and "modern" in origin and would consider contemporary art in China as a manifestation of a less developed, Asian, and putatively socialist region of the world. In this chapter, however, I do not assume that the current global economy arose simply or even first in the West or that contemporary Chinese art has lost its moorings in Chinese heritage and is largely a belated knock-off of erstwhile Western contemporary art. Instead I posit that some of the leading contemporary artists of Chinese descent who have incorporated their bodies into their work are reflecting elements of the Chinese past and present as well as their own experience in addressing the different culture of their adopted abodes. In this sense, the walls between two Chinese communities, near and far, have come down and the influences are flowing abundantly in both directions to a perhaps unprecedented extent.

Zhang Huan from Henan

We begin with Zhang Huan, a behavioral artist whose career was spawned in central China, who emigrated to the United States in the 1990s, and who now bases his practice both in the West and in China. Among the three immigrants discussed in this chapter, he originated closest to the center of territorial China, in the heart of the central plain

---

1   I use this anachronistic English-language translation of the Chinese term for "China" (which is no longer a kingdom) to suggest the tenacity of historic imaginings on the part of outsiders about the mysterious allure of that polity. The current, most common Chinese term for what Westerners call China continues to be *zhongguo*, which is now perhaps better translated as the "Central State(s)." "Central" in English, like *zhong* in Chinese, is more intimately involved with 360 degrees of periphery than "middle," which suggests a point on a line between two poles. "State(s)," like *guo* in Chinese, can denote either a single- or a multiple-state system, both of which have existed during long stretches of Chinese history.

(*zhongyuan*), an important synecdoche for China (see Chapters 2 and 3 in this volume). Of the three immigrants, he is also the most recently arrived in North America. For all these reasons, perhaps, he maintains the strongest ties to mainland China and now spends a fair amount of his time in Shanghai, a Chinese metropolis that makes its own claims to cultural centrality (see Chapter 5 in this volume). This brief history would suggest that Zhang Huan is likely to be the most fully culturally "Chinese" among the four artists under review.

Zhang Huan, whose original name was Zhang Dongming, was born in 1965 into a factory worker's family in Anyang, in northern Henan province, China. Adjacent to the famous ruins of the last Shang capital, Anyang is the city ostensibly featured in Wang Chao's film, *Anyang Orphan* (see Chapter 12 in this volume). Zhang Huan, though not orphaned himself, was sent at age one to live with his paternal grandmother in the Henan countryside. Although at that time the Chinese economy was beginning to recover from the "Three Hard Years" of 1959–1962,[2] Henan was China's most populous province and suffered from persistent poverty. The province was also the epicenter of many radical experiments, from the communes in the Great Leap Forward to the rustication of cadres during the Cultural Revolution.[3] Zhang seems to have experienced poverty and illness during his early childhood, but he soon returned to Anyang to attend elementary school, where he excelled in art and soon won recognition for his talent.[4]

At the age of fourteen, in the same year that Deng Xiaoping initiated the new policies of reform and opening, Zhang began to study drawing and painting. In 1984 he gained admission to the art department of newly renamed Henan University in Kaifeng, where he was influenced by Western masters such as Rembrandt and Millet. He graduated in 1988 on the eve of the urban demonstrations for more democracy, and taught art history at the Zhengzhou Institute of Education for the next two years. In 1991 he left Henan for the first time

---

2   The "Three Hard Years" between 1959 and 1962 were caused by a series of poor harvests and foreign pressures as well as by state mismanagement of the Great Leap Forward. One result was widespread famine and the death of up to thirty million people.

3   Domenach, *Origins*; Chen, *Year*.

4   Wu, *Transience*, pp. 104, 198.

and moved to Beijing, where he enrolled in the graduate program at the Central Academy of Fine Arts. There he pursued his interest in the European classical and Renaissance traditions with an emphasis on emotional balance and technical perfection. In 1992, a year before graduating from the two-year program, he suddenly turned away from oil painting and took up behavioral art in the Da Shan Zi neighborhood of Beijing. He was one of the first artists to reside in a poor section of that neighborhood, which was known for its low rents and copious garbage. In 1993 it became a Mecca for poor artists and was dubbed the East Village (Dongcun), in apparent imitation of the artist colony of the same name in New York City.[5]

Zhang's masters project at the Academy was "Weeping Angels," a mixed-media installation featuring a plastic child suspended on a wall covered with felt. Zhang has explained his turn away from classical European art to contemporary Chinese themes as a result of his having witnessed much poverty and hardship growing up in Henan. He was especially moved by the travails of young unwed mothers forced to give up their children.[6] Authorities in the Academy were not pleased. They fined Zhang for "Weeping Angels," forced him to apologize as a condition for exhibiting the work, and then closed the exhibition anyway. To avoid such censorship, Zhang Huan and small groups of his peers began to do behavioral art in people's homes, industrial spaces, and other unconventional settings.

Zhang's early solo work centered on endurance and pain as possible vehicles for transcending the self and identifying with others. In 1994 he performed "12 Square Meters," which involved sitting for one hour in a local public toilet with his bare body covered in fish oil and honey to attract an onslaught of flies. Zhang then "cleansed" himself by walking into an adjacent pond that was so polluted that the flies died. It was an obvious protest against the living conditions of his poor neighbors, who had no choice but to use such degrading facilities and who eked out an existence by sorting through huge piles of urban garbage to find items worth selling. Since he had performed in the nude, Zhang was criticized by some locals for engaging in what they considered to be pornography. Even some fellow experimental artists dis-

---

5   Ibid., p. 199.
6   Ibid., pp. 104–5.

missed Zhang's kind of art as being itself "garbage," a label he did not contest. In Zhang's view, however, his art involved not just masochism and exhibitionism but self-sacrifice and empathy in an effort to bring social problems to public notice.

According to one skeptical American critic writing in 2000, Zhang Huan's 1994–1995 ordeal art was in "a style no longer fashionable here (in the U.S.A)."[7] This comment seemed to imply that Zhang's art was little more than an imitation of past Western art movements. In my view, the critic's statement was a good example of a general Western disregard for the contexts of history, geography, and society in the production of Chinese art. It ignored the specificities of Zhang's case and glibly presumed that such Chinese contemporary artists were simply and belatedly producing works that were derivative of contemporary Western art.

Just as the Central Academy of Art in Beijing often followed the models of European classical art, Western critics continued to privilege that same artistic heritage, or, at best, the so-called ancient or "traditional" art of China and Japan. This tendency was manifested in some appraisals of Asian-American art as well as that of contemporary Chinese artists in China. In Elaine H. Kim's words,

American cultural expression is still seen by many as being properly rooted in European artistic traditions that Asian Americans are not permitted to claim. Thus Asian American art has customarily been susceptible to comparison with Chinese and Japanese art as [it] was known in the West, where art audiences have focused almost exclusively on the ancient as opposed to the contemporary. Even today, modern Asian art is frequently thought of as too derivative of Western art forms to be as interesting as the more anthropologically and commercially appealing Asian art of the distant past.[8]

Some Western critics assume that "modern art" is a wholly Western product. Despite early multitudinous cultural exchanges among many parts of the world, incorporating colonizers, the colonized, or, in the case of China, the semicolonized, such observers often draw a false

7   Carr, "On Edge."
8   Kim, "Interstitial Subjects," *Fresh Talk,* p. 4.

divide between "authentic traditional" ethnic cultures and the "derivative contemporary" art that emerges from regions outside the West. In Dilip Menon's ironic phrases, Asian-American and Asian artists are too often regarded as "hitchhikers on the grand narrative of western civilization" and "illegal immigrants in the project of modernity."[9]

Following his "endurance art" period, Zhang Huan began enacting what Gao Minglu describes as "behavioral art" (or *xingwei yishu*), homologous with—but not identical to—performance art.[10] Whereas in the West "performance art" can include intensely solipsistic work that pits the individual against external forces, "behavioral art" that is more characteristic of the work coming out of China implies the linking of art practice to the Confucian tradition, where "there is no such thing as purely individual behavior, all individual behavior (being) social and all behavior reflect[ing] some type of social relationship."[11] Although this formulation may risk unduly reifying the oversimplified East-West binary of collectivism versus individualism, it offers a useful distinction that may help in analyzing Zhang Huan's work and that of some of his peers.[12]

Zhang Huan demonstrated his concern for society through a series of works in 1997 involving the choreographing of multiple bodies. In a piece called "To Raise the Water Level in a Fishpond," Zhang organized forty of his fellow male residents in Da Shan Zi, ranging in age from four to sixty and consisting mainly of itinerant laborers, to raise the water level in a neighborhood fishpond by adding the volume of their bodies. Zhang Huan's comment on the piece was: "That the water in the pond was raised by one meter is an action of no avail."[13] This statement perhaps refers to the ultimate futility of the exercise in that there was no perceivable practical benefit to the community. Yet the project required a communal effort that was moving as well as fruitless. Zhang's close relationship to nature, nurtured from the time he spent in the

---

9   Lowe, "Out of the West," *Fresh Talk*, p. xx.

10 Gao, "Private Experience."

11 Ibid, pp. 1–2. For a contemporary look at the Confucian concept of the self, see Yu, *Ethics*, esp. chapter 7.

12 For the complexity of these issues, see Munro, *Individualism*; Hegel and Hessney, *Expressions*; Murck, *Artists*.

13 Zhang, "To Raise the Water."

Figure 1 Pilgrimage—Wind and Water in New York, 1998, Zhang Huan (1965–)

Inside Out: New Chinese Art exhibition, P.S.1 Contemporary Art Center, New York City, 1998. Performance. © Zhang Huan.

www.pacewildenstein.com

countryside as a child, probably entered into his choice of site and interaction, but we cannot escape the dire undercurrent of rapacious urban development in this tableau of social and natural displacements. The performance tends to undermine the romantic agricultural collectivism associated with Maoism, wherein much labor was sometimes expended with few enduring results. Yet it also appears to reflect the belief, characteristic of Daoism and to a lesser extent of Confucianism, that human action does not require gainful results to be significant.

It is revealing to juxtapose these earlier works with the first behavioral event that Zhang Huan carried out in the West after emigration to the United States in 1998. As part of the 1998 Inside Out exhibition curated by Gao Minglu for P.S.1 Contemporary Art Center in New York City, Zhang Huan created "Pilgrimage–Wind and Water in New York." His props consisted of a Ming dynasty–style bed padded by an ice mattress and surrounded by leashed pet dogs (volunteered by their owners), now a symbol of the middle class in China. Zhang Huan approached the furnishings via a series of Tibetan-Buddhist-like prostrations and then attempted to melt the ice with his body heat.

It was, I think, in this New York performance that Zhang Huan began performing ethnicity. The use of cultural stereotypes within the performance was manifest not only in his presentation of himself as an ethnic Other but also in his response as curious outsider to a dominant culture. He included canine pets in his performance in reaction to what was for him an absurd and culturally specific Western animal-human relationship that was now making its appearance (or in some cases reappearance) in China. The appropriation of Tibetan Buddhist practice raises the question of the artist's view of Han Chinese culture as itself being in a dominant role. Although a Han Chinese from the heart of the central plain, Zhang had since childhood been spiritually influenced by Tibetan Buddhism.[14] In comparing Zhang's earlier works with this piece, the influence of location is clear: Zhang Huan performed "Chineseness" only after he left China. Positioning oneself as an ethnic Other can occur only in juxtaposition with a dominant culture.[15] This condition underlies the change that occurred in Zhang

14 Goldberg, "Interview with Zhang Huan."
15 For a similar point, see Harrell, *Cultural Encounters*, p. 6.

Huan's work subsequent to his relocation to the West. Inadvertently, his move had plunged him more directly into the authenticity debate.

The appropriation of specific features of other cultures had never previously entered into Zhang's behavioral art and had not been part of his lexicon. The use of gestures and props borrowed from preexisting cultural rituals was a clear departure from his earlier behavioral works, where the focus instead had been on gestures that stem from the commonplace and the everyday. Also, Zhang had performed previous works in already functioning sites, like the latrine, the pond, and factories, as opposed to the formally designated and rarified environment of an art gallery. Beyond the dictates of the apparent economic and political limitations of his previous working conditions in China, Zhang Huan's early works were less about spectacle than about the expression of a shared humanity. There was no need to differentiate himself culturally from his viewers. That kind of situation resulted in work that used commonality as a point of departure. In the situation he faced when making work in the West, the pressure was on to entertain and "teach." As spectators at P.S.1 watched Zhang's performance, there was surely an undeniably high level of expectation for this artist fresh from China to inform and enlighten them about ways "Chinese." The body of work that Zhang Huan created in the West cannot be assessed without considering the public's penchant for, simultaneously, obfuscating mysticism and reductive authenticity, as well as the artist's own need to reposition himself in a demanding foreign context.

If Zhang Huan has kept his roots deep in China while adjusting to the different environment and demands of North America, the next three artists under discussion here have acculturated to greater degrees to the West. Indeed it might be said that they have reached the point where their adopted culture has become "home" and China has become "foreign."

Chinese migration to North America has a long and convoluted history. Before World War II, both the United States and Canada accepted very few Asian immigrants and then only in restricted capacities. In the United States, laws named Chinese, as well as other Asians, as "aliens ineligible to citizenship."[16] In Canada, after the need declined

---

16   Lowe, "Out of the West," *Fresh Talk,* p. xxi. Lowe quotes from American laws dating
     from before World War II.

for the Chinese laborers brought into the country to help build the national railroad, a hefty head tax was levied on each immigrant. The result in both countries was a disenfranchised Asian population disallowed entry into the dominant cultural and political circles of society. Coupled with the strong bonds of the Chinese to motherland (e.g., those who ventured forth from China were called "sojourners" [*hua qiao*] to signify their continuing commitment to an eventual return to China), this discriminatory legislation discouraged these immigrants from fully engaging with the host culture.

It was not until the late 1960s to early 1970s that the discriminatory immigration quotas were changed and a broad civil rights movement spurred the development of ethnic studies in the United States. Significantly, Tehching Hsieh and Tseng Kwong Chi, two U.S.-based artists of Chinese descent who caught Zhang Huan's attention during his early encounters with contemporary art from outside China,[17] produced their signature work in the late 1970s and early 1980s.

Tehching Hsieh from Taiwan

Tehching Hsieh was born in Taiwan in 1950. The island territory had developed separately from the mainland for millennia before being incorporated into the Chinese central state as a province during the Qing dynasty. After China was defeated by Japan in war in 1895, Taiwan became a Japanese colony for fifty years. By agreements ending World War II, Taiwan was returned to the authority of the waning Republic of China in 1945. Although Taiwan was about to fall to the forces of the People's Republic in early 1950, the Korean War intervened and resulted in U.S. support for the rump Republican government on the island, support that continues with only minor modification to this day. Cut off from the mainland in 1950, the year of Hsieh's birth, Taiwan existed precariously from year to year heavily dependent on the United States. Then known as the Republic of China, it is now known in diplomatic circles as Chinese Taipei.

It was in this context that Tehching Hsieh spent his formative years. The Hsieh family had deep ancestral roots in Taiwan that can be traced

---

17   Zhang Huan's conversation with the author, Buffalo, New York, 2003.

Figure 2 Outdoor Piece, 1981–82, Tehching Hsieh (1950–)
from the series "One Year Performances" 1978–1999, New York City. Performance.
© Tehching Hsieh. www.TehchingHsieh.com

back hundreds of years. Tehching grew up in a large family and was
strongly influenced by his mother. Without finishing high school, he
began painting at the age of seventeen. At that time in Taiwan, there
was limited access to information on Western avant-garde and contemporary art. The situation was only marginally better than on the
mainland, where the study of Western art was largely confined to late-
nineteenth- and early-twentieth-century canonical figures such as Van
Gogh and Picasso. In the absence of a broad spectrum of Western art,
Hsieh was more influenced by nineteenth-century German philosophy (e.g., Nietzsche) and Russian literature (e.g., Dostoevsky).

Eventually sensing that painting was too limiting for his needs,
Hsieh began performing art with his body. In 1973 he took the dramatic
step of jumping out of a second-story window in Taipei. In retrospect,
this act prefigured another that he took the following year. Making a
much bigger leap, he jumped ship and arrived in the United States as

an illegal immigrant. His low status in the new society resulted in hardship and isolation that would mark his subsequent performance work. Living as an illegal alien in New York City, struggling with English, doing menial labor, and always looking over his shoulder, he gravitated to making art that expressed the idea of confinement and extreme limitation. Coming from a large, close-knit family but now immersed in an environment where he could freely articulate his thoughts and express his emotions, he found the sense of solipsism overwhelming at times. He nonetheless persisted, refusing to return to Taiwan because, despite the adversities, New York City offered him more possibilities as an artist.[18] He continued to live there precariously for the next fourteen years before finally being granted amnesty in 1988.

Hsieh produced the main body of his work between 1978 and 1999. It consisted of a series of five performances, each given the formal generic name "One Year Performance," because each lasted an entire year. Each was subtitled with the year: 1978–1979, 1980–1981, 1981–1982, 1983–1984, and 1985–1986. After more than a decade of other work, Hsieh embarked in 1999 on a new project he called "Earth." He announced he would make art only in private without showing it publicly for the next thirteen years. In 2000, he went even further to announce that he would stop making art and would just "do life." As a result, it is so far primarily in Hsieh's series of one-year performances that we can see his approach to behavioral art.

For present purposes, the third and fourth one-year pieces are especially revealing. In the third, known informally as the "Outdoor Piece," Hsieh lived out-of-doors in Manhattan for an entire year in 1981–1982. During that time, he resolutely barred himself from entering any structures. Steven Shaviro interprets this project to be an exploration of

> solitude and isolation. It questions the inner limits of identity and being. Hsieh stripped himself down to the bare minimum of subsistence. . . . What does it mean to reduce the self to its narrowest possible compass? Hsieh's willing embrace of such a state of deprivation

---

18   Tehching Hsieh's conversation with the author, 2008.

remains mysterious and unsettling . . . How does one's (home) con-
tribute to one's identity? . . . Without a home, one becomes nearly
invisible, anonymous. Is there a freedom to such homelessness, as
well as a deprivation? There are many involuntarily homeless people,
compelled to live on the streets of New York City; what did it mean
for Hsieh to willfully share their plight?[19]

We are also left to wonder if Hsieh had any intention of alluding to the
condition of invisibility—or the converse of racial profiling—
experienced by some minority populations in large urban centers.

In Hsieh's fourth piece, informally known as "Art/Life," he
collaborated closely with American artist, Linda Montano. Indeed,
they raised "collaboration" to new levels by living tied to one another
by eight feet of rope for an entire year in 1981–1982. The two artists
documented their interactions during that year with daily photographs
and audio recordings. They have since made the photographs available
for public viewing but they have kept the audio recordings sealed on
the grounds that the details of the day-to-day experiences would
distract from the main concept of the piece. Any such intimate
collaboration between two persons would have been very challenging,
but Hsieh and Montano chose to complicate it by reaching across
cultural, racial, and gender walls.

Hsieh does not consciously comment on ethnicity in these works or
in any other. In the extremely disciplined minimalism of his works, he
intentionally avoids clichés and any specific references to his ethnic
identity or cultural orientation. Perhaps we can interpret this as a
tactical maneuver, downplaying his obvious condition of being a member of both an ethnically and culturally "visible minority," a trespasser
and nonconformist in the terrain of the norm. On the other hand,
Hsieh's projects may be, as he claims, not ethnic but ontological con-
templations. By creating the conditions of deprivation and Sisyphean
endurance, he seeks to explore human existence pared down to its bare
essence and most basic needs. Indeed, we can view his works about
confinement as suggesting methods of escape: from the complicated
demands of daily existence, from the exploitative pressures of the

---

19   Shaviro, "Performing Life," *One Year Performances*, pp. 3–4.

capitalist economy, or from the lived reality of Hsieh's personal conditions. His experiences of living in Taiwan, a polity of undetermined international status, of being literally a man without a "national" home, and then of moving illegally from that polity to another on which it was largely dependent for its very international existence, may well have given him cause to think about homelessness and the constraints that arise out of the inequitable distribution of wealth and power among states and persons.

Although Tehching Hsieh did not spend much of his adult life in Taiwan, he has remained close to the culture and the society. The simmering political tension that has existed between the island of Taiwan and the mainland of China since the 1940s has spawned a generation of artists preoccupied with identity and boundary issues.[20] Although Hsieh identifies more with being Taiwanese (and American) than with being Chinese, he does not consider himself to be either a Chinese or Taiwanese contemporary artist because he has lived in New York for thirty-four years. He has never intended his work to be reflective of any Chinese identity, and he feels more kinship with other diasporic East Asian artists, especially those who are themselves immigrants (i.e., those born in East Asia and become émigrés to the West).

Whatever Hsieh's motives and intentions, his performances are very popular among at least some art communities in China.[21] They are representative of a larger gravitation toward endurance-based performance practice that marks the generation of artists in China since the 1980s. Inflicting pain and hardship on the self in public is unsettling and even taboo in many cultures, but this very fact helps to explain the popularity of this form of performance art among some artists in China today. Behavioral art began in the 1980s because it offered an opportunity for social critique. It gained added appeal in the eyes of some by causing anxiety among Chinese officials and conservatives,

---

20 Gao, "Toward a Transnational Modernity," *Inside Out*, p. 22.

21 My awareness of this arose from discussions with members of the art communities in Chongqing, following a screening there of Hsieh's work in 2006.

who viewed it as "a form of dangerous social subversion."[22] It has continued to thrive and grow to this day in part because it gets noticed in an age often characterized by self-indulgence.

Tseng Kwong Chi from Hong Kong

The body of the artist as an intellectual, sensorial, emotive and political vehicle has been a presence in Western art making since the beginning of the twentieth century. It was not until much later in the century, though, that the embodiment of gender, ethnicity, and culture became an important concept within performative practice. Though primarily considered a photographer, Tseng Kwong Chi utilized performance and performativity in his everyday life to a degree that effectively crossed over into his photographic work, in particular his series of self-portraits in landscapes that became an exploration of identity.

Born in the same year as Tehching Hsieh, 1950, Tseng Kwong Chi spent his early years in the British colony of Hong Kong. The sparsely inhabited island had been seized by force from the Qing in 1842. Adjacent territory on the mainland crucial for its development had been leased from China for ninety-nine years in 1898. Hong Kong, continental Kowloon and the New Territories together became a major commercial metropolis for a century before their return to China in 1997.

When the People's Republic was established in 1949, Tseng's parents left Shanghai for Hong Kong. Having come from privileged backgrounds, his mother from an intellectual family and his father from a merchant family, and having been educated in the West, they judged that they would not fare well under Mao's revolutionary rule. Then, in 1966, when reverberations from the Cultural Revolution reached Hong Kong, the Tsengs made another move, this time to Canada. Like many emigrants from Hong Kong and Taiwan at that time, Tseng's parents sought in North America what they considered to be better educational opportunities for their children.

Tseng Kwong Chi had emerged as a prodigy in Chinese painting and calligraphy in Hong Kong even before leaving for Canada at age

---

22   Gao, "Private Experience," *Pilgrimage to Santiago*, p. 2.

sixteen. In high school in Vancouver, British Columbia, he showed great talent in painting and music. After one year of study at the University of British Columbia, Tseng was admitted to L'Ecole Supérieure d'Art Graphique at the Académie Julien in Paris. There he began a four-year program in painting but switched to photography by the end of his first year. Unable to obtain a visa to stay in France on completion of his studies, he followed his sister, choreographer and dancer Muna Tseng, to New York City in 1978. In the 1980s he settled in the East Village, where he pursued his career in photography until his untimely death in 1990.[23]

Tseng produced documentary and commercial photography but my focus here is on his identity series. In 1979, he embarked on a project featuring the "Ambiguous Ambassador," his own newly emerging artistic persona. In this series of portraits that extended over a decade, Tseng depicted himself dressed in the classic, simply collared Sun Yat-sen (*zhongshan*) suit (often misleadingly identified as the Mao suit), sporting sunglasses, and identified with a label "SlutforArt." At first glance, the "Ambiguous Ambassador" appears as a kind of imposer or at least cultural misfit in the presence of global tourist sites that are both iconic and clichéd. His more than ninety self-portraits, entitled the "Expeditionary Series" or "East Meets West," reflected the tensions among his different allegiances—to his Chinese family, the gay community, and the art world of the East Village. In an ironic twist, Tseng fully embraced clichés (such as the inscrutable Asian, the stiff Communist cadre, the camera-toting tourist) in order to thwart any tidy containment of his own possible identities (such as good comrade, queer artist, fetishistic object, narcissistic subject). The strength of Tseng's work lies in its skillful use of camp, sly humor, and witty irreverence in exploring complex subject matter and culturally loaded imagery.

The impact of Tseng's images hinges on the juxtaposition of an exoticized body with a normalized landscape, the alien tourist with commonplace symbols of nationhood (e.g., the Statue of Liberty, Grand Canyon, Hollywood Hills, Disneyland, Eiffel Tower). It is in the very context of the foreign body that normalcy becomes *un*hinged,

23 Schlegel, "Improbable Pilgrim," p. 4.

Figure 3 Hollywood, California, 1979, by Tseng Kwong Chi (1950–1990) from "East Meets West: The Expeditionary Self-Portrait Series: 1979–1989."

Silver Gelatin photograph, 36 x 36 inches / 91.4 x 91.4 cm. © Muna Tseng Dance Projects, Inc. New York. www.tsengkwongchi.com / www.paulkasmingallery.com

Photograph by Tseng Kwong Chi. © 1979 Muna Tseng Dance Projects, Inc. New York.

thrown off balance. Intriguingly, the juxtapositions have the potential to make absurd not so much the artist's body but the environment in which it is sited. The selected landscape becomes subject to scrutiny and social critique; what has usually been taken for granted becomes destabilized.

As with the embodiment articulated in Zhang Huan's "Pilgrimage—Wind and Water in New York" and Hsieh's "One Year Performances," the scenarios presented in Tseng's "Expeditionary Series" draw our attention to the ultimately skewed environments that surround and extend from the artist's body. By deregulating and rechoreographing their bodies' behavior within these restraining spaces, the artists encourage us to turn our gaze onto ourselves, our conditioned behavior, routine actions, and standard habitats. It is through the conscious altering of perspective that we gain awareness of our normalized relationships to locality. In other words, it is only in this state of attentiveness that we can appreciate alternative points of view.

Patty Chang from the United States

It is revealing to compare Tseng Kwong Chi's practice to that of Chinese-American Patty Chang, the youngest artist of the four and the only nonimmigrant. Of the group, these two were the only ones to spend part or all of their youthful formative years being educated in the West. The effect of this on their work can perhaps be seen in the way they both utilize a particular type of camp humor and satiric irreverence in their generation of images that essentially question the notion of Chinese authenticity.

Patty Chang approaches the gendered and racialized body via pro-vocative acts incorporating performance, video, film, and photography. She was born in San Francisco in 1972 and is currently based in New York City. Her parents, originally from the China mainland, grew up in Taiwan and arrived in the United States in the 1960s. Her father studied mechanical engineering and worked in restaurants while he was a student.

Patty Chang enrolled in studio art at the University of California at San Diego and studied painting. Dissatisfied with that, however, she started making performances in her last year at school. Early on in her experiments with performance, she was influenced by spoken-word poets in San Diego like Quincy Troupe, as well as stage performance artists like Karen Finley and Holly Hughes. She also found inspiration in Marina Abramovic's work, as well as that of Linda Montano and Tehching Hsieh. Later on she became aware of Ana Mendieta and Carolee Schneemann's performance practices.[24]

---

24 Patty Chang's communication with the author, 2008.

By turns humorous and unsettling, Chang pushes her body to physical extremes as a means of exploring and exploding the physical and ideological ways in which women's bodies are coerced into a socially constructed "femininity." In Chang's own words, "seduction and breakdown" are the central concepts of her work. Influenced by female predecessors within Western performance art history such as Abramovic, Mendieta, and Schneeman, Chang uses her body to address issues surrounding the objectification of women and their representation in art history and popular culture. While continuing aspects of the practices of her predecessors, such as engaging in endurance, testing the limits of the body, and performing ritual, identity, gender politics, and sexuality, Chang differs from them with her insistent resort to humor, satire, and self-mockery.

Chang does not name any significant influences on—or precedents for—her approach to the ethnic body, but she acknowledges the inevitable presence of her Asian identity in her productions: "The fact that I am in almost all the pieces makes it very difficult not to reference Asian female identity; either as fitting within the confines of Asian female representation or else consciously rejecting that identity."[25] Do Chang's satirical strategies consciously challenge ethnographic habits or are they an accidental consequence of her not having a fully formed "Chinese" identity?

Speaking about the context in which Chinese-American women writers such as Maxine Hong Kingston and Amy Tan negotiate their "Chinese" identities, Zhong Xueping writes:

Their (mis)use of Chinese myths and history (which is often a point of contention especially among different groups of Chinese) is conditioned by their own historical reference points [that] . . . orient around American dominant culture in negotiation for an ethnic identity. In this sense, one can argue that these Chinese American women writers focus more on the synchronic relationships between ethnic groups and the dominant culture, between one ethnic group and another, and among people within the same ethnic group [than on the history of any single, "pure" ethnic type]. The synchronicity is

25   Chang in Oishi, "Passionate Interaction," p. 6.

conditioned, once again, by the ethnic politics in the United States, and it is part of the history of this country. Throughout American history, different diasporic communities have struggled to coexist and to be recognized. The notion of Chineseness is therefore often essentialized, in different ways, by both Chinese Americans (as part of their struggle) and [members of] the dominant culture (largely due to ignorance). . . . In this sense, the depth and intricate layers of Chinese history are also necessarily flattened into a spatial existence conditioned by the relationships between the American dominant culture and various Chinese diasporic groups.[26]

Patty Chang has effectively utilized the tactic of diasporic flattening to acknowledge and ultimately contest the problematics broached by Zhong Xueping. Inspired by the contortionists and acrobats she witnessed during a trip to China, the 2000 video piece "Contortion" combines sly charm with slapstick trickery. Chang was as mesmerized by the almost superhuman abilities of the Chinese contortionists as anyone outside (or even inside) that culture would be, but she was also aware of how these qualities easily fall into clichés about ethnic authenticity, Asian inscrutability, and exotic female powers. In the video, she intentionally plays into pat assumptions by gazing coyly and knowingly at the camera as she appears in the transparently illusory pose of a Chinese acrobat with (someone else's) legs resting on her shoulders. The camp mockery subverts the stereotype of the ethnographic spectacle and the objectification of female sexuality.

In Chang's video installation, "In Love" (2001), one monitor plays footage of Chang's face pressed against that of her mother while a second monitor pairs her with her father. The two screens document the intimate and uncomfortable process of Chang passing an onion from her mouth to each of her parents' mouths, but with the film run in reverse so that the onion appears to pass from the parents to their daughter and the tears that are shed ultimately return to the eyes that shed them. At the beginning of the video there is a potent illusion of a deep kiss between Chang and each of her parents.

---

26   Zhong, "Multiple Readings and Personal Reconfigurations," *Chinese Women*, p. 114.

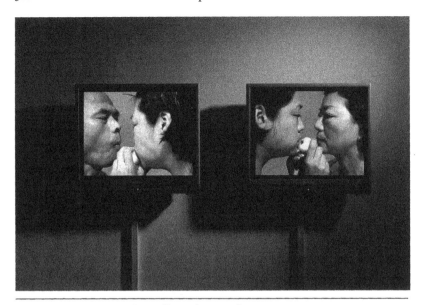

Figure 4 In Love, 2001, Patty Chang (1972–   )
Video installation. © Patty Chang.

Photograph by Tim Mcconville, Chinese Arts Centre, Manchester, UK.

It is always discomfiting to explore the sexuality and conflicts inherent in any parent-child relationship. This is particularly true in a
Chinese context in which, "traditionally," parents are expected to nurture their children warmly but with restrained physical intimacy.
Compounding this already difficult imagery is the often especially
prickly relationship between immigrant Chinese parents and their
American or Americanized children. According to Chang, "Sharing an
awful experience with another person binds you together. . . . As I
thought about this awful yet exquisitely touching act, I imagined the
least likely people I would want to do it with . . . my parents. . . . I was
extremely nervous about approaching them to do the piece."[27] It was
perhaps a measure of Patty Chang's "Chineseness" that she was troubled by the act she wished to perform and record; and it may have been

---

27   Chang in Oishi, "Passionate Interaction," pp. 4–5.

an indication of her parents' "Americanization" that they agreed to participate in the interest of their daughter's art.

When considering Zhong's point of view that information is reduced and the audience becomes under- or mis-informed due to a lack of authentic knowledge, do we not find the writer falling back on yet another stereotype concerning authenticity? How is one geographic and cultural formulation of life experience more legitimate or pure than another? Where we as cultural producers or as cultural consumers trip up is in our persistent but erroneous assumption that the condition of authenticity automatically provides genuine information in terms of *the unadulterated, originary culture*. The problem is that such a culture is in and of itself an impossible entity to define, not least because it probably never existed.

Sharon K. Hom writes about her misgivings concerning

> the politics of authentication, especially for ethnic "minorities" inhabiting a diasporan space. In his eloquent [and] passionate reflections on the doubling effects and challenges of inhabiting postcolonial locations, R. Radhakrishnan asks, "If a minority group were left in peace with itself and not dominated or forced into a relationship with the dominant world or national order, would the group still find the term 'authentic' meaningful? . . . Who . . . is checking our credentials [and by what authority]? Is 'authenticity' a home we built for ourselves or a ghetto to satisfy the dominant world?"
>
> When I wonder if I have "passed" or whether I am still just intellectually cross-dressing, I find a shift from authenticity debates to multiple performance possibilities to be a trans-form-ing strategic move.[28]

The most pertinent question here concerns the function of art: is it to educate and inform? How history and culture are to be interpreted is inherently contentious and subjective. For the reader/viewer/audience of cultural works, interpretation cannot be based solely on the literal or factual. For cultural producers, I believe, the goal is not so much to educate and persuade—in the guise of the "expert" or

---

28 Hom, "(Per)forming Law," *Chinese Women*, pp. 140–41.

"specialist"—as to question and provoke, and to engage in analysis of the multiplicity of our heterocultural condition.

This same heterocultural condition that can be so liberating, however, does have the potential to be reductive, not in terms of the problematics of the authenticity debate but in terms of the effects of globalization. The term "contemporary art" entails a savvy practice that is predicated on certain privileges such as awareness of global issues and access to geographical mobility. This applies not only to those who are longtime residents in the West but also to artists from less privileged world regions who have gained international attention for their work. Carol Becker cautions us against the effects of globalization on the practitioners of contemporary art:

> [Nomadic elites] ultimately do very well in this global art world, living on the boundaries of culture, versed in several languages, constructing and deconstructing their identities at every turn. They are the future. But they are more and more formed and informed by the West, and as their work becomes more and more about their complex, multiple realities, they find it harder to connect to those at "home" who never left.
>
> Romance surrounds this theoretical transmigration. Idealizing transnationality as the social order of the future is convenient, now that we've seen the end of the hope of Marxism and the rampant acceptance of global capitalism. Isn't it easier to think of yourself as a citizen of the world than as citizen of a neighborhood where gang violence, unemployment, pollution, racism, [and] a defunct educational system may prevail? Global ideas are just abstract enough to counter the need for real social action. They also fit nicely into the future already chartered by global capitalism.[29]

How can resistance to an uneven globalization be mounted and maintained? Does a resolution lie in the locational identity of the body, i.e., Chinese in China or Chinese in North America? Is the body the ultimate site of rebellion as it convulses against the indigestible speed of technological development, environmental contamination, social

---

29 Becker, "If It's Tuesday," pp. 50–52.

alienation, and the increasingly brutal, eroding canyon between haves and have-nots? How can the concept of embodiment be utilized to overcome these social and physical lesions? Katherine Hayles recognizes that market forces will likely ensure that "we will increasingly live, work, and play in environments that construct us as embodied virtualities."[30] Under these circumstances, she proposes that it is possible to interpret information in a way that acknowledges its own material existence. Information is embodied, and that embodiment enables resistance and contestation.

> Whereas the body is an idealized form that gestures toward a Platonic reality, embodiment is the specific instantiation generated from the noise of difference. Relative to the body, embodiment is other and elsewhere, at once excessive and deficient in its infinite variations, particularities, and abnormalities. . . . Embodiment is thus inherently destabilizing with respect to the body. . . . Embodiment is . . . inherently performative, subject to individual enactments, and therefore always to some extent improvisational. Whereas the body can disappear into information with scarcely a murmur of protest, embodiment cannot, for it is tied to the circumstances of the occasion and the person. As soon as embodiment is acknowledged, the abstractions of the Panopticon disintegrate into the particularities of specific people embedded in specific contexts. Along with these particularities come concomitant strategies for resistances and subversions, excesses and deviations.[31]
> . . . embodiment is always instantiated, local, and specific. Embodiment can be destroyed, but it cannot be replicated. . . . As we rush to explore the new vistas that cyberspace has made available for colonization, let us remember the fragility of a material world that cannot be replaced.[32]

Embodiment entails performativity, defined by Judith Butler "not as a singular or deliberate 'act,' but, rather, as the reiterative and cita-

---

30 Hayles, "Virtual Bodies and Flickering Signifier," *How We Became Posthuman*, p. 48.
31 Ibid. pp. 196–98.
32 Ibid., p. 49.

tional practice by which discourse produces the effects that it names."[33] Performativity operates in the everyday, most often as unwitting, conditioned gestures that integrate us into the general social fabric. The instances in which those gestures are deliberately amplified, inverted or recontextualized are defined as performance practice. Performative art work surfaces in situations where cultural expressions must exist under the radar of authoritarian rule or in conditions where individuals or collectives are compelled to protest oppressive conditions, to agitate the status quo, to disrupt complacency. As a strategy for grappling with the complexities of the postmodern condition of global dispersion, relocation, and mobility, practice that is grounded in embodiment—via the mutable, temporal, portable body—has the potential to counter, in the words of Miwon Kwon, "both the nostalgic desire for a retrieval of rooted, place-bound identities on the one hand, and the antinostalgic embrace of a nomadic fluidity of subjectivity, identity, and spatiality on the other."[34]

In order for truly critical, contemporary art practice to thrive in China, does its cultural reconstruction necessitate the adoption of this kind of perspective? Would that mean working against China's historic grain—that is, one of being "earthbound," central and hierarchical?[35] Or is that cluster of supposed traits problematic or, if not, potentially productive on the global scene? Does the solution lie in "the potential to transgress the 'boundedness' of an identity-based framework in order to rethink this community of not belonging"?[36] In pondering the need for development of a revised Confucian humanism in the wake of Tiananmen, Tu Wei-ming contemplated the ideal condition for China's "modernization," emphasizing the growing importance of diaspora to the future health of the entire culture:

> The center no longer has the ability, insight, or legitimate authority
> to dictate the agenda for cultural China. On the contrary, the trans-

---

33   Butler, *Bodies*, p. 2.

34   Kwon, "Introduction," *One Place*, pp. 8–9.

35   Wang, *Chinese Overseas*.

36   Min, "Last Asian American Exhibition," *One Way*, p. 40. The context for this comment is the current state of curating identity-based exhibitions in the United States. This seems relevant to the problems with forming a unified Chinese cultural identity.

formative potential of the periphery is so great that it seems inevitable that it will significantly shape the intellectual discourse on cultural China for years to come. It is perhaps premature to announce that "the center is nowhere, the periphery is everywhere," but undeniably, the fruitful interaction of a variety of economic, political, social, and cultural forces at work along the periphery will continue to shape the dynamics of cultural China.[37]

We may doubt how often the Chinese "center" ever "dictated the agenda for cultural China," but shifts in the relative power of the Chinese center and its peripheries have occurred frequently over the course of history. There is no reason why such a change should not recur in the twenty-first century, and very possibly more than once. A potentially reciprocal manifestation has formed "along the periphery" that suggests a shift in focus in Western countries like the United States and Canada, where "now there is an overwhelming pressure to see the Asian American experience through a diasporic lens rather than from a cultural national perspective. In Asian American communities, the goals of 'claiming America' for themselves and of being recognized as 'American' are no longer priorities as they once were."[38] As we ponder the possible power shifts occurring in the game of global cultural domination and influence, the youth in China are increasingly looking to other Asian youth, especially in Tokyo, Seoul, and Taipei, rather than in the West, for models in shaping the popular psyche. We must wait to see how social phenomena like this affect an increasingly confident and bold nationalism and how that nationalism in turn affects China's relation to its "sojourners."

Of late, China has loomed large politically, economically, and culturally on the international media scope, making up for decades if not centuries of disregard and abuse. Yet this kind of media spotlight may only serve to throw up another wall around cultural production, spurred by the momentum of the international art market and driven by the selective economic engine of globalization. There is a dearth of analyses of the intricate interrelationship of China, its artists who have stayed, its artists who have left, and the variously differentiated cultural

---

37 Tu, *Living Tree*, pp. 33–34.
38 Min, "Last Asian American Exhibition," *One Way*, p. 39.

life in both geographically near and far diasporic art communities. How encompassing or exclusive, vague or specific is a term like "contemporary Chinese artists" when considering ancestry, geography, nationality, nationhood, dispersion, relocation, and mobility? What of the Asian body in diaspora, visually nonspecific in its locational identity but still irrefutable in its ethnicity? What contextual information does the viewer require to be able to untangle its complexities? Despite the differences in the diverse works of the four artists discussed in this essay, it is the racialized, gendered, and class embodiment of these artists that conveys their art. They therefore determine their bodies to be simultaneously the vehicles, the places, the situations, and the decoys in their negotiations between assimilation and intrusion and in their explorations of our shared human conditions.

Works Cited

Becker, Carol. "if it's tuesday, this must be ihla do sal," *Utne Reader* (July–August 2000), pp. 50-52. Adapted from *Art Journal* (Summer 1999), College Art Association, New York.

Butler, Judith. *Bodies That Matter: On the Discursive Limits of "Sex."* New York: Routledge, 1993.

Carr, C. "On Edge: Stripped Down: China's Foremost Ordeal Artist Emerges in America," *Village Voice* (May 3-9, 2000), p. 1

Chen, Jack. *A Year in Upper Felicity: Life in a Chinese Village During the Cultural Revolution.* New York: Macmillan, 1973.

Domenach, Jean-Luc. *The Origins of the Great Leap Forward: The Case of One Chinese Province.* Boulder: Westview, 1995.

Gao, Minglu. *Inside Out: New Chinese Art.* Berkeley: University of California Press, 1998.

———. "Toward a Transnational Modernity: An Overview of *Inside Out: New Chinese Art*," In *Inside Out: New Chinese Art*, edited by Gao Minglu. Berkeley: University of California Press, 1998.

———. "Private Experience and Public Happenings, the Performance Art of Zhang Huan." http://www.zhanghuan.com/ShowText.asp?id=26&sClass ID=1

Goldberg, Roselee. "Interview with Zhang Huan." http://www.zhanghuan. com/ShowText.asp?id=7&sClassID=3

Harrell, Stevan. *Cultural Encounters on China's Ethnic Frontiers.* Seattle: University of Washington Press, 1995.

Hayles, N. Katherine. *How We Became Posthuman*. Chicago: University of Chicago Press, 1999.

Hegel, Robert E., and Richard C. Hessney, eds. *Expressions of Self in Chinese Literature*. New York: Columbia University Press, 1985.

Hom, Sharon K. "(Per)forming Law: Deformations and Transformations," In *Chinese Women Traversing Diaspora: Memoirs, Essays, and Poetry*, Sharon K. Hom, ed. New York: Garland, 1999.

Hsieh, Tehching. *One Year Performances: Art Documents 1978–1999*. DVD-ROM. New York: Tehching Hsieh, 2000.

Kim, Elaine H., "Interstitial Subjects: Asian American Visual Art as a Site for New Cultural Conversations." In *Fresh Talk Daring Gazes: Conversations on Asian American Art*, Elaine H. Kim, Margo Machida, and Sharon Mizota, eds. Berkeley: University of California Press, 2003.

Kwon, Miwon. *One Place After Another: Site-Specific Art and Locational Identity*. Cambridge, Mass.: MIT Press, 2002.

Lowe, Lisa. "Out of the West: Asian Migration and Modernity." In *Fresh Talk Daring Gazes: Conversations on Asian American Art*, Elaine H. Kim, Margo Machida, and Sharon Mizota, eds. Berkeley: University of California Press, 2003.

Min, Susette S. "The Last Asian American Exhibition in the Whole Entire World." In *One Way or Another: Asian American Art Now*, Melissa Chiu, Karin Higa, and Susette S. Min, eds. New Haven, Conn.: Asia Society and Yale University Press, 2006.

Munro, Donald, ed. *Individualism and Holism: Studies in Confucian and Taoist Values*. Ann Arbor: Center for Chinese Studies, University of Michigan, 1985.

Murck, Christian, ed. *Artists and Traditions: Uses of the Past in Chinese Culture*. Princeton, NJ: Art Museum of Princeton University and Princeton University Press, 1976.

Oishi, Eve. "Passionate Interaction: Interview with Patty Chang," *X-Tra* 5(4:2003).

Schlegel, Amy Ingrid. "Improbable Pilgrim: The Photographs of Tseng Kwong Chi." http://www.munatseng.org/tsengkwongchi.htm

Shaviro, Steven. "Performing Life: The Work of Tehching Hsieh," *One Year Performances: Art Documents 1978–1999*. DVD-ROM. New York: Tehching Hsieh, 2000.

Tu Wei-ming, ed. *The Living Tree: The Changing Meaning of Being Chinese Today*. Stanford: Stanford University Press, 1994.

Wang, Gungwu. *The Chinese Overseas from Earthbound China to the Quest for Autonomy*. Cambridge, Mass.: Harvard University Press, 2000.

Wu, Hung. *Transience: Chinese Experimental Art at the End of the Twentieth Century.* Chicago: University of Chicago Press, 2004.

Yu, Jiyuan. *The Ethics of Confucius and Aristotle: Mirrors of Virtue.* New York and London: Routledge, 2007.

Zhang, Huan. "To Raise the Water Level in a Fishpond." http://www.zhanghuan .com/ShowWorkContent.asp?id=39&iParentID=21&mid=1

Zhong, Xueping. "Multiple Readings and Personal Reconfigurations Against the 'Nationalist Grain.'" In *Chinese Women Traversing Diaspora: Memoirs, Essays, and Poetry*, Sharon K. Hom, ed. New York: Garland, 1999.

CHAPTER ELEVEN

Confronting the Walls

Efforts at Reconstructing World History in China at the Turn of the Twenty-First Century

Luo Xu

Introduction

WRITING HISTORY HAS LONG BEEN an important part of Chinese civilization. From early times, in the absence of any significant belief in a radically transcendent, omnipotent creator deity, most Chinese believed that the human experience, understood in the context of the natural world (heaven and earth), was the most valuable source of wisdom. They therefore developed many different forms of historiography, including annals, biographies, chronicles, treatises, local histories, comprehensive histories (*tongshi*), standard histories of dynasties (*zhengshi*), and accounts of series of events from beginning to end.[1] None of these kinds of history made any sharp distinction between their main focus, China (the central state[s], *zhongguo*), and the known world (all under heaven, *tianxia*) extending in all four directions. Indeed, it can be argued that from Han times on, comprehensive histories, which purported to cover the entire human experience over

---

1   Ng and Wang, *Mirroring the Past*; Wang, *Inventing China*.

time and space, came as close to world histories as was possible before
the unification (or reunification) of the globe since the fifteenth century
of the common era.[2] Standard dynastic histories continued to describe
known peoples and states, both near and far, and usually in the form
of special biographies, or what amounted to prosopographies cum
ethnographies, down through the Ming.[3]

With the vast expansion of the world known to China during the
Qing, however, it became necessary to pay closer attention to the relationship between Chinese history and the history of the rest of the
world. When the draft history of the Qing was compiled in 1927, it no
longer included accounts of such states as Japan, Portugal, and Hol-
land among its "biographies."[4] Indeed, a virtual wall was gradually
constructed between histories of China on the one hand and histories
of the rest of the world on the other. The distinction probably originated in diaries and monographs written by Chinese who traveled
abroad as early as the Han dynasty, but it grew much sharper in geog-
raphies and histories written by individuals from the late-Qing on.[5]
These works, based largely on "Western" sources, naturally reflected
various Euro-American views of the world and focused on the West
that seemed to offer the largest potential threat to—and model for—
China. These accounts also provided much valuable information on
the rest of the world, but they did not deal with Chinese history—let
alone integrate it effectively into world history. Subsequent generations
of Chinese historians were keenly aware that China's destiny was increasingly bound up with that of the rest of the world, but the wall
between Chinese history and world history in the academy seemed to

---

2   See, for example, the Han-period comprehensive history, Sima Qian's *Shiji*. For an ex-
     cellent translation in process, see Nienhauser, *Grand Scribe's Records*. For a good study
     of the perception of the world in Chinese historiography, see Wang, "History." The first
     unification of the globe might be said to have occurred tens of thousands of years ago
     when homo sapiens spread over the surface of the earth, populating almost every in-
     habitable place. Fernandez-Armesto, *World*, ch. 1. Of course there was little communi-
     cation of any kind, not to speak of writing among those relatively small and far-flung
     communities, but it is well to remember that communication remained difficult even
     in the second unification and it is far from complete even today in the age of the world-
     wide web.

3   Zhang et al., *Mingshi*, juan 313–32.

4   Zhao, *Qingshi gao*, juan 512–29.

5   For early Chinese travelers, see Mirsky, *Great*; for late Qing accounts, see Wei, *Haiguo
     tuzhi*; Xu, *Yinghuan zhilue*. See also Leonard, *Wei Yuan*; Drake, *China Charts*.

get only higher and thicker.[6] To be sure, some historians tried to write world history, but the result was simply "histories of various countries," mainly European, that did not include China.[7] Symptomatically, up through the 1940s, there was no "world history"—only "Chinese history" and "Western history"—in the curricula of China's secondary and tertiary schools.[8]

In the late 1950s and early 1960s, Chinese historians began to try to depict world history according to a universal pattern of development of human society. A collective effort led to the first multivolume, "official" world history text, which was published in 1962.[9] That text has recently been dubbed "a milestone in the development of China's world history."[10] To the extent that it analyzed the history of much of the world in a coherent and integrated fashion it was indeed a step forward. But it followed the Marxist stages of social history universalized in Soviet historiography: from communal society through slavery, feudalism, and capitalism, to socialism and, ultimately, communism.[11] Since that theory of social evolution was based largely on European historical experience, the Chinese text imbued with it was necessarily Eurocentric and focused on the countries and events that best illustrated the orthodox five stages.[12] Moreover, partly due to its concentration on demonstrating the supposed underlying "laws of historical development," the text largely neglected horizontal relationships (con-

---

6   For the most representative figure of the last decade of the Qing, see Levenson, *Liang Ch'i-ch'ao*; Chang, *Liang Ch'i-ch'ao*; Huang, *Liang Ch'i-ch'ao*; Zhang, *Liang Qichao*; Duara, *Rescuing History*; Tang, *Global Space*; Karl, *Staging the World*; Huters, *Bringing the World*. For other Republican-era historians, see Wang, *Inventing China*.

7   One important exception was the work by Zhou Gucheng, who tried to change the Eurocentric approach that had dominated the writing of world history, and to incorporate the historical experiences of various nations (including that of China) in his narrative of the world as a whole. See Zhou Gucheng, *Shijie tongshi*.

8   Liu, "Woguo 'shijie tongshi,' " p. 9.

9   Zhou and Wu, *Shijie tongshi*. See also Littrup, "World History," pp. 43–44; Croizier, "World History"; Martin, *Making*; and Wang, "Encountering the World."

10 Liu, ed., *Lishixue bainian*, p. 482.

11 For a study of the emergence of Marxist historiography in China, see Dirlik, *Revolution and History*. See also Feuerwerker, "Chinese History," Feuerwerker, *History,* and Unger, *Using the Past*.

12 For example, in the Modern Section (vols. 3–4) of the 1972 revised edition of the 1962 text, European history occupied about 58 percent of the space. See Zhou and Wu Yujin, *Shijie tongshi*.

temporaneous interactions among different regions and cultures).[13] For all its effort to be systematic and comprehensive, the text completely excluded Chinese history.[14]

Beginning in the 1980s and reflecting the diversification of Chinese society, more and more historians called for a critical reevaluation of the entire academic field of world history in China. This field was deemed important, perhaps even central, in part because Chinese historians have described a pattern of history in which China was intimately involved with the rest of the world during its "modern" (*jindai*) history, i.e., since the 1840s. Ironically enough, a wall had arisen in the academy between Chinese and world history just when it was recognized that those two histories had actually became inextricably intertwined during the last century. Similarly and with equal irony, a wall arose in scholarship between so-called ancient (*gudai*) Chinese history and "modern/contemporary" Chinese history just when it became essential to understand the actual relationships—the continuities as well as changes—between the two periods. The challenge was to recognize the important role of the "West" in general and Euro-America in particular in shaping "modern" history, including modern Chinese history, without falling into an excess of Eurocentrism and eliding China from the story of its own recent experience. In the new era of reform and opening, Chinese historians have attempted to confront these two walls—between China and the rest of the world and between the past and the present—in part by drawing, again ironically, on Western efforts to write world history.[15] Most recently Chinese historians have begun to take account of Western scholarship devoted to developing a less Eurocentric account of modern world history.[16] In the process, the very theory of Marxism-Leninism that had once played such a positive role in stimulating the field of world history in China

13   For the importance of this approach, see Fletcher, "Integrative History"; Karl, *Staging the World*.

14   For a useful analysis of these problems in the textbook, see Martin, "China."

15   See, for example, McNeil, *Rise of the West*; Stavrianos, *World Since 1500* and *World to 1500*; Braudel, *Civilization and Capitalism*; Wallerstein, *Modern World System*; Bentley and Ziegler, *Traditions and Encounters*; among others. For theoretical discussions of world history studies, see Geyer and Bright, "World History"; Costello, *World Historians*; Bentley, *Shapes of World History*; and Manning, *Navigating World History*.

16   Frank, *ReORIENT*; Wong, *China Transformed*; Pomeranz, *Great Divergence*.

may be emerging in some historians' minds as yet another obstacle to the merging of Chinese and world historiography. At the same time, academic historians' turn to Weberian modernization theory may yet be called into question by public intellectuals' critiques of "neoliberalism."[17]

Wu Yujin and the Rise of Global History Theory in China

Professor Wu Yujin initiated the venture to reconstruct world history "with Chinese characteristics" in 1978. After about two decades, Wu's theory became established as almost a new orthodoxy in China's world history field. In fact, nearly all of the published world history texts since the early 1990s have more or less followed Wu's pioneering work.[18]

Trained at Harvard University in the 1940s,[19] Wu Yujin had long been exposed to Western historiography.[20] In the early 1960s, he served as one of the two editors-in-chief of the first multivolume world history text. During the process of compiling the 1962 text, he had questions about the Soviet model of historiography, which led to his long search for alternative ways to write world history. After the Cultural Revolution (1966–1976), Wu began to advocate his own ideas of world history that departed from the model adopted from the Soviet Union.

---

17 See Wang, *China's New Order*; Huang and Cui, *Zhongguo*; Yang, *Da Hezuo*.

18 For example, Wu and Qi, *Shijie shi*; Ma, *Shijie shigang*; Qi, *Shijie tongshi*; and Wang, *Shijie tongshi*.

19 Wu received his M.A. in 1944 and Ph.D. in 1946.

20 Among Western scholars, Geoffrey Barraclough had the earliest and therefore most consequential influence. In 1959 Wu Yujin published a long review of Barraclough's 1955 book *History in a Changing World* (Wu, *Wu Yujin*, pp. 231–54). Professor Qi Sihe, another prominent historian, also cited Barraclough in his essay "Luelun kaizhan shijieshi yanjiu gongzuo." Partly due to their introduction, Barraclough became well known among Chinese historians. Later in 1982 the *Times Atlas of World History* that Barraclough edited was translated into Chinese, and his *Main Trends in History* (1978, Chinese edition in 1987) and *An Introduction to Contemporary History* (1964, Chinese edition in 1996) were often cited by Chinese historians when they criticized Eurocentrism in historical works, Chinese or foreign, and searched for a broader global history approach. As a comparison, interestingly, William McNeill, "the premier figure of modern world history" (words of Bruce Mazlish, "Comparing Global History") had less influence in China. I have found only one essay focusing on McNeill's work and his contribution to the field of world history. See Guo, "Ping Maikenier."

Among China's world historians, Wu was the first systematically to criticize the Soviet model of historiography. While still giving it considerable credit for taking the changes in socioeconomic formations as the standard for periodizing the world's past, emphasizing the role of the masses in historical evolution, paying attention to the histories of repressed and conquered peoples, and deriving the underlying "laws of history" from changes in the modes of material production, he argued that the Soviet model had serious flaws. At the very least, the Soviet model and Chinese world history texts stemming from it were not really free from the influence of Eurocentrism. They continued to periodize world history according to European historical experiences, and they attempted to put world history into a fixed pattern of socioeconomic development, which was then often applied mechanically to all areas and nations. This sometimes resulted in the distortion of the historical experiences of non-Western countries to fit the model. Moreover, Wu observed, the world history compiled within this framework was often little more than a list of periods and countries put together without any effort to show the organic development of interrelations and interactions among different regions, nations, and societies over time.

Wu's world history theory included the following components. First, "world history" cannot be comprehensive in the sense of including everything, and it should not be merely the sum of all existing national and regional histories. Rather, it is a special subfield of the historical profession with clear and limited goals. The study of world history aims at exploring the *process* through which fragmented and largely isolated parts of the world in earlier times grew into the fully interconnected and interactive global community of more recent times. From this point of view, "world history" cannot be limited to the history of "foreign countries outside China"; it must include and take account of Chinese experience. In short, Wu argued, "world history" (or "global history," including more interaction among different peoples and cultures) did not exist in ancient times (*gudai*); rather, it resulted only from the development of human history. Therefore the main task of "world history" as a subfield of the historical discipline is not just to discover and demonstrate universal rules of historical change defined either by Marxist historical materialism or by non-

Marxian grand synthesizers such as Spengler and Toynbee, but to explain how the *history of human groups* became a *world history*. Using other terms, Wu was to a large extent interested in the "history of globalization."

Second, Wu argued that "world history" must relinquish all kinds of "centrism" caused by national or ideological "bias," whether Eurocentric or Sinocentric. "World history" researchers should transcend the confines of a single nation or one particular ideology, and acquire a worldwide view. Whether or when a nation, a region, or an event should be given more attention than others depends on the role it played at the time in the process of world historical development. For example, Wu's reconstruction of "modern" world history started with the major events and developments of the fifteenth and sixteenth centuries, which in his (and many others') view proved to be the turning point in the process of *history* becoming *world history*.[21] Since in Wu's view Western Europe was the driving force of this historical turning point that accelerated the process of human interaction at a global level, the changes that occurred at the western end of the Eurasian continent and factors that nurtured these changes should be the primary focus of world history.

Third, the long period over which the history of human groups developed into a world history included two fundamental dimensions: longitudinal (*jing*) and horizontal (*wei*). Longitudinal development (or development through time) refers to the evolution in the modes of production and the corresponding changes in society over time, which remained in Wu's analysis somewhat in line with the Marxian stages of social evolution. Horizontal development is the process in which scattered and relatively isolated parts of the world gradually broke various barriers and became increasingly connected, eventually merging into a closely knit global community. According to Wu, the common basis and ultimate propelling force of both longitudinal and horizontal development was the progress in material production that turned the history of human groups into world history.

---

21 Some scholars have argued that "world history" has been around for a much longer time than the last five hundred years. See, for example, Abu-Lughod, *Before European Hegemony*; and Frank and Gills, *World System*.

Finally, Wu argued that both Western synthesizers such as Spengler and Toynbee and Soviet world historians concentrated on one or the other "universal" pattern of human history. Their overemphasis on uniformity and eagerness to prove universal theories made them sometimes overlook the variations and diverse situations in history. Moreover, neither Western synthesizers nor Soviets considered horizontal history an equally important subject and neither gave it proper treatment, though to some extent both touched upon the issue in different ways. To Wu, since world history as a subfield belongs to macrohistory, the goal of which is to reveal how the world became integrated, world historians should base their studies on national, regional, and other histories, but they must go beyond these "specific" histories and view the world as a whole, looking at transnational, transcultural subjects. He personally led the research team at Wuhan University to study world history in the fifteenth and sixteenth centuries, using macro- and comparative approaches to explore issues across large geographical areas.[22]

While criticizing the Soviet model of world history studies, Wu continued to assert his belief in Marxist theory and historiography. In fact, he wrote that to search for a solution to the problems of the old Soviet as well as Western non-Marxist models and to reconceptualize world history as a whole, he "sought advice from the classics of Marxism."[23] Beginning in 1978, in most of his writings and open speeches, Wu repeatedly quoted the following words of Karl Marx:

World history has not always existed; history as world history [is] a result.[24]

The further the separate spheres, which act on one another, extend in the course of this development and the more the original isolation of the separate nationalities is destroyed by the advanced mode of production, by intercourse and by the natural division of

---

22   This discussion draws on Wu, *Wu Yujin xueshu lunzhu zixuanji*, pp. 16–29, 30–51. Also see An, "Cong shijieshiguan kan"; Zhang, "Luelun shijieshi"; and Li, "Wusi fengxian." For a good discussion of some of Wu's ideas in English, see Littrup, "World History."

23   Wu, *Wu Yujin*, p. 576.

24   Marx, *Grundisse*, 109.

labor between various nations arising as a result, *the more history becomes world history.*[25]

It (big industry) *produced world history for the first time*, insofar as it made all civilized nations and every individual member of them dependent for the satisfaction of their wants on the whole world, thus destroying the former natural exclusiveness of separate nations.[26]

Wu claimed that it was these ideas of Marx that inspired him to reconceptualize world history. But it was also possible that he felt he had to put his global approach to world history in a "politically correct" framework, considering the fact that he began to advocate his "new" concept of world history less than two years after the ideology-dominated, but also somewhat heterodox Cultural Revolution. Even though he often cited many other Western scholars, these quotations of Marx appeared repeatedly in Wu's writings on world history. Perhaps he felt that, without the "spiritual support" of Marx, it would have been more difficult to convince his younger colleagues, who were trained in the Marxist tradition after 1949 and had little access to other theories, to convert to his "new" concept of world history. Moreover, the above quotations seemed to point to another dimension in the Marxist view of world history: Marx not only emphasized the *stages* of social evolution (longitudinal development), but also highlighted the *process* in which history became a world history (horizontal development). Wu obviously believed, with good reason, that the latter had thitherto been overlooked in world history works, Soviet and Chinese.

It is also fair to say that Wu's ideas of world history revealed a much greater influence from contemporary Western authors and their works. Indeed, except for a rather thin veneer of theoretical "guidance" from Marx, which was prudently integrated into his narrative, Wu's (and others') speeches and essays on world history were full of citations and interpretations of world history theories by such contemporary Western historians as Spengler, Toynbee, Braudel, Stavrianos, Wallerstein,

---

25 Marx, *German Ideology*, p. 58. Emphasis added.
26 Ibid., p. 81. Emphasis added.

and especially Barraclough.[27] In an essay published in 1964, he mentioned Barraclough and Toynbee as examples of Western historians who were critical of Eurocentrism.[28] Wu cited Marx's short note mentioned above on "history as world history [is] a result" for the first time in 1978, and he interpreted this note and Marx's "the more history becomes world history" only in 1982.[29] In the 1980s, while Wu continued to quote these comments of Marx,[30] in his writings, he also paid great attention to the ideas and approaches of L. S. Stavrianos and Immanuel Wallerstein.[31] Perhaps Wu's educational background in English and his special interest in Western historiography can help to explain his familiarity with those Western historians. It is not inconceivable that he had already developed his global perspective on world history based on what he learned from these "bourgeois" scholars before he found the relevant quotations in Marx.

Marx's comments on "history becoming world history" certainly inspired Wu, but they also served as an ideological cover for his attempt to "rewrite" world history. With these comments he was able to demonstrate that the Western "bourgeois" approaches to world history that he borrowed and adopted were not at odds with Marx's own ideas. In other words, Marx's view of horizontal development in world his-

---

27 Many Chinese historians believed that Barraclough first proposed the global perspective on world history in his *History in a Changing World* (1955). See, for example, Yu, "Quanqiuhua."

28 Wu, *Wu Yujin*, pp. 12, 231–54.

29 Ibid., pp. 28, 576.

30 Ibid., pp. 44, 64, 92, 548–49. Following Wu's pioneering work, many other historians in China turned to Marx for inspiration in their efforts to reconstruct world history. But most of them did not (could not) find in Marx/Engels' works anything more than what Wu had already dug out. Most of the published essays that I have read in this respect simply cite the same two sentences by Marx and interpret them in the same manner as Wu had done, and few went further. Perhaps that is why Wu felt very glad when Professor Qi Shirong, coeditor-in-chief for the 1994 world history text, told him that he (Qi) found another similar sentence in Marx's work (possibly the one also from *The German Ideology*) about big industry producing world history for the first time. (Cited in Professor Liu Xincheng's e-mail to me on January 2, 1999.)

31 Ibid., pp. 48, 60. Long before Stavrianos's two volumes of global history were translated into Chinese (Shanghai, 1992), in the 1980s the photocopies of the English edition had already been available at major foreign language bookstores in China. Wallerstein's *The Modern World System* also has its Chinese edition.

tory somehow made it easier for him to bypass the powerful ideological "wall" of the Soviet (and Chinese) interpretation of Marxism, which had always laid special emphasis on the "fundamental, determining" course of longitudinal progress and tended to ignore the horizontal process of globalization.[32]

Employing the New Theory: World History Texts of the 1990s

In the mid-1980s, the State Education Commission authorized Wu Yujin at Wuhan University and Qi Shirong at Capital Normal University to compile a new multivolume text of world history, which was eventually completed and published in 1994.[33] The new text was constructed according to Wu's concept of world history, and was intended to reveal both the *stages* of social evolution and the *process* by which scattered and relatively isolated human groups developed into a closely connected and well-integrated global community.[34] To get a better picture of continuity and change in China's world history studies, we need to look closely at this new multivolume text. Since its publication, it has been compared with the 1962 edition and praised as "another milestone in the development of world history in China."[35] It has also been

---

32 Compared with other fields of history (modern Chinese history, for example), the "ideological wall" in world historiography seemed "thicker" and harder to break through, especially among the senior historians who were trained in the 1950s to 1970s. This observation is based on my reading of dozens of research articles published in China in the last twenty years and my conversations with several Chinese world historians. For example, an essay published in 2000 still criticized the new world history approach initiated by Wu Yujin for confusing the causal relations between the longitudinal and horizontal developments of history, because, according to the author, the longitudinal development was always the determining force of history and the motivating dynamic that caused horizontal development in history. See Yu, "Shijie jindaishi."

33 Wu and Qi, *Shijie shi*. Although there were two general editors for both the 1962 text and the one published in 1994, Wu played the leading role in both projects. For Wu's contribution to the 1962 text, see Zhou, *Bijing*, pp. 188–89. For the 1994 text, Professor Qi Shirong stated that Wu was the leader and he was Wu's "assistant." See Zhang Hongyi's interview with Qi in *Shixueshi yanjiu*, 1994, No. 3.

34 Wu's long essay, titled "Shijie lishi" [World history] and written for *The Chinese Encyclopedia* [Zhongguo dabaike quanshu] in 1988, was included in all six volumes of the new text as the "General Introduction."

35 Liu, *Lishixue bainian*, p. 483.

described as "representing the highest level of world history compilation in this country in recent times."[36]

According to Chinese world historian Liu Xincheng, this new
world history "straightened out the essential relations of historical
materialism" by giving the "forces of production" their due position
as the determining factors behind the "relations of production."[37] In
other words, the new text no longer took class relations and class
struggles as the ultimate impetuses of historical change; instead, it
depicted progress in productive forces, such as the "agricultural revolution" and "scientific-technological revolution" as the key developments. These "revolutions," prominent in Western bourgeois historiography, were to be seen as the ultimate benchmarks of fundamental
changes in history.[38]

Corresponding to the theoretical revision, the structure and periodization of the 1994 text were also altered. Unlike the 1962 world history text, which was divided into ancient, medieval, and modern sections on the Soviet model, the new text devoted two volumes to each of
three periods: ancient (*gudai*), modern (*jindai*), and contemporary
(*xiandai*). The section on ancient history now covered the standard
Marxist stages of communal, slave, and feudal societies worldwide, but
its focus was on the more general Western "bourgeois" postulated phenomena such as the rise, development, and changes in the "agricultural
civilizations" on the Eurasian continent. The text abandoned the European and Soviet concept of the "medieval period," and modified the
Soviet practice of squeezing the experiences of non-European nations
into the Marxist framework of social evolution (especially into the
"slave" and "feudal" categories). Instead it used more general and vague
concepts such as "prefeudal" and "precapitalist." In addition to modify-
ing previous approaches to these old issues, the authors made efforts to
record the contacts, communications, and clashes through migration,

---

36 Liu, "Woguo 'shijie,'" p. 12.

37 Ibid.

38 This new emphasis on productive forces as the ultimate determinant of history was
    clearly in line with the post–Cultural Revolution change in the state policy from Mao's
    ideology-oriented continuous revolution to Deng's economy-centered modernization.

trade, war, and the spread of religion among different groups, nations, and countries in the "old world" (i.e., Eurasia).[39] Departing from Soviet practice of beginning the modern era with the English revolution of 1640, the Chinese historians followed the more fundamental Marxist view that modernity began with the rise of capitalism around 1500 CE. The modern history section then describes the emergence, rise, and worldwide expansion of capitalism, the last phase of which was primarily attributed to the "industrial revolution." To Wu Yujin (and numerous Western historians), the year 1500 holds special significance as a key turning point in world history. Western European maritime expansion to the furthest reaches of both the "old" and "new" worlds at that time was crucial; indeed, "without the great geographical discoveries, there would not have been the industrial revolution and the growth of capitalism, and consequently there would not have been the fundamental transition of world history into an integrated unit."[40] What distinguishes this Chinese text from most Western works of modern world history is that the modern history section ends at 1900, which is defined as the beginning of "contemporary history," whereas most Western texts do not separate the twentieth century from the rest of "modern history" beginning at 1500.

Before the 1990s China's world history texts usually started their "contemporary history" volume/section with the 1917 Russian Revolution, which, according to the Soviet interpretation, ushered in a new historical era in which capitalism was in decline and on its way to eventual demise, while socialism was beginning its march toward victory on the world stage. Since the history of the late twentieth century more or less belied this prophecy, the new text instead describes the twentieth century as the beginning of a "long-term coexistence, competition, and mutual influence between capitalism and socialism." The most important developments of this century were "the establishment of the socialist system, the collapse of colonialism, as well as rapid

---

39   In this and other newly published world history texts, "ancient history" (or *gudaishi* in Chinese) operates more like "traditional times" than "ancient history" in the West since it also includes the entire medieval period.

40   Wu and Qi, *Shijie shi*, vol. 3, p. 1. For more recent and different interpretations of the "origins of the modern world," see Wong, *China Transformed*; Frank, *ReORIENT*; Pomeranz, *Great Divergence*; Marks, *Origins*; and Hobson, *Eastern Origins*.

progress in science-technology and massive growth of the economy."[41]
While the transition from capitalism to socialism was held in abey-
ance, the transition to world history was completed. In the authors'
words: "Only during the twentieth century was world history in a complete sense finally shaped." That is because, although "world history" as
Wu Yujin defined it had already begun to form during the "modern"
period, not until the twentieth century were all the parts of the world
closely bound together in all respects. In this sense, the authors argued,
"contemporary history is world history" in its entirety.[42] In other words,
the history of the twentieth century was nothing but world history, and
world history in its full form exists only since the beginning of the
twentieth century.

Evidently the authors of the 1994 text sought to reconstruct world
history based on a blending of historical materialism, including the
Marxist stages of social change, and contemporary Western "bourgeois" world/global history theories. In many chapters the new text
took a broad view and a comparative approach to illustrate long-term
and transregional trends of development and to explain their historical
significance. The authors took pains to absorb the most recent scholarship by both Chinese and non-Chinese historians, making revisions
wherever they were deemed necessary and appropriate, and giving
consideration to all major aspects of history, in order to present a
richer and more balanced picture of the world's past.

Because of the continuing influence of the theoretical models of
Marx and Weber, however, the 1994 text arguably overemphasized material "productive forces" as the sole determinant in history. As Liu
Xincheng commented, it seems that the authors "stressed only economic integration, and saw the progress in productive technology as
the only driving force [of history]; and they paid less attention to the
coexistence of different cultural systems as well as the relations, exchanges, and clashes among them and the impacts of all these [activi-
ties] on the longitudinal and horizontal developments in world
[history]."[43] The "new" world history, in short, retained some of the
economic determinism of the old.

---

41   Wu and Qi, *Shijie shi*, vol. 3, p. 5.
42   Ibid., p. 1.
43   Liu, "Woguo 'shijie,' " p. 20.

Eurocentrism: An Insurmountable Wall?

Perhaps the most serious problem of the 1994 text continued to be, ironically, the very Eurocentrism that characterized pre-1980s historiography and that the authors sought to eschew in their new approach. In fact, especially in its modern history section, the 1994 text was in some ways even more Eurocentric than its 1962 predecessor. For example, in the 1972 revised edition of the 1962 text, the two volumes of the modern section (1640–1918) together had 274 pages (31 percent of a total of 890 pages) devoted to Asia, Africa, and Latin America. The rest (69 percent) was about European and North American experiences. In comparison, the two volumes of the modern history section (1500–1900) of the 1994 text have only 183 (21 percent of the total of 910 pages) focused on Asia, Africa, and Latin America. The rest (79 percent) was about Europe and North America. Volume I of the modern history section spent fifty pages describing British history from 1640 to 1742, and it devoted only forty-three pages to the entire history of China, Japan, India, and Turkey in the sixteenth and seventeenth centuries. Volume II provided a detailed discussion (eighteen pages) of the American Civil War (1860–1864), but only a brief description (two and a half pages) of the Taiping Uprising in China (1851–1864), which was the largest and longest civil war of the nineteenth-century world. Obviously the reconstructed text followed the same old way of compiling world history—Europe as the center and others as peripheries—and went even further to emphasize Europe's key role. While the authors argued that "modern world history was mainly the history of the rise, development, and worldwide expansion of Western capitalism,"[44] they did not even try to explain exactly how this Western focus differed from the old-fashioned Eurocentrism they consistently denounced.

One explanation for the endurance of Eurocentrism among Chinese historians of the world can be found in the theory prevalent among them regarding the main theme and general direction of modern world history (1500–1900). The theory includes three interconnected and mutually reinforcing aspects. First, influenced by Wu Yujin, China's world historians focused more and more on the pro-

---

44 Wu and Qi, *Shijie shi*, vol. 3, p. 3.

cess by which various scattered and relatively isolated parts of the world were increasingly interrelated, interactive, and integrated. To a large extent they have seen this accelerating course of *history* becoming *world history* (or the process of globalization)—impelled primarily by the European maritime "exploration" of the world around 1500—as the chief attribute of the modern world. Second, many Chinese world historians believe that modern world history has been mainly the history of "capitalism," including its origins and growth in Europe and its expansion to and conquest of the rest of the world. They have continued to insist that the capitalist era commenced in the sixteenth century, as Marx said. Since then, the new economic system drew new blood from the increase of global trade facilitated by European contacts with other parts of the world. It set in motion the commercial revolution and the industrial revolution, which in turn led to the worldwide spread of capitalism and the establishment of the capitalist world market. This was the primary component of the globalization process and the main theme of modern world history.[45] Third, in the course of the "modernization fervor" that has overwhelmed Chinese society since the 1980s, various studies of past experiences and present theories, both Chinese and Western, have swayed many fields of social science in China including history. For world historians, "modernization" refers to the same process of *history* becoming *world history*. Guided by this modernization discourse, some historians took it as their priority to demonstrate how Europe gave birth to the economic, political, and cultural archetypes of modernization and how modernity, with minor alterations, has diffused to other regions of the world.[46] Professor Qian Chengdan, a leading scholar of modern history, proposed recently to restructure the entire "modern" and "contemporary" history of the world along the line of modernization.[47]

---

45 Ibid. Also see Ma, *Shijie shigang*, vol. 1, pp. 21–22; and Qi, *Shijie tongshi*, vol. 2, p. 2. Some historians disagree with the idea that modern history began around 1500 and have remained faithful to the pre-1980s periodization. But they still believe that "modern" history started with the English revolution of 1640 and ended in 1918. They tend to assert even more strongly that modern world history has been the history of the capitalist era. See Pan and Lin, *Shijie jindaishi*.

46 See, for example, Wang, *Shijie tongshi*, pp. 3–4.

47 Qian, "Yi xiandaihua."

In this grand narrative of modernization, the "modern history sections" of many recently published texts of world history describe European, and especially Western European, nations as advanced, progressive, open-minded, innovative, and eager for change, whereas Asian and African countries are depicted as backward, stagnant, isolated, conservative, and antireform. For example, the 1994 text stated that Europe in the sixteenth century witnessed the "dawn of capitalism," while, at the same time, China and Japan "remained feudal societies and came to a standstill." During the seventeenth and first half of the eighteenth centuries, while Western Europe "was making big strides forwards toward capitalism," Eastern countries largely fell into "stagnation and decline."[48] What has transpired in China's world history field in the last twenty-five years seems consistent with André Gunder Frank's observation: "Eurocentrism marks and limits even the severest critics of received Eurocentric social theory." Frank adds: some historians still "only look under the European street light, whose illumination is ever dimmer as they work from Europe outward to examine its 'expansion' as it 'incorporated' the rest of the world."[49]

In short, this dominant discourse, which equates modernization with one-way expansion and diffusion of European capitalism to the rest of the world and which regards the process as an advanced stage of historical evolution, has made Eurocentrism into a wall that many of

---

48 Wu and Qi, *Shijie shi,* vol. 3, pp. 1, 94, 109, 230.
49 Frank, *ReORIENT, pp.* 46, 48. Perhaps Chinese historians' ambivalent feeling toward Marx and Marxism also contributed to the persistence of Eurocentrism. On the one hand, people knew very well that many of Marx's ideas were rather Eurocentric, such as his theory of "Asiatic mode of production" with its judgments of Asia as being "the cruelest form of state, Oriental despotism" and of the Asian economy as being "traditional, backward, and stagnant" until the incursion of Western capitalism woke it out of its otherwise eternal slumber (cited from ibid., pp. 14–15). But when they listed representatives of Eurocentrism such as Hegel, Ranke, and Weber, they were usually careful not to mention Marx. Indeed, the acknowledged unacceptability of the Eurocentrism of Marx's "Asiatic mode of production" seems actually to have obscured in their eyes the Eurocentrism of his five-stage theory of history. Either out of the need to be politically correct or because of true belief, so far few Chinese historians have openly acknowledged in print the historical limitations of Karl Marx and the theoretical problems of Marxism. Moreover, in their effort to demonstrate modernization/globalization as inevitable and progressive, they could not help being inspired by Marx, who claimed to give this process a "scientific" formation.

China's world historians have found difficult to scale or skirt let alone dismantle.

Chinese History and the "ReORIENTation" of Chinese Historians

In addition to the seemingly insurmountable wall of Eurocentrism, Chinese historians have encountered another major challenge in their collective effort to reconstruct world history from a global perspective: how to incorporate Chinese experiences in the narrative of the world's past.

At the institutional level, for decades before and after the Cultural Revolution, history departments at universities and colleges have been divided into two mutually exclusive academic sectors: Chinese history and world history. While undergraduates take courses in both fields, graduate students and faculty normally specialize in one field or the other.[50] Due to this sharp distinction between fields, Chinese history texts and teachers have paid attention to parts of the world outside China only insofar as they are intimately related to China. World history texts and teachers focus on the rest of the world and leave Chinese history to the historians of China to teach. For example, the 1962 multivolume world history text, which was widely used for decades, excluded all of Chinese history except for some of China's most obvious economic and cultural relations with other countries (e.g., the silk trade, the Jesuit missions). Even in the past twenty-five years, despite many world historians' enthusiastic embrace of the global perspective and great efforts to portray the experience of the whole world, some world history texts have continued to exclude Chinese history from the narrative.[51] As a result of this rigid institutional and curricular divide, with few exceptions Chinese historical studies have

---

50 Historians in a field of non-Chinese history may be trained as specialists in British history, Russian history, Latin American history, etc., but they are all referred to as "world historians" even though some never teach a world history survey. Perhaps that was one of the reasons why Wu Yujin repeatedly stressed the special feature of "world history" as more than a collection of various countries' histories. Perhaps his point was that not everyone who studies non-Chinese history is qualified to be a world historian. Rather, only those who study the process of history becoming world history can call themselves "world historians."

51 See, for example, Qi, *Shijie tongshi jiaocheng*; and Wang, *Shijie tongshi*.

for long been divorced from their larger regional and global contexts,[52] and "world" histories have been little more than the combined records of foreign (especially Western) polities.

It has recently become common sense that any work of "world history" will not be complete without including the Chinese experience, but incorporating Chinese history into world history texts has proven to be a complicated and difficult task in China. China's world historians believe that the responsibility for writing world history rests on their shoulders and on theirs alone, but many of them do not have the training necessary to include the Chinese record in their purview. Under the circumstances they will need to retool to bring themselves up to speed in Chinese history or they will have to reach out and cooperate with specialists in Chinese history. Although the authors of the 1994 world history text tried to incorporate the Chinese experience in their account, they were not, I think, very successful. They contented themselves with some brief entries about China in various chapters, and did not take Chinese views and actions as important elements in the main process of *history* becoming *world history* that they described and analyzed. For example, the Boxer Movement and Boxer Protocol, which occurred at an important historical moment and had significant impacts on both Chinese and world history, were only briefly mentioned as the product of imperialist invasion and were never explored in their broader historical and international contexts.[53] Overall in the modern history section (1500–1900) of the 1994 text, China occupied only

---

52 In recent years some Chinese historians have tried to examine their research subjects against the world history background, and they have achieved exciting results. Perhaps the best example is Professor Fan Shuzhi's *Wanming Shi*. In this two-volume comprehensive study of the last seventy-one years of the Ming dynasty, he applies a global perspective to evaluate the historical changes that took place in Chinese society, including the growth of the commercial economy in Southeast China, the flourishing of overseas trade from the coastal areas, and the coming of the Jesuits. He provides a much more complex picture of how the global developments in the sixteenth and early seventeenth centuries profoundly influenced Chinese economy and society, and how the Ming dynasty, although the center of the world economy, went step by step to its doom in the global context. See also Shen, *Ming Qing zhiji,* on the same period.

53 We may contrast here the development of Boxer studies in the United States in recent years that emphasize the movement's world historical importance. See Esherick, *Ori-*

about 4 percent of the book, whereas the pages given to European history constituted 58 percent. This imbalance is even greater than that in L. S. Stavrianos's *The World Since 1500: A Global History,* which devotes 44 percent of the pages to Europe and 6 percent to Chinese history.

At a deeper, conceptual level, in the modern history section, Chinese history of the sixteenth to eighteenth centuries was tailored to fit the larger interpretive framework of "Europe advanced and China (Asia) declined" in supporting the grand narrative of capitalist modernization. The authors argued that, from the beginning of the sixteenth century to the mid–eighteenth century, Europe prevailed over Asia in the struggle for social evolution. They offered four important reasons for the European advantage: European geographical "discovery" led to large overseas colonies, which financed their capitalist economy; the Renaissance provided the newly emerging bourgeois class with new values and meanings of life; the Reformation liberated people's economic spirit from Catholic and feudalistic restrictions; and state power and new political institutions in Europe protected and promoted the new capitalist economy (e.g., mercantilism). Then, why did the East "fall behind"? The authors gave four main reasons: the strengthening of feudalistic centralized rule (*fengjian zhuanzhi*); the centuries-long belief and practice of valuing agriculture over commerce; the state policy of isolation from the outside world; and the stifling effect of "traditional" (*chuantong*) culture and ideology.[54]

This line of reasoning touches upon an essential issue: how to weigh the positions and advantages (especially economic) of major (especially Eurasian) countries or regions in the world between 1500 and 1800. In recent years, the conventional view on this issue endorsed by the modernization discourse in general and the authors of the 1994 text in particular has undergone serious challenge from a group of Western historians, including R. Bin Wong, André Gunder Frank, James Lee, and Kenneth Pomeranz.[55]

---

gins; Cohen, *History*; Liu, *Tokens*; Hevia, *English*; Liu, *Clash*; Bickers and Tiedemann, *Boxers*.

54 Wu and Qi, *Shijie shi,* vol. 3, pp. 279–81.

55 The Chinese translations of Wong's *China Transformed,* Frank's *ReORIENT,* Lee and Wang's *One Quarter,* and Pomeranz's *Great Divergence* were published in 1998, 2000,

It would not be an exaggeration to say that Frank's book calling for a major reinterpretation of world history from 1500 to 1800 (and to a lesser extent Pomeranz's as well) sent a "shock wave" through the Chinese historical profession. But it is interesting that, although the translator of Frank's book was a world historian, most Chinese scholars who have been involved in the "ReORIENT sensation" have been specialists in Chinese history.[56] This might suggest that it has been easier for Chinese historians of China than for Chinese historians of the world to take Frank's call for a more Asian- (if not Chinese-) centered history seriously. It is also important that, similar to what has happened in the Western academic world, the ideas and approaches of Frank and Pomeranz were not only widely noted but also vigorously debated as soon as they became widely accessible.[57]

Many were impressed and excited by the anti-Eurocentric stance of Frank and Pomeranz, by their comparison of China and Europe in the larger context of the global economy, and by their conclusion that, during the early modern period, China's economy was not stagnant but continued to grow. Frank believed that, between 1500 and 1800, the center of the world economy and international trade was not Europe, but Asia; Europe's role in the existing "global system" was rather marginal; and, without trade with the Asian economies, the rise of Europe would not have occurred. Professor Liu Beicheng, translator of Frank's *ReORIENT*, argued that, reading the book, people should face up to two facts of world history between the fifteenth and eighteenth centuries: that Asia included the biggest economies in the world; and that Asia played a crucial role in the rise of Europe. Given these two facts, he wrote, people cannot continue to see Asia, including China, as static and irrelevant to early modern world history, and they must question the conventional wisdom about the dynamic forces in the

for both Frank's and Lee/Wang's), and 2003, respectively. Other works in this group that have been translated into Chinese include Marks, *Origins (2006)*; and Hobson, *Eastern Origins* (being translated into Chinese). Also see Goldstone, "Neither Late," and Goody, *Theft*.

56 The translators of Wong's and Pomeranz's books are all specialists in Chinese economic history.

57 One online reviewer mentioned forty-five essays on Frank's *ReORIENT* written by thirty-six authors and twenty-one essays on Pomeranz's *Great Divergence* written by fifteen authors. See He, *"Baiyin ziben," "Da fenliu."*

early modern world.[58] More importantly, as Liu He (Lydia Liu) wrote, Frank provided people with a global perspective to question all the existing knowledge and conclusions about modernity. From this global perspective, when examining the historical causes for Europe's "advancing" and Asia's "falling behind," researchers should not concentrate only on "internal" factors; they should also look for answers in the positions of Asia and Europe in the world economic system and in the changes in those positions.[59] Along the same line, another Chinese scholar disputed the conventional view that it was Europeans who created the modern world:

> Only in a very limited sense does the judgment that modern capitalist civilization was created by Westerners hold water. A more accurate expression would be that this form of civilization happened to first emerge in the West. From a grand global perspective and in a broader, deeper sense, modern capitalism was brought about by various civilizations together.[60]

In the eyes of many Chinese scholars, Pomeranz's *The Great Divergence* similarly deconstructed the dominant discourse of Eurocentrism about the early modern world. Based mainly on a detailed comparison of England and China's Yangzi delta, he argued that Europe was not more "advanced" than China during the seventeenth century; in fact, the two ends of the Eurasian continent were similar in many aspects of socioeconomic development up to the end of the eighteenth century. The "great divergence" between China and Europe began at the beginning of the nineteenth century, and the reason for the economic "take-off" of Europe was not any internal social or cultural advantage, but the exploitation of American colonies and the easy access to coal in England. Pomeranz and R. Bin Wong not only evaluate Chinese history in the light of European experiences but also appraise what happened (or did not happen) in Europe in the light

---

58 Liu, "Chonggou shijie." For comments on Frank's book, see also Chen, "Chonggou quanqiu"; Zhou, "Fulanke sixiang"; He, "Zhouqi lilun"; Jiang, "*Baiyin ziben*"; and Wei, "*Baiyin ziben.*"

59 Liu, "Ouzhou ludeng."

60 Ruan, *Wenming de biaoxian*, p. 28.

of Chinese experiences. Rejecting the conventional question of "why China did not become England," which implies that the English model of development was "standard" and "universal" and China simply "strayed from the right path," Pomeranz reversed the question and asked: Why did England not become China?[61] Many scholars seized upon this new perspective to tear down the wall of Eurocentrism and reconstruct their understanding of the early modern world.[62]

While being inspired by the new approach, some Chinese historians frowned on Frank's and Pomeranz's research methods and some of their arguments. They pointed out the paucity of primary sources in both of their works. Some thought that Frank's study was not persuasive because of an allegedly wide gap between his intended goal and his evidence.[63] Others believed that Frank overestimated the level of economic development in pre–nineteenth-century China.[64] Still others questioned if Frank, because of his anti-Eurocentrism agenda, improperly ignored local factors such as culture and their impact on the historical development of local areas.[65] Professor Qin Hui focused criticism on what he took to be a major logical and historical problem in Frank's work—using a trade surplus to prove the economic advance of a country. He also argued that Frank fell into an impasse due to his "unprogressive view of history." Frank sought to uncover universal values and achievements transcending the East and West, but he also wanted to explain why the East and West had different fates, and his explanations always evaded cultural and sociopolitical explanations.[66] Indeed, to many Chinese historians, lacking an analysis of the roles of political and cultural institutions in economic development was a major flaw of the Frank-Pomeranz approach. For example, Professor

---

61 The Chinese scholar Li Bozhong also argues that, even in Europe, the case of Britain's modernization was unique and therefore should not be regarded as a universal model. See Li, "Yingguo moshi."

62 For comments on Pomeranz's *Great Divergence*, see, among others, Shi, "Chongxin shenshi"; Wu, "Da fenliu"; Zhang, "Peng Mulan"; Zhong, "Da fenliu"; and Zhou, "Zhongguo he Ouzhou." Here, again, specialists in Chinese history were more involved in the debates than specialists in world history.

63 Wang, "Ludeng, Yujing."

64 See, for example, Li, "'Xianjin' yangai."

65 He Weibao, "Zhouqi lilun."

66 Qin, "Shui, mianxiang."

Wang Jiafan argued that the most problematic part of Pomeranz's methodology was that it totally ignored the sociopolitical system as an important factor in—and indispensable context of—any economy.[67]

In addition to pointing out such technical and methodological problems, some scholars voiced serious concerns about the likely political and ideological consequences of Frank's and Pomeranz's theory. Frank and Pomeranz reiterated common knowledge that China had a great, mature economy before the rise of the West, but neither of them offered any convincing answer to the pointed question of why China fell behind and suffered at the hands of the West in the nineteenth century. Moreover, their ideas somehow led people to reminisce about and even embellish China's past glory while at the same time ignoring problems that were deeply embedded in the Chinese system. For this reason, Wang Jiafan disagreed with some of his Chinese colleagues who were too eager to use Frank and Pomeranz as new weapons to challenge the accepted image of China's past. Wang believed that such Chinese scholars were intoxicated with an exaggerated and misleading sense of China's glorious past. As a result, they ignored the keenly felt pain inflicted on the Chinese people by the political corruption and social polarization that were deeply rooted in their national history. They therefore consciously or unconsciously risked downplaying the need to change the "traditional" sociopolitical system.[68]

Some scholars sensed so intensely the "subversive effect" of Frank's work on the common understanding of nineteenth- and twentieth-century Chinese history that they bluntly rejected his entire thesis. For example, Xu Youyu, a leading liberal scholar, stated:

If the theory of *ReORIENT* is tenable, then [the efforts of] several generations of Chinese since Yan Fu and especially the New Cultural Movement of the May Fourth time to learn from and draw on Western experiences, and to reflect upon and criticize the outdated elements in their own tradition, have all been futile and wrong. People like Chen Duxiu, Li Dazhao, Lu Xun, and Hu Shi were all wrong in appraising and promoting "Mr. Democracy" and "Mr. Science," [be-

---

67 Wang, "'Xixue dongjian.'"
68 Ibid.

cause] all of them were just fooled and victimized by the fallacy of Eurocentrism.[69]

While this conclusion seems exaggerated, it points out the potential stakes in the debate over the origins of the generally acknowledged "great divergence" between Asia and Europe in the nineteenth century.[70] Wang Jiafan looked at this controversy from a psychological perspective. He repeatedly reminded people that "historians' states of mind" inevitably influence their studies. He argued that Frank, Pomeranz, and others

> in their researches displayed a state of mind totally different from that of Chinese historians. They tried their best to look for each and every bright development in pre-nineteenth century Chinese history and to ignore the dark side, because only in this way can the light of Eurocentrism that they oppose be dimmed. But they are unable to understand how the Chinese people suffered from hardships during the transformation to modernity at the turn of the nineteenth to twentieth centuries, and this [Chinese] state of mind did not come from conceptions, but from real life experiences. They therefore are unable to understand why we look at the pre-nineteenth century history painfully and regretfully and are determined to get to the bottom of it, questioning what went wrong in the existing mechanism of social development and what the root cause was. [The difference between the two mindsets] may be called "the well-fed doesn't know how the starving suffers." This is one situation and that was another.[71]

Again, this criticism may be hyperbolic and emotional, but it underscores our need to take seriously Chinese perspectives in the present as well as in the past, especially among those of us who presume

---

69 Xu, "Zhiyi *Baiyin*."
70 For a work doubting the extent of such a divergence in the Chinese cultural domain, see Elman, *On Their Own*. For the problem of analyzing history in terms of continents, see Lewis and Wigen, *Myth*.
71 Wang, "*Da fencha*."

to offer a non-Eurocentric view from our still somewhat privileged purchases here in the "West."

In my own view, as an ethnic Chinese living and working in the United States, both the fulsome Chinese praise for and harsh Chinese criticism of Frank and Pomeranz have stemmed largely from the same nationalistic stance. Advocates of the new approach have often been animated by a desire to acknowledge and take pride in China's arguably belated assumption of its "rightful place" in modern world history and historiography, whereas critics have frequently felt that the new scholarship (from the West!) might lure contemporary Chinese into complacency in the quest to regain China's standing in the world. In a 2004 essay to celebrate the fortieth anniversary of the World History Institute of the Chinese Academy of Social Sciences, Yu Pei, director of the institute, stated that from its very beginning, China's world history field has manifested a strong national spirit, the core and quintessence of which is patriotism. Although today's China is very different from that of the mid–nineteenth century, Yu concluded, patriotism remains the "soul" of China's world history studies.[72]

By acclaiming the national spirit upheld by historians of the world, Professor Yu (and others) may be defending them from latent or potential charges of excessive cosmopolitanism or even Eurocentrism. But Yu and others have typically failed to specify how their patriotic "soul" should guide their historical research and whether it means that they should always observe world history from a Sinocentric perspective. Moreover, these champions of patriotism seem to have overlooked the potential contradiction between the nationalistic spirit and the truly global perspective that they have also earnestly endorsed. Indeed, no matter how much Chinese historians want to employ a truly global perspective, as long as they continue to envision what happened in the world's past in the light of either their Eurocentric or Sinocentric worldview, they will not be able to approach the more genuinely "objective" perspective that Stavrianos described and that they have also highly extolled. Is nationalism really compatible with "the viewpoint of an observer perched on the moon, surveying our planet as a whole, rather than that of someone who is ensconced in London or Paris, Peking or Delhi"?[73]

72   Yu, "Hongyang zhongguo."
73   Stavrianos, *World to 1500*, p. 3. In another essay, Yu Pei highly commended this global perspective (see Yu, "Quanqiuhua," p. 6). Wu Yujin also highlighted the need for world

In some ways the recent debate over Frank/Pomeranz in China signified an ambivalent state of mind among Chinese when defining their own country's place in the world after 1500. On the one hand, many are more than ready to accept the main conclusion of recent scholarship from the West that Asia in general and China in particular were the center of world history long before Europe was able to seize that position, and China continued to be the leader of the world economy as late as the mid–eighteenth century. On the other hand, they also feel the need to explain why and how such a rich and powerful country failed to become "modernized" and, as a result, fell victim to the "modern" West in the mid–nineteenth century. The dilemma in conceptualizing China's historical place comes from mixed feelings of pride and shame in their nation's past as well as impatience for China to regain her lost glory. This self-imposed tension has sometimes made it more difficult for historians to reveal the full picture of the "rise of the West" and the "decline of China" from a global perspective. In the same way, underneath the seemingly unsolvable Eurocentrism in China's modern world discourse with its focus on the successful experiences of the West and the systemic defects of China that allegedly held the country back, one can still see a "Sinocentric" mindset determined to find out "what went wrong" and "how to catch up" through studying history.[74]

Conclusions

As Ralph Croizier noted in his pioneering 1990 essay, "World history in China faces some of the same challenges as in America: how to make sense out of the larger historical patterns that have shaped our interconnected modern world, and how to relate one's own national identity to those patterns."[75] But Chinese historians have had some ad-

---

historians to "transcend national narrow-mindedness" (Wu, *Wu Yujin,* p. 42). For a recent reaffirmation of the value of such a celestial view of the globe, see Fernandez-Armesto, *World,* passim.

74 This utilitarian approach to world history studies that intends to serve China's modernization cause is clearly demonstrated in the following books: Hao et al., *ZhongXi;* Chen et al., *Shiwu shiji;* and Qi, *Shiwu shiji.* The first book attempts to explore the systemic factors that brought about the "rise of the West" and the "decline of China," and the last two focus on the historical experiences of major world powers since the fifteenth century.

75 Croizier, "World History," p. 151.

ditional challenges of their own, particularly the struggle to construct a world history that would show, from the perspective of historical materialism, the rules that underlie the development of the world. In the 1950s through the 1970s, the world history texts they compiled were heavily Eurocentric, rigidly following the Marxian five-stage model of social evolution and virtually excluding the history of their own polity. Since the late 1970s, led by Professor Wu Yujin, Chinese historians have made great efforts to reconstruct world history with Chinese characteristics, an important part of which is to insert Chinese experiences into the global record. During the 1980s they learned more about recent developments in the field of world history in the West, and they took seriously the theories and approaches of their Western colleagues. As of 1990, to cite Croizier again, "The Marxist theoretical framework was still there but less obtrusive."[76]

Since 1990, China's world historians have continued to strive to interpret world history in a new framework. They have combined the revised Marxist theory of societal stages with the contemporary Western global history perspective emphasizing the process by which the history of disparate human groups became a history of an integrated world. The multivolume text published in 1994, together with other similar works, showed both the advantages and the limitations of this new model. While those studies broadened the scope of world history to include more of Chinese history and changed the periodization of world history, they continued to regard Europe as the main origin of—and principal player in—the modern world system of capitalism. To that extent they arguably remained Eurocentric.[77] More recently, Western assaults on Eurocentrism in the study of world history have became known in China and have confirmed Chinese efforts to write a less Eurocentric world history. But some positive as well as negative Chinese appraisals of this recent Western (mainly American) scholarship seem to be driven more by nationalism than by cosmopolitanism,

---

76 Ibid., pp. 163–64.

77 A paragraph associating this residual Eurocentricity with the continuing power of the Marxist paradigm was cut by the journal editor from my recent essay (Xu, "Ping jin-nianlai") before publication.

by a patriotic effort to celebrate or criticize Chinese history more than by any strong desire to see world history from a global perspective. In this context, in my view, a lingering Eurocentrism might be the price we have to pay to avoid a resurgent Sinocentrism that would be no less harmful to the project of writing an "objective" world history.

Another possibility, suggested by some other essays in this volume, might be to transcend the remaining walls between Chinese and world history and between the ancient past and the modern present that figure in both Marxian materialism and Weberian modernization by taking several steps toward a theory more consistent with what we know about both Chinese and world history. The first step would be to acknowledge that there have been centers in both Chinese and world history but that they have shifted in space over time. Thus we could recognize that China may have played a central role in world history from, say, the Tang through the Ming or high Qing (thus the refrain of "China's glorious past"), but China yielded that role to Europe by 1800 just as Europe (and Asia) were forced to relinquish the status to North America by 1945. The second step would be to hypothesize that there are different ways of being "central" in the world (as in any part of it!). These ways constitute various cultures or civilizations that have all made significant contributions to world history over time and space (e.g., East Africa was the chief—if not sole—center that produced humanity; the Middle East and Mediterranean were the centers that initiated "powerful"—if not "higher"—civilizations). The third step would be to entertain the possibility that each of these successive "central" world regions has made contributions that will prove to be of equal significance in the emerging global civilization of the twenty-first century. In other words, as we face the future, all periods and places of human history will be equal in the eyes of heaven/nature. Or as the 2008 Olympic slogan had it: One World, One Dream.

Acknowledgment

The author is most grateful to Roger Des Forges, Donald Wright, and Michael Lazich for their valuable comments and suggestions on earlier versions of this article.

Works Cited

Abu-Lughod, Janet. *Before European Hegemony: The World System A.D. 1250–1350*. New York: Oxford University Press, 1989.

An, Changchun. "Cong shijieshiguan kan woguo shijieshi xueke jianshe" [The construction of the world history field in our country in light of the concept of world history], *Wuhan daxue xuebao* [Journal of Wuhan University], 4(1993), pp. 13–18.

Barraclough, Geoffrey. *History in a Changing World*. Oxford: Blackwell, 1955.

———. *An Introduction to Contemporary History*. New York: Basic Books, 1964.

———. *Main Trends in History*. New York : Holmes & Meier, 1978.

———, ed. *Times Atlas of World History*. Maplewood, N.J.: Hammond, 1989.

Bentley, Jerry H. *Shapes of World History in Twentieth-Century Scholarship*. Washington, DC, 1996.

———. and Herbert F. Ziegler. *Traditions and Encounters: A Global Perspective on the Past*. McGraw Hill, 2000.

Bickers, Robert, and R. G. Tiedemann. *The Boxers, China, and the World*. Lanham, Md.: Rowman and Littlefield, 2007.

Braudel, Fernand. *Civilization and Capitalism 15th–18th Century* (3 vols.). New York: Harper & Row, 1982–1984.

Chang, Hao. *Liang Ch'i-ch'ao and Intellectual Transition in China, 1890–1907*. Cambridge, Mass.: Harvard University Press, 1971.

Chen, Xiaolu, et al. *Shiwu shiji yilai shijie zhuyao fada guojia fazhan licheng* [The course of development of the major developed countries in the world since the 15th century]. Chongqing: Chongqing chubanshe, 2004.

Chen, Yangu. "Chonggou quanqiu zhuyi de shijie tujing" [The prospect of reconstructing the world of globalism]. Pp. 1–11 in *ReORIENT* (Chinese edition, *Baiyin ziben*). Beijing: Zhongyang bianyi chubanshe, 2000.

Cohen, Paul A. *History in Three Keys: The Boxer Rebellion as Event, Experience, and Myth*. New York: Columbia University Press, 1997.

Costello, Paul. *World Historians and Their Goals: Twentieth-Century Answers to Modernism*. DeKalb, Ill.: Northern Illinois University Press, 1993.

Croizier, Ralph. "World History in the People's Republic of China," *Journal of World History*, 1(No. 2, 1990), pp. 151–69.

Dirlik, Arif. *Revolution and History: Origins of Marxist Historiography in China, 1919–1937*. Berkeley: University of California Press, 1978.

Drake, Fred W. *China Charts the World: Hsu Chi-yu and His Geography Of 1848*. Cambridge, Mass.: Harvard University Press for East Asian Research Center, 1975.

Duara, Prasenjit. *Rescuing History from the Nation: Questioning Narratives of Modern China*. Chicago: Chicago University Press, 1996.

Fan, Shuzhi. *WanMing shi* [A history of the Late Ming]. Shanghai: Fudan daxue chubanshe, 2003.

Elman, Benjamin. *On Their Own Terms: Science in China, 1550–1900*. Cambridge, Mass.: Harvard University Press, 2006.

Esherick, Joseph. *The Origins of the Boxer Uprising*. Berkeley: University of California Press, 1987.

Fernandez-Armesto, Felipe. *The World: A History*. Upper Saddle River, N.J.: Pearson, Prentice-Hall, 2007.

Feuerwerker, Albert. "Chinese History in Marxian Dress," *American Historical Review*, 66(2,1961), pp. 323–53.

———, ed. *History in Communist China*. Cambridge, Mass.: MIT Press, 1968.

Fletcher, Joseph. "Integrative History: Parallels and Interconnections in the Sixteenth and Seventeenth Centuries," *Journal of Turkish Studies*, 9 (1,1985), pp. 37–58.

Frank, Andre Gunder. *ReORIENT: Global Economy in the Asian Age*. Berkeley: University of California Press, 1998.

———, and Barry K. Gills, eds. *The World System: Five Hundred Years or Five Thousand?* New York: Routledge, 1993.

Geyer, Michael, and Charles Bright. "World History in a Global Age," *American Historical Review*, 100(4,October 1995), p. 1034–60.

Goody, Jack. *The Theft of History*. Cambridge: Cambridge University Press, 2006.

Goldstone, Jack. "Neither Late Imperial Nor Early Modern: Efflorescences and the Qing Formation in World History." Pp. 242–302 in *The Qing Formation in World-Historical Time*, Lynn A. Struve, ed. Cambridge, Mass.: Harvard University Asia Center, Harvard University Press, 2004.

Guo, Fang. "Ping Maikenier de *Xifang de xingqi*" [A review of McNeill's *The Rise of the West*], *Shixue lilun yanjiu* [Studies in Historical Theory], 2(2000), p. 95–102.

Hao, Xiajun, et al., eds. *Zhong Xi 500 nian bijiao* [A comparison between China and the West over 500 years]. Beijing: Zhongguo gongren chubanshe, 1996.

He, Aiguo. "*Baiyin ziben* yanjiu zongshu" [A summary of comments on silver capitalism (*ReORIENT*)], online essay on *Shiji zhongguo* [Century China, www.cc.org.cn], January 20, 2005.

———. "*Da fenliu* yanjiu zongshu" [A summary of comments on *The Great Divergence*], online essay on *Shiji zhongguo* [Century China, www.cc.org.cn], May 17, 2005.

He, Weibao. "Zhouqi lilun yu changshiduan" [Cyclical theory and the long Durée], *Shixueshi yanjiu* [Studies in Historiography], 3(2003).

Hevia, James L. *English Lessons: The Pedagogy of Imperialism in Nineteenth-Century China*. Durham, N.C.: Duke University Press, 2003.

Hobson, John M. *The Eastern Origins of Western Civilization*. Cambridge: Cambridge University Press, 2004.

Huang, Philip. *Liang Ch'i-ch'ao and Modern Chinese Liberalism*. Seattle: University of Washington Press, 1972.

Huang, Ping, and Cui Zhiyuan, eds. *Zhongguo yu quanqiuhua: Huashengdun gongzhi haishi Beijing gongzhi* [China and globalization: The Washington consensus, the Beijing consensus, or what?]. Beijing: Shuihui kexue wenxian chubanshe, 2005.

Huters, Theodore. *Bringing the World Home: Appropriating the West in Late Qing and Early Republican China*. Honolulu: University of Hawaii Press, 2005.

Jiang, Hua. "*Baiyin ziben*: zhongshi jingji quanqiuhua zhong de dongfang" [Silver capitalism (*ReORIENT*): Taking the East seriously in economic globalization], *Guowai shehui kexue* [Social Sciences Outside China], 3(2001).

Karl, Rebecca. *Staging the World: Chinese Nationalism at the Turn of the Twentieth Century*. Durham, N.C.: Duke University Press, 2002.

Lee, James Z., and Feng Wang. *One Quarter of Humanity: Malthusian Mythology and Chinese Realities*. Cambridge, Mass.: Harvard University Press, 1999.

Leonard, Jane Kate. *Wei Yuan and China's Rediscovery of the Maritime World*. Cambridge, Mass.: Harvard University Press, 1984.

Levenson, Joseph. *Liang Ch'i-ch'ao and the Mind of Modern China*. Berkeley: University of California Press, 1959.

Lewis, Martin W., and Kären E. Wigen. *The Myth of Continents: A Critique of Metageography*. Berkeley: University of California Press, 1997.

Li, Bozhong. "Yingguo moshi, Jiangnan daolu yu zibenzhuyi mengya" [British model, Yangzi Delta road, and capitalist sprouts], *Lishi yanjiu* [Historical Research], 1(2001), pp. 116–26.

Li, Genpan. "'Xianjin' yangai xia de luowu" [The falling behind covered by "advance"], online essay on *Zhongguo jingjishi luntan* [China Economic History Forum, http://economy.guoxue.com], January 31, 2003.

Li, Zhinan. "Wusi fengxian, kaituo jinqu: shenqie huainian Wu Yujin laoshi" [Selfless dedication and pioneering effort: Cherishing the memory of Professor Wu Yujin], *Shixue lilun yanjiu* [Studies of Historical Theory], 1(1994), pp. 36–42.

Littrup, Leif. "World History with Chinese Characteristics," *Culture and History*, Vol. 5 (1989), 39–64.

Liu, Beicheng. "Chonggou shijie lishi de tiaozhan" [The challenge of reconstructing world history], *Shixue lilun yanjiu* [Studies of Historical Theories], 4(2000).

Liu, He (Lydia), ed. *Tokens of Exchange: The Problem of Translation in Global Circulations.* Durham, N.C.: Duke University Press, 1999.

———. "Ouzhou ludeng guangcai yiwai de shijie" [The world outside the glow of European streetlight], *Dushu* [Reading], 5(2000).

———. *The Clash of Empires: The Invention of China in Modern World Making.* Cambridge, Mass.: Harvard University Press, 2004.

Liu, Xincheng. "Woguo 'shijie tongshi' bianzuan gongzuo de huigu yu sikao" [Reflections on the compilation of "world history" in our country], in *1995 nian zhongguo lishixue nianjian* [The 1995 yearbook of China's historical studies]. Beijing, 1995.

———, ed. *Lishixue bainian* [A hundred years of historical studies]. Beijing: Beijing Chubanshe, 1999.

Ma, Shili, ed. *Shijie shigang* [The outline of world history], vols. 1–2. Shanghai: Shanghai renmin chubanshe, 1999.

Manning, Patrick. *Navigating World History: Historians Create a Global Past.* New York: Palgrave Macmillan, 2003.

Marks, Robert B. *The Origins of the Modern World.* Lanham: Rowman and Littlefield, 2002.

Martin, Dorothea A. L. "China: Finding a Place for Itself in Modern World History," *History Teacher*, 28(2, Feb. 1995), pp. 152–55.

———. *The Making of a Sino-Marxist World View: Perceptions and Interpretations of World History in the People's Republic of China.* Armonk, N.Y.: M. E. Sharpe, 1990.

Marx, Karl (with Friedrich Engels). *The German Ideology.* Amherst, New York: Prometheus, 1998.

Marx, Karl. *Grundisse: Foundation of the Critique of Political Economy* (Rough Draft), translated with a foreword by Martin Nocolaus. London: Allen Lane, 1973.

Mazlish, Bruce. "Comparing Global History to World History," *Journal of Interdisciplinary History*, 28(Winter 1998).

Mirsky, Jeanette. *The Great Chinese Travelers.* Chicago: University of Chicago Press, 1964.

McNeill, William H. *The Rise of the West: A History of the Human Community.* Chicago: University of Chicago Press, 1963.

Ng, On-cho, and Q. Edward Wang. *Mirroring the Past: The Writing and*

Use of History in Imperial China. Honolulu: University of Hawaii Press, 2005.

Nienhauser, William H. Jr., ed., *The Grand Scribe's Records*, Tsai-fa Cheng, Zongli Lu, William H. Nienhauser, Jr., and Robert Reynolds, trans., vols. I, II, V.1, VII. Bloomington: Indiana University Press, 1994.

Pan, Runhan, and Lin Chengjie. *Shijie jindaishi* [Modern world history]. Beijing daxue chubanshe, 2000.

Pomeranz, Kenneth. *The Great Divergence: China, Europe, and the Making of the Modern World Economy*. Princeton, N.J.: Princeton University Press, 2000.

Qi, Shirong, ed. *Shiwu shiji yilai shijie jiuqiang de lishi yanbian* [The historical evolution of nine world powers since the 15th century]. Guangzhou: Guangdong renmin chubanshe, 2005.

Qi, Sihe. "Luelun kaizhan shijieshi yanjiu gongzuo" [On the development of world history studies], *Guangming ribao* [Guangming Daily], January 17, 1961, p. 2.

Qi, Tao, ed. *Shijie tongshi jiaocheng* [A course in world history], Vols. 1–3. Jinan: Shandong daxue shubanshe, 2001.

Qian, Chengdan. "Yi xiandaihua wei zhuti goujian shijie jinxiandaishi xinde xueke tixi" [Creating a new theoretical structure of modern and contemporary world history around the theme of modernization], *Shijie lishi* [World History], 3(2003), pp. 2–11.

Qin, Hui. "Shui, mianxiang nage dongfang?" [Who, and which east to face?], online essay on *Zhongguo jingjishi luntan* [China Economic History Forum, http://economy.guoxue.com], February 7, 2003.

Ruan, Wei. *Wenming de biaoxian* [Performances of civilizations]. Beijing daxue chubanshe, 2001.

Shen, Dingping. *Mingqing zhiji Zhong Xi wenhua jiaoliu shi* [A history of the cultural interaction between China and the West during the Ming-Qing transition]. Beijing: Shangwu yinshuguan, 2001.

Shi, Jianyun. "Chongxin shenshi Zhong Xi bijiaoshi" [Reassessing the comparative history of China and the West], *Jindaishi yanjiu* [Studies of Modern (Chinese) History], 3(2003).

Sima, Qian. *Shiji* [Historical records], 10 vols. Beijing: Zhonghua shuju, 1959.

Stavrianos, L. S. *The World Since 1500: A Global History*. Englewood, N.J.: Prentice-Hall, 1966.

———. *The World to 1500: A Global History*. Englewood, N.J.: Prentice-Hall, 1970.

Tang, Xiaobing. *Global Space and the Nationalist Discourse of Modernity: The*

Historical Thinking of Liang Qichao. Stanford: Stanford University Press, 1996.

Unger, Jonathan ed. *Using the Past to Serve the Present: Historiography and Politics in Contemporary China.* Armonk, N.Y.: M. E. Sharpe, 1997.

Wallerstein, Immanuel J. *The Modern World System,* 3 Vols. Academic Press, New York, 1974–1988.

Wang, Hui. *China's New Order: Society, Politics, and Economy in Transition.* Theodore Huters, ed. Cambridge, Mass.: Harvard University Press, 2003.

Wang, Jiafan. "*Da fencha* yu Zhongguo lishi chonggu" [*The Great Divergence* and the reevaluation of Chinese history], *Wenhui bao* [Wenhui Newspaper], February 9, 2003.

———. "'Xixue dongjian' haishi 'xixue dongbian': Peng Mulan de *Dafenliu* dapo 'Ouzhou zhongxin zhuyi' lema" [Western learning influenced the East or Western learning was misused in the East?: Did Pomeranz's *The Great Divergence* Break Eurocentrism]? *Wenhui bao* ([Wenhui Newspaper], May 16, 2004, p. 8.

Wang, Q. Edward. "History, Space, and Ethnicity: The Chinese Worldview," *Journal of World History,* 10(2, Fall 1999), pp. 285–305.

———. *Inventing China Through History: The May Fourth Approach to Historiography.* Albany: State University of New York Press, 2001.

———. "Encountering the World: China and Its Other(s) in Historical Narrative, 1949–1989," *Journal of World History,* 14(3, 2003), pp. 327–58.

Wang, Side, ed. *Shijie tongshi* [A comprehensive history of the world]. Shanghai: Huadong shifan daxue chubanshe, 2001, vols. 1–3.

Wang, Zeke. "Ludeng, Yujing, *Dushu* zazhi" [Streetlight, context, and *Reading* magazine], online essay on *Shiji Zhongguo* [Century China, www.cc.org. cn], August 25, 2000.

Wei, Si. "*Baiyin ziben* daodu" [An introduction to silver capitalism (*ReORIENT*)], online essay (http://www.booker.com.cn/gb/paper217/1/class 021700002/hwz178429.htm).

Wei, Yuan. *Haiguo tuzhi* (Illustrated record of states across the sea). 1844–1852. Zhengzhou: Zhongzhou guji chuban she, 1999.

Wong, R. Bin. *China Transformed: Historical Change and the Limits of European Experience.* Ithaca, N.Y.: Cornell University Press, 1997.

Wu, Chengming. "'Da fenliu' dui bijiao yanjiu fangfa de gongxian" [The contribution of *The Great Divergence* to methods of comparative studies], *Zhongguo xueshu* [China Scholarship], 1(2003).

Wu, Yujin. *Wu Yujin xueshu lunzhu zixuanji* [Self-selected academic works by Wu Yujin]. Beijing: Shoudu shifan daxue chubanshe, 1995.

———, and Qi Shirong, eds. *Shijie shi* [World history], Vols. 1–6. Beijing: Gaodeng jiaoyu chubanshe, 1994.

Xu, Jiyu. *Yinghuan zhilue* [Record of the ocean circuit], 10 juan, 1850 Taibei, 1967.

Xu, Luo. "Ping jinnianlai shijie tongshi bianzhuan zhong de 'Ouzhou zhongxin' qingxiang" ["Eurocentrism" in China's world history writings of recent years], *Shijie lishi* [World History], 3(2005), pp. 93–106.

Xu, Youyu. "Zhiyi *Baiyin ziben*" [Doubts about *Silver Capitalism (ReORIENT)*], *Nanfang zhoumo* [Southern China Weekend], June 1, 2000.

Yang, Jiemian. *Da Hezuo: Bianhua zhong de shijie he Zhongguo guoji zhanlue* [Grand cooperation: The changing world and China's international strategy]. Tianjin: Tianjin renmin chubanshe, 2005.

Yu, Jinyao. "Shijie jindaishi shi zibenzhuyi shidai de lishi" [Modern world history is the history of the capitalist era], *Shijie lishi* [World History], 6(2000), pp. 95–104.

Yu, Pei. "Quanqiuhua he quanqiu lishiguan" (Globalization and the global history perspective), in *Shixue jikan* (Collected Essays of History), 2(2001), pp. 1–12.

———. "Hongyang Zhongguo shijieshi yanjiu de minzu jingshen" [Uphold the national spirit of China's world history studies], *Shijie lishi* [World History], 5(2004), pp. 4–11.

Zhang, Guangzhi. "Luelun shijieshi zai ershi shiji de chonggou" [On the reconstruction of world history during the twentieth century], *Xuexi yu tansuo* [Study and Exploration], 5(1992), pp. 124–31.

Zhang, Hongyi. "Xiongzhong ziyou yibu shijieshi: Qi Shirong jiaoshou tan shijieshi yanjiu" [Professor Qi Shirong on World History Studies], *Shixueshi yanjiu* [Historiographical Studies], 1994, no. 3, pp. 1–8.

Zhang, Zhilian. "Peng Mulan, Wang Guobin dui Zhong, Ou fazhan daolu de kanfa" [The opinions of Pomeranz and Bin Wong on the developmental roads of China and Europe], *Qingshi yicong* [Translations of Qing History Studies], 1(2004).

Zhang, Pengyuan. *Liang Qichao yu Qingji geming* [Liang Qichao and the revolution at the end of the Qing]. Taibei: Zhongyang yanjiu yuan, Jindai shi yanjiu suo, 1982.

Zhang, Tingyu, et al., comp. *Mingshi* [History of the Ming], 28 vols., 332 juan. 1739 Beijing: Zhonghua shuju, 1974.

Zhao, Ersun, et al., comps. *Qingshi gao* [Draft history of the Qing], 529 juan, 48 vols. 1927 Beijing: Zhonghua shuju, 1977.

Zhong, Weimin. " 'Da fenliu' yu 'neijuanhua' " [*The Great Divergence* and

"involution"], online essay on *Zhongguo jingjishi luntan* (China Economic History Forum, http://economy.guoxue.com), September 30, 2003.

Zhou, Gucheng. *Shijie tongshi* [World history], vols. 1–3. Beijing: Shangwu yinshuguan, 1949.

Zhou, Lihong. "Fulanke sixiang de zhuanhang yu beilun" [Transition and paradox in Frank's ideas], *Shixue yuekan* [History Studies Monthly], 1(2002).

Zhou, Wu. "Zhongguo he Ouzhou heshi lakai chaju" [When China and Europe diverged], *Wenhui bao* [Wenhui Newspaper], January 26, 2003.

Zhou, Yiliang. *Bijing shi shusheng* [After all (I am) a scholar]. Beijing shiyue wenyi chubanshe, 1998.

———, and Wu Yujin, eds. *Shijie tongshi* [World history], vols. 1–4. Beijing: Renmin Chubanshe, 1962.

PART FIVE

Walls in Cinema and Painting

HAVING WORKED OUTWARD FROM MATERIAL walls in China and within its cities to virtual walls in China's relations with its neighbors near and far, we come in the last part of this book to material and virtual walls in the transcultural realms of cinema and painting. The similar forms of the two media make them especially relevant to any discussion of walls and gates. The content of a film becomes visible by being projected onto a screen that functions as a wall and is frequently mounted on one, but it can also serve the viewer as a virtual window on the world. A painting is usually made on the opaque surface of a canvas that is typically hung on a wall, but it, too, can at least appear to function as a transparent window allowing the viewer to see the world beyond the wall.

As we would expect, the content of films in China's "new era" of "reform and opening" and of painting in the West's "postmodernist" age of irony and skepticism can differ markedly. Films like Wang Chao's *Anyang Orphan* depict the difficult lives of the men, women, and children who are being left behind in the rush to economic "development" that is often described as a feature of "market socialism" but that looks to some more like the most brutal aspects of "monopoly capitalism." Paintings like those in Brice Marden's series titled *The Propitious Garden of Plane Image* experiment with deepening the surfaces of modernist painting associated with American abstract painters of an earlier time without returning to the three-dimensional perspectivist art stemming from the "modernity" of the European Renaissance.

But Wang's and Marden's aesthetics are strikingly similar in other, perhaps more important ways. Wang draws on the European auteurist school of cinematography, in which the author directs a small crew of nonprofessional, relatively obscure actors and actresses in a natural setting in an effort to break down the usual wall between fine art and daily life. Marden is inspired by Chinese calligraphy and paintings on walls to transcend the supposed wall between Western and Chinese painting and to help reinvent what we might call modernism with Chinese characteristics.

In the contemporary oeuvres of both artists, we find walls playing many different but important roles. In *Anyang Orphan*, city walls remind us of stability and order in a time of flux and chaos, factory walls recall industrial jobs that have disappeared, apartment walls reminiscent of the socialist era now host capitalist activities, and dikes of the Yellow River symbolize the fragility of even the stoutest human defenses against disaster. Marden compared his paintings with his father's stone walls, witnessed André Malraux's project of cleaning up the walls of Paris, and recalled that he was "driven up the wall" by the postmodern rumor of the death of painting. He also reinvented the metaphor of paintings as walls on which images of the world can be posted, and incorporated architectural surface and space into his paintings so as to go beyond the formalist predictions of the absolutely flat picture plane.

Both Wang's film and Marden's paintings indicate the continuing, or perhaps recurrent, force of gender and religion in late- twentieth-century Chinese aesthetics. In *Anyang Orphan* the only protagonist who survives is Feng Yanli, the young mother who had become a prostitute to support her father, resident in an impoverished village, and her lover, an unemployed factory worker who comes to look after her son while helping to make ends meet by repairing bicycles. Although she encounters one tragedy after another, she draws inspiration at the end in the possibility that her lover, executed for having killed a gangster pimp, has been reincarnated as the protector of her lost child. Marden, for his part, was drawn to Asian models by his Californian wife, and he became intrigued with Buddhist-inspired art, including the famous frescoes on the walls at Dunhuang.

Indeed, it is not just women and religion that play important roles in these two artists' works but the specific culture of the Tang dynasty, when these two elements of Chinese civilization were arguably in flood tide. It may not be just chance that Wang's gangster villain dresses in Tang-dynasty–style clothing in an effort to enhance his respectability in the last days of his life. Nor is it surprising that Marden's chief inspiration comes from the Daoist- and Buddhist- as well as Confucian-informed calligraphy, poetry, and painting of the Tang age. Just as the putatively populist, revolutionary, and nativist Han and Ming models that played important roles in the early People's Republic faded after the death of Mao Zedong in 1976, the more elitist, reformist, and cosmopolitan orders of the Tang and Qing seem logically to have become more appealing in the presumably new era of reform and opening.

CHAPTER TWELVE

Amid Crumbling Chinese Walls

The Changing Roles of Family and Women as Revealed in Wang Chao's *Anyang Orphan*

Xiaoping Lin

WANG CHAO'S CRITICALLY ACCLAIMED BUT hitherto unanalyzed *Anyang Orphan* (2001) is an excellent example of the so-called sixth generation of Chinese films that focus on the seamier side of China's widely acclaimed quest for "modernization" since 1979.[1] It features a single, unemployed factory worker, Yu Dagang, who makes ends meet by looking after the infant son of a prostitute, Feng Yanli, while she is at work. Soon Dagang's and Yanli's relationship develops beyond the business deal; he moves in with her and sets up a bicycle repair stand nearby, where he works while also watching "their" baby. The

---

1   Chinese cinema was arguably born in Shanghai in the early twentieth century and went through successive generations: the second during the late 1940s, the third during the early People's Republic, the fourth during the Cultural Revolution, the fifth during the 1980s and 1990s, and the sixth from the 1990s to the present. See "Cinema of China"; Lin, "New Chinese Cinema." For other examples of the sixth generation of filmmakers, see Huang, "Screening Cinematic." Wang's film is not mentioned in either of these essays but it was screened at the 2001 Cannes Film Festival as part of the Directors' Fortnight series. According to one American critic, Tom Vick ("Review"), the film "establishes first-time director Wang Chao as one of the most talented of China's 'Sixth Generation' filmmakers."

heartwarming story of a new kind of "family" and the promise of a better life for all three protagonists, however, soon turns into a tragedy. Yanli's pimp, the gangster Liu Side, is diagnosed with incurable leukemia. Confronting his own mortality, he claims the baby as his own in an effort to recover the resources flowing to Dagang and to honor his own elderly mother's wishes by continuing the family line. Dagang tries to defend his constructed "family," but in the process deals a mortal blow to Side. He is arrested on the charge of murder, and is quickly executed for his crime. Yanli, driven from her trade in a police raid, loses her baby and is trundled off to the countryside to redeem herself. Amid the crumbling walls of an erstwhile "socialist" society, in short, we see changes in the nature and the status of the Chinese family unit. We also glimpse, I think, what we may call the uncanny power of a kind of Chinese matriarchy. Although itself distorted, this female authority seems to survive the assault on male self-esteem during the incipient stage of "socialism with Chinese characteristics" or what we may more accurately call the recent upsurge of capitalism in China with global characteristics.[2]

In Wang Zhao's view, his film offers us an "auteurist" gaze at the newly revived—if that is the right word—world of unemployed but dogged workers, exploited but enterprising prostitutes, and powerful but pitiful gangsters.[3] Critics like André Bazin in France and Andrew Sarris in the United States use the term "auteurist" for films that are the product of "a single AUTHOR or auteur, whose ideas, values, and worldview the film expresses."[4] In such films, the author is also the director, the script and acting are often improvised, the setting includes natural sights and sounds, the actors are nonprofessional, young, and relatively unknown, and the crew is small so the cost is limited.[5] If some of the artistic inspiration for Wang's film comes from Europe, however,

---

2   As Slavoj Žižek wrote: "China . . . seems to embody a new kind of ruthless capitalism: disregard for ecological consequences, disregard for workers' rights, everything subordinated to the ruthless drive to develop and become the superpower" (*Welcome*, p. 147).

3   Director Wang Zhao used the word "auteurist" during an interview with Cheng Qingsong on May 12, 2001, in Beijing. For the transcript, see http://www.xmusics.net/files/news/2001-7/wangchao.htm

4   See Childers and Hentzi, *Columbia Dictionary*, p. 21.

5   See Huang, "Screening Cinematic," p. 275.

many of the film's social motifs have their origins in—and reflect—the Chinese historical context. The first generation of Chinese films, for example, included a family drama, *Orphan Rescues Grandfather* (1923), and a story of a prostitute, *The Goddess* (1934).[6] More important for our purposes, Wang Chao consciously or unconsciously deploys various kinds of walls to offer settings in time and space. Walls in this film symbolize the endurance of old structures and the evanescence of new ones. They also suggest continuities in infrastructure surviving changes in social behavior from one kind of economy to another.

Walls as Symbols of Anomie, Persistence, and Change

In the opening shots of the film, the protagonist, Yu Dagang, a laid-off (*xiagang*) factory worker, contemplates various walls in what purports to be Anyang, an ancient city in northern Henan province that had become an important industrial center in the People's Republic.[7] A strikingly wide shot takes in a massive gray brick urban wall that mantles the entire frame. A few faceless elderly men appear to be crushed into the ground by the wall as a spiritless figure enters the scene from the right. It is Dagang, who stops to look at some birdcages displayed by the old men. Jobless, Dagang now is rich only in time as he wanders through the city. The precise nature of the wall in this scene is unclear, but by its size and impassivity it seems to suggest the puny endeavors and lonely fate of the middle-aged as well as elder denizens of a late (or is it not yet even incipient?) socialist society.

The original city of Anyang was the last capital of China's first, fully historical dynasty, the Shang. The ruins of the Shang capital, called Yinxu, had long served as a powerful metaphor for the evanescence of political authority and cultural efflorescence.[8] Oddly enough, despite extensive excavations since the late 1920s, the original city walls of that early Anyang have not yet been found, and it is possible that they may never have existed! Today's Anyang nearby, however, is surrounded by

6 "Cinema of China."

7 The story is set in Anyang but the film was actually shot in Kaifeng, in eastern Henan.

8 The ruins include Xibeigang, where the royal tombs of the kings were first discovered in the 1930s, and Xiaotun, best known for its palace foundations, Neolithic pottery, oracle bones, and the tomb of Lady Fu Hao. See Dillon, *China*, pp. 12, 370.

Figure 1   Yu Dagang Passes By a Typical Wall in the City of Anyang.

walls that are sufficiently old to suggest durability, at least in comparison
with the more volatile patterns of daily life. After passing by a noisy
chicken coop on the street, Dagang soon appears alone in a deserted
park reading a fenced-in gravestone of some important but unspecified
historical figure. In the background the battlemented city wall emerges
from below a low wintry sky. A deep, long shot of a barren hillside
within the wall follows. Again the camera focuses on the relatively
minute figure of Dagang walking through the secluded area until he
blends into the dark, naked trees that surround him. In these bleak yet
vigorous cityscapes, the protagonist seems to be questioning his fate:
How had he lost his job and why? He seems to be appealing for an
answer in Anyang's past represented by its city walls, symbols of
permanence in a time of flux.[9] One gets the sense that Dagang may

---

9   One is reminded here of the ancient Mesopotamian epic of Gilgamesh, in which the
     city wall emerges as a consolation prize for the hero in his vain quest for immortality.
     Foster, *Epic*, p. 95.

Figure 2   Yu Dagang Stands Before a Wall of His Closed-Down Factory.

never have noticed the ancient elegance and grandeur of those remnant city walls until his recent layoff as a factory worker. Now, as a resident of this ancient city, Dagang seems to be desperately seeking inspiration and even "protection" from the walls that he used to ignore with impunity. But all is deadly silent.

In a following scene, we see the much more contemporary walls of a factory that has been shut down. Dagang returns to the empty yard that they enclose and where he once worked. In one long shot, Dagang walks along in front of the bankrupt state-owned factory kicking a glass bottle that emits an ominous sound. In a succeeding medium shot, Dagang confronts us: still in his work clothes, he is leaning against a different wall, now bathed in a glorious sunset.

Once again Dagang is significantly linked to a wall. If the solemn city wall symbolized a durability that has been denied to Dagang's career, the factory wall in golden sunshine revives a fading "memory" of the good old days when Dagang at least had a job. A short while before, Dagang had seemingly inquired about his bitter fate in front of the ancient city wall. Now he has returned to his abandoned factory for a clue. Dagang had devoted all his adult life to working here, yet in the end he has become utterly alienated from this place. In a long shot of a monumental factory building the façade seems to soar against a glowing sunset while the demure figure of Dagang passes by like a frightened ghost. Sunk in this twilight "postsocialist" industrial landscape, Dagang seems resigned to his alienation and issues not a word of protest.

Wang Chao's ample use of industrial landscapes to depict man's alienation from his environment is akin to that of Michelangelo Antonioni's *The Outcry* (1953), one of the best Italian neorealist films. At the close of that film, Aldo (Steve Cochran), a skilled worker at a sugar refinery who had quit his job for pointless wandering, eventually returns home, only to find that his factory has been shut down by the local authorities and replaced by a defense industry. Distraught, Aldo first roams through the grisly empty yard, then climbs a tower, faints, and plunges to his death. In both films we find that the alienation of a workman from his milieu can be disastrous for him. As Peter Bondannella has remarked regarding *The Outcry*: "The emotional impact of this work is achieved by completely understated methods. Very little musical accompaniment is employed and dialogue is often sparse or elliptical; silence rather than words accompanies the director's stark images of alienation."[10] It would seem that in the sedate opening of *Anyang Orphan* Wang Chao combines a few "Antonionian" elements, such as the solitary working-class character and the desolate local landscape.[11] Yet his Chinese protagonist's alienation must also be understood in the sociopolitical context of "postsocialist" China's market-driven economy.

Walls as Erstwhile Supports That Now Change Their Functions

Dagang's disaffected "wandering" in the city and the factory is followed by an episode that is both devastating and comical. As the long winter

---

10   Bondanella, *Italian Cinema*, p. 113.

11   Vick also noted: "The film's general atmosphere and blighted cityscapes recall the neorealism of Roberto Rossellini, [Wang] Chao's way of coaxing sensitive and moving performances from non-actors brings to mind Robert Bresson, and his long takes, rigorous visual compositions, and exquisite use of natural light and color bear something of a relationship to James Benning's experimental landscape films." See http://www.allmovie.com.

night falls, Dagang stops for supper at a noodle shop in his neighborhood. When he reaches in his pocket for the money to pay for his meal, he finds only a meal ticket. In socialist China, the meal ticket had been used as a substitute for money within the work unit, where workers ate at the public canteen. But the meal ticket was not currency acceptable to food markets outside the supportive walls of one's unit even in "socialist" China, let alone in the new era. Embarrassed, Dagang rushes back home and, unaccountably, searches for some valid money within the four walls of his dingy one-room apartment. Of course he finds none.

Dagang thus begins a tragicomic search for real money that will at least enable him to confront the chilly evening with a full stomach. In the dim hallway of his apartment building, he knocks on the doors of his neighbors one after another, asking for cash in exchange for his meal tickets, ostensibly worth thirty-four *yuan*. One well-fed man gives Dagang a sly answer: "I no longer eat at the factory but bring my own lunch," a tangle of non sequiturs, as if his factory were still functioning, and/or as if he could do without money and so had none. One woman declares more forthrightly but from behind a closed door that she, too, is out of work and has not been paid for her previous labors for several months. The last person that Dagang pleads with is off screen, but we hear his dry voice: "I'll exchange them for you since we are old buddies." Here, of course, the pretense is that the meal tickets continue to have value and can be "exchanged" for money, saving Dagang's face in accepting what amounts to a gift or at best a free loan. At this moment we may heave a sigh of relief for our hungry protagonist, but some people more familiar with China may also laugh bitterly. How could this factory worker remain so dependent on his erstwhile unit that he has not yet begun to think of a life outside the supportive walls of the socialist system?

Allegorically, this tragicomic scene of "meal ticket exchange" takes place in the wake of the breakdown of a stern Maoist "socialism," especially its work unit system modeled on those in the Soviet Union in the 1950s. (The system was reminiscent, too, as we have seen, of earlier cellular structures in Chinese society such as the wards of Tang Chang'an.) According to the political scientist Martin King Whyte, the Chinese urban unit system was more highly accentuated than that in the Soviet Union owing to the absence of any market distribution of basic goods and services. In this respect, Chinese workers depended more upon their work units than their Russian comrades did. In China, moreover, the political control systems and monitoring of the private life of employees made "personal autonomy and privacy virtually impossible."[12] Vital to this vigilant unit system were the so-called internal canteens where workers used "meal tickets" to buy their food. According to Yunxiang Yan, the central message delivered through such "family-style" canteens was that the work unit, which represents the party-state, provides food to its employees, "just as a mother feeds her children." In other words, there was "a patronizing relationship between the feeder and the fed, rather than a relationship of service provider and customers."[13]

As a devoted employee of his factory, Dagang had always trusted in the system, like a child who relies on his parents. Once dismissed from his work unit, however, Dagang loses access to the "motherly" internal canteen, which used to feed him so generously. He becomes, in short, an orphan. Now, with thirty-four *yuan* in his hand, Dagang hurries back to the noodle shop glittering in the cold dark night. Almost certainly for the first time in his life, he pays for his meal with a currency acceptable in a "free market," or, more precisely, a money economy. From now on, he must survive on food supplied by the market rather than the workplace controlled by the party-state.

Out of the blue, the sympathetic shop owner, busy cooking Dagang's soup, suddenly hands him a baby that had been left in the shop recently by a customer. As he eats, Dagang reads a note asking for someone to take care of the child in exchange for a payment of two hundred *yuan* each month. Realizing that the small amount of money he had just received from his coworker would not last very long, Dagang decides to bring the baby home as a new means of earning his living. This is the second step taken by the confused ex–factory worker to fight for his livelihood in the absence of the system that had once fed him and all others. The walls of his small apartment now become the shelter of another "orphan," one even less independent than himself. In an odd twist, the apartment that had been provided to him under the socialist system but had never been his to own, now becomes the principal base

---

12   Whyte, "Changing Role," p. 177.
13   Yan, "Hamburger," p. 209.

of his operations in the new system in which erstwhile public goods are gradually being transformed into private capital.

Dagang's unconscious search for a new "feeder" soon leads to the mother of the child. She turns out to be a prostitute named Feng Yanli. Yanli had left the baby with a note that included her beeper number. When Dagang and Yanli first meet in one of the new "market-driven" restaurants, the outspoken young woman acts as a truly caring "mother" to both the quiet worker and the baby he is awkwardly holding. When Yanli asks if the baby has eaten, the "first time father" Dagang replies that he has been giving him milk. Satisfied, the young woman then asks if *he* has eaten, and Dagang admits that he has not. Yanli then calls out: "Waiter! Two bowls of noodles!" The meeting between the two protagonists is a most significant scene in the film. Abandoned by his work unit, Dagang has become an "orphan" along with the child, and Yanli will nourish him as a way to care for her child. Evidently, this somewhat bittersweet scene demonstrates a shift in power from the party-state, with its own matriarchal aura, to the capitalist economy in which a prostitute, although herself dependent on others, has sufficient wealth and power to nurture a male "nanny" as well as her own male child.

On an allegorical level, I suggest, the Yanli character represents what we may call the persistence under new conditions of the uncanny power of Chinese matriarchy. That matriarchy, which Marxists believe had once existed in ancient societies, had in any case previously informed the party-state that had provided for its workforce "just as a mother feeds her children." It now survives the demise of that order and takes the form of a sex worker who provides for two dependent males. However, this emerging form of Chinese matriarchal power is fundamentally flawed. It is a "by-product" of the widespread unemployment that, as Jennifer Lin has reported, "hit hardest against" female workers. While women made up 39 percent of the workforce in the state sector in the spring of 1998, 60 percent of laid-off state workers in that year were women (most over the age of thirty-five).[14] Such massive layoffs of woman workers in the 1990s contrasted sharply with the previous rapid growth of the female labor force during the 1960s and

---

14   According to the semiofficial All-China Women's Federation. See Lin, "About Face," cited in Meisner, *Mao's China*, p. 548, note 45.

1970s.[15] Hence appears as an alternative the hoary "force of pleasure" (i.e., prostitution) for a great many young unemployed female factory workers. Yanli is simply a cinematic representation of this feminine economic force that Pan Suiming, a renowned scholar of the sex industry, has termed the "misses economy (*xiaojie jingji*)."[16] He notes that the economy is even supported by some local government officials, who argue that there are three "good reasons" to bolster "sexual service (*xing fuwu*)." (1) It employs many young female laid-off workers; (2) it stimulates the consumption of cosmetics, clothing, housing, and tourism; and (3) it enables the rich to "support" the poor,[17] boosting "a corner of the Chinese economy."[18] An article in the New York Times also reports that the sex trade is "an industry that has served as a financial backdrop for millions of China's rural migrants."[19] (By "backdrop" the writer probably meant "fall-back," leaving open, apparently, its moral legitimacy.) In any event, this "misses economy" may also confirm what Karl Marx had said more than a century and a half earlier about prostitution in a capitalist society: "Just as the woman passes from marriage to general prostitution, so the entire world of wealth (that is, of man's objective substance) passes from the relationship of exclusive marriage with the owner of private property to a state of universal prostitution with the community [in the public marketplace]."[20] And in Marx's view, "Prostitution is only a specific expression of the general prostitution of the laborer."[21]

---

15 As Barry Naughton put it: "In the 1950s, women had difficulty entering the urban labor force. . . . But as strict limits on city growth came into effect after the mid-1960s and industrialization continued . . . female labor force participation rates increased steadily. By the late 1970s, almost all urban women entered the labor force after leaving school, and high female labor force participation became an essential characteristic of urban society." See "Cities," pp. 75–76.

16 Pan, "Phenomenon."

17 Huangpu, "About a Closure." The idea that "the rich feed the poor" was, of course, a fundamental "bourgeois fallacy" that Chinese socialist "thought reform" had been designed to destroy.

18 Zhong, "Does 'Sex Industry.' "

19 Rosenthal, "Migrants."

20 Marx and Engels, "Communist Manifesto," pp. 100–1.

21 Ibid., p. 100.

At that meeting in the restaurant, "Miss" Yanli gives Dagang two hundred *yuan* and sympathetically watches him tuck into his noodle soup. It appears that, for Dagang, the four walls of this small noodle shop define a new social space that is far outside the boundaries of his "work unit." Here he has found an alternative "feeder." The film does not indicate whether Yanli is a factory worker who has lost her job. As soon as the "business deal" about the care of the baby is over, however, Yanli rushes to a post office to remit some money to her father. In a close-up of the money order, we see that he lives in a village in Heilongjiang on the northeastern frontier. Obviously, Yanli is one of those girls from the countryside "specializing" in sex services to support her impoverished rural family. We understand that Yanli has to prostitute herself to support her father, who is as vulnerable as her son and her newfound friend in the city.

By effectively "feeding" two men (and a baby), Yanli perhaps unwittingly poses an additional challenge to an already severely damaged Chinese masculinity. It seems that her father and the timid Dagang would otherwise be defenseless in the face of the new market forces. In *Anyang Orphan*, there is an ever-fresh portrayal of the brutal "market forces" that besiege almost the entire city. Street life is crammed with gaudy advertisements—from ubiquitous food stands to garish women's clothing to children's toys. Throughout the film, we often catch sight of Dagang and Yanli walking along busy streets, as they visit a shopping center, a Buddhist temple, and a photo shop. In line with the "auteur style," we hear no background musical score but only the loud pop songs that break out at random in the marketplace. Soon Dagang finds his own "place" in this market-driven economy. After receiving the first payments from Yanli, he draws on his small capital to set up a bicycle repair stall on the street. In this way, Dagang starts a new life as a laid-off worker turned "self-employed entrepreneur" (*getihu*), the solution enthusiastically endorsed by the government during the 1990s.[22] In the meantime, a policeman who knows Dagang well stops by and asks about his life since being laid off. Dagang, himself a former state employee, replies: "It's better than before." In this somewhat ambivalent answer (just how good is "better than before,"

---

22 We are reminded here of the equally promising—and ultimately tragic—career of the Republican-era rickshaw puller immortalized in Lao She's *Camel*.

and which "before"?), we may again sense the power of the new Chinese matriarchy in the form of Yanli that has brought timely relief to Dagang. Yanli's feminine help should be merely "supplemental" to a man like Dagang, struggling to mend his economic deficiency. By China's patriarchal traditions, Dagang ought to become a man of independent means in order to "replenish" his masculinity, which has been depleted by unemployment. His efforts to reclaim his masculinity might reasonably include getting married and having a normal family.

When Dagang brings the baby to meet with Yanli again, they arrive by taxi in a more thriving district of the city. In the scene that follows, we find the two protagonists eating in a spacious, tidy restaurant, which is far more attractive than the dingy noodle place of their first "business meeting." At the dinner table Dagang is retiring as usual, but his eyes widen as Yanli breastfeeds the crying toddler. It would seem that the once emasculated laid-off worker is finally reclaiming his libidinal drive along with his new employment. To our surprise, however, the sexually deprived man addresses Yanli with the words: "Miss, I want to give you back the baby." Since it is the child that ties Dagang with his object of desire—the "maternal" prostitute—such a request seems somewhat incomprehensible to the spectator.

In the next scene, however, it becomes clear that Yanli has interpreted Dagang's wish in the most positive light. Without any intervening scene or exchange, Dagang and Yanli are depicted lying side by side in bed like a loving couple. As in Antonioni's *The Outcry*, the dialogue between the protagonists is often elliptical. We never learn how Yanli responded to Dagang's express wish and we do not know why she refused to take back the child except that she would have to quit—or at least reduce—her work to take care of the infant. But this eventual "union" between the two people is only natural and "logical" if we consider each protagonist's own troubled life. Now, acting as a more self-respecting "husband," Dagang urges Yanli: "Don't be a 'miss' (*xiaojie*) any more."[23] The "would-be wife" Yanli answers coolly: "I don't do it for myself." At this point Yanli's seeming refusal to adopt a cleaner, better life almost provokes a crisis in the couple's new relationship. Yet Dagang seeks a compromise, saying: "Then do it at my place. And I will

---

23 In Chinese *xiaojie* means "miss," which is now a popular name for young women working in China's expanding sex industry.

take care of the baby." There is a "perverse" undertone in this blunt talk, masking Dagang's humiliation with an assertion of pragmatism. But we also discern in Dagang's "business proposal" that he is determined to survive in the crazy market-driven economy at whatever price.

In fact, Dagang's "place" is the tiny, single-room apartment he had rented cheaply from his factory in the Mao era. According to David Fraser, the Maoist party-state had "decommodified" housing and made it a state-provided social good under the socialist welfare system. The party-state had transformed housing into an element of the re-distributive economy, allowing individual work units to allocate accommodations.[24] Mockingly, the now self-employed Dagang re-commodifies his housing with the income from China's revived sex industry. The four walls of his apartment remain unaltered, but their function has shifted from containing a home to providing space for the world's oldest profession.

Following the bedroom scene is a wide shot in which Dagang is standing at his bike repair stall in front of an immense gray brick wall, a striking image similar to those we saw in the opening scenes of the film. This time, however, the wall is not the nondescript wall of the city that had reinforced the despair of the newly unemployed Dagang. Nor is it the massive old city wall that had offered him an image of durability or the sunset-lit wall of his defunct factory that reminded him of better days. It is instead an unidentified yet newly "supportive" wall that happens to be opposite to his own apartment building. Against the backdrop of this wall, or literally "with his back to the wall," Dagang is able to attend to three things simultaneously and efficiently: (1) to work as a bicycle repairman; (2) to baby-sit the child placed in a basket; and (3) to watch Yanli's customers come and go. A one point, Dagang takes advantage of his strategic location to express his personal emotions and advance his business interests. He casually walks across the street and pierces the tire of a bike parked there by one of Yanli's present customers. It is a charming vignette in Dagang's daily struggle to build his unorthodox family. His and Yanli's concerted efforts to survive help us to overlook the negative social consequences of prostitution and vandalism. Under the circumstances we can but share the hard-working

24 Fraser, "Inventing Oasis," p. 30.

Figure 3   The Wall across from Yu Dagang's Apartment.

couple's hope for a better life. And, as we have seen, this new life begins right across the street from his apartment building, which belongs to the bygone socialist era but now "helps" put Dagang back on his feet. It is in a private business adjacent to this past public wall that the former factory worker and present bicycle repairman has finally found at least a provisional "answer" to his query about life, love, and family (see Figure 3).

Shortly thereafter another episode affectingly reveals the couple's everyday existence. Across the street from his building, Dagang stands dutifully fixing a tire while watching the child. Inside their apartment, Yanli is awakened from sleep by the alarm clock, and she sends her customer away (she is paid by the hour). Then she changes the sheet and makes a new bed for the night. Afterward Yanli, dressed in a pure white sweater (when working she is always attired in brassy red), sits before the mirror and applies her lipstick thoughtfully. As the night falls, Dagang packs up his tools and carries the baby home, where Yanli gives him a warm welcome. In bright lamplight the entire "family" eats a simple dinner at the table without talking, and Yanli's fresh white dress seems to speak of a spiritual cleansing. Soon after all three— Dagang, Yanli, and the baby—are "lying in bed side by side" in a medium shot that, according to a critic, "brings the point home with a poignant simplicity that few contemporary directors are able to achieve."[25] At this very moment Yanli promises Dagang: "I will quit this spring."

The scene then cuts to a close-up of a Buddhist statue of the Goddess of Mercy (Guanyin),[26] and in the next shot Dagang and Yanli are praying in a Buddhist temple filled with burning incense. The shrill chanting of sutras is heard, which continues even after they leave the temple and walk through a noisy crowd on the street. Like Yanli's "immaculate" white dress, this haunting Buddhist chanting signifies a "purification" that paves the way for a new "wholesome" life, as the couple stops by a photo studio to have their *quanjiafu* ("whole happy family") picture taken. In this staged scene, Dagang, Yanli, and the baby all play a role in a tight, well-governed family. Dagang is a solemnly responsible "husband," dressed in his erstwhile factory uniform. Yanli wears a dark gray jacket, having shed her "prostitute look" and assumed a new identity as a virtuous "wife." The little boy is wrapped in white and blue clothes, and he remains quiet as an "obedient son." Such cool and dull colors chosen for the occasion seem to shield this would-be family from any sensual distractions. Behind the three devoted family members is a balmy and dreamy landscape. In it a farmhouse, a wheat field, and sunflowers are painted in velvet red, green, and yellow. The scenery serves as a backdrop pertinent to the family in search of a redeemed humanity in a natural setting. Although this imagery is one of the most commonplace in commercial photography, its very banality arouses a sweet desire for a tranquil and ordinary life—a rarity in the maddened capitalistic and urban world.

---

25 See Tom Vick's review.

26 Guanyin is the Chinese female form of Avalokiteśvara (Bodhisattva of Compassion) in the Buddhist religion. For how an Indian god became a Chinese goddess, see Yü, *Kuan-yin*.

The Evanescence of Walls and Dikes

One day the family's bucolic dream is disrupted, however, when a crimson car pulls up in front of Dagang's apartment building. Four young men in dark blue suits jump out, and two of them come to Dagang's stand across the street. Without a word, they look at the boy in the basket and walk back to the car. In a second, a burly bald man emerges from the car and comes to see the baby for himself. The infant, surprisingly, gives the man a welcoming smile. The man seems to be touched by the child's "greeting" and goes back to his vehicle in silence. At first Dagang is on the alert for the potential consequences of this unexpected visit by strangers, but after they leave he goes right back to his work as if nothing had happened. The bald man is Liu Side, a gangster who owns the "singing and dancing" building where Yanli used to work. In a flashback, we see Side walk into the karaoke bar in that building and yell brashly for the "misses" to appear, demanding in particular Yanli. Having just served a customer upstairs, Yanli soon comes down to the bar exhausted. The "pimp" Side derisively demands the "fee" she has just earned for her services. Yanli refuses, explaining to the gangster: "The money I earn is to raise *your* bastard son!" Humiliated and angered by this disclosure, Side hits Yanli in the face with a steel fork and instructs his men that she is to be dismissed from the premises. Coming out of the building, Side all of a sudden faints by his car. He is soon checked into a hospital, where he is diagnosed as having cancer. Here we seem to have a case of "instant" retribution in Buddhist terms. After Side has injured Yanli in a vicious attack, he is punished by the uncanny power of Chinese matriarchy for his bad karma.[27]

Unlike Dagang, the representative worker whose status "has rapidly declined" under China's "market socialism,"[28] Side is one of those mobster bosses who "have taken advantage of new market opportu-

---

27 In Indian philosophy, karma (Sanskrit for "action" or "work") is "the principle that a person's actions have consequences meriting reward or punishment. Karma is the moral law of cause and effect by which the sum of a person's actions are carried forward from one life to the next, leading to an improvement or deterioration in that person's fate." Crystal, *Penguin Encyclopedia*, p. 827.

28 See Goldman and MacFarquhar, *Paradox*, p. 18.

nities to gain access to private industrial and commercial resources."[29] Similar to their counterparts around the world, Chinese gangs engage in drug trafficking, gambling, prostitution, robbery, and extortion. And such gang activities attract many young people who "are looking for any means to get rich quickly."[30] So in Side's company there are always silent young men dressed in neat navy blue suits, who look like the mob characters in Kitano Takeshi's *yakuza* films. After the visit to Dagang's bike repair shop, Side joins those young men in a public bath, where they agree that the boy must be Side's son.

Side's urge to "recognize" his son by Yanli does not mean that the dying gangster has developed any affection for the prostitute he had once grossly abused. In fact, his emotions have more to do with filial piety. As soon as Side had learned of his terminal illness, he had called on his mother who lived in the countryside. During Side's visit, his mother sat at a table installed with an old photo of her deceased husband. Noticing that her son was losing his hair as had his father who had also died of cancer, she instructed him to have a family and, especially, to produce an offspring (*hou*). That was the origin of Side's sudden inquiry into the identity of Yanli's little boy. Here we see how Chinese matriarchy exerts its influence even over a gangster who tends to ignore all the other "rules" in a Chinese society under rapid economic transformation.

Wang portrays Side as a rogue who is curiously also bound by "traditions." In his karaoke bar he snubs modern pop music but sings along with Chinese folk songs. Right after the ominous hospital checkup, he goes to pay homage to the Yellow River, which, with its massive wall-like dikes, often serves as a symbol of the continuity of Chinese civilization.[31] In this scene Side sustains a crushed dignity as a result of his ill health while his crass lieutenants urinate on the dikes, symbolizing their contempt for culture (or at least for public infra-

---

29 Ibid., p. 325.

30 Ibid., pp. 324–25.

31 See, for example, the 1988 Chinese television series titled *Heshang*, which depicted the Yellow River as a symbol of Chinese stagnancy, as opposed to the blue ocean of Western dynamism: Su and Wang, *Deathsong*. Side's visit to the Yellow River was facilitated by the shooting of the film in Kaifeng; it seems less reasonable for someone based, as Side was supposed to be, in more distant Anyang.

Figure 4 Liu Side on the Dike of the Yellow River.

structure!). Side's "costume" in this scene merits our attention. He is wearing a pseudoclassical jacket called Tang-style attire (*tangzhuang*), which has recently been popular among wealthy Chinese and favored by leaders such as President Jiang Zemin (see Figure 4).[32] However, this

---

32 *Tangzhuang* can mean the Tang people's dress or, more generally, Chinese costume. Luo *Hanyu*, vol. 1, p. 1598. According to Stephen Wong: "Discussion about *hanfu* [i.e., Chinese-style dress] started in 2001 after China hosted the Asia Pacific Economic Conference (APEC) summit in Shanghai, where each participant was presented with a *tangzhuang*, a Tang-style suit. The clothing gained such publicity at the event that it was soon widely recognized as China's national costume. But Han dress (*hanfu*) lovers do not agree. They say *tangzhuang* is not the costume of the Han-dominated Tang dynasty, as its name suggests. Rather it is a variety of the costume of the Manchurians, who forced the Han people to wear it for 300 years ago [*sic*]"(available at http://www.atimes. com). In fact, we may add, the Tang ruling family was of Turkish as well as Han descent

Figure 5   Feng Yanli Visits Yu Dagang in Prison.

iconographic reference to Chinese *nouveaux riches* and the power elite constitutes a mocking parody, since Side's doom has been sealed by his infirmity.

In order to fulfill his mother's wish, Side returns to Anyang and to Dagang's apartment accompanied by his thugs to demand of Yanli the custody of her child. This time Dagang is watching the situation more vigilantly from his stand across the street. Soon he realizes he must go back to his apartment, where the mobster is pressing Yanli to give up the child. Dagang enters the room and stands by his woman in silence. Unable to brush off Dagang, the ruffled Side resorts to violence. The

and the Qing ruling family included Han and Mongol as well as Manchu elements. For the argument that both the Tang and Qing may be understood as examples of "elitist-reformist" orders going back to the Zhou, see Des Forges, "Toward Another." This might help to explain why the clothing of those periods appeals to some members of what we may call the reformist elite of contemporary China.

two men engage in a fistfight in the dark hallway (off screen) that ends with a bang. A moment later we learn that Side has been killed in the fight, and Dagang has been arrested and jailed on charges of murder. Yanli and the child pay a last visit to Dagang, now on death row in prison (see Figure 5).

Speaking from behind the wire netting, a composed Dagang tells Yanli: "If I die, take care of the baby. He is my offspring." In the next shot, we see the shop front of the noodle place where the two protagonists had first met. Now Yanli alone walks into the restaurant carrying the baby. What follows is an exceedingly long take, in which Yanli eats a bowl of noodles to the very end, with the baby dangling from her arm. On the table there is another bowl of noodles— apparently an "offering" to the spirit of the absent Dagang. Suddenly, Yanli bursts into tears. We are given to understand that this prolonged meal is Yanli's ritual honoring of her erstwhile lover on the day of his execution.

"Battering Down All Chinese Walls"

The grim demise of Side and Dagang raises a question critical to our understanding of Wang Chao's *Anyang Orphan*. Who indeed will be the father to Yanli's child? To put it another way, is there any patriarchal power that has survived the brute force of "market socialism" and can play this role? In fact, both men's failure to become the father denotes a grave masculinity crisis in "postsocialist" Chinese society. Not only has the longstanding wall between patriarchy and matriarchy come down, with consequences both positive and negative, but also the equally venerable walls of those two forms of authority against human suffering have been greatly weakened, with results that seem to me more harmful than helpful.

In Dagang's case, he has been forced to use his inherited "socialist housing" as a venue for prostitution in order to survive and attempt to have a family. His transgression mirrors a troubled socialist state whose proper functions have been impaired in a frantic "free-market" economy. As Marx and Engels' *Communist Manifesto* famously described "the bourgeois mode of production": "All that is solid melts into air, all that is holy is profaned, and man is at last compelled to face with sober senses his real conditions of life and his relations with his kind."[33] As they also pointed out: "The cheap prices of its commodities are the heavy artillery with which it batters down all Chinese walls, with which it forces the barbarians' intensely obstinate hatred of foreigners to capitulate."[34] In a Marxian sense, Dagang is perhaps a classic example of "the proletarians" who "have nothing to lose but their chains."[35] However, as a man confronting "his real conditions of life" in that ruthless capitalistic mode of production, Dagang appears "complicit" in tearing down "all Chinese walls" of social orders and moral principles, as he turns his home into a brothel, another commodity in the marketplace, and eschews any sentimentality.

Similarly, Side's profitable prostitution "business" is also a transgression reflective of a weakened socialist state that has failed to provide for its citizens. Side's incurable illness, however, sounds like a Buddhist karmic result of his unlawful way of life. In any case, both men's paternal inadequacy seems to be effected and insured by a socialist state that has been largely undermined by the "manic logic of global capitalism."[36] On the one hand, the state is incapable of caring for redundant workers such as Dagang. On the other, it falls short of regulating crooked "businessmen" like Side. In short, the troubled socialist state itself is a waning patriarchal power that willy-nilly instigates social fragmentation and breakdown. Even a strong-willed woman like Yanli cannot find a father for her child among either "losers" (Dagang) or "winners" (Side) in the game of "market socialism." And her hope to build a "normal" happy family has been shattered twice: first, by the impoverishment of her home village under the market reforms; second, by a harsh state legal apparatus blind to human suffering and individual circumstances. The capital punishment of Dagang for killing the gangster is nothing but a manifestation of a common hoary principle: "a life for a life" (*sharen changming*). In this case it indiscriminately cancels out Yanli's search for a father for her baby. In this respect, the demise of both potential

33   Marx and Engels, "Communist Manifesto," p. 212.
34   Ibid., p. 213.
35   Ibid., p. 243.
36   I borrow this expression from Greider, *One World*.

fathers in *Anyang Orphan* dramatically reflects the larger masculinity crisis in a China increasingly driven by various "market forces."

In the final sequence of *Anyang Orphan*, Director Wang Chao continues to remark on a coercive state power that undermines Yanli's troubled hope. Seen from a deep archway, Yanli and other "misses" are being chased out of their workplaces by the uniformed police. During her hurried effort to escape the net of the law, Yanli gives her baby to a stranger on the street to look after. After successfully eluding the police she returns to the scene to look for the stranger and to get back her child. Unfortunately the man has vanished without a trace. Yanli runs along the street in desolation, stopping only to ask a young man about the stranger "with a baby." Without any warning another man jumps out from behind her with a handcuff—he is a plainclothesman who has been lurking in the shade of a shoe repair stand and waiting for the escaped "misses." Yanli screams for help but the cop grabs her hair and ties her up.

In the subsequent wide shot, we see a "new" Anyang city cleansed of its social evils. Against a clear blue sky a train station comes into sight. Although it appears to be a socialist monument with revolutionary slogans of the Mao era it differs from the previous cityscapes in the movie that were dreary and murky. Now, with the "bad elements" all gone, Anyang is reborn, like a phoenix rising from the ashes. A police van and a truck arrive in a public square next to the train station. A following medium shot shows vacant-faced young prostitutes (some are teenagers), including Yanli, who steps down from the truck under the policemen's watch. By Chinese law they are to be detained and "reeducated" and then sent back to their hometown to begin a new life. The girls are packed into a cargo train. A dazzling sun shines in through a small window in one wall of the freight car. Trapped in this claustrophobic space, Yanli stares up at the window—the only link with the outside world. And we see what Yanli sees in the last matching shot (Figure 6): a "resurrected" Dagang holding their child against the background of a sunny street in Anyang. Is Yanli under an illusion that she has found a father for her baby in the next life?

This rather "surrealist" ending of Wang Chao's film reflects China's everyday reality and its cultural resources. Earlier in the movie, Dagang and Yanli had gone to a Buddhist sanctuary seeking "purification" of their somewhat tainted lifestyles. In the final shot, Yanli has a vision of

Figure 6   Yanli's Vision of Dagang Holding Their Child.

Dagang, which is his "reincarnation" as defined by the Buddhist religion. The Buddhist doctrine of karma "states that what one does in this life will have its effects on the next life" and "the karma of the deceased conditions the birth of a new self."[37] In this way, Dagang is able to become the father of the child in his next life because of the good deeds he performed for Yanli and her child in this life. Obviously, this Buddhist "happy ending" defies the oppressive realities so force-fully conveyed through most of the film.

Perhaps we can best understand this paradox in the context of Confucianism, a Chinese ideology that stresses a strong bond between the individual, the family, the state, and the world. According to *The Great Learning*, one of the Four Books that became the orthodox keys to the Five Classics in the Song period: "When the personal life is cultivated, the family will be regulated; when the family is regulated, the state will be in order; when the state is in order, there will be peace

---

37   Doniger, *Merriam-Webster's*, p. 913.

throughout the world."[38] In *Anyang Orphan*, however, the sacred links among the four realms in the Confucian concept have broken down: the bankrupt state factory disposes of its loyal employee; the forlorn worker goes astray to befriend a prostitute; and the hapless prostitute strains herself in order to carry out filial duties. Moreover, in the so-called free-market economy, neither the personal life nor the family is "regulated" by any "traditional" value systems. Hence disorder, violence, and "the humiliated father," to borrow Žižek's psychoanalytical term.[39]

Central to Wang Chao's *Anyang Orphan* is the problematic "Confucian trinity" of the individual, the family, and the state. It is a revered ideological trinity that has been pulverized by crushing market forces. As we have witnessed in the film, the severing of the trinity fatally affects all three protagonists' lives. Dagang is twice "humiliated" by the state: first when it throws him out into the street and second when it puts him to death as an utter criminal (which he certainly is not). Even though Side profits from "market socialism," he too is "humiliated" not only by that "providential" illness, but also by the country's sex industry, which he helps to build. (In Yanli's words, "The money I earned is to raise *your* bastard son!") Both men's masculinity is completely "washed out" when they die toward the end of the film. The destruction of Dagang and Side can be seen as a result of the usurpation of Confucian paternal-maternal authority by a ruthless Chinese (and global) capitalism that seems to defy all human values. In this context, Yanli is probably the strongest character emerging from Wang Chao's film if only because she survives under such harsh circumstances. That is to say, Yanli is still *alive* and even *visionary*, an altogether worthy representative of an enduring Chinese matriarchal power. But can the woman, strong as she is, ever succeed in having a family in a pathetically heartless world? Or will even the victory of Chinese matriarchy prove to be Pyrrhic under the conditions of the putatively wall-less world of globalization?

An alternate version of this chapter was published in *Third Text* (London), vol. 23, issue 2, March 2009, pp. 197-210.

---

38   Chan, *Source Book*, pp. 86–87.
39   Slavoj Žižek, *Enjoy*, p. 149.

Works Cited

Bondanella, Peter. *Italian Cinema: From Realism to the Present.* New York: Continuum, 1999.

Chan, Wing-tsit. *A Source Book in Chinese Philosophy.* Princeton, N.J.: Princeton University Press, 1963.

Childers, Joseph, and Gary Hentzi, eds. *The Columbia Dictionary of Modern Literary and Cultural Criticism.* New York: Columbia University Press, 1995.

"Cinema of China." Wikipedia, the free encyclopedia (http//en.wikipedia.org/wiki/CinemaofChina#The_Sixth_Generation_and_beyond.2C_1990s_-_present

Crystal, David. ed. *Penguin Encyclopedia.* London: Penguin, 2004.

Davis, Deborah S., Richard Kraus, Barry Naughton, Elizabeth J. Perry, eds. *Urban Spaces in Contemporary China: The Potential for Autonomy and Community in Post-Mao China.* New York: Woodrow Wilson Center Press, Cambridge University Press, 1995.

Des Forges, Roger. "Toward Another Tang or Zhou? Views from the Central Plain in the Shunzhi Reign." Pp. 73–112 in *Time, Temporality, and Imperial Transition: East Asia from Ming to Qing,* Lynn Struve, ed. Honolulu: University of Hawai'i Press, 2005.

Dillon, Michael, ed. *China: A Cultural and Historical Dictionary.* Surrey: Curzon, 1998.

Doniger, Wendy, ed. *Merriam-Webster's Encyclopedia of World Religion.* Springfield, Illinois: Merriam-Webster, 1999.

Foster, Benjamin R. *The Epic of Gilgamesh.* New York: W. W. Norton, 2001.

Fraser, David. "Inventing Oasis: Luxury Housing Advertisements and Reconfiguring Domestic Space in Shanghai." Pp. 25–53 in *The Consumer Revolution in Urban China,* Deborah Davis, ed. New York: Cambridge University Press, 1995.Goldman, Merle, and Roderick MacFarquhar, eds. *The Paradox of China's Post-Mao Reform.* Cambridge, Mass.: Harvard University Press, 1999.

Greider, William. *One World, Ready or Not: The Manic Logic of Global Capitalism.* New York: Simon & Schuster, 1998.

Huang, Bingyi. "Screening Cinematic Space—On Chinese Experimental Films from the Last Decade." Pp. 275–95 in Ming-lu Gao, *The Wall: Reshaping Contemporary Chinese Art/Qiang: Zhongguo dangdai yishu lishi yu bianjie.* Beijing: Millennium Art Museum; Buffalo: Albright-Knox Art Gallery; University at Buffalo Art Galleries, 2005.

Huangpu Qingshan. "About a Closure of the Four Famous Mansions." Available at http://www.sd.cnifo.com

Lao She. *Camel Xiangzi*. Beijing: Foreign Languages Press, 1986.

Lin, Jennifer. "About Face: China's Economic Reforms Hit Hardest against Women," *Chicago Tribune*, April 26, 1998, Section 13, p. 9.

Lin, Xiaoping. "New Chinese Cinema of the Sixth Generation: A Distant Cry of Forsaken Children," *Third Text*, 16.3(2002).

Luo, Zhufeng, ed. *Hanyu dacidian* (The unabridged dictionary of the Chinese language). Shanghai: Hanyu dacidian chubanshe, 1997.

Marx, Karl, and Friedrich Engels. "The Communist Manifesto." In *Economic and Philosophic Manuscripts of 1844 and the Communist Manifesto by Karl Marx and Friedrich Engels*. Martin Milligan, trans. New York: Prometheus, 1988.

Meisner, Maurice. *Mao's China and After: A History of the People's Republic*. New York: Free Press, 1999.

Naughton, Barry. "Cities in the Chinese Economic System." Pp. 25–53, in Davis, *Urban Spaces*.

Pan, Suiming. "The Phenomenon of 'Misses Economy.'" In *Kexue Shibao (Scientific Daily)*. Available at http://www.mlist.myrice.com

Rosenthal, Elisabeth. "Migrants to Chinese Boom Town Find Hard Lives." *New York Times*, July 2, 2002. Available at http://www.ntimes.com

Su, Xiaokang, and Wang Luxiang, *Deathsong of the River: A Reader's Guide to the Chinese TV Series, Heshang*, Richard W. Bodman and Pin P. Wan, trans. Ithaca, New York: Cornell University East Asia Series, 1991.

Vick, Tom. "Review of *Anyang Orphan*." Available at http://www.allmovie.com

Whyte, Martin King. "The Changing Role of Workers." Pp. 173–96 in *The Paradox of China's Post-Mao Reform*, Merle Goldman and Roderick, MacFarquhar, eds. Cambridge, Mass.: Harvard University Press, 1999.

Wong, Stephen. Discussions about Hanfu (Chinese dress available at http://www.atimes.com).

Yan, Yunxiang. "Of Hamburger and Social Space: Consuming McDonald's in Beijing." Pp. 201–25 in *The Consumer Revolution in Urban China*, Deborah Davis, ed. New York: Cambridge University Press, 1995.

Yü, Chün-Fang. *Kuan-yin: The Chinese Transformation of Avalokitesvara*. New York: Columbia University Press, 2000.

Zhong, Wei. "Does 'Sex Industry' Boost a Corner of the Chinese Economy?" In *Zhonggguo baodao zhoukan* (China Report Weekly). Available at http://www.mlist.myrice.com

Zizek, Slavoj. *Enjoy Your Symptom! Jacques Lacan in Hollywood and Out*, rev. ed. New York: Routledge, 2001.

———. *Welcome to the Desert of the Real*. London and New York: Verso, 2002.

CHAPTER THIRTEEN

Writing on the Wall

Brice Marden's Chinese Work and Modernism

Liu Chiao-mei

TO TALK OF A WALL—that is, a surface that blocks the gaze from proceeding into a deeper visual field—is to engage with the major issues in the modernist theory of painting. In this chapter we take up the work of the American artist Brice Marden (1938–), who was trained in the United States when "modern" painting of the "Cold War" variety reached its height and began to encounter post-modern criticism and even the suggestion that painting was dead. By tracing Marden's personal experiences in Europe and in Asia, we shall show how he incorporated ideas and techniques into his own practice to reinvent the American modernist metaphor of the painting as a wall. Resisting any return to an earlier modern view of paintings as windows on the world and going beyond the more contemporary idea of paintings as nothing but opaque planes, Marden drew on the Chinese artistic heritage in particular to develop a middle position treating his canvases as walls on which images can be projected but also having texture and even some depth. Unlike some previous studies of Marden's work that divide his oeuvre into Western and Chinese compartments, we shall attempt to break down that wall by analyzing the complex interaction between his Western formation and perspective and the Eastern—and par-

ticularly Chinese—art and philosophy that came to his attention and
engaged his interest. In the process we shall see the many ways that
other walls have helped to shape his work, from the stone walls built by
his father to the limestone walls cleaned by André Malraux, from the
virtual wall he was driven up by post-modern claims to the material
walls on which Chinese artists have inscribed their calligraphy and
painting from early times to the present.

Walls in American Modern Art of the "Cold War" Period

In the wake of World War II, the American art critic Clement Greenberg promoted what he called the freshness of American abstract
painting (also known as Abstract Expressionism or Action Painting)
vis-à-vis the declining easel painting of a supposedly decadent
bourgeois Europe. He observed among American avant-gardes a
persistent urge "to go beyond the cabinet picture, which is destined to
occupy only a spot on the wall, to a kind of picture that, without
actually becoming identified with the wall like a mural, would *spread*
over it and acknowledge its physical reality."[1] Greenberg identified a
contradiction between the public, architectural setting of the wall and
the private, intimate circles in which such advanced art was produced.
He described that contradiction as a crisis in contemporary mainstream painting—a crisis that he had earlier named "the dynamic of
modernism." Vis-à-vis the synesthetic (or multisensory) developments
of the early twentieth century, he insisted on the strict separation of
the arts and held that avant-garde painting involved "a progressive
surrender to the resistance of its medium," i.e., of paint on a flat
surface. In his view, truly "modern" or abstract painting turned away
from the illusory/illusionistic depth of the early-modern Renaissance
perspective toward the purity of the picture plane.[2] For Greenberg, the
principal drama of modern painting since 1850 was this struggle
between depth (a window on the world) and flatness (a wall on which
images of the world would be mounted) for the soul of any individual
picture. In 1960, he once more claimed "the integrity of the picture
plane" to be the precondition of pure painting, as the essence of

1   Greenberg, "Situation at the Moment" (1948), pp. 194–95.
2   Greenberg, "Towards a Newer Laocoon" (1940), p. 34.

Modernism was in "the use of characteristic methods of a discipline to criticize the discipline itself, not in order to subvert it but in order to entrench it more firmly in its area of competence."[3]

During the "Cold War," Greenberg's kind of modernism, which has been commonly described as "formalist," was influential in establishing the hegemony of Abstract Expressionism of the New York School and in dissociating it from prewar "leftist" avant-gardes in Europe and America.[4] Greenberg's formalism was further purified by the critic Michael Fried, who emphasized the integrity of the picture plane in such artists as Morris Louis. Fried also repudiated the effort of some artists to appeal to the viewers' imaginations to help arrive at the meaning of a work of art. His targets included the sense of theatricality in Minimalist works of the 1960s.[5]

Others soon came to see such formalist criticism as too dogmatic. Meyer Schapiro, a major art historian based at Columbia University disagreed with Greenberg and referred to "modern art" (since 1830) as the work of those "who take seriously the challenge of new possibilities and wish to introduce into their work perceptions, ideas and experiences which have come about only in our time."[6] Schapiro did not believe change in contemporary painting and sculpture to be limited to "a simple studio experiment or an intellectual play with ideas and with paint." It was instead "related to a broader and deeper reaction to basic elements of common experience and the concept of humanity, as it developed under new conditions."[7] T. J. Clark saw *flatness* as substance, "a barrier to the ordinary bourgeois' wish to enter a picture and dream, to have it be a space apart from life in which the mind would be free to make its own connections."[8] Nowadays art historians tend to consider modern painting as avant-garde practices in both subject matter and

---

3   Greenberg, "Modernist Painting" (1960), pp. 85, 87.

4   Guilbaut, *How New York*, pp. 165–94. We put "Cold War" in quotation marks to remind
    us that two of the surrogate wars of that period, in Korea and in Vietnam, were far from
    "cold."

5   Fried, "Art and Objecthood" (1967), pp. 148–72.

6   Schapiro, "Recent Abstract Painting" (1957), p. 213.

7   Ibid., p. 217.

8   Clark, "Greenberg's Theory," p. 81.

form, more or less in the spirit of Baudelaire's essay, "The Painter of Modern Life" (1863).

Avant-garde artists of the 1950s also revolted against Greenberg's theory of flatness. Jackson Pollock (1912–1956), a leading practitioner of the Abstract Expressionism exemplified in Greenberg's so-called all-over paintings (1947–1951), returned to painting symbolic figures in a later phase of his career. In 1962, the art critic Leo Steinberg noted Jasper Johns's sovereign disrespect for "the integrity of the picture plane," an icon of Greenberg's modernism, in his broken strokes reminiscent of Cézanne.[9] In 1972, Steinberg observed that the upright surface of the Renaissance picture plane, permitting distinctions among the observer, the surface, and the virtual space lying behind the plane, persisted in Abstract Expressionism. Moreover, Robert Rauschenberg's picture plane that incorporated all kinds of materials offered a new model for post-modernist (meaning after the modern era) painting. His work, simulating opaque flatbed horizontals rather than vertical visual fields (even if it would be hung on a wall), was related to making rather than just seeing, and letting the world in again.[10] Nevertheless, Greenberg's analogy between the picture plane and the wall underlies even "off-the-wall" practices since the 1960s, as avant-gardes turned away from the gallery walls, and in some cases, from painting altogether.

The Roles of Walls in Brice Marden's Modernism: An Overview

Receiving his training in art at Yale University in the 1960s, Brice Marden began his career as a modernist, even a minimalist. Maintaining "the indisputability of the plane" (1974)[11] and honoring the example of Pollock's late work (1952–1956),[12] he soon joined in the debate

---

9   Steinberg, "Jasper Johns," pp. 42–43.

10 Steinberg, "Other Criteria," pp. 72–73, 82–91. For a comparison of Steinberg's view and Michel Foucault's poststructuralist view on classical perspective, see Owens, "Representation," pp. 88–107.

11 Marden, *Grove Notebook*, summer 1974, in *Grove Group*, p. 25. Marden worked as Rauschenberg's studio assistant in the 1960s, but turned more to Johns's pictures.

12 Richardson, *Brice Marden*, p. 39.

between Greenberg and Steinberg on the role of the picture plane.[13] His adherence to modernism was only confirmed when he encountered the post-modern argument for "the death of painting" that has become popular art talk in support of nonpictorial experiments since the 1970s. In 1986 he declared that the related post-modernist idea of everything having been done (in painting) drove him "up the wall."[14] As we shall see, this was true in several senses: it caused him to mount and even transcend the often imagined wall between "Western modern" and "Asian traditional" art, to adopt elements of Chinese wall painting, and to reinvent the metaphor of paintings as walls on which images of the world can be posted.

Indeed, "up the wall" was a logical place for a painter of Marden's interests to go. At first categorized as a Minimalist painter, he nonetheless worked on "plane images" (this was also the name of his studio) until the early 1980s, whereas most of the Minimalists in the 1960s used (fabricated) objects as their artistic medium.[15] In 1977, Marden compared his own paintings with his father's stone walls: "My father . . . used to build beautiful dry stone walls and everything has to fit together right in order for it to stand, and I make paintings and everything has to fit together right in order for it to stand."[16] His *Grove Group I* (1972–1973), a grayish green canvas evoking Greek land and sea was mounted on a stretcher of about seven centimeters in depth (Figure 1). As such, it referred to the physicality of a wall. This was an early indication of how Marden's travels would come to broaden and enrich his art.

But Marden apparently came to think that the physicality of his monochrome picture planes risked excessive momentousness, and he consequently went through a period of inactivity around 1985. With his portfolio of *Etchings to Rexroth* (1986–1987) and his series on the theme of the *Cold Mountain* (1988–1991), Marden soon shifted to line drawing

---

13   Marden, however, says that he was never interested in formalism, thus putting some distance between himself and Greenberg; Wei, "Talking Abstract," p. 83.

14   Marden, "Brice Marden: Interview," p. 71; quoted in Shiff, "Force." I am indebted to Richard Shiff for providing me with a copy of his manuscript in June 2006.

15   For an overview of Minimalist objects, see Goldstein, *Minimal Future?*

16   Marden, on the sound track to Howard and Haimes, *Brice Marden.*

Figure 1 Brice Marden, *The Grove Group I*, 1972–1973. Oil and beeswax on canvas, 182.9 x 274.3 cm. The Museum of Modern Art, New York. Courtesy of the artist.

inspired by Chinese calligraphy and poetry.[17] More recently, his works have been inspired by inscriptions on Tang-period walls, tomb stones, and garden rocks. Calling the revolt against his own Minimalist style of the 1970s a midlife crisis, he uses Asian calligraphy because it is a pure form of expression, energetic and elegant, while painting has less line but tends to be defined by color, pigment, and form.[18] Withal, he has reinvented Greenberg's wall metaphor by endowing his flat paintings with more depth, without returning to the illusory/illusionist perspective of the earlier "modern" West.

Marden's cross-cultural creativity has encountered both resistance and support among contemporary art critics. On the one hand, Yve-Alain Bois argues that the comparison of the formal structure of Marden's painting with that of Chinese calligraphy is more distracting than illuminating. He sees Marden's multiprocedure painting as being based on discontinuous temporality, not on the forward movement of writing or sketching, and proposes instead the model of the body's internal structure as an explanation of the pictorial effect of Marden's glyphs.[19] Bois, moreover, dismisses the idea that the contents of Chinese poetry had any effect on Marden's calligraphic style. In this resistance to the example of cohabitation offered by Chinese poetry and painting we may see an echo of Greenberg's insistence that twentieth-century arts grow out of their own media and cannot serve another medium (hence his rejection of Surrealist painting as too "literary"). Bois' identification of calligraphy with literariness and linearity, however, is not self-evident. A prominent historian of Chinese art, Jonathan Hay, contends that the practice of calligraphy is founded on "the tensions between the grid and its decomposition, between unilinear temporality and a pictorial negation of that temporal order, and between graphic flatness and surface depth." In other words, we may observe, it participates in the same struggles that Greenberg ascribed to avant-garde painting. Hay also notes an expansion of Marden's Chinese frame of reference since 1993, paralleled by a further engagement

---

17 Marden, *Thirty-Six Poems by Tu Fu*.
18 Gardner, "Call It," *Art News* 93:4 (April 1994), pp. 140–43.
19 Bois, "Marden's Doubt," pp. 19, 35, 37. He considers Richardson's monograph (1992) as a representative case of a perfunctory mode of critical entry through calligraphic reading since 1987 (17, n. 2).

with the body or corporeal form.[20] Marden's recently adopted studio name, Propitious Garden of Plane Image, combines a Chinese reference (propitious garden) with the core concept of modern art and modernist criticism (plane image).

Unlike some previous studies that have more or less compartmentalized Marden's paintings into Western and Chinese styles, we shall analyze Marden's Chinese work in relation to the fundamental artistic and spiritual quests evident in his early abstract paintings. We shall emphasize their ground, or their handling of the pictorial support—canvas, paper, etc.—and we shall focus on the exchange between window and wall metaphors inspired by Piet Mondrian's (1872–1944) wallworks and Abstract Expressionism. We shall then offer more details on the relationship between word and image in his *Cold Mountain* works, a group of paintings and drawings inspired by the poems of Hanshan (fl. 627–649). We shall then go on to relate Marden's "writing" to the Chinese tradition of writing poetry on walls or rocks. In his most recent China-related work, Marden revives the dance subjects of wall decorations in Western modern art and thus rediscovers pictorial foundations common to Western and Chinese cultures. By means of *painterly* drawing inspired by Chinese calligraphy, Marden paradoxically reinvents the modernist wall metaphor—no longer as a synonym for flatness but as a pictorial support for virtual volume and depth, in the sense of openness and breaking through modernist and postmodernist dogmas.

Tiles and Walls

Marden was first known as a minimalist painter because of the literalness and conceptual complexities of his monochrome panels, whose physicality (what Michael Fried called "objecthood") inspire the spectator's poetic imagination.[21] Until the mid-1980s, Marden worked on subdued color planes or panels, on a scale comparable to the human figure. To avoid too much brightness on the picture plane, he used

---

20 Hay, *Brice Marden*, pp. 10–11.

21 Marden's statements in Carl Andre, "Line Work," *Arts Magazine* (May 1967); quoted and commented in Goldstein, *Minimal Future?*, p. 276.

beeswax mixed with oil paint.[22] Marden's use of wax also indicates his interest in the sense of slowness in Jasper Johns' painting. Johns first consistently used wax to allow the paint to dry faster so that he could put on another stroke without altering the first.[23] But color plane was not Marden's sole artistic penchant. While a student at Yale (1961–1963), Marden had already become interested in drawing and he acknowledged more influence from Esteban Vicente, an old-world Spanish painter, than from Josef Albers, who promoted abstract color interactions.[24] As we shall see, his interest in drawing turned out to be crucial to his cross-cultural contributions to painting in the 1980s.

In the 1960s, Marden multiplied the axial bisections of his surface to form a compositional grid, giving varied textures to each equally divided rectangle. Compositional grid pattern had been much exploited by Mondrian and Dutch De Stijl artists, and it has become an emblematic form of abstraction. Marden's grid pattern at this point recalled Johns' number paintings, which Marden had studied closely at the Jewish Museum in 1963. Many of his earlier paintings were of a monochromatic field with a three-sided border. *Decorative Painting* (1964) was intended to fit in a space on a wall in his New York studio.[25] This practical motive makes the reference to the wall an interactive process for painting, not a one-way circuit as Greenberg described it. In other words, a wall and a painting designed for it articulate each other. However, Marden actually began making grid drawings in Paris in 1964, at first by doing rubbings of kitchen tiles, simply because he had no place to paint. He painted a blank surface over a preliminary grid of the kitchen tiles and developed his multiple layering of color planes (Figure 2). He tended to leave unpainted a lower edge of one-half to one inch wide, where drips of paint accumulated and thus left traces of the painting process.[26]

---

22 For the view that Marden's color planes are postminimalist, see Shearer, "Brice Marden's Paintings," pp. 9–27.

23 Crichton, *Jasper Johns*, p. 28. The sense of slowness is comparable to Cézanne's conspicuously separate brushstrokes.

24 John Yau, "Interview," p. 55.

25 Ibid., p. 45. Garrels, *Plane Image*, no. 8.

26 For a detailed description of Marden's technique until 1973, see Smith, "Brice Marden's Painting," pp. 36–41.

Figure 2 Brice Marden, Untitled, 1964–1965. Charcoal on paper, 50.2 x 56.5 cm. Collection of the artist. Courtesy of the artist.

During his four-month stay in Paris in 1964, Marden became fascinated with the massive project to clean up the old exterior walls of both public and private buildings (an initiative of Minister of Culture André Malraux). He sat and watched workers scrub and sandblast stone walls all day, resulting in a "fantastic accumulation of drips" on the old walls. At the same time, he read the journal *Art International*, in which Greenberg championed Morris Louis's and Kenneth Noland's works as the new models of modernist painting, on account of the optical identification between color and ground (canvas) in their paintings. Marden also saw his first Nolands and Louises in Paris, at

Lawrence Rubin's gallery. Marden compared Jasper Johns's grid paintings with his own experimental efforts in that direction, and he said that the grid should be "equally divided."[27] Thus, the reference to everyday life in Johns' art provided a counterpoint to Greenberg's pure abstraction. However, the modular grid also reflects the influence of Mondrian's Parisian compositions and Marden's handling of color was in the monochromatic vein of Franz Kline (1910–1962). The conjoined influence of Mondrian and Kline accounts for the temporality (in the sense of in process) and the meditative quality of Marden's early work.

The experience of viewing old but revitalized Parisian walls appears to have inspired his subsequent work on painterly action. Returning to New York, he came to conceive of paintings as "large areas of one color, maybe two strips down the outside, or just like two rectangles . . . put on with a brush and worked with a palette knife, lots of varnish, [with a] very oily kind of surface."[28] In the 1970s, arranging several panels of identical shapes in each painting allowed Marden to emphasize the variations in color. The *Annunciation* series, five groups of assembled vertical panels, focused on the permutation of color values and forms to depict the five states of mind of the Virgin Mary—*Conturbatio* (disquiet), *Cogitatio* (reflection), *Interrogatio* (inquiry), *Humiliatio* (submission), and *Meritatio* (merit)—as interpreted in Michael Baxandall's sociological study of fifteenth-century Florentine painting.[29] The painting was conceived during the pregnancy of Marden's wife, Helen,[30] reminding us that art and life have almost always been associated in Marden's painting. Moreover, different from Baxandall's idea of a period eye specific to fifteenth-century Florentines, Marden's abstract color panels seem to hint at cross-cultural and intertemporal correspondences.[31]

27 Cummings, "Interview with Brice Marden." See also Greenberg, "Louis and Noland," pp. 97, 99. Marden probably read also Fried's "New York Letter: Louis" (1962) and "New York Letter: Noland" (1963), both published in *Art International*.
28 Cummings, "Interview with Brice Marden."
29 Lebensztejn, "From." Baxandall, *Painting and Experience*, pp. 45–56. See Kertess, *Brice Marden*, pp. 98–102, plates.
30 Wylie, *Brice Marden*, p. 28.
31 According to Marden, "art is not about sociology or criticism, art is about art," cited in Wei, "Talking Abstract," p. 83.

Since the mid-1970s, Marden has regularly traveled with his family to the Aegean island of Hydra and has drawn inspiration from Greek architecture and mythology.[32] In the early 1980s, Marden's multipanel Greek paintings often involved subtle variations of the picture plane. One of his best-known "post and lintel paintings," *Thira* (1979–1980, Musée National d'Art Moderne, Paris), composed of eighteen panels, refers to the myth of Theseus, the Minoan palace of Knossos, and the classical Doric style of architecture.[33] The arrangement recalls the painted walls and labyrinthine division, enclosure and opening, of a reconstructed Minoan palace.[34] *Thira* is the ancient name for the island of Santorini, while the homophonic Greek word *thyra* means door.[35] *Thira* is intended to make a space through color variations of value among the panels, while, according to Marden, "modernist painting has been about how the color comes up closer to the surface and how that affects the viewer."[36] For Greenberg, who preferred the optical identification between color and ground in modernist painting to the tactile or spatial effect of Cubist light and dark, "Color meant areas and zones, and the interpenetration of these, which could be achieved better by variations of hue than by variations of value."[37] The critic also regretted the immediate perception of illusory space "behind the frame" in Abstract Expressionism.[38] In the four *Elements* (1983–1984), Marden also combines the column with the beam of classical Greek architecture.[39] The reference to architecture and space becomes a major theme in his Greek work.[40] Marden's color and surface produce the physicality and spatiality of walls.

---

32 Keller, "Brice Marden at Daros," p. 19.

33 Hale, "Of a Classic Order: Brice Marden's *Thira*," pp. 152–53. Garrels, *Plane Image*, no. 83.

34 Scully's *Earth* has been one of Marden's favorite readings; Yau, "Interview," p. 49.

35 The author would like to thank Haun Saussy for his instruction in Greek terms, October 2005.

36 Marden's statement in Yau, "Interview," p. 51.

37 Greenberg, "Louis and Noland," pp. 96–97.

38 Greenberg, "After Abstract Expressionism," p. 124.

39 Keller, "Brice Marden at Daros," pp. 20–21.

40 Marden is also interested in artifacts from other "ancient" cultures, such as the false doors in an Egyptian tomb that provide a sense of blocked openings; Lewison, *Brice Marden*, p. 42.

In the early 1980s, too, Marden comes closer than before to the spiritualist abstraction that had inspired Mondrian's choice of a grid structure.[41] In the commissioned studies for the stained-glass windows at the Basel cathedral (1978–1985), Marden stopped using wax and focused on line drawings brightened by almost transparent color, but he introduced the diagonal to combine the colors in lines and planes. For example, he produced three colors in linear figures (red, yellow, blue) and four monochromatic panels (red, green, yellow, blue) in *Second Window Painting* (1983).[42] The diagonal lines are distributed according to three axes falling along the central axis and two vertical borders of the central panel, which is rendered with mixed and diluted colors of the other four panels. The variations of colors and angles of the diagonals make the grids underlying each panel more translucent and interrelated. Marden treats his canvases as walls, doors, windows, and grids—in short, his painting incorporates architectural surface and space, or diverging from Greenberg's formalist theory of the absolutely flat picture plane predetermined by the wall (Figure 3).

Marden discovered Asian calligraphy in the early 1980s with help from his wife, Helen, a Californian with a particular affinity for Asian culture. Once again, Helen played the role of cross-cultural muse. After traveling for two or three months with his family in Asia in 1984, Marden became fascinated with Eastern calligraphy.[43] He was most impressed by the exhibition of Japanese masters of calligraphy at the Asia Society and the Japan House galleries in New York that same year.[44] His calligraphic-style paintings from 1985 to 1987 came out of the drawings he made during a trip to Thailand in 1985. Looking at calligraphy as painting to be observed, rather than as writing to be read, he nonetheless tried to follow the particular stroke order of the script to see how characters are made. This yielded a completely new "reading" to Marden, one in his view "much closer [than he had perceived before] to the real energy of [the script]—the complexity and the control—and this is when it [the Chinese inspiration for him] really

---

41 On interpretations of Mondrian as a formalist or spiritualist, see respectively Bois, "Iconoclast," pp. 313–72, and Blotkamp, *Mondrian*.

42 Yau, "Interview," p. 51.

43 Gardner, "Call It," p. 143.

44 Richardson, *Brice Marden*, p. 49. See the exhibition catalogue, Shimizu and Rosenfield, *Masters*.

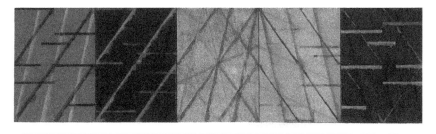

Figure 3 Brice Marden, *Second Window Painting*, 1983. Oil on linen, 66 x 50.8 cm each panel (5 panels). Collection of the artitst. Courtesy of the artist.

starts soaring."[45] This "new reading" actually corresponds to a degree to the longstanding Chinese synthesis of writing and painting. Marden developed in his glyphs (1986) a further link with the gestural painting of Abstract Expressionism.[46] For him, they were like the skeletons or structures of his early paintings.[47]

Marden did not approach Chinese poetry and painting as a specialist. "I don't know anything about the (Chinese) language, but Ezra Pound (1885–1972) says if you are in any way receptive, you'll get it."[48] His initiation into Chinese poetry came from Pound's *Cathay* (1915) and Kenneth Rexroth's translations of thirty-six poems by Du Fu (712–770), as well as the travelogue writer Peter Matthiessen's *Nine-Headed Dragon River: Zen Journals 1969–1982.*[49] Matthiessen mentions the Zen idea of Oneness of existence that Bodhidharma (ca. 440– ?) came to realize through nine years spent in *zazen*—literally, sitting Zen or, in Matthiessen' words, "facing the wall."[50] Thus Marden's appreciation of Chinese art is informed by a spirituality that previous "Westerners" have found in "Eastern" aesthetics and philosophy.

Between 1988 and 1991, Marden did six renderings of *Cold Mountain*, together with a series of drawings. They were based on Red Pine's (i.e., Bill Porter's) translations of the poems by Hanshan, which had the Chinese text on one page and the English translation on the other.[51] Marden's efforts in visualizing Hanshan's poems proved to be crucial to his pictorial transformation. He had first come across Hanshan's poems through Gary Snyder's (b. 1930) translation when he was in college in the early 1960s.[52] Snyder's translation was very popular among the Beats: in fact, Jack Kerouac (1922–1969) dedicated *The Dharma Bums* (1958) to Hanshan and quoted Snyder's Hanshan repeatedly in his own book.[53] For Marden, who had been carrying around Arthur Waley's

45 Hay, *Brice Marden*, pp. 24–25.
46 Kertess, "Plane Image," pp. 42–44.
47 Gardner, "Call It," p. 142.
48 Wei, "Talking Abstract," p. 83.
49 Richardson, *Brice Marden*, pp. 51, 76.
50 Matthiessen, *Nine-Headed*, p. 9.
51 Hanshan, *Collected Songs*.
52 Richardson, *Brice Marden*, p. 51. Snyder, "Cold Mountain Poems," Snyder, *Riprap*, pp. 35–67.
53 Kerouac, *Dharma Bums*, pp. 21–22, quotations of Snyder, #8, #3, #10.

(1889–1966) *The Way and Its Power* (1958) for years, "The poems of Hanshan, his life, the landscape, [and] its spirituality" took on a very real focus. In contrast to Snyder's dense rendition, Red Pine's translation is in a more Zen–like style—very short sentences composed of everyday words without any signs of punctuation—in which the meaning depends on the syntactical break of each line, so as to enhance its openness.

Take for instance, the poem about the path to Cold Mountain in the two versions. Gary Snyder #8 reads:

> Clambering up the Cold Mountain path,
> The Cold Mountain trail goes on and on:
> The long gorge choked with scree and boulders,
> The wide creek, the mist-blurred grass.
> The moss is slippery, though there's been no rain
> The pine sings, but there's no wind.
> Who can leap the world's ties
> And sit with me among the white clouds?

Red Pine #32 reads:

> Who takes the Cold Mountain Road
> takes a road that never ends
> the rivers are long and piled with rocks
> the streams are wide and choked with grass
> it's not the rain that makes the moss slick
> and it's not the wind that makes the pines moan
> who can get past the tangles of the world
> and sit with me in the clouds[54]

In short, Red Pine's translations conformed more than Snyder's to the original Chinese texts and to Marden's ideal of plane/plain images.

The transposition of Chinese calligraphy to abstract painting had long since been accomplished within European modernism. In his quest for a new art free of inherited representational conventions,

---

54 Red Pine's translation approaches the Daoist noninterference promoted by Yip in his *Ezra Pound's Cathay*. See also Chapter 9 in this volume.

Roger Fry (1866–1934) looked to certain non-European traditions, including the Egyptian, the Byzantine, and the Chinese, for compositional principles (i.e., related to the pictorial surface) in non-representational art. He believed that useful objects attract no particular attention—only certain things such as Chinese decorative objects or jewelry could arouse aesthetic thinking.[55] Fry posited that Chinese art is concerned with compositional equilibrium, and he thought that some contemporary European art had more affinity to Chinese art than to the "grand tradition" of European art. He identified three characteristics of Chinese art: the linear rhythm of calligraphic drawing, the rhythmic continuity on the pictorial surface (i.e., a regular compositional pattern), and round shapes such as globe, egg, and cylinder.[56]

After World War II, some accomplished artists such as Henri Michaux (1899–1984), Mark Tobey (1890–1976), and Franz Kline drew inspiration from Chinese calligraphy. For example, Pierre Soulages (1919–), inspired by Victor Segalen's (1878–1919) *Stèles*, simulated ideograms on a large shiny surface.[57] Many Western artists have tended to be fascinated with the rhythmic and gestural (or corporeal) quality of Chinese calligraphy. Marden, on the other hand, had a special interest in visual organization. Seeing Kline's intention of appropriating "flying white" strokes as efforts in a single element, Marden chose to study the notion of "skeleton (bones)" in Chinese calligraphy.[58]

Cold Mountain and the Wall for Meditation

Marden followed the classical principles of Chinese calligraphy that connect abstraction with figuration. In the supposed words of the primordial master calligrapher Wang Xizhi (ca. 321–379), calligraphy should be

---

55   Fry, "Essay in Aesthetics," p. 18.

56   Fry, *Chinese Art*, pp. 1–5.

57   Michael Sullivan compares Kandinsky's theory of resonance to the principle of spiritual resonance in Chinese painting, and suspects the close parallels between the existentialist gestures of Pollock, Kline, or Soulages and Zen ink painting to be more than coincidence. See *Meeting*, pp. 244–46.

58   Yau, "Interview," pp. 57–58.

music without sound, image without form, every horizontal stroke is like a mass of clouds in battle strength, every dot like a falling rock from a high peak, every turning of the stroke like a brass hook, every drawn-out line like a dry vine of great old age, and every swift and free stroke like a runner on his start.[59]

The figural evocation calls to mind Daisetz Suzuki's (1870–1966) comparison of the world of Zen to the artist's world of creating "forms and sounds out of formlessness and soundlessness."[60]

The line drawings in Marden's six paintings of *Cold Mountain* show a development from vertical figural drawings based on calligraphic couplets toward intricate web weaving. Marden himself says that he was thinking in terms of a calligraphic hand scroll.[61] In *Cold Mountain I*, he simulated four couplets on a grid module, a very common way of presenting the Chinese regular style of writing (*kaishu*). From *Cold Mountain II* to *Cold Mountain IV*, he moved toward the constantly changing characters of Zen writing, not unlike the "wild cursive" (*kuangcao*) of the *Autobiographical Scroll* (777) by the famous Chan (Japanese *Zen*) monk-calligrapher Huaisu (ca. 725–785).[62] In *Cold Mountain IV*, some vague human figures emerge from the web of drawing and look as if they are moving toward one side or the other. In *Cold Mountain VI*, the horizontal and the diagonal connecting the columnar figures become stronger, evoking more balanced and interrelated movement from one side to the other.

Marden's rendering of the ground in this series is distinguished from that in earlier paintings. In general, the picture planes appear lighter and occasionally have some transparent spots due to thin over-painting. In *Cold Mountain II*, smudges and dripping of faded dark green tones under brighter lines add to the sense of immediacy of the act of painting, in contrast to the finished quality of the controlled line drawing. Such incidental marks also allude to natural traces on exterior or garden walls. Marden works the ground more or less like a house painter. He thins the paint with terpineol, a very strong solvent, which demands to be done in one go for a large canvas. He works top to

---

59   Wei, "Talking Abstract," p. 83.

60   Suzuki, *Zen*, p. 17.

61   The artist's statement, in Richardson, *Brice Marden*, p. 56.

62   See Na, *Choice Works*, pp. 61–62, plate 4. See also Chiang, *Chinese Calligraphy*, p. 97.

bottom, which results in dripping. He then reworks the canvas, "putting the paint on with a house-painting brush, and scraping the excess off with a knife," to prevent excessive buildup. The process of scraping down, because of the nature of the solvent, dissolves as well some of the layer beneath. Different layers of ground colors will mix, yielding an opaque color.[63]

Although Marden's *Cold Mountain* paintings are not precisely illustrations of the poetry, he did subtitle three paintings of the six and suggested, without specifying, their meanings. In the plain style of Zen verse, Hanshan wrote about various emotions experienced on his quest for the true path (*dao*, or *tao* in Red Pine's transliteration)—frustration, independence, nostalgia, doubt, and openness. Marden seems to relate Hanshan's poems to his own artistic quest, a relatively isolated and "archaizing" path in the contemporary art world. *Cold Mountain I (Path)* has a subtitle *(Path)* revealing Marden's reflection on the verbal tendency in contemporary art. Red Pine's translations use the word "path" sparingly (#89, #207), while most of the words corresponding to *dao* in Chinese are rendered as "way" (#16), "road" (#32), or "trail" (#35). One of the rare instances of the word "path" is in a poem about the Buddhist practice of reciting:

> They don't walk the Noble Path
> They say they believe as they go astray
> Their tongues don't stop before buddhas
> Their hearts overflow with envy
> In private they eat fish and meat
> In public they chant *O-mi-to-fo*
> If this is how they cultivate
> How will they deal with disaster (#76)

Hanshan mocks practitioners who take the common path of recitation, instead of the higher path of Zen meditation (see below).[64] Marden noted in 1974 the situation of a painter in New York: "I've heard it said, / Painting is dead. / Too much mouth / Not enough eyes." Marden

---

63 Hay, *Brice Marden*, p. 19.

64 Gary Snyder first translated the word *tao* as path (Kerouac, *Dharma Bums*, p. 21), and changed it to trail in the final version (1958, 46); Leed, "Gary Snyder," p. 192.

personally heard this chant uttered, often by artists on completion of a new piece, in downtown Manhattan. Moreover, it was accompanied by "a gleeful soft step dance too complicated to define," but clearly signifying joy.[65] The robust materiality in Marden's *Grove Group* thus marks his reflection on the origins of painting at a Greek site, as a way out of the hypersophisticated art world in contemporary New York.

In *Cold Mountain I (Path)*, the semicalligraphy follows a clear pattern on the right, turning into freer strokes and shapes toward the left. The last vertical line simulates three or four characters—not five as it is in the poem, to leave an opening on the lower left. Thus, the figural drawing appears with gesticulation, each columnar figure pointing at another, and gradually merging into the void on the lower margins. The indeterminate figuration appearing through gray wash indicates a movement leading into and out of the pictorial space, recalling the elusive trail in such late Pollock paintings as *White Light* (1954, Museum of Modern Art, New York) that Marden admired. In other words, the ambivalent figuration of human size in the *Cold Mountain* paintings enacts the virtual space of the picture plane, relating the wall metaphor to transparent pictorial depth, which invites the spectator to trace the interwoven trails in it.

Marden's resolve in his spiritual quest can be seen in *Cold Mountain V (Open)* (1989–1991) (Figure 4). In his words, he was bent on producing paintings that "offer open situations that are not infinitely open but are rather more open than a lot of other situations." The painter would not be able to just "attain" such situations but would have to come across them in the process of painting. He would have to avoid identifying himself with his painting; he would have to forget himself.[66] The resulting unmade openness would be at the same time monumental and vulnerable to change.

The subtitle *Open* related to the description of Hanshan's dwelling, material and spiritual:

> Cold Mountain owns a house
> with no partitions inside
> six doors open left and right

65   Marden, *Grove Group*, p. 21.
66   For the artist's statement, see Richardson, *Brice Marden*, p. 74.

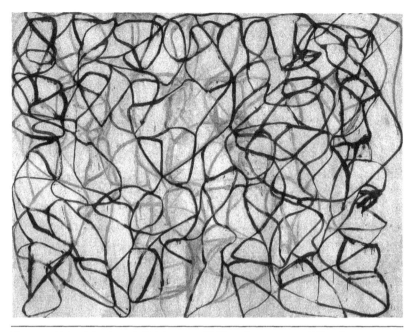

Figure 4 Brice Marden, *Cold Mountain V (Open)*, 1989–1991. Oil on linen, 274.3 x 365.8 cm. Robert and Jane Meyerhoff Collection, Phoenix, Maryland. Courtesy of the artist.

> from the hall he sees blue sky
> wherever he looks it's bare
> the east wall greets the west
> nothing stands between them
> no need for anyone's care. (Red Pine #167)

The "six doors" refer to the six senses of the eyes, ears, nose, tongue, body, and will in Buddhist terminology. Hanshan's poem leads us to interpret the walls as the external structure, or shell, of the human body, open to nature. For a Zen Buddhist temple, two rooms are essential: the meditation-(or Zen) hall (Chinese *chantang*, Japanese *zendō*) and the recitation hall (Chinese *nianfotang*), representing two different paths for spiritual exercise. Most practitioners choose the path of chanting *O-mi-to-fo* (the Amitabha Buddha). However, illustrious monks have almost always performed Zen sittings for five or six years before reaching enlightenment. The Zen meditation hall, with one opening as the sole entrance and exit, is sparsely furnished with a stone bank along the four walls. During their meditation sessions, two seasons every year, practitioners sit on the bank, facing the wall, to inquire through the six senses, in memory of Bodhidharma's meditation, which involved nine years of sitting facing a rock wall.[67] Red Pine characterizes Bodhidharma's teaching of wall meditation as the equation of Zen with buddhahood along with the everyday mind, and his "walls of emptiness connect all opposites, including self and other, mortal and sage." Bodhidharma's meditation was that of Mahayana Zen, not Hinayana Zen—symbolized by the sword of wisdom, not the meditation cushion.[68] Hanshan claims to have written all of his six hundred poems on rock walls (Red Pine #268), apparently alluding to Bodhidharma's meditation. In the eighth century, the Chan monk Huaisu expanded the practice, writing on walls, rocks, and various other more banal surfaces,[69] apparently engaging in typical Zen activity.

In all six *Cold Mountain* paintings, the repeated scraping and sanding made the canvas ground appear similar to old walls or ancient rocks.[70] Marden's color drawing thus approaches Hanshan's act of writing on walls. *Cold Mountain, Zen Studies 1,* in its early state (1990) communicates some anxious twisting confined to a regular grid pattern, some of the large dark strokes showing dramatic movements and sudden stops or turns.[71] In *Cold Mountain 5 (Open),* the fluid movement of the figural evocation over the whole pictorial space, produced by means of interweaving black and grayish blue lines,

---

67   The author is indebted to Chou Po-Kan for his instruction on Buddhist practice, October 2005. After translating Hanshan's poems, Gary Snyder also turned toward the *zendo*; Snyder, *Riprap*, p. 66.

68   Red Pine, *Zen Teaching*, xi–xv, 3, 115, n. 2. Bodhidharma, the (legendary) patriarch of Zen Buddhists, was a Brahman prince by birth who converted to Buddhism. He supposedly brought Zen to Southern China around 475 CE.

69   Na, ed., *Choice Works*, pp. 103–4.

70   See also Richardson, *Brice Marden*, p. 67.

71   Ibid., p. 121, illustration.

appears solemnly organized and is therefore distinguished from the frantic interlacing of the previous four *Cold Mountain* paintings.

Marden's earlier paintings had already manifested a contemplative quality. In the vertical monochrome panels of *Fave* (1968–1969) and *For Pearl* (1970), Marden intended to "stop the flow of sensation."[72] Referring to Goya's seemingly static female presence in a tripartite verticality in *D'après la Marquise de la Solana* (1969, Solomon R. Guggenheim Museum, New York), the narrow gap between the panels, emphasized by the dark color on the sides, produces an ambivalent effect somewhere between closing and opening, between moving and stopping, like stone walls and gates in an enchanted palace. With the earlier monochrome paintings, the spectator contemplating the physicality of the picture plane experienced temptation and enlightenment, illusion, and disillusion.

In contrast, after his "brush" with Chinese calligraphy, Marden is able to assert firmer control over the fluid meditation. The modular grid in *Cold Mountains* is based on the ground structure in regular Chinese writing and printing. Calligraphers strove to render the spiritual resonance of the universe in complex skeins of handwriting. The calligraphers' *qi* (literally, "breath") communicates from one line to the next, emerging from and going beyond the grid.[73] This spirituality actually involves coordinated body movement and breathing. Putting down vertical lines from right to left, the calligrapher usually maintains the brush at a certain distance from the paper, the wall or some other support, to allow the writer to have an optimum perspective on the handwriting. In so doing, the calligrapher breaks up the boundary between art and nature, as the writing surface structured by a grid recaptures the body movement of the calligrapher in harmony with nature. In using the grid system of Chinese calligraphy, Marden reinforces the stability of his work. Moreover, the direction in which the drawing is done (from top to bottom) relates to Marden's earlier work, where there was dripping along the bottom edge.[74] In short,

---

72 On *Fave, For Pearl*, and other monochrome paintings, see Marden's conversation with Shiff, February 12, 2006; Shiff, "Force," p. 59.

73 Concerning *qi* or *qihou*, see the ninth-century author Zhang Huaiguan's theory on *cao* (cursive) script, as commented on in Hay, "Human Body," pp. 87–88.

74 Yau, "Interview," p. 58.

Marden's Chinese work enhances his articulation of the spatiotemporal structure of the picture plane.

Inter-textual Writing on the Wall

With the layering of drawing and painting, the six *Cold Mountain* paintings appear as monumental surfaces of memory, but not to be remembered, only to be looked at.[75] Drawing that simulates writing is intended to be seen, not read, as traces of man becoming one with nature. There is apparently a psychological *double entendre* in Marden's handwriting of Chinese characters, or, the artist's presence through Chinese *characters*. Chinese calligraphy is, after all, about energy or vitality materializing through the brush into the ink-trace.[76] In Marden, the energy embodied in the materiality of Chinese calligraphy is metamorphosed into the act of drawing. In the *Cold Mountain* paintings, some shimmering surfaces are interlaced with the skeins of drawings, and the color washes take on a shamanistic aspect. Marden painted things out, making corrections by painting over with white. In this way, "What was painted out also became a positive image. It was sort of like a ghost image."[77] The act of erasure turns into a positive act with its own trace, indicating the presence of something beneath, behind, or beyond.

The aesthetics of presence (not representation) relates Marden's drawing to the Chinese tradition of writing on walls. Writing poems on walls, a Chinese literary tradition starting from the seventh century, turns the wall into a site of memory. Inspired by the site, literati would leave their handwriting on a wall, usually in public spaces, which in turn might inspire literary acquaintances or newcomers with corresponding states of mind to express their thoughts in poetry. Recording poems through chance spiritual encounters and losing them through time, the inscribed wall turns into a memento of continuity and discontinuity of human emotion. Poems inscribed on walls, *tibishi*, tend to elicit a melancholy response to the evanescence

---

75 Hay, *Brice Marden,* p. 20.
76 Hay, "Human Body," p. 89; quoted as being from *Theories of Art in China* [*sic*] in Shimizu and Rosenfield, *Masters,* p. 33. Shimizu and Rosenfeld's exhibition catalogue is one of Marden's favorite references.
77 Steir, "Brice Marden."

of life and the inevitability of loss. However, the materiality of writing on a wall related to a strong spiritual presence, and was sometimes associated, particularly in the seventeenth century, with ghosts whose intense emotions made them restless revenants.[78]

One could imagine that, in the same spirit, the tradition of New York painting becomes the historical inscription *in* the wall that Marden contemplates and writes through. Pollock could become both a material and a phantasmagoric presence in Marden's line-based paintings after 1989. Creating Marden's own historicity through the reminiscence of Pollock's picture plane, Marden used his drawing to probe in depth the wall/ground of painting and writing. On the other hand, the modular grid refers to a formal device that has been much exploited in abstract art from Mondrian and Dutch De Stijl artists.[79] In the grid system of *Victory Boogie Woogie* (1944, Gemeente-museum, The Hague), Mondrian reinforces the flickering light at the crossing of different color bands. The jumpy surface relates at the same time to materiality and spirituality. Mondrian's New York works are particularly relevant for Marden, who professes a rooted identification with the lights in the city.[80] Marden made a "boogie-woogie print," begun in 1973, carried on until 1979, and finally released in 1988. The layering of Mondrian's *Broadway Boogie-Woogie* might have inspired one of Marden's *Homage to Art* drawings (1973–1974).[81]

Marden's calligraphic drawing stresses the act of writing itself, not the resulting script, and thus approaches the first definition of writing in the *Oxford English Dictionary*: "The action of one who writes, in various senses," before "the penning or forming of letters or words; the using of written characters for purposes of record, transmission of ideas, etc."[82] Focused on the action at the expense of legibility, Marden's *Cold Mountain* paintings thus constitute a counteraction to other contemporary artists' cynical use of language to teach the death of

---

78 Zeitlin, "Disappearing Verses," pp. 73–125.

79 Krauss, "Grids," pp. 8–22.

80 For the artist's statement, see Richardson, *Brice Marden*, p. 79.

81 Lewison, *Brice Marden*, nos. 35, 148, 45; Saul Ostrow, "Brice Marden Interview," *BOMB* (Winter 1988); both quoted in Bois, "Marden's Doubt," pp. 27, 29, n. 7.

82 The second definition is quoted as applicable to conceptual artists in Morley, *Writing*, p. 6.

painting, a demise now enthusiastically embraced by magazines, galleries, and museums. In Marden's view, "Art isn't about cynicism; it's about faith and hope."[83] Breaking down the boundary between drawing and writing, Marden's line drawing comes close to Roland Barthes's (1915–1980) idea of graphism: "The artist's gesture (artist as gesture) does not break the causal chain of the acts, what Buddhists call the *karma*, . . . but blurs it and relaunches it until its meaning gets lost." Graphism is, in short, an act of rupture reminiscent of the *satori* (enlightenment) in Zen.[84] Reminiscent of André Masson's (1896–1987) intertextual, cross-cultural writing, Marden's graphism also refers to various manners of inscription not so much bound to spelling out characters as to conveying the fluid energy of the artist's body.[85] In the same vein, Henri Michaux also remarks on the general tendency of eschewing the primitive ideographic legibility in different Chinese styles of writing and calligraphers' pursuit of liberty in gestural quality: *Voie par l'écriture.*[86]

In the 1990s, Marden drew on Chinese calligraphy and Greek classicism in his quest for natural forces. He noticed that, as he shaped his calligraphic work in the form of couplets, figures started to appear. As he worked, his paintings became much more about the movement of the body, making gestures. This led to a group of paintings and drawings about the nine figures of the Muses.[87] In the *Muses* (1991–1993), Marden maintained the grid as a compositional principle, though he also drew on the imaginary Maenads, predecessors of the Muses, who were not depicted in grid form.[88] Marden based his series of *Muses* on the interpretation of Robert Graves, who described them as *Bacchantes* intent on performing orgiastic dances, figures of Dionysian madness. Marden thus connects to the ancient theme of

---

83 Wei, "Talking Abstract," p. 83. For an introduction to conceptual art, see Tony Godfrey, *Conceptual Art.*

84 Barthes, "Cy Twombly," pp. 160–61. On *satori*, see Suzuki, *Zen*, pp. 6, 10, 218–21.

85 Barthes, "Semiography," p. 154.

86 Michaux, *Idéogrammes*, n.p. Marden also owns a work of Henri Michaux; Lewison, *Brice Marden: Prints*, p. 50.

87 Hay, *Brice Marden*, p. 26.

88 Yau, "Interview," p. 59; Garrels, *Plane Image*, no. 137.

dance and riot, order and disorder.[89] In this series, he extends the act of writing toward what Jacques Derrida (1930–2004) described as "not only the physical gestures of literal pictographic or ideographic inscription," but "all that gives rise to inscription in general, whether it is literal or not and even if what it distributes in space is alien to the order of the voice: cinematography, choreography, of course, but also pictorial, musical, sculptural 'writing.'"[90] Marden's calligraphic drawing transformed the Maenads' physicality into a springboard for spirituality.

On the other hand, in *Chinese Dancing* (1993–1996), the interweaving curvilinear movement of relatively even lines of color evokes the ribbon dance.[91] The even distribution of paint on each single line ensures the physicality of the movement, which is consolidated by the layered rubbings of gray tones over some preceding colored lines. Billowing ribbons in Chinese dance are associated with clouds, evoking at the same time sensuality and spirituality—the "breath" or atmosphere of body movement. In Chinese visual culture, ribbons and clouds stand for male and female physicality, according to the conditioning terms with which they are associated. Ribbons with lively rhythm represent physical and psychological movement in Chinese painting, as seen in *Admonitions of the Palace Instructress* (British Museum, London), probably a Tang copy of a work by Gu Kaizhi (ca. 344–ca. 406). Floating ribbons in particular invoke a superhuman state associated with female rather than male subjects.[92]

In the eighth century (mid–Tang dynasty), Chinese artists, painting on the grotto walls of Dunhuang, preserved the immediacy of the sketch in rendering bodies in action in close relationship to the forces of nature. As Fraser points out, this new level of spontaneity was canonized during the ninth and tenth centuries (late Tang, Five Dynasties, and early Song) and was supported by the three spheres of

---

89 Hay, *Brice Marden,* p. 26; Mario Codognato, "A Cut through the Frieze of Time," in Codognato, *Brice Marden,* p. 19.

90 Derrida, *De la grammatologie,* p. 19; trans. by Spivak, *Of Grammatology,* p. 9.

91 Wylie, *Brice Marden,* fig. 7.

92 Hay, "Body Invisible," pp. 52–56.

literati calligraphy, Chan meditation, and Daoist action.[93] Marden himself explained the corporeality of his figural painting of specific dances from the caves of Dunhuang as "a transference of your [the artist's] own dance to the canvas."[94] Because of its Buddhist overtones, Chinese art of the eighth century such as the cave paintings at Dunhuang explicitly depicted elements of nakedness, especially of foreign bodies.[95] In the eighth and ninth centuries, nakedness was associated with foreign bodies in Buddhist paintings, while physicality was characteristic of the figure paintings in subjects of court life. For example, Zhou Fang, a major court painter active in the late eighth century, was known for his depiction of court ladies with bodily lines and shapes. Such physicality, however, diminished in and then disappeared from mainstream Chinese figure paintings after the tenth century. Thus Marden's choice of Dunhuang paintings is specifically conducive to his multicultural creation. In this perspective, "Chinese dance" for Marden was a metonym of *Bacchante* sensuality and physicality. Marden's robust line drawing in *Chinese Dance* registers such physicality incisively and rediscovers the aesthetics of spontaneity of the Tang.

Marden transposed the dance on the wall in the caves of Dunhuang to the dance on the canvas. Dance on the canvas is also an apt metaphor of European modern painting, calling to mind Henri Matisse's (1869–1954) dance subjects for wall decoration. In addition to these pieces, Marden was also fascinated by the figure of the Hour in Botticelli's (1444–1510) *Birth of Venus*, whose feet "both do and do not touch the ground."[96] In this way, Marden continues to develop broader inter-cultural and intertemporal references.

---

93 Fraser, *Performing the Visual*, pp. 197–229. For example, Wu Daozi (ca. 685–758) was canonized by the art historian Zhang Yenyuan on account of his "sparse style" of calligraphic drawing; Zhang, *Lidai Minghuaji*, pp. 25–27.

94 Hay, *Brice Marden*, p. 21.

95 Hay, "Body Invisible," p. 59.

96 Marden also reported having seen, one summer in the late eighties, his daughters dancing in the light-filled room of his studio at Hydra, a vision of late childhood and the impending loss of their virginity; conversation with Brenda Richardson, about #3 at the Baltimore Museum of Art (1987–1988), 1991; Richardson, "Brice Marden, Lifelines," p. 95.

Marden moved further into cross-cultural painting with his trip to Suzhou in November 1995, when he was most impressed by the past influence of scholars in this city.[97] He also observed firsthand the famous rocks from Lake Tai, such as the *Cloud-Capped Peak* rock in the Garden of Lingering in Suzhou.[98] His *Suzhou, Before and After* (1995–1996) was inspired by and reflected the weird shapes of these rocks hollowed out by the action of strong currents in the lake.[99] The "physiognomy" of the rock, the foraminate texture and upright stance, evokes the human body in motion.[100] Such rocks, as garden walls, were the frame of a garden and, as symbols of mountains, the principal agent of spatiotemporal transference.[101] By painting such rocks, Marden introduced further abstraction to his picture planes, but always with a natural reference.

Marden may also have been inspired by Suzhou to recoup some of the work of the modernists. Consciously or unconsciously, the capricious flow inward and outward of the picture plane in *Suzhou, Before and After,* seems to paraphrase the stormy surge of Pollock's *The Deep* (1953, Musée National d'Art Moderne, Paris). Furthermore, the abstractness of rocks was also a favorite subject of Cézanne, whom Marden once called "my hero."[102] In Marden's *Red Rocks (1)* (2000–2002), red traces interpenetrate with the olive green ground (Figure 5). The movement of the yellow and gray-blue lines is balanced by the large but hollow shape of red and yellow. The title and composition of this painting clearly refer to Cézanne's *Red Rock* (Musée de l'Orangerie, Paris), in which the rock seems to hover as an abstract impression of orange color in the Provençal shimmering verdure. Marden's *Red, Yellow, Blue Drawing* also recalls the rich color and changing aspects of Cézanne's *Trees and Rocks near the Caves of the Château Noir* (1902–1906, Musée d'Orsay, Paris).

In Marden's *Extended Window Painting* (1986–2001), solid curvilinear lines of yellow, red and black are painted over a grayish-white

---

97   Wylie, *Brice Marden*, p. 42.

98   Hay, *Brice Marden*, p. 21.

99   Wylie, *Brice Marden*, no. 21.

100 On the association of Taihu rocks with the human body, see Hay, *Kernels*, pp. 20–22.

101 Ibid., pp. 15–17.

102 Marden, "Past Recent Now," in Fairbrother, *Brice Marden: Boston*, p. 30; quoted in Richardson, *Brice Marden*, p. 46.

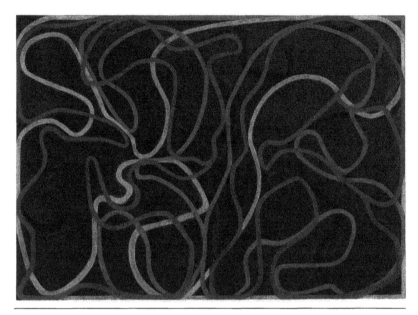

Figure 5 Brice Marden, *Red Rocks (1)*, 2000–2002. Oil on linen, 190.5 x 271.8 cm. Collection of the artist. Courtesy of the artist.

wash, which in turn is painted over some red lines on the left and a rectangular window grid, most visible on the right.[103] The four corners of the picture are painted over with yellow and black, which reconfigure the original grid. In *Red Rocks (1)* (2000–2002), the curvilinear movement is integrated into a fundamental grid structure. *Red Rocks (1)* is enacted by a strong flow of energy, invoked by geological structure. The dark purple ground appears as an infinite site of this inner mobility. The lower left corner is left open for the passage of energy flow, and the other three corners are definitely enclosed. With the undulation of color lines around the edge, the picture plane itself becomes a sculpted body evoking a Taihu rock. In both works, the picture plane becomes the site of a dialectic between movement and stasis, a fusion of materiality with human rhythm through the framework of spirituality.

Since 1985, Marden has been working on "inter-textual" writing on the modernist metaphor of the wall surface, using Chinese calligraphy

103 Marden, *Extended Window Painting*, in *Brice Marden: Attendants, Bears, and Rock*, no. 48.

to articulate the spatiotemporal variations of the picture plane in contrast to the presumption of a single flat surface. In Marden's most recent work, three versions of *The Propitious Garden of Plane Image* (2000–2006), each composed of six panels, the color lines flowing inward and outward of the panels of spectral colors constitute a wall of light, recapturing the architectonic structure of *Thira*.[104] The interweaving acts of reclusion and expansion configure an imaginary space of eremitism in the modern city. The multiple pictorial spaces correspond to the complex structure of Cézanne's rocks on the one hand, and the spatiotemporal shifting in the garden imagery of Suzhou on the other.

According to Fry and others, linearity, rhythm, and spirituality have been the major resources that Western artists have drawn from Chinese art. For Marden, the relationships among lines and between lines and the ground are equally fundamental. He distinguishes his line from Pollock's: Pollock's line falls on the surface to make the plane, while his own is embedded in the plane.[105] To talk of embeddedness is to invoke Rauschenberg's "all-purpose picture plane" as Steinberg called it. Marden has an urge to transcend the weight of the gallery wall. To enhance the sense of embeddedness, he prefers to hang paintings low, instead of, as usual, at a hypothetical eye level, because an eye-level picture seems to sit on (as well as hang from) a wall. Doing monochrome triptychs that are also figural, he sought to evoke an empathetic response from the spectator standing there.[106] In other words, the spectator is induced to look at Marden's paintings close up, and to get inside his paintings through meditative viewing. In his words, the picture serves as a "trampoline to bounce on spirituality," or, more precisely, a trampoline of spirituality on which to bounce.[107] In retrospect, we may say that his earlier color panels were conceived as planes of spiritual resonance, similar to the walls of Hanshan's dwelling.

In sum, in Marden's hands, and with his persistent effort to fuse the materiality and spirituality from both Chinese and Western cultures, modernist painting becomes an art of inclusion, not exclusion. Marden induces viewers to rethink the physicality and materiality

---

104 See also Brenda Richardson, "Even a Stone," pp.101–5.
105 Yau, "Interview," p. 58.
106 Hay, *Brice Marden*, p. 22.
107 Marden, *Grove Notebook*, Summer 1974, in *Grove Group*, p. 21.

of Chinese art, and the abstractness and spirituality of Western modern art.[108] Insistently tracing his figures on a cultural wall, Marden creates a vision of material and spiritual transaction between East and West. Incorporating but also going beyond Clement Greenberg's antirepresentational purism, he reinvents and reinvigorates the multiplicity of modern painting.

Acknowledgments

The present study has been made possible by a research grant from the National Science Council, Taipei, during 2004–2005. The author would like to thank Roger Des Forges and Haun Saussy for reading and editing an early draft.

Works Cited

Barthes, Roland. "Cy Twombly: Works on Paper." Pp. 157–76 in *The Responsibility of Forms*, Roland Barthes (Richard Howard, trans.). Oxford: Blackwell, 1986.

———. "Semiography of André Masson." Pp. 153–56 in *The Responsibility of Forms*, Roland Barthes (Richard Howard, trans.). Oxford: Blackwell, 1986.

Baxandall, Michael. *Painting and Experience in Fifteenth-Century Italy. A Primer in the Social History of Pictorial Style*, 2nd ed. Oxford: Oxford University Press, 1988.

Blotkamp, Carel. *Mondrian. The Art of Destruction*. New York: Abrams, 1994.

Bois, Yve-Alain. "Marden's Doubt." Pp. 13–67 in *Brice Marden: Paintings 1985–1993*, Yve-Alain Bois and Ulrich Loock, eds. Bern: Kunsthalle Bern, 1993.

———. "The Iconoclast." Pp. 313–72 in *Piet Mondrian: 1872–1944*, Yve-Alain Bois, ed. New York: Museum of Modern Art, 1994.

Chiang, Yee. *Chinese Calligraphy. An Introduction to Its Aesthetic and Technique*, 3rd ed. Cambridge, Mass.: Harvard University Press, 1979.

Clark, Timothy Y. "Greenberg's Theory of Art." Pp. 71–86 in *Pollock and After: The Critical Debate*, Francis Frascina, ed. New York: Harper & Row, 1985; London: Routledge, 2000 [2nd ed].

Codognato, Mario, ed. *Brice Marden. Works on Paper 1964–2001*. London: Trolley, 2002.

108 Arthur Danto is pleased to see the term "spirit" appear in contemporary discourse, as in Richardson and Garrel's comments on Marden; "Surface Appeal," p. 34.

Crichton, Michael. *Jasper Johns*. New York: Abrams, 1977.

Cummings, Paul. "Interview with Brice Marden," October 3, 1972. *Smithsonian Archives of American Art*.

Danto, Arthur. "Surface Appeal," *Nation*, 284: 4(January 29, 2007), pp. 32–36.

Derrida, Jacques. *De la grammatologie*. Paris: Minuit, 1967. [English ed., *Of Grammatology*, Gayatri C. Spivak, trans. Baltimore, Md.: Johns Hopkins University Press, 1976.]

Fairbrother, Trevor. *Brice Marden: Boston*. Boston: Museum of Fine Arts, 1991.

Fried, Michael. "New York Letter: Louis, Chamberlain and Stella, Indiana," *Art International*, 6(November 1962), pp. 53–55. [Reprinted in *Art and Objecthood: Essays and Reviews*, Michael Fried. Chicago: University of Chicago Press, 1998, pp. 281–86.]

——. "Art and Objecthood." Pp. 148–72 in *Art and Objecthood: Essays and Reviews*, Michael Fried. Chicago: University of Chicago Press, 1998.

——. "New York Letter: Noland, Thiebaud," *Art International*, 7(May 1963), pp. 69–70. [Reprinted in *Art and Objecthood: Essays and Reviews*, Michael Fried. Chicago: University of Chicago Press, 1998, pp. 297–303.]

Fraser, Sarah E. *Performing the Visual: The Practice of Buddhist Wall Painting in China and Central Asia, 618-960*. Stanford: Stanford University Press, 2004.

Fry, Roger. "An Essay in Aesthetics." *New Quarterly*, 2(April 1909), pp. 171–90. [Reprinted in *Vision and Design*, J. B. Bullen, ed. (London: 1920) New York: Dover, 1998, pp. 12–32.]

——. *Chinese Art: An Introductory Handbook to Painting, Sculpture, Ceramics, Textiles, Bronzes and Minor Arts*. *Burlington Magazine* monograph, 1925. [New edition, with an introduction by Madame Quo Tai-Chi. Taipei: Southeast Asia, 1967.]

Gardner, Paul. "Call It a Mid-Life Crisis," *Art News*, 93:4(April 1994), pp. 140–43.

Garrels, Gary, et al. *Plane Image. A Brice Marden Retrospective*. New York: Museum of Modern Art, 2006.

Godfrey, Tony. *Conceptual Art*. London: Phaidon, 1998.

Goldstein, Ann, et al. *A Minimal Future? Art as Object: 1958-1968*. Los Angeles: Museum of Contemporary Art, 2004.

Greenberg, Clement. "Towards a Newer Laocoon" (1940). Pp. 23–38 in *The Collected Essays and Criticism*, vol. 1, *Perceptions and Judgments, 1939-1944*, John O'Brian, ed. Chicago: University of Chicago Press, 1986.

——. "The Situation at the Moment" (1948). Pp. 192–96, in *The Collected Essays and Criticism*, vol. 2, *Arrogant Purpose, 1945-1949*, John O'Brian, ed. Chicago: University of Chicago Press, 1986.

————. "Modernist Painting" (1960). Pp. 85–93 in *The Collected Essays and Criticism*, vol. 4, *Modernism with a Vengeance, 1957–1969*, John O'Brian, ed. Chicago: University of Chicago Press, 1993.

————. "Louis and Noland," *Art International* (May 1960). Pp. 94–100 in *The Collected Essays and Criticism*, vol. 4, *Modernism with a Vengeance, 1957–1969*, John O'Brian, ed. Chicago: University of Chicago Press, 1993.

————. "After Abstract Expressionism," *Art International* (October 1962). [Reprinted in *The Collected Essays and Criticism*, vol. 4, *Modernism with a Vengeance, 1957–1969*, John O'Brian, ed. Chicago: University of Chicago Press, 1993, pp. 121–34.]

Guilbaut, Serge. *How New York Stole the Idea of Modern Art: Abstract Expressionism, Freedom, and the Cold War*, Arthur Goldhammer, trans. Chicago: University of Chicago Press, 1983.

Hale, Niki. "Of a Classic Order: Brice Marden's *Thira*," *Arts Magazine* (October 1980), pp. 152–53.

Hanshan. *The Collected Songs of Cold Mountain*, Red Pine, trans. Port Townsend, Washington: Copper Canyon, 1984; 2000, rev. ed..

Hay, John. "The Human Body as a Microcosmic Source of Macrocosmic Values in Calligraphy." Pp. 74–102 in *Theories of the Arts in China*, Susan Bush and Christian Murck, eds. Princeton, N.J.: Princeton University Press, 1981.

————. *Kernels of Energy, Bones of Earth: the Rock in Chinese Art*. New York: China House Gallery: China Institute in America, 1985.

————. "The Body Invisible in Chinese Art?" Pp. 42–77 in *Body, Subject and Power in China*, Angela Zito and Tani E. Barlow, eds. Chicago: University of Chicago Press, 1994.

Hay, Jonathan. *Brice Marden, Chinese Work*. New York: Mathew Mark, 1998.

Howard, Edgar and Theodore Haimes. *Brice Marden*. New York: Tuckeruck Productions, 1977.

Keller, Eva. "Brice Marden at Daros." Pp. 18–23 in *Brice Marden*, Eva Keller and Regula Malin, eds. Zurich: Daros, 2003.

Kerouac, Jack. *The Dharma Bums* (1958). New York: Penguin, 1976.

Kertess, Klaus. *Brice Marden: Paintings and Drawings*. New York: Abrams, 1992.

Krauss, Rosalind. "Grids." Pp. 8–22 in *The Originality of the Avant-garde and Other Modernist Myths*, Rosalind Krauss. Cambridge, Mass.: MIT Press, 1985.

Lebensztejn, Jean-Claude, trans. by Joachim Neugroschel. "From," in *Brice Marden: Recent Paintings and Drawings*, Brice Marden. New York: Pace Gallery, 1978, n.p.

Leed, Jacob. "Gary Snyder, Hanshan, and Jack Kerouac," *Journal of Modern Literature*, 11:1 (March 1984), pp. 185–93.

Lewison, Jeremy. *Brice Marden: Prints 1961–1991. A Catalogue Raisonné.* London: Tate Gallery, 1991.

Marden, Brice. *Brice Marden: Recent Paintings and Drawings.* New York: Pace Gallery, 1978.

——. *Brice Marden: Marbles, Paintings, and Drawings.* New York: Pace Gallery, 1982.

——. *Thirty-six poems by Tu Fu translated by Kenneth Rexroth, with twenty-five etchings by Brice Marden.* New York: Peter Blum Edition, 1987.

——. "Brice Marden: Interview with Robert Storr on October 24, 1986." P. 71 in *Abstract Painting of America and Europe*, Rosemary Schwarzwärder, ed. Klagenfurt: Ritter, 1988.

——. *The Grove Group.* New York: Gagosian Gallery, 1991.

——. *Brice Marden: Recent Drawings and Etchings.* New York: Matthew Marks, 1991.

——. *Brice Marden: Attendants, Bears, and Rocks.* New York: Matthew Marks Gallery, 2002.

Matthiessen, Peter, *Nine-Headed Dragon River: Zen Journals 1969–1982.* Boston: Shambhala, 1998.

Michaux, Henri. *Idéogrammes en Chine.* Paris: Fata Morgana, 1975.

Morley, Simon. *Writing on the Wall: Word and Image in Modern Art.* Berkeley: University of California Press, 2003.

Na, Zhiliang, ed. *Choice Works of Calligraphy in the National Palace Museum.* Taipei: National Palace Museum, 1969.

Owens, Craig. "Representation, Appropriation, and Power." Pp. 88–113 in *Beyond Recognition: Representation, Power, and Culture*, Craig Owens, ed. Berkeley: University of California Press, 1992.

Red Pine, trans. *The Zen Teaching of Bodhidharma.* New York: North Point, 1987.

Richardson, Brenda. *Brice Marden: Cold Mountain.* New York: DIA Center for the Arts, 1992.

——. "Brice Marden, Lifelines." Pp. 85–104 in *Abstraction, Gesture, Ecriture. Paintings from the Daros Collection.* Zurich: Scalo, 1999.

——. "Even a Stone Knows You." Pp. 76–109 in *Plane Image. A Brice Marden Retrospective*, Gary Garrels et al. New York: Museum of Modern Art, 2006.

Schapiro, Meyer. "Recent Abstract Painting." (1957) Pp. 213-26 in *Modern Art: 19th and 20th Centuries*, Meyer Schapiro. New York: George Braziller, 1979.

Scully, Vincent. *The Earth, the Temple, and the Gods: Greek Sacred Architecture.* New Haven, Conn.: Yale University Press, 1979, rev. ed.

Segalen, Victor. *Stèles.* Paris: G. Crès, 1914. [Edition with annotations by Christian Doumet (1982). Paris: Librairie Générale Française, 1999.]

Shearer, Linda. *Brice Marden.* New York: Solomon R. Guggenheim Museum, 1975.

Shiff, Richard. "Force of Myself Looking." Pp. 28–75 in *Plane Image. A Brice Marden Retrospective,* Gary Garrels et al. New York: Museum of Modern Art, 2006.

Shimizu, Yoshiaki, and Rosenfield, John M. *Masters of Japanese Calligraphy: 8th to 19th Century.* New York: Asia Society Galleries; Japan House Gallery, 1984.

Smith, Roberta Pancoast. "Brice Marden's Painting," *Arts Magazine,* 47:7 (1973), pp. 36–41.

Snyder, Gary. *Riprap and Cold Mountain Poems.* Washington, DC: Shoemaker & Hoard, 1958.

———. "Cold Mountain Poems," *Evergreen Review* (August 1956) [Reprinted in *Riprap and Cold Mountain Poems,* Gary Snyder, Washington, DC: Shoemaker & Hoard, 1958, pp. 35–67.]

Steinberg, Leo. "Jasper Johns: The First Seven Years of His Art." Pp. 17–54 in *Other Criteria. Confrontations with Twentieth-Century Art,* Leo Steinberg. Oxford: Oxford University Press, 1972.

———. "Other Criteria." Pp. 55–91 in *Other Criteria. Confrontations with Twentieth-Century Art,* Leo Steinberg. Oxford: Oxford University Press, 1972.

Steir, Pat. "Brice Marden. An Interview," in *Brice Marden: Recent Drawings & Etchings.* New York: Matthew Marks, 1991, n.p.

Sullivan, Michael. *The Meeting of Eastern and Western Art.* Berkeley: University of California Press, [1989] 1997.

Suzuki, Daisetz. *Zen and Japanese Culture.* New York: Bollingen Foundation, 1959.

Wei, Lilly. "Talking Abstract," *Art in America* 75:7 (July 1987), pp. 80–97.

Wylie, Charles. *Brice Marden: Work of the 1990s; Paintings, Drawings, and Prints.* Dallas: Dallas Museum of Art, 1998.

Yau, John. "An Interview with Brice Marden." Pp. 44–60 in *Brice Marden,* Eva Keller and Regula Malin, eds. Zurich: Daros, 2003.

Yip, Wai-lim. *Ezra Pound's Cathay.* Princeton, N.J.: Princeton University Press, 1969.

Zeitlin, Judith T. "Disappearing Verses. Writing on Walls and Anxieties of Loss." Pp. 73–125 in *Writing and Materiality in China. Essays in Honor of*

Patrick Hanan, Judith T. Zeitlin and Lydia H. Liu, eds. Cambridge, Mass.: Harvard University Press, 2003.

Zhang Yenyuan. Lidai minghuaji [Record of famous painters through the ages, *ca.* 845–47]. Pp. 5–135 in *Huashi congshu* [History of painting series], Yu Anlan, ed. Taipei: Wen-shi-zhe, 1974.

Conclusion: Bricks and Tiles

[Pnin] was less strong than his powerfully puffed-out chest might imply, and the wave of hopeless fatigue that suddenly submerged his topheavy body, detaching him, as it were, from reality, was a sensation not utterly unknown to him . . . I do not know if it has ever been noted before that one of the main characteristics of life is discreteness. Unless a film of flesh envelops us, we die. Man exists only insofar as he is separated from his surroundings. The cranium is a space-traveler's helmet. Stay inside or you perish. Death is divestment, death is communion. It may be wonderful to mix with the landscape, but to do so is the end of the tender ego. The sensation poor Pnin experienced was something very like that divestment, that communion. He felt porous and pregnable. He was sweating. He was terrified. A stone bench among the laurels saved him from collapsing on the sidewalk.

—VLADIMIR NABOKOV, *PNIN*

As I reflect on the essays collected in this volume, what comes to mind is not a particular list of shared positions or conclusions but a set of perspectives opened by several days of concentrated discussion and developed through concerted communication over weeks and months. Though spared Pnin's sweating and terror, I have found myself newly appreciative of the virtues of "discreteness."

435

In our hyper-networked era it is too easy to forget that discreteness is also one of the main characteristics of social and political life.[1] Individuals have their identities; groups have their defining properties and rituals of membership; a jurisdiction has to begin and end somewhere; even communication assumes distinct entities that do the sending and receiving.

This discreteness can never be a matter of sheer logic. It must be instantiated somehow, through artifacts—through walls, as we are calling them. The essays in this volume explore the physical envelope of the Chinese state (or polity) and the envelopes of groups (cities, jurisdictions, families, bodies) subordinated or connected to it. One must add, as soon as physical walls have been mentioned, that in another of its dimensions "China" names a culture, indeed a culture-state, the boundaries of which do not perfectly align with any set of material barriers.[2]

The era in which this book has been written is one dominated by the "divestment," the "communion," of which Nabokov speaks with mixed fear and fascination. The late twentieth century saw the dismantling of many formerly fiercely defended political and legal units. Certain walls melted into the landscape (and others went up). Everyone who has had the experience of living or traveling in, let us say, the two Germanys, the Soviet Union, South Africa, Eastern Europe, or China before and after 1990, knows how much has changed. The European Union has abolished internal border controls. Within China, the regimen of work units and household registration has loosened (as Xiaoping Lin reminds us). People, money, and goods flow abundantly, if not quite freely, between Taiwan and the mainland, and, more recently and to a lesser extent, between north and south Korea. These examples of opening do not amount to a universal trend, as any inhabitant of the West Bank or the Mexican side of the southern border of the United States can aver; but if there is a sum total of world anxiety over borders, it seems to have diminished, or at least become more

---

1   For the growth and intensification of human communication over time, see Mc Neill and Mc Neill, *Human Web,* and Castells, *Rise of the Network Society.*

2   For the idea of a culture-state, see the work of Tu Weiming, including *Living Tree.*

narrowly focused on specific zones and interchanges.[3] Barbed wire and its analogues are now special-order items, it seems.

Certainly the rhetoric of fortification has changed in register since the days of the Ming and of Maginot, with walls now being perceived as implicitly futile and dishonest, their maintenance a defensive strategy that can itself be spoken of only in defensive tones. The cause, broadly speaking, is the overall dominance of economics and the poverty of politics in our era. For international economic exchange, protectionism is an obstacle that is not necessarily conducive to protection. The redeployment in recent years of the German wartime slogan *Festung Europa* (Fortress Europe) to designate European Union efforts to block entry of videocassette recorders, asylum-seekers, or jobless Third World people carries a tone of implicit criticism, even sarcasm. To describe a policy as wall-like is most often to brand it with illegitimacy. Walls, as usually conceived of, have nothing in common with the skins and self-preservation instinct of living things; indeed, the imaginative vocabulary of liberal democracies pits the wall as a lifeless barrier against the living humans pent up within it and yearning, as the poem has it, to breathe free.[4] One might even expect a volume on Chinese walls to join in this chorus: if China is imagined as walled or defined by walls, it must be closed, ignorant, deluded, autistic, at odds with the rest of the world.[5] That is, of course, precisely the imagining of China that has prevailed in many quarters, even among some Chinese, and its prevalence is one reason the authors of this book have taken another tack. Instead, we ask: What if the relation between the human animal and the walled community did not simply amount to opposition and struggle? What if walls were (and are) the skins surrounding forms of collective life?

Taking a longer historical view, as we do, and espousing a greater variety of critical languages than is usual, we are able to see more than

---

3   But see Brown, *Regulating Aversion*, for a different understanding of "openness."

4   "Give me your tired, your poor, / Your huddled masses yearning to breathe free," Emma Lazarus, "The New Colossus," inscribed on the pedestal of the Statue of Liberty. This sonnet was for years a memorization piece in United States schools.

5   Fortunately, many volumes identify China by its walls without taking the image too seriously. See, for example, Rodzinski, *Walled Kingdom*. The misconception of China as historically "closed" is directly controverted by Valerie Hansen, *Open Empire*.

one side of the question of walls. To consider walls in a biological or somatic context automatically nudges us toward implications that the architectural or political vocabularies would overshadow. We are invited to take note of the existence of barriers and to ask about their functions. What conditions of viability do they seek to ensure? What internal processes of change are made possible by "separation" of an inside from its "surroundings"? (One must assume that the presence of an encircling wall does not block all change, if only because there are usually gates. As Laozi pointed out long ago, a house without doors or windows is useless for dwelling.[6]) What kinds of nesting and differentiation happen among subdomains within the boundary? In what way do the internal domain and the surrounding context continue to respond to one another despite the interposition of a wall? Do walls mediate—as well as separate—the realms that they mutually divide? How can a wall be displaced? Under varying kinds of pressure, do walls tend to weaken, become porous, get overrun, or simply collapse? Under what conditions are walls erased and rebuilt, or old stones reemployed in new masonry? Questions analogous to these are posed, at varying levels of abstraction and in differing historical contexts, by each of the chapters in this volume.

In short, our common procedure has been to put aside the assumption, customary in contemporary rhetoric, that the universal tendency goes in one direction and mandates that all barriers be broken down, so as to open up a single globalized economic space (with politics left to follow suit as best it can).

* * *

The somatic metaphor makes it seem that a political boundary, for example, that of "China," is definitional and a condition for survival for that entity. The sneakiness of the body metaphor for a state lies in the fact that our bodily boundaries are given us even before we can think about ourselves as different from the world around us, whereas the quasi-somatic boundaries of a state are constructed as a consequence of state-formation processes and are always affected by rivalries with

---

6   Laozi (attr.), *Daode jing*, chapter 11.

neighboring polities or disaffected factions within the same polity. Thus, in order to forestall the kind of acceptance that precludes questioning—that is, in order to use our metaphors knowingly—we need to think of boundaries as the outcome of events. That, at least, was the conclusion we reached in compiling this volume, a selection of revised versions of papers presented at the conference over three years ago.

At earlier moments in Chinese history, the building of walls was a victory in itself, a hedge against chaos and a token of the civilizing process that is widely, if problematically, identified as "Confucian."[7] As such, the wall was an event, an event needing constant renewal. The "Fang ji" [On dikes] section of the classical work the *Records of Ritual* (*Li ji*) begins thus:

> The Master [Confucius] said: "The Way of a Gentleman, may it not be compared to the raising of dikes (*fang*)? It constrains (*fang*) that wherein the populace is lacking. However much the noble person exerts himself in the building of constraints, the people will still leap over them. So the gentleman uses ritual to constrain virtue; he uses punishments to constrain excess; he uses commands to constrain desire."[8]

In this vision, the absence of dikes and walls is a "state of nature" without the slightest law. Just as material subsistence is guaranteed by walls solid enough to keep out invaders and dikes firm enough to prevent floods, so civilization as the gentleman knows it depends on the building of "mind-forg'd" barriers[9] on boundaries and interdictions aimed at lawless desire. Contrariwise, the dweller among civilized people who breaks the rules of the community is assimilated to the peoples and animals outside the walls, and may find him or herself banished to join them.[10] Thus a walled city gave most Chinese in most

---

7   "Confucianism" is sometimes described as a permanent fixture of the Chinese mind or culture, but needs to be understood in its historical emergence. See Jensen, *Manufacturing Confucianism,* and Brooks and Brooks, *Original Analects.*

8   *Li ji,* "Fang ji," in Ruan Yuan, ed., *Shisan jing zhushu,* 51/7b–8a.

9   William Blake, London, *Collected Poetry and Prose,* p. 26.

10 See Waley-Cohen, *Exile.*

periods the feeling of "ein' feste Burg," security against disorder from within and without. Both constraining *to* (virtue) and constraining *from* (vice), the goodness of defenses was self-evident on many metaphorical planes at once—as is also, to a post-Freudian ear, the hint of repression in the *Li ji*'s praise of "constraint" (*fang*).

More generally: it is good to remember that boundaries are constructed for a purpose. The purpose may fail or be superseded, as Arthur Waldron has emphasized, but the trace of the boundary still attests to it. Being purposeful, walls require engagement. That is, they are part of human signifying behavior. They have to be maintained, repaired, and at times replaced (this is true of the physical ones as well as of the semantic ones). A line drawn frequently needs to be redrawn— reaffirmed in the face of semiotic decay or redesigned to answer new needs. The essays by Roger Des Forges and Desmond Cheung on city walls demonstrate the rise and fall of boundaries as well as the repeated replacement of their meanings from the Ming to the present, or what are widely but not unproblematically known as the late imperial and republican periods.

A wall inscribes a division in space. It also presents surfaces for inscription. If a wall is the material realization of a political decision (say, the decision to differentiate the inside of a city from its outside), the vertical faces of the wall offer spaces for public reflection on the jurisdictions thus created. Less technically put, graffiti, advertisements, official slogans, even laundry put out to dry, endow the barrier with commentary. Gao Minglu, in an essay related to this volume, examines this reflective process at work in the graffiti that mark Beijing under reconstruction.[11] Liu Chiao-mei, from another starting point, inserts the wall-like paintings of Brice Marden into the multiple heritages of twenty-first century art history.

Walls have thickness. They are not pure boundaries, not categories that merely exclude and include; they can be lived in or upon. In other words, there is an interstitial dimension to walls, room for "regimes of exception" that thrive on the energy and material that must be invested in order to create distinctions.[12] Walls, multiplied, become mazes; or

11 Gao, *Wall*, chapter 7.
12 See Agamben, *State of Exception*.

walls contain mazes whenever the wall's function is explicable from more than one perspective. The mazelike dimension is investigated in Tahirih Lee's study of extraterritorial law in Shanghai and in Keyang Tang's reading of a Tang *chuanqi* tale that discovers worlds within the wards of Chang'an, the principal capital city during much of China's early and middle periods. In other ways, the maze is investigated in Junhao Hong's study of the police force mobilized to maintain the "Great Firewall," and by Adam Cathcart's study of wall imagery in political cartooning of the early People's Republic.

One hears—repeatedly, since Karl Marx and Kang Youwei—of a world in which all barriers are down.[13] Pathogens dream, if they dream, of a world in which all barriers are permeable. Richard Lee's study of SARS and its political fallout traces the parallels between two forms of competition: that of disease agents and medical strategy, and that of the control and circulation of information. Certain artists, too, are no doubt pathogens, potential threats to the cultural integrity that is one of the paramount interests of national institutions. Such artists include those described by Millie Chen, who perform ethnicity within established genres of behavioral art, and the translator, theorist and poet Wai-lim Yip, whose efforts to carry the spark, or the virus, of Asian poetics into the English language are discussed by Jonathan Stalling. Meanwhile, world historians, like those analyzed by Luo Xu, confront paradigmatic and disciplinary walls in search of a perspective from which multiple interacting communities can be narrated at once. Xu finds that "the view from the moon" eludes them, as no doubt it must elude us all. Can world history be written without centers or protagonists? That is to say, without a "tender ego" at its core or a "space helmet" on its periphery?

Walls are a vehicle for thinking about historical continuity and change, as fossils are a vehicle for thinking about biological evolution and mutation. It is too simple and unrewarding to think of walls as good or bad, as comforting or constraining. We have instead tried to

13 "The bourgeoisie has through its exploitation of the world market given a cosmopolitan character to production and consumption in every country. . . . National one-sidedness and narrow-mindedness become more and more impossible." Marx and Engels, "Manifesto," pp. 38–39; Kang, *Datongshu*; Moore, *World Without Walls*.

discover and elucidate the opportunities, negotiations, frustrations, and reinventions that they stimulate.

* * *

These essays amply repay the wager with which we started out: that walls would provide more than a convenient figure of speech; that they would prove a methodological and historical thread. At a minimum, they complicate the putative antithesis of traditional positions (arguing the necessity of strong defenses) and modern ones (arguing the virtues of openness). Inevitably, we devise definitions as boundaries between concepts and we revise them when necessary, just as when learning a foreign language we discover that the near-equivalences with concepts we had previously held are only near-equivalences. In fact all intellectual work can be seen as a wall-building enterprise, the task of erecting and dismantling definitions, with bricks and tiles reused many times. Chunks of former structures resurface in unforeseen ensembles, just as, in the political world, the outlines of now dismantled material walls may yet be traced in new forms of information-collecting and intellectual policing. The story of walls is far from over.

> *Wall.* Thus have I, Wall, my part discharged so;
> And, being done, thus Wall away doth go.
> *Theseus.* Now is the mural down between the two neighbors.
> *Demetrius.* No remedy, my lord, when walls are so willful to hear without warning.

> ——William Shakespeare, *A Midsummer Night's Dream*

HS for the editors

Works Cited

Agamben, Giorgio. *State of Exception,* Kevin Attell, trans. Chicago: University of Chicago Press, 2004.

Blake, William. *Complete Poetry and Prose.* David V. Erdman, ed. New York: Anchor, 1997.

Brooks, A. Taeko, and Bruce Brooks. *The Original Analects.* New York: Columbia University Press, 1997.

Brown, Wendy. *Regulating Aversion: Tolerance in the Age of Identity and Empire.* Princeton, N.J.: Princeton University Press, 2006.

Castells, Manuel. *The Rise of the Network Society.* New York: Wiley-Blackwell, 2000.

Gao, Minglu. *The Wall: Reshaping Contemporary Chinese Art/Qiang: Zhongguo dangdai yishu de lishi yu bianjie.* Beijing and Buffalo: The Millennium Museum, University at Buffalo Art Galleries, Albright-Knox Art Gallery, 2005.

Hansen, Valerie. *The Open Empire: A History of China to 1600.* New York: Norton, 2000.

Jensen, Lionel. *Manufacturing Confucianism: Chinese Traditions and Universal Civilization.* Durham, N.C.: Duke University Press, 1997.

Kang Youwei, *Datongshu* [Book of the great harmony], Qian Anding, ed. Shanghai 1935, reprinted Beijing 1956, Taipei 1958.

Marx, Karl, and Friedrich Engels. "Manifesto of the Communist Party." *Selected Works in One Volume.* New York: International Publishers, 1968.

Mc Neill, William, and John Mc Neill. *The Human Web: A Bird's Eye View of World History.* New York: Norton, 2003.

Moore, Mike. *A World Without Walls: Freedom, Development, Free Trade, and Global Governance.* Cambridge: Cambridge University Press, 2003.

Nabokov, Vladimir. *Pnin.* New York: Avon, 1969.

Rodzinski, Witold. *The Walled Kingdom: A History of China from Antiquity to the Present.* New York: Free Press, 1984.

Ruan Yuan, ed. *Shisan jing zhushu.* Taipei: Dahua, 1988. Reprinted.

Tu, Weiming. *The Living Tree: The Changing Meaning of Being Chinese Today.* Stanford: Stanford University Press, 1994.

Waley-Cohen, Joanna. *Exile in Mid-Qing China: Banishment to Xinjiang, 1758–1820.* New Haven, Conn.: Yale University Press, 1991.

Glossary

ALL ROMANIZATIONS ARE GIVEN IN the *pinyin* system. Where the traditional form of the character differs from the simplified form, the simplified form is given in parenthesis.

Ah Yang 啊楊(啊杨)
An Jinhuai 安金槐
Andong 安東(安东)
Anyang ying'er 安陽嬰兒(安阳婴儿)
Anyi 安邑
Anyuan men 安湲門
Ao 隞

Badaling 八達嶺
Bai Xingjian 白行簡
bao 堡
bing zhongyuan 冰中原
Bo 亳
bugao 布告
buzheng 布政

Canglang shihua 滄浪詩話
Caomen 曹門
Changyuan xian 長垣縣
chantang (zendô) 禪堂
Chen Maoling 陳懋領
Chongqing 重慶

dagudu 大古都
daliyuan 大理院

dalu 達虜
danwei 單位(单位)
Daode jing 道德經
Da Qing Lüli 大清律例
Dashigu 大師姑
Daxing 大興
Dengfeng 登封
Ding Fang 丁方
ditai 敵台
Dongdajie 東大街

Fan xian 范縣
fang 坊
"Fang ji" 坊記
Fang Qiang 方強
fangli 坊裏
fanpiao 飯票 (饭票)
fanshen 翻身

Gaogouli/Goguryo 高句麗
getihu 個體戶 (个体户)
Gong xian 鞏縣
Gu 顧
Gu Wenda 谷文達
Guan 管

445

Guan Jiong 關炯
Guangshan xian 光山縣
Guanyin 觀音 (观音)
Guchengzhai 古城寨
gudu qun 古都群
Guide gucheng 歸德古城
Gun 鯀
Guo Moruo 郭沫若
Guo Xiang 郭象
guoqi gaizao 國企改造 (国企改造)
Gushi xian 固始縣
Gusi qu 古寺曲

Han Wudi 漢武帝
Han Xuandi 漢宣帝
hang tu 夯土
Hanshan 寒山
He Yunchang 何云昌
Hejian Liu Biejia 河間劉別駕
hou 后
Hou Hanru 侯瀚如
Hu Cheng 胡成
Hua Junwu 華君武
Huainanzi 淮南子
Huaisu 懷素
Huang Limin 黃禮民
Hui xian 輝縣
huishen gongtang 會審公堂
huishen gongxie 會審公廨

Jiangsu gaodeng fayuan di'er fenyuan
    江蘇高等法院第二分院
Jiangsu gaodeng fayuan disan fenyuan
    江蘇高等法院第三分院
Jing Fang 景芳

kaishu 楷書
Kaogong ji 考工記
kuangcao 狂草

Lanyang xian 蘭陽縣
Lidai Minghuaji 歷代名畫記
Li ji 禮記
Li Wa Zhuan 李娃傳
Li Zhanyang 李占洋
Liang Qichao 梁啟超
Liang Xiaowang 梁孝王
Liangyuan qü 梁園區
lianhuanhua 連環畫 (连环画)
lijia 里甲
lin rang 臨襄
lingshi gongtang 領事公堂
Linzhang xian 臨漳縣
Liu Bocheng 劉伯承
Liu Shun'an 劉順安
Liu Xie 劉勰
Liu Yong 劉湧 (刘涌)
Liu Zhi 劉峙
liu 流
Longqing 隆慶
Lu Ji 陸機
Lu Xun 魯迅
Lü Shengzhong 呂勝中
Luan Xing 欒星
Lushan xian 魯山縣

Ma Haitao 馬海濤
Ma Yupeng 馬玉鵬
Meng Haoran 孟浩然
Meng Jiangnü 孟姜女
Mengzi 孟子

Nanjing 南京
Nei Ye 內業
neibu shitang 內部食堂
Neihuang xian 內黃縣
nianfotang 念佛堂
Nie Qigui 聶緝槼
Niu Jianqiang 牛建強

Pingkang 平康

Qi (of Xia) 啟 (夏)
qiang 牆
qianhu suo 千戶所
qianwei (avant-garde) 前衛
qianwei (money-oriented) 錢衛
qihou 氣候
Qin Shihuang 秦始皇
Qin Yufen 秦玉芬
Qin-Han 秦漢
Qingming shanghe yuan 清明上河園
Qiuran Ke Zhuan 虬髯客傳
quanjiafu 全家福
Qujiang 曲江

Renhe men 仁和門
Riben guizi 日本鬼子

Sanfu huangtu 三輔黃圖
Sanshan buxian, wumen budui
　三山不顯，五門不對
shan shui 山水
Shangcheng xian 商城縣
Shanghai linshi fayuan 上海臨時法院
Shanghai tequ difang fayuan
　上海特區地方法院
Shangqiu shi 商邱市
shangren 商人
Shangshan men 上善門
Shanhaiguan 山海關
sharen shangming
　殺人償命 (杀人偿命)
Shengye 勝業
Shenpanting 審判庭
Shenqiu xian 沈丘縣
Shi Shangzhao 師尚詔
Shifo 石佛
shou xun 守巡

Shuxian 淑鮮
Sikong Tu 司空圖
Sima Qian 司馬遷
Song Haidong 宋海冬
Su Xiaokang 蘇曉康
Su Yangyang 蘇陽揚
Sui Yangdi 隋煬帝
Suiyang qu 睢陽區
Sun Tongxuan 孫桐萱
Sun Zhigang 孫志剛

Taihu 太湖
Taikang xian 泰康縣
Tang (ruler) 湯
tangzhuang 唐裝
Teng 滕
Tonghua 通化
Tongxu xian 通許縣
tu 徒
Tudizhangcheng 圖地章程

Wang Chao 王超
Wang Jin 王晉
Wang Jingsong 王勁松
Wang Xizhi 王羲之
Wangchenggang 王城崗
wei (guard) 衛
Wei (state) 衛
Wei Qianzhi 魏千志
Weijingfa 違驚法
weng cheng 甕城
Wenxin Diaolong 文心雕龍
woniu cheng 臥牛城
Wu (ruler) 武
Wu Jian 吳翦
Wu Shan 巫山
Wu Yujin 吳于廑
Wu Zun 吳遵
wuwei 無為

wuwo 無我

wuyan 無言

wuzhi 無知

xiancheng 縣城

Xiangcheng xian 襄城縣

xianzhang 縣長

xiaojie jingji 小姐經濟 (小姐经济)

xiaokang 小康

Xiayi xian 夏邑縣

Xie Lingyun 謝靈運

Xifengkou 喜峰口

xingfuwu 性服務

Xingqing 興慶

Xingyuan 杏園

Xinmi 新密

Xinxiang xian 新鄉縣

Xinzhai 新砦

Xinzheng 新鄭

Xiongnu 匈奴

Xishan 西山

Xu Bing 徐冰

Xu Hongming 徐紅明

Xu Ni 徐霓

Xuanyang 宣陽

Yalu River (Yalujiang) 鴨綠江

Yan Yu 嚴羽

Yancheng xian 郾城縣

Yang Kuan 楊寬

Yangcheng 陽城

Yangjingbang (Yangjingbin) sheguan 洋涇浜設官

Yangjingbang (Yangjingbin) Zhangcheng 洋涇浜章程

yangma qiang 羊馬牆

Yangshao 仰韶

Yangwu xian 陽武縣

Yanling xian 鄢陵縣

Yanshi xian 偃師縣

Yao Qing 姚卿

Ye Minlei 葉敏磊

Yifeng xian 議封縣

Yingyang 滎陽

Yongcheng xian 永城縣

Yu (ruler) 禹

Yushi xian 尉氏縣

Yuwen Kai 宇文愷

Zhang Dali 張大力

Zhang Ding 張丁

Zhang Huaiguan 張懷瓘

Zhang Jihong 張繼紅

Zhang Juzheng 張居正

Zhang Xinbin 張新斌

Zhang Yanyuan 張彥遠

Zhenyang xian 真陽縣

Zhong Nanshan 鍾南山 (钟南山)

Zhongding 仲丁

Zhongyuan chengshi qün 中原城市群

zhongzhou 中州

Zhou Fang 周昉

Zhu Rong 祝融

Zijingshan dadao 紫荊山大道

ziran 自然

Zisheng si hou qu 資勝寺後曲

Zou Heng 鄒衡

Contributors

Thomas W. Burkman is Research Professor of Asian Studies at the University at Buffalo, where he teaches Japanese and East Asian international history. He edited three collections of conference papers on the Allied Occupation of Japan and has authored, most recently, *Japan and the League of Nations: Empire and World Order, 1914–1938* (Hawaii, 2008).

Adam Cathcart teaches East Asian History at Pacific Lutheran University in Tacoma, Washington. He has recently published "Peripheral Influence: The Sinuiju Student Incident and the Soviet Occupation of North Korea, 1945–1947" (*Journal of Korean Studies,* 2008); and "Atrocities, Insults, and 'Jeep Girls': Depictions of the U.S. Military in China, 1945–1949" (*International Journal of Comic Art,* 2008).

Millie Chen teaches contemporary art practice and theory in the Department of Visual Studies at the University at Buffalo. She has published in *Performance Research, Espace, Artexte, Musicworks* and *Fuse;* she has curated exhibitions for Mercer Union Centre for Contemporary Art, Center for Exploratory and Perceptual Arts, and Tank Loft Contemporary Art Center; and she has exhibited in North and South America, Europe, and Asia. Her website is www.milliechen. com.

Desmond Cheung is a doctoral candidate in Chinese history at the University of British Columbia in Vancouver, Canada, where he is preparing a dissertation on the socio-cultural history of famous sights in Hangzhou. Under the name Zhang Haihao, he has published "The

Christian Poetry of Chinese Convert Zhang Xingyao [1633–1715]" (in Chinese, Wang Ding'an, trans.), in *Logos & Pneuma, Chinese Journal of Theology*, 2007.

Roger Des Forges teaches Chinese, Asian, and World History at the University at Buffalo. His recent publications include *Cultural Centrality and Political Change in Chinese History: Northeast Henan in the Fall of the Ming* (Stanford, 2003); with John S. Major, *The Asian World, 600–1500* (Oxford, 2005); and "Time and Space in Chinese Historiography: Concepts of Centrality in the History and Literature of the Three Kingdoms," in *The Many Faces of Clio: Cross-Cultural Approaches to Historiography* (Q. Edward Wang and Franz L. Fillafer, eds., Berghahn, 2007).

Minglu Gao is Professor of Art History at the University of Pittsburgh. His major publications include *Zhongguo dangdai meishu shi* (A History of Contemporary Art in China, Shanghai renmin chubanshe, 1991), *Inside/Out: New Chinese Art* (San Francisco: San Francisco Museum of Modern Art, 1998), and *The Wall: Reshaping Contemporary Chinese Art* (Albright Knox Art Gallery, 2005).

Junhao Hong teaches in the Communication, Media and Society, and Information Technology programs at the University at Buffalo. His publications include *The Internationalization of Television in China: The Evolution of Ideology, Society, and Media Since the Reform* (Praeger, 1998), and, with Lawrence Sherlick, *Internet Popular Culture and Jewish Values: The Influence of Technology on Religion in Israeli Schools* (Cambria, 2008).

Richard V. Lee, a grandson of Yan Phou Lee who came to the United States with the Chinese Educational Mission in 1872, is Professor of Medicine at the University at Buffalo, holding adjunct appointments in Pediatrics, Obstetrics, Anthropology, and Social and Preventive Medicine. He teaches a graduate course on Geographic Medicine and advises the medical student exchange program between the University at Buffalo and Capital Medical University in Beijing. He wrote the introduction and foreword for a reprint of his grandfather's *When I*

Was a Boy in China (1887) and has published over two hundred papers, essays, and book chapters in medicine.

Tahirih V. Lee teaches Chinese law and international business law at Florida State University College of Law. Her publications include *Chinese Law: Sociological, Political, Historical, and Economic Approaches* (Garland, 1997); "The Future of Federalism in China," in *The Limits of the Rule of Law in China* (Karen Turner et al., eds., Washington, 2000); "The United States Court for China: A Triumph of Local Law," *Buffalo Law Review*, 2004; and "Exporting Judicial Review From the United States to China," *Columbia Journal of Asian Law*, 2005.

Xiaoping Lin teaches Asian art and Cinema at Queens College of the City University of New York. He has published extensively on contemporary Chinese visual arts and films in *Third Text* and other journals. He is the author of *Children of Marx and Coca Cola: Chinese Avant-garde Art and Independent Cinema* (Hawaii, forthcoming).

Liu Chiao-mei teaches modern art and culture at the National Taiwan University (Taipei). Her publications include: "Poetry-Painting Relationships in Late Ming Suzhou Painting," *Study of the Arts* (Taipei, 1991); *Cézanne: la série de Château Noir* (Presses Universitaires du Septention, 2001) and "*Cette belle viande*: Cézanne's bathers and the Concept of Correspondences in Mid-Nineteenth Century," *Historical Inquiry* (National Taiwan University, 2002).

Haun Saussy is Bird White Housum Professor of Comparative Literature and East Asian Languages and Literatures at Yale University, where he also chairs the Council on East Asian Studies. His books include *The Problem of a Chinese Aesthetic* (Stanford, 1993); *Great Walls of Discourse* (Harvard East Asia Center, 2001); and "Fenollosa Compounded: A Discrimination," in *Ernest Fenollosa and Ezra Pound, The Chinese Written Character as a Medium for Poetry: A Critical Edition*, coedited with Jonathan Stalling and Lucas Klein (Fordham, 2008).

Jonathan Stalling is Assistant Professor of English Literature at the University of Oklahoma, specializing in twentieth-century American poetry and East-West poetics. He is the assistant editor of *World Literature Today* and the coeditor of *Ernest Fenollosa and Ezra Pound, The Chinese Written Character as a Medium for Poetry: A Critical Edition* (Fordham, 2008). He has published articles, translations, poems, and reviews in *Boston Review, CLEAR (Chinese Literature: Essays, Articles, Reviews), World Literature Today,* and *Jacket.* He is currently working on a monograph entitled *Poetics of Emptiness* and a book of translations entitled *Winter Sun: The Poetry of Shi Zhi 1966–2007.*

Keyang Tang is an urban designer who is currently curator at the National Art Museum of China. He has published *Chinese Gardens for Living* (Staatlichen Kunstsammlungen, 2008), *A Garden Rising from Ruins* (Sanlian, 2009), and is translating *Delirious New York* (SDX Joint Publishing, forthcoming).

Arthur Waldron is Lauder Professor of International Relations in the Department of History at the University of Pennsylvania. In addition to many publications on the problem of the Great Wall of China and twentieth-century China, he is currently at work on *The Chinese* for the series *Peoples of the World* (Blackwell, forthcoming).

Luo Xu teaches Chinese, Asian, and World History at the State University of New York at Cortland. His recent publications include *Searching for Life's Meaning: Changes and Tensions in the Worldviews of Chinese Youth in the 1980s* (Michigan, 2002); "Farewell to Idealism: Mapping China's University Students of the 1990s," *Journal of Contemporary China,* 2004; and "Eurocentrism in China's World History Writing of Recent Years and an Alternative Approach to the Early Modern World," *World History,* 2005.

Index

Page numbers in italics refer to figures and illustrations.

CORNELL EAST ASIA SERIES

4   Fredrick Teiwes, *Provincial Leadership in China: The Cultural Revolution and Its Aftermath*
8   Cornelius C. Kubler, *Vocabulary and Notes to Ba Jin's Jia: An Aid for Reading the Novel*
16 Monica Bethe & Karen Brazell, *Nō as Performance: An Analysis of the Kuse Scene of Yamamba*
18 Royall Tyler, tr., *Granny Mountains: A Second Cycle of Nō Plays*
23 Knight Biggerstaff, *Nanking Letters, 1949*
28 Diane E. Perushek, ed., *The Griffis Collection of Japanese Books: An Annotated Bibliography*
37 J. Victor Koschmann, Ōiwa Keibō & Yamashita Shinji, eds., *International Perspectives on Yanagita Kunio and Japanese Folklore Studies*
38 James O'Brien, tr., *Murō Saisei: Three Works*
40 Kubo Sakae, *Land of Volcanic Ash: A Play in Two Parts*, revised edition, tr. David G. Goodman
44 Susan Orpett Long, *Family Change and the Life Course in Japan*
48 Helen Craig McCullough, *Bungo Manual: Selected Reference Materials for Students of Classical Japanese*
49 Susan Blakeley Klein, *Ankoku Butō: The Premodern and Postmodern Influences on the Dance of Utter Darkness*
50 Karen Brazell, ed., *Twelve Plays of the Noh and Kyōgen Theaters*
51 David G. Goodman, ed., *Five Plays by Kishida Kunio*
52 Shirō Hara, *Ode to Stone*, tr. James Morita
53 Peter J. Katzenstein & Yutaka Tsujinaka, *Defending the Japanese State: Structures, Norms and the Political Responses to Terrorism and Violent Social Protest in the 1970s and 1980s*
54 Su Xiaokang & Wang Luxiang, *Deathsong of the River: A Reader's Guide to the Chinese TV Series Heshang*, trs. Richard Bodman & Pin P. Wan
55 Jingyuan Zhang, *Psychoanalysis in China: Literary Transformations, 1919-1949*
56 Jane Kate Leonard & John R. Watt, eds., *To Achieve Security and Wealth: The Qing Imperial State and the Economy, 1644-1911*
57 Andrew F. Jones, *Like a Knife: Ideology and Genre in Contemporary Chinese Popular Music*
58 Peter J. Katzenstein & Nobuo Okawara, *Japan's National Security: Structures, Norms and Policy Responses in a Changing World*
59 Carsten Holz, *The Role of Central Banking in China's Economic Reforms*
60 Chifumi Shimazaki, *Warrior Ghost Plays from the Japanese Noh Theater: Parallel Translations with Running Commentary*
61 Emily Groszos Ooms, *Women and Millenarian Protest in Meiji Japan: Deguchi Nao and Ōmotokyō*
62 Carolyn Anne Morley, *Transformation, Miracles, and Mischief: The Mountain Priest Plays of Kyōgen*
63 David R. McCann & Hyunjae Yee Sallee, tr., *Selected Poems of Kim Namjo*, afterword by Kim Yunsik
64 Hua Qingzhao, *From Yalta to Panmunjom: Truman's Diplomacy and the Four Powers, 1945-1953*
65 Margaret Benton Fukasawa, *Kitahara Hakushū: His Life and Poetry*
66 Kam Louie, ed., *Strange Tales from Strange Lands: Stories by Zheng Wanlong*, with introduction
67 Wang Wen-hsing, *Backed Against the Sea*, tr. Edward Gunn
69 Brian Myers, *Han Sōrya and North Korean Literature: The Failure of Socialist Realism in the DPRK*
70 Thomas P. Lyons & Victor Nee, eds., *The Economic Transformation of South China: Reform and Development in the Post-Mao Era*
71 David G. Goodman, tr., *After Apocalypse: Four Japanese Plays of Hiroshima and Nagasaki*, with introduction
72 Thomas Lyons, *Poverty and Growth in a South China County: Anxi, Fujian, 1949-1992*
74 Martyn Atkins, *Informal Empire in Crisis: British Diplomacy and the Chinese Customs Succession, 1927-1929*
76 Chifumi Shimazaki, *Restless Spirits from Japanese Noh Plays of the Fourth Group: Parallel Translations with Running Commentary*
77 Brother Anthony of Taizé & Young-Moo Kim, trs., *Back to Heaven: Selected Poems of Ch'ŏn Sang Pyŏng*
78 Kevin O'Rourke, tr., *Singing Like a Cricket, Hooting Like an Owl: Selected Poems by Yi Kyu-bo*
79 Irit Averbuch, *The Gods Come Dancing: A Study of the Japanese Ritual Dance of Yamabushi Kagura*
80 Mark Peterson, *Korean Adoption and Inheritance: Case Studies in the Creation of a Classic Confucian Society*
81 Yenna Wu, tr., *The Lioness Roars: Shrew Stories from Late Imperial China*
82 Thomas Lyons, *The Economic Geography of Fujian: A Sourcebook*, Vol. 1
83 Pak Wan-so, *The Naked Tree*, tr. Yu Young-nan
84 C.T. Hsia, *The Classic Chinese Novel: A Critical Introduction*
85 Cho Chong-Rae, *Playing With Fire*, tr. Chun Kyung-Ja
86 Hayashi Fumiko, *I Saw a Pale Horse and Selections from Diary of a Vagabond*, tr. Janice Brown
87 Motoori Norinaga, *Kojiki-den, Book 1*, tr. Ann Wehmeyer
88 Chang Soo Ko, tr., *Sending the Ship Out to the Stars: Poems of Park Je-chun*
89 Thomas Lyons, *The Economic Geography of Fujian: A Sourcebook*, Vol. 2
90 Brother Anthony of Taizé, tr., *Midang: Early Lyrics of So Chong-Ju*
92 Janice Matsumura, *More Than a Momentary Nightmare: The Yokohama Incident and Wartime Japan*
93 Kim Jong-Gil tr., *The Snow Falling on Chagall's Village: Selected Poems of Kim Ch'un-Su*
94 Wolhee Choe & Peter Fusco, trs., *Day-Shine: Poetry by Hyon-jong Chong*
95 Chifumi Shimazaki, *Troubled Souls from Japanese Noh Plays of the Fourth Group*
96 Hagiwara Sakutarō, *Principles of Poetry (Shi no Genri)*, tr. Chester Wang

CPSIA information can be obtained
at www.ICGtesting.com
Printed in the USA
LVHW070437151119
637261LV00002BB/2/P

9 781933 947143